P9-DDE-268

The Gary Snyder Reader

POETRY:

Riprap and Cold Mountain Poems

Myths and Texts

The Back Country

Regarding Wave

Turtle Island

Axe Handles

Left Out in the Rain

No Nature

Mountains and Rivers Without End

PROSE:

Earth House Hold

He Who Hunted Birds in His Father's Village

Passage Through India

The Practice of the Wild

A Place in Space

The

Gary Snyder

Reader

Prose, Poetry,

and Translations

1952–1998

Gary Snyder

V1.99

COUNTERPOINT
WASHINGTON, D.C.

Library of Congress Cataloging-in-Publication Data
Snyder, Gary, 1930-
[Selections. 1999]
The Gary Snyder reader : prose, poetry, and translations, 1952–1998.
p.   cm.
ISBN 1-887178-90-2 (alk. paper)
1. Snyder, Gary, 1930-   . 2. Poets, American—20th century Correspondence.
3. Environmentalists—United States Biography.   4. Chinese poetry—Translations into
English.   5. Poets, American—20th century Interviews.   6. Poets, American—20th
century Diaries.   7. Beat generation Poetry.   8. Zen poetry, American.   I. Title
PS3569.N88A6   1999
811'.54—dc21
[B]   99-20918
CIP

FIRST PRINTING

The author wishes to acknowledge permission
to reprint the following previously published material:
New Directions Publishing Corporation: From *The Back Country* (1968), *Earth House
Hold* (1969), *Regarding Wave* (1970), *Turtle Island* (1974), *Myths & Texts* (1978), *The Real
Work* (1980). North Point Press, a division of Farrar, Straus and Giroux: From *Riprap
and Cold Mountain Poems* (1965), *Axe Handles* (1983), *Left Out in the Rain* (1986), *The
Practice of the Wild* (1990). Grey Fox Press: From *He Who Hunted Birds in His Father's
Village* (1979), *Passage Through India* (1983). Pantheon Books: From *No Nature* (1992).

Frontispiece photograph by Allen Ginsberg, © 1999

Printed in the United States of America on acid-free paper that meets
the American National Standards Institute Z39-48 Standard.

COUNTERPOINT
P.O. Box 65793
Washington, D.C. 20035-5793

Counterpoint is a member of the Perseus Books Group.

10   9   8   7   6   5   4   3   2   1

For Philip Zenshin Whalen

K'ung said:

To learn and then put it in practice—isn't that a delight?

To have friends come from afar—isn't that a joy?

The Lun Yü

Contents

POETRY

Foreword by Jim Dodge

As the Secretary of Foolishness in the Gary Snyder Appreciation Society, and as a Reverend in the Reborn Again Taoist Dirt-Pagan Church of the Ravishingly Real, I'm loath to preach to the choir. Therefore, this introduction isn't directed at the folks already conversant with Gary Snyder's Pulitzer Prize–winning poetry, his marvelous translations, sharp and playful letters, insightful travel journals, and illuminating essays on culture, ecology, and "wild mind"—except to note that this Reader constitutes something akin to Gary Snyder's Greatest Hits, and it's handy to have them gathered in a single volume. *The Gary Snyder Reader* includes some new work as well: previously unpublished early correspondence with Philip Whalen and Will Petersen; a few new poems; and a strong selection of recently published but uncollected essays which alone are worth the price of admission. Gary and Jack Shoemaker, his sterling editor, selected the work for this volume, and to my mind their choices are impeccable, displaying the full breadth and depth of a writer widely regarded as one of the most influential thinkers of the last fifty years.

Gary more modestly views his work as simply inhabiting "the mythopoetic interface of society, ecology, and language," a work, as the choir knows, that Gary accomplishes with exceptional intelligence, superb imagination, and consistent excellence. But whatever his ultimate place in the pantheon of American poets and revolutionary thinkers, I direct this introduction to those who haven't yet discovered what I consider the essential power and basic pleasure in Gary Snyder's work: he enlarges one's delight in existence and amplifies the élan vital, the life force, coursing through it all. And if in so doing he also, as Freeman House put it, "gives you the permission to use your senses and offers tools to take on the more destructive aspects of Western Civilization," all the better.

I first discovered Gary Snyder's work when I was a 20-year-old student at Humboldt State University in northern California, majoring in fisheries management because I loved to fish—or, more exactly, loved to ramble the short-run rivers and gnarly streams of the west slope Coast Range—and also because I had to major in something to receive the proper credentials to take my place as a productive member of society.

Unfortunately, I'd spent the two previous summers working as a seasonal aide for the California Department of Fish and Game at a trout hatchery, where most of my days were occupied spraying sacks of food pellets to thousands of trout. When the fish reached "catchable" size, I helped transport them to various streams and dump them by the buckets-full into easily accessible pools where, according to our occasional creel surveys, 95% were caught in two days.

Basically, I worked at a trout factory in the company of good men who were demoralized to the point of cynicism—the toxic reflux of powerlessness—by a Fish & Game bureaucracy that seemed pathologically committed to providing a "successful fishing experience" for license holders rather than addressing the obvious decline in wild native fish, a decline that even I, as a beginner biologist, linked to the profound degradation of watersheds. As I entered my junior year, a heavy shadow had fallen between the ideal and the reality of my chosen vocation.

Then, with what strikes me now as serene inevitability, two poems changed my life. The first was D. H. Lawrence's "The Fish," which I chanced upon about a week before a midterm exam in Organic Chemistry. In the poem, Lawrence has seen a large pike slash through a school of small fish:

> And I said to my heart, there are limits
> To you, my heart;
> And to the one God.
> Fish are beyond me.
>
> Other gods
> Beyond my range . . . gods beyond my God . . .

For all my fishing and study of fish, I had never considered the limits of my heart. The poem haunted me for a week, making it impossible to concentrate on the Organic Chemistry exam, leading directly to a score of 19 and the classic professorial notation, "See me." I saw him, acknowledged his observation that my heart wasn't in it, accepted his kind invitation to drop the course, submitted the paperwork, and slumped homeward wondering what I was going to do for a major, much less a life.

On the way to my apartment I passed Northtown Books, a new store in town operated by Jack Hitt and Jeremiah Gorsline. All I knew of contemporary poetry I'd learned from a former girlfriend who'd favored the efforts of East Coast academics, so I wasn't being completely disingenuous when I swerved into the store and asked Jeremiah if he carried any poetry that wasn't about statues in Italy written while on sabbatical, or about sailing off Cape Cod and ending with a reference to crossing the Styx.

Jeremiah spread his arms in joyous welcome and proclaimed, "The Beats, my man, the Beats!" And promptly directed me to a poetry section that easily comprised a quarter of their inventory (my eternal gratitude, Jack and Jeremiah). Featured face-out on a shelf was Gary Snyder's *Riprap.* I knew what riprap was, having hung out briefly with a trail crew while conducting a creel census that summer, and provoked by the odd title, I opened the book randomly right to what remains my favorite Snyder poem, "Hay for the Horses." In a judgment perhaps clouded—though I'd argue deepened—by sentiment, I consider "Hay for the Horses" a flawless poem, wholly realized: lucid, graceful, true, risky, and resonant.

> *Hay for the Horses*
>
> He had driven half the night
> From far down San Joaquin
> Through Mariposa, up the
> Dangerous mountain roads,
> And pulled in at eight a.m.
> With his big truckload of hay
>   behind the barn.
> With winch and ropes and hooks
> We stacked the bales up clean
> To splintery redwood rafters
> High in the dark, flecks of alfalfa
> Whirling through the shingle-cracks of light,
> Itch of haydust in the
>   sweaty shirt and shoes.
> At lunchtime under the Black oak
> Out in the hot corral,
> —The old mare nosing lunchpails,
> Grasshoppers crackling in the weeds—
> "I'm sixty-eight," he said,
> "I first bucked hay when I was seventeen.
> I thought, that day I started,
> I sure would hate to do this all my life.
> And dammit, that's just what
> I've gone and done."

My initial response, as I stood there in the bookstore, was a murmured "Holy shit." Someone was speaking my language, knew my people, understood the gritty joy of bucking hay, the satisfaction and bone-deep dignity of a hard day's work, including the obligatory complaint at persisting in such folly, a typically flat, fatal Western humor that serves to confirm acceptance.

I bought *Riprap,* Lawrence's *Selected Poems,* and, if memory serves, Gregory Corso's *Gasoline.* A few weeks later, after discovering a tiny footnote in the college catalogue, I changed my major from fisheries management to interdisciplinary studies, incorporating biology, English, and journalism. Inspired primarily by Gary Snyder's subject matter and his use of natural American speech, I'd decided I wanted to be a writer, a poet, and with all the fervor of a fresh convert sallied forth into that noble foolishness. Thirty years later, blessing Gary with the blame, I can say with perplexed certainty, dammit, that's just what I've gone and done. Many others, in their own ways, along their own paths, have been similarly moved by Gary Snyder's inspiration, a word rooted in the Latin *inspirare,* literally "to breathe," which has come to mean "exerting a guiding, animating, enlivening, or exalting influence," and, metaphorically, providing breath for our individual and collective songs. New readers are properly cautioned.

"Hay for the Horses" also displays a virtue that I particularly value in Gary Snyder's work and would emphasize for new readers: both his poetry and prose are amazingly direct. Clarity, especially in poetry, requires conceiving of your work as a collaborative act of imagination with the audience, thus affording them the deepest respect. I've heard Gary read many times to diverse audiences and he's never failed to connect; the audiences seem to respond as much to his work's excellence as to the generosity of spirit that informs it and the pains taken to make it available. I think Gary's commitment to clarity stems from his blue-collar Wobbly (I.W.W.) roots, his egalitarian disposition, and his well-founded sense that poetry is traditionally an oral/aural community art-form meant for a live audience. If poets/singers can't move their friends and neighbors, tribe and kin, art truly becomes academic. Not long after he received the Pulitzer Prize and the media attention that goes with it, I kidded Gary, "How famous do you want to be?" He replied, "Five miles." That sense of work centered in place, of addressing a community that includes plants and animals as well as people, is one of the reasons Gary's work is so widely read. I can't prove it, but I'd bet coins against cornflakes that Snyder's work is assigned in anthropology, religion, sociology, science, and environmental studies classes as often as it is in English curricula.

As Scott McLean has pointed out, Gary's work speaks "to the fundamental questions of our lives." Like how to live them with understanding, equanimity, and elegance. This isn't to suggest that Snyder has all the answers, but he cuts cleanly to the center of common concerns and voices them with uncommon eloquence. He possesses that knack for making the simple luminous without reducing it to the simplistic. And simple doesn't mean it's easy. The essence of Snyder's work is Nature—especially "wild nature," "wild mind"—and often when you wade in Snyder's pond you find yourself up to your ass in alligators.

Having achieved the "mythopoetic interface of society, ecology, and language" that he chose as his fields of inquiry, his point of multiple attention, Gary Snyder is justly honored as an elder in the environmental movement, a revolutionary social critic, an excellent translator, a Buddhist scholar and eminent practitioner, and, of course, a premier poet. He is also a nature writer of surpassing lucidity for the "is-ness" and "such-ness" of individual beings and living systems, while never losing sight of the human political and spiritual implications. Snyder is esteemed as one of the great synthesizing intellects of our age, possessed of a breathtaking ability to reveal clear associations among disparate areas of knowledge. His originality resides in taking the best of "old" ideas (from Aldo Leopold to the Paleolithic) and combining and refining them into new configurations, fresh possibilities. And while those are all admirable accomplishments and considerable contributions to our lives, what I really love about Gary is that he's a Warrior of the Imagination in a time of what pundits on both sides have called the Cultural Wars, but which Diane di Prima was among the first to identify more accurately as The War Against Imagination.

Kenneth Rexroth called human imagination "the organ of communion," and that seems right to me. I've come to think of imagination as the psychic nexus of the physical body, emotion, intellect, and spirit, but who knows? Artists and shamans have variously described it as a mode or state of participatory consciousness, extended identity, psychic simultaneity, voluntary incarnation. By any description, it denotes a realized connection between the Self and Other, an empathetic merging (however brief), a sense of shared immanence—basically, the predication for love, or at least a deep and true regard for someone or something beyond the self. The nature of imagination tends toward integration, inclusion, and intimacy, and as such is inimical to the alienation and homogeneity of corporate global capitalism, centralized government, and the other forces of darkness that regard the planet as dominion rather than domicile, markets instead of hearths. As his essays prove and his poems embody, Gary Snyder is among the most ferociously imaginative proponents of the biocentric ("life-centered") view over the egocentric ("self-centered") model. I'm glad Gary is on my side, and though it looks like long odds on short money, Gary's work represents a compelling counterforce, and exemplifies what's meant by a "fighting chance."

Reading some commentators on Snyder's work, you might think he's the best 20th-century Chinese poet writing in English. While he has wisely yielded to the more salubrious influences of Asian aesthetics (and drawn eclectically from others) I will argue until the Fire Goddess serves sno-cones that Snyder's voice, from root to flower, decidedly belongs to the West, as in West of the Rockies, and the Pacific Northwest in particular.

I offer as proof my first visit to Kitkitdizze, the Snyder home in the Sierra foothills, just after its construction in the early '70s. As I recall, a group of Goddard students was there, along with our contingent, and we ate a simple meal of road-kill venison stew seated cross-legged on the floor Japanese-style at a long table. We finished our meal by swabbing our wooden bowls clean with a dill pickle, then eating the pickle. People rinsed and stacked their bowls, then repaired to the living room for some conversation. The whole meal and clean-up struck me as oddly formal in its efficiency and dispatch, and I was thinking maybe Gary had gone over to Asian ways, that I had been misguided by his Northwest vernacular, when Gary emerged from the pantry with a large cardboard box and glee-fully announced, "Dessert is served," and began handing out packages of Hostess Ding-Dongs, the ultimate confirmation of Western roots, and a clear testament that he understood purity was the end of possibility.

Like his work, Gary engages, provokes, inspires, and invariably sur-prises. That last time I saw him, at a recent Stanford symposium culmi-nating a year-long study of his book-length poem *Mountains and Rivers Without End,* the audience had a strong component of passionately com-mitted environmental activists. After a full day of scholarly panels and speakers on various aspects of the poem, Gary concluded the day's discus-sion with some general responses and comments, then took a few ques-tions from the audience. The last came from a young man who wanted to know what Gary had meant by the paradoxical statement that ends the seminal *Four Changes:* "Knowing that nothing need be done is the place from which we begin to move." Gary replied—and here I'm working from memory—that Nature bats last, is eminently capable of caring for herself against destructive human foolishness, and no doubt will remain long after our demise. Nature doesn't need us to save her.

I could feel the audience sag, then bristle. Someone called out, "Then why work to stop the destruction?"

Gary grinned hugely, leaned slightly forward, and replied without a quiver of hesitation, "Because it is a matter of character. " Then, with an absolutely wild glitter of delight in his eyes, added, "And it's a matter of style."

You'll find that wild glittering throughout this book.

Author's Note

This table of contents is like looking at a cutbank exposing the strata, with its deposits, intrusions, sediments, and amalgamations laid in era by era—just a few years, though, amounting to one brief life.

Jack Shoemaker has been friend and colleague thirty years now, and often my editor. His venture and vision have always matched whatever I had of my own, and so the appearance of this book, like a number of my others before it, is in good part a result of his sure-footed willingness to try. My deep thanks to him for his convivial and practical guidance, and for this Reader.

But to go back to beginnings. Lawrence Ferlinghetti funded my first book, *Riprap;* LeRoi Jones (Amiri Baraka) got *Myths and Texts* into print with the help the Wilentz Brothers at the Eighth Street Bookshop in Greenwich Village. Donald Allen (Grey Fox Press) and James Laughlin (New Directions) brought out another round of my publications through the seventies. I joined North Point Press in the early eighties, and found myself with Counterpoint Press—Jack Shoemaker—in the nineties.

The foundation on which poetry books are built is the little magazines. Early on I worked with Barney Rossett's *Evergreen Review,* Cid Corman's *Origin,* Diane di Prima's *Floating Bear,* James Koller's *Coyote's Journal,* and Clayton Eshleman's *Caterpillar,* to mention a few.

In addition to being a generous sampling from published books, this Reader also draws on fugitive and unpublished material. I have made a strong case in recent years for people choosing a home place—and now I can see how much I have knocked about in the world, on tankers, freighters, third-world buses, beat-up cars, by foot and by jumbo jet— midnight bars and dawn mosques. Although it's hard to maintain the perspective, the whole earth is one watershed.

I grew up in the rural Northwest. It will be clear my roots are not just Reed College, Beat or North Beach, but feckless redneck as well, which helps make eight months on a tanker, or a summer and fall in a logging camp pass peacefully.

The mix of ideas, images, meters, archetypes, and propositions here is out of the nervy (in retrospect) but deliberate life I put myself to, all in the spirit of quest, of making art, seeking knowledge, courting wisdom, and nourishing home place Dharma practice and community. Lately research, teaching, keeping up with requests and queries, tune-ups, meetings, mail—just like everyone else. And further handy work wants to be done. My great thanks to the Lannan Foundation for the support which is giving me the time to think my way through this collection and plan the next project.

And finally nine bows to Philip Zenshin Whalen, retired Abbott of the Hartford Street Zen Center in San Francisco. Phil has been a friend and mentor since undergraduate days. He first showed me the difference between talking about literature and doing it, and pointed the way into Asian philosophy and art. Later we both came to Zen meditation. Over the years we've shared bare-floor flats in Portland, Berkeley and San Francisco, tight quarters in Kyoto, plus some huge and funny spaces of the mind.

1.III.99

The Gary Snyder Reader

Prose

FROM

Earth
House Hold

Lookout's Journal

A. Crater Mountain

22 June 52   Marblemount Ranger Station
                Skagit District, Mt. Baker National Forest

Hitchhiked here, long valley of the Skagit. Old cars parked in the weeds,
little houses in fields of bracken. A few cows, in stumpland.

Ate at the "parkway café" real lemon in the pie
            "—why don't you get a jukebox in here"
            "—the man said we weren't important enough"

                        ☙

28 June

                        Blackie Burns:
"28 years ago you could find a good place to fish.
GREEDY & SELFISH   NO RESPECT FOR THE
    LAND
            tin cans, beer bottles, dirty dishes
            a shit within a foot of the bed
one sonuvabitch out of fifty
fishguts in the creek
the door left open for the bear.
If you're takin forestry fellas keep away
from the recreation side of it:
first couple months you see the women you say
            'there's a cute little number'
the next three months it's only another woman

after that you see one coming out of the can
           & wonder if she's just shit on the floor

ought to use pit toilets"

⟡

Granite creek Guard station   9 July

    the boulder in the creek never moves
           the water is always falling
      together!

A ramshackle little cabin built by Frank Beebe the miner.
Two days walk to here from roadhead.
             arts of the Japanese: moon-watching
                        insect-hearing
Reading the sutra of Hui Nêng.

    one does not need universities and libraries
    one need be alive to what is about

saying "I don't care"

⟡

11 July

cut fresh rhubarb by the bank
the creek is going down
last night caught a trout
today climbed to the summit of Crater Mountain and back
high and barren: flowers I don't recognize
ptarmigan and chicks, feigning the broken wing.

    Baxter: "Men are funny, once I loved a girl
    so bad it hurt, but I drove her away. She was
    throwing herself at me—and four months later she
    married another fellow."

A doe in the trail, unafraid.
A strange man walking south
A boy from Marblemount with buckteeth, learning machine shop.

6 ⟡ PROSE

Crater Mountain   Elevation: 8049 feet   23 July

Really wretched weather for three days now—wind, hail, sleet, snow; the FM transmitter is broken / rather the receiver is / what can be done?

Even here, cold foggy rocky place, there's life—4 ptarmigan by the A-frame, cony by the trail to the snowbank.

hit my head on the lamp,
the shutters fall, the radio quits,
the kerosene stove won't stop, the wood stove
won't start, my fingers are too numb to write.

& this is mid-July. At least I have energy enough to read science-fiction. One has to go to bed fully clothed.

The stove burning wet wood—windows misted over giving the blank white light of shoji. Outside wind blows, no visibility. I'm filthy with no prospect of cleaning up. (Must learn yoga-system of Patanjali—)

Crater Shan   28 July

Down for a new radio, to Ross Lake, and back up. Three days walking. Strange how unmoved this place leaves one; neither articulate nor worshipful; rather the pressing need to look within and adjust the mechanism of perception.

A dead sharp-shinned hawk, blown by the wind against the lookout. Fierce compact little bird with a square head.

—If one wished to write poetry of nature, where an audience?
Must come from the very conflict of an attempt to articulate the vision poetry & nature in our time.

(reject the human; but the tension of
human events, brutal and tragic, against
a nonhuman background? like Jeffers?)

Pair of eagles soaring over Devil's Creek canyon

ᘐ

31 July

This morning:
                    floating face down in the water bucket
          a drowned mouse.

*"Were it not for Kuan Chung, we should be wearing our hair unbound and our
clothes buttoning on the left side"*

          A man should stir himself with poetry
          Stand firm in ritual
          Complete himself in music
                    Lun Yü

ᘐ

Comparing the panoramic Lookout View photo dated 8 August 1935:
with the present view. Same snowpatches; same shapes. Year after year;
snow piling up and melting.

          "By God" quod he, "for pleynly, at a word
          Thy drasty ryming is not worth a tord."

ᘐ

Crater Shan   3 August

How pleasant to squat in the sun
Jockstrap & zoris

form—leaving things out at the right spot
ellipse, is emptiness
                         these ice-scoured valleys
                         swarming with plants
     "I am the Queen Bee!
                    Follow Me!"

ᘐ

Or having a wife and baby,
    living close to the ocean, with skills for
    gathering food.

QUEBEC DELTA 04 BLACK

Higgins to Pugh (over)
  "the wind comes out of the east
    or northeast,
    the chimney smokes all over the room.
    the wind comes out of the west;
    the fire burns clean."

Higgins L.O. reads the news:
  "flying saucer with a revolving black band
    drouth in the south.
Are other worlds watching us?"
The rock alive,   not barren.
    flowers   lichen   *pinus albicaulis*   chipmunks
mice   even grass.

—first I turn on the radio
—then make tea & eat breakfast
—study Chinese until eleven

—make lunch, go chop snow to melt for water,
read Chaucer in the early afternoon.

    "Is this real
     Is this real
      This life I am living?"
                —Tlingit or Haida song

                        🦅

"Hidden Lake to Sourdough"
  —"This is Sourdough"
  —"Whatcha doing over there?"
  —"Readin some old magazines
            they had over here."

                        🦅

6 August

Clouds above and below, but I can see Kulshan, Mt. Terror, Shuksan; they blow over the ridge between here and Three-Fingered Jack, fill up the valleys. The Buckner Boston Peak ridge is clear.

What happens all winter; the wind driving snow; clouds—wind, and mountains—repeating

this is what always happens here,

and the photograph of a young female torso hung in the lookout window, in the foreground. Natural against natural, beauty.

two butterflies
a chilly clump of mountain
flowers.

zazen   non-life.   An art: mountain-watching.

leaning in the doorway whistling
a chipmunk popped out
listening

❦

9 August

Sourdough: Jack, do you know if a fly is an electrical conductor? (over)
Desolation: A fly? Are you still trying to electrocute flies? (over)
Sourdough: Yeah   I can make em twitch a little. I got five number
    six batteries on it (over)
Desolation: I don't know, Shubert, keep trying. Desolation clear.

❦

10 August

First wrote a haiku and painted a haiga for it; then repaired the Om Mani Padme Hum prayer flag, then constructed a stone platform, then shaved down a shake and painted a zenga on it, then studied the lesson.

                    a butterfly
                scared up from its flower
          caught by the wind and swept over the cliffs
                              SCREE

Vaux Swifts: in great numbers, flying before the storm, arcing so
close that the sharp wing-whistle is heard.

                    "The śrāvaka
disciplined in Tao, enlightened, but on the wrong path."
summer,
              on the west slopes creek beds are brushy
                north-faces of ridges, steep and
                    covered late with snow

          slides and old burns on dry hills.

(In San Francisco: I live on the Montgomery Street drainage—at the top
of a long scree slope just below a cliff.)

                              ℘

sitting in the sun in the doorway
picking my teeth with a broomstraw
listening to the buzz of the flies.

                              ℘

12 August

          A visit all day, to the sheep camp, across the glacier and into
Devil's park. A tent under a clump of Alpine fir; horses, sheep in the
meadow.

              take up solitary occupations.

Horses stand patiently, rump to the wind.
              —gave me one of his last two cigars.

Designs, under the shut lids, glowing in sun

              (experience! that drug.)
Then the poor lonely lookouts, radioing forth and back.

_____

After a long day's travel, reached the ridge,
followed a deer trail down
                              to five small lakes.
in this yuga, the moral imperative is to COMMUNICATE.
Making tea.

fewer the artifacts, less the words,
                              slowly the life of it
a knack for nonattachment.

Sourdough radioing to the smoke-chaser crew

"you're practically there
you gotta go up the cliff
you gotta cross the rock slide
look for a big blaze on a big tree"
            [two climbers killed by lightning
            on Mt. Stuart]
"are you on the timber stand
or are you on the side of the cliff?
Say, Bluebell, where are you?
A patch of salmonberry and tag-alder to the right"
            —must take a look.

⚕

Cratershan   15 August

   When the mind is exhausted of images, it invents its own.

            orange juice is what she asked for
                bright chrome restaurant, 2 A.M.
            the rest of us drinking coffee
            but the man brought orange pop.   haw!

late at night, the eyes tired, the teapot empty, the tobacco damp.

Almost had it last night: *no identity.* One thinks, "I emerged from some
general, nondifferentiated thing, I return to it." One has in reality never
left it; there is no return.
                    my language fades.   Images of erosion.

"That which includes all change never changes; without change time is meaningless; without time, space is destroyed. Thus we arrive at the void."

⟡

"If a Bodhisattva retains the thought of an ego, a person, a being, or a soul, he is no more a Bodhisattva."

> You be Bosatsu,
> I'll be the taxi-driver
> Driving you home.

The curious multistratified metamorphic rock. Blue and white, clouds reaching out. To survive a winter here learn to browse and live in holes in the rocks under snow.
Sabi: One does not have a great deal to give. That which one does give has been polished and perfected into a spontaneous emptiness; sterility made creative, it has no pretensions, and encompasses everything.

Zen view, OK?

⟡

21 August

Oiling and stowing the tools. (artifact / tools: now there's a topic.) When a storm blows in, covering the south wall with rain and blotting out the mountains. Ridges look new in every light. Still discovering new conformations—every cony has an ancestry but the rocks were just here.

Structure in the lithosphere / cycles of change in rock / only the smallest percentage sanded and powdered and mixed with life-derived elements.

Is chemical reaction a type of perception??—Running through all things motion and reacting, object against object / there is more than enough time for all things to happen: swallowing its own tail.

⟡

Diablo Dam   24 August

Back down off Crater in a snowstorm, after closing up the lookout. With Baxter from Granite Creek all the way to the dam for more sup-

---

from Earth House Hold ⟡ 13

plies. Clouds on the rocks; rain falls and falls. Tomorrow we shall fill the packs with food and return to Granite Creek.

☙

In San Francisco: September 13.

Boys on bicycles in the asphalt playground wheeling and circling aimlessly like playful gulls or swallows. Smell of a fresh-parked car.

B. Sourdough

Marblemount Ranger Station   27 June 53

The antique car managed it to Marblemount last week, and then to Koma Kulshan for a week of gnats, rain, & noise.
    The Philosophy of the Forest Service: Optimistic view of nature—democratic, utilitarian. "Nature is rational." Equals, treat it right and it will make a billion board feet a year. Paradox suppressed. What wd an Aristocratic F.S. be like? Man traps?

Forest equals crop / Scenery equals recreation / Public equals money. :: The shopkeeper's view of nature.

> Hail Mr. Pulaski, after whom the Pulaski
> Tool is named.

—the iron stove, the windows, and the trees. "It is, and is not, I am sane enough." Get so you don't have to think about what you're doing because you *know* what you're doing.
J. Francis: Should I marry? It would mean a house; and the next thirty years teaching school."   LOOKOUT!
    Old McGuire and the fire of 1926: 40,000 acres on the upper Skagit, a three-mile swathe.   Going to scrub my clothes & go down to Sedro-Woolley now with Jack.

☙

28 June

A day off—went to Bellingham and out to Gooseberry Bay, the Lummi reservation. Past a shed with three long cedar canoes in it. Finally to where the

Lummi Island ferry stops, and this was about the end of the road, but we could drive a little farther on, and it was there we went through the Kitchen Midden. Through it, because the road cut right through shells and oysters and all. While looking at this a lady in a house shouted out to us; then came closer, & said if you're interested in the kitchen midden "as such" come out in back and "look where we had it bulldozed." And I said how do you like living on somebody's old kitchen heap, and she said it made her feel kind of funny sometimes. Then I said, well it's got about 3000 years in it vertical, but that might be dead wrong. It was 10 feet high, 45 feet wide, and 325 feet long, with one cedar stump on it about 110 years old, to show when (at least) it was finished with. Full of oyster, butter clam, cockle, mussel, snail and assorted shells.

We went back by the same road and at the outskirts of Bellingham Jack pointed out a ratty-looking place called Coconut Grove where he said he had spent time drinking with a "rough crowd." They drank beer out of steins and called the place the Cat's Eye instead.

Outskirts of Bellingham, something of clear sky to the west over the waters of Puget Sound, the San Juan islands; and very black clouds up the Skagit, toward the vast mountain wilderness of the North Cascades. We turned off 99 to go into that black, wet hole, and it did start raining pretty quick after we went up that road. Coffee in Sedro-Woolley, a sign "No Drinks Served to Indians" and there are many Indians, being strawberry-picking season, and Loggerodeo is next week. Marblemount Ranger Station about 8.30 & in the bunkhouse found a magazine with an article about an eighteen-year-old girl who could dance and paint and compose and sew and was good looking, too, with lots of pictures.

❦

Story: a Tarheel at Darrington had this nice dog. One day he was out dynamiting fish—threw a stick of powder into the water, all lit and ready to go. The dog jumped in, retrieved it, and ran back with it in his mouth. The logger took off up a tree shouting
—Git back, Dog! Then it blasted. Tarheel still limps.
—Blackie.

—And then there was this young married couple, who stay locked in their room four weeks—when friends finally break in all they find is two assholes, jumping back and forth through each other.

❦

The foamy wake behind the boat *does* look like the water of Hokusai. Water in motion is precise and sharp, clearly formed, holding specific postures for infinitely small frozen moments.

Four mules: Tex, Barney Oldfield, Myrtle, Bluejay. Four horses: Willy, Skeezix, Blaze, Mabel.

ᘓ

Sourdough Mountain Lookout   Elevation: 5977 feet 17   July 53

"GREENEST Goddam kid I EVER saw. Told him he couldn't boil beans at that altitude, he'd have to fry them. When I left I said, now, be careful, this is something you gotta watch out about, don't flog your dummy too much! And he says real serious, Oh no, I won't. Hawww—"

"And then he was trying to fry an egg and he missed the pan and he missed the stove and landed the egg on both feet, he didn't know whether to run, shit, or go blind!"

Just managed to get through to Phil Whalen, on the radio, him up on Sauk Lookout now.

Rode up here on Willy the Paint, a pleasant white-eyed little horse that took great caution on rock and snow. Had to lead him across the white-water at Sourdough Creek. Horses look noble from the side, but they sure are silly creatures when seen from the front. Mules just naturally silly— Whenever we stopped, Myrtle would commence kicking Bluejay & Bluejay would kick Barney, all with great WHACKS on the forkies, but Tex behaved, being neither kicked nor kicking. Shoeing Willy required the twitch, anvil, nails, three of us, and great sweating groaning and swearing. Blackie whacks him with a hammer while Roy twists his nose to make him be good.

This is the place to observe clouds and the gradual dissolution of snow. Chipmunk got himself locked in here and when I tried to shoo him out he'd just duck in a corner. Finally when I was sorting screws he came out and climbed up on the waterbucket looking I guess for a drink—hung on, face down, with his hind legs only to the edge of the pail, inside, for a long time, and finally fell in. Helped him out, splashing about—nobody been there he'd have drunned.

Keep looking across to Crater Mountain and get the funny feeling I am up there looking out, right now, "because there are no calendars in the mountains" —shifting of light & cloud, perfection of chaos, magnificent *jiji mu-ge* / interlacing interaction.

ℂ

Sourdough Mountain Lookout   19 July

Up at a quarter to six, wind still blowing the mist through the trees and over the snow. Rins'd my face in the waterhole at the edge of the snow-field—ringed with white rock and around that, heather. Put up the SX aerial on a long pole made by some lookout of years past, sticks & limbs & trunks all wired and tied together. Made a shelf for papers out of half an old orange crate, and turned the radio receiver off. Walked down the ridge, over the snow that follows so evenly the very crest—snow on the north slope, meadows and trees on the south. Small ponds, lying in meadows just off the big snowfields, snags, clumps of mountain hemlock, Alpine fir, a small amount of Alaska cedar.

Got back, built a fire and took the weather. About six, two bucks came, one three-point, one four-point, very warily, to nibble at huckleberries and oats and to eat the scraps of mouldy bacon I threw out. Shaggy and slender, right in the stiff wind blowing mist over the edge of the ridge, or out onto the snowfield, standing out clear and dark against the white. Clouds keep shifting—totally closed in; a moment later across to Pyramid Peak or up Thunder Creek it's clear. But the wind stays.

Now I've eaten dinner and stuffed the stove with twisted pitchy Alpine fir limbs. Clumps of trees fading into a darker and darker gray. White quartz veins on the rocks out the south window look like a sprinkling of snow. Cones on the top boughs of the Alpine fir at the foot of the rocks a DARK PURPLE, stand perfectly erect, aromatic clusters of LINGAMS fleshy and hard.

Lookout free talk time on the radio band: Saul called Koma Kulshan, Church called Sauk, Higgins is talking to Miner's Ridge.   Time to light the lamp.

ℂ

23 July

Days mostly cloudy—clouds breaking up to let peaks through once in a while.   Logan, Buckner, Boston, Sahale, Snowpeak, Pyramid, Névé, Despair, Terror, Fury, Challenger. And the more distant Redoubt and Glacier Peak. As well as Hozomeen and Three-Fingered Jack. Right now look-ing down on the Skagit—pink clouds—pale rose-water pink, with soft shadings of gray and lavender, other combinations of pastel reds and blues, hanging over Pyramid Peak.

Fretting with the Huang Po doctrine of Universal Mind. What a thorny one.

❧

25 July

Last night: thunderstorm. A soft piling of cumulus over the Little Beaver in late afternoon—a gradual thickening and darkening. A brief shower of hail that passed over & went up Thunder Creek valley: long gray shreds of it slowly falling and bent in the wind—while directly above Ruby Creek sunlight is streaming through. Velvety navy blue over Hozomeen, with the sun going down behind Mt. Terror and brilliant reds and pinks on the under-clouds, another red streak behind black Hozo-meen framed in dark clouds. Lightning moving from Hozomeen slowly west into red clouds turning gray, then black; rising wind. Sheet light-ning pacing over Little Beaver, fork lightning striking Beaver Pass.

This morning a sudden heavy shower of rain and a thick fog. A buck scared: ran off with stiff springy jumps down the snowfield. Throwing sprays of snow with every leap: head held stiffly high.

❧

9 August

Sourdough radio relay to Burns:

to: Ray Patterson, District Assistant, Early Winters
        Ranger Station.
from: Jud Longmoor.
        "Kit, Ted and Lucky went out over Deception Pass
        probably headed for airport. Belled but not
        hobbled. Horse took out in night, August 3, above
        Fish Camp. The Shull Creek trail is not passable now.
        Mt. Baker string will pack us to Skypilot Pass
        Thursday August 5. Have Ken Thompson meet us there
        with pack string and saddle horse for Loring. We
        will have pack gear and riding saddle."

Lightning storm again: first in twilight the long jagged ones back of Ter-ror & Fury, later moving down Thunder Creek, and then two fires: right after the strikes, red blooms in the night. Clouds drifting in & obscuring them.

𐤒

Discipline of self-restraint is an easy one; being clear-cut, negative, and usually based on some accepted cultural values. Discipline of following desires, *always* doing what you want to do, is hardest. It presupposes self-knowledge of motives, a careful balance of free action and sense of where the cultural taboos lay — knowing whether a particular "desire" is instinctive, cultural, personal, a product of thought, contemplation, or the un-conscious. Blake: if the doors of perception were cleansed, everything would appear to man as it is, infinite. For man has closed himself up, 'til all he sees is through narrow chinks of his caverns. Ah.

> the frustrate bumblebee turns over
> clambers the flower's center upside down
> furious hidden buzzing
> near the cold sweet stem.

In a culture where the aesthetic experience is denied and atrophied, genuine religious ecstasy rare, intellectual pleasure scorned — it is only natural that sex should become the only personal epiphany of most people & the culture's interest in romantic love take on staggering size.

The usefulness of hair on the legs: mosquitoes and
deerflies have to agitate it in drawing nigh the
skin — by that time warned — Death to Bugs.

(an empty water glass is no less empty than a universe full of nothing) —
the desk is under the pencil.

𐤒

Sourdough Mountain Lookout   12 August

3:55 P.M.   Desolation calls in his weather.
4:00   Sourdough starts calling Marblemount.
4:00   Sam Barker asks for the air: "Dolly, call the doctor at Concrete
              and have him go up to Rockport. There's a man got hurt up
              here."

from Earth House Hold 𐤒 19

4:01	Marblemount: "Up where?"
4:01	Barker: "Up here on Sky Creek. A fellow from Stoddard's logging outfit."
4:01	Marblemount: "Okay Sam. Marblemount clear."
4:10	Sourdough calls his weather in to Marblemount.
4:11	Barker: "Dolly, did you make that call through?"
4:11	Marblemount: "You mean for the doctor?"
4:12	Barker: "Yeah. Well the man's dead."
4:12	Marblemount: "Who was he?"
4:12	Barker: "I don't know, the one they call the Preacher."
4:13	Somebody I couldn't hear, calling Marblemount.
4:13	Marblemount: "The Sky Creek trail. I don't know. Somebody they call the Preacher." Marblemount clear.

ℰ

14 August

11:30 Hidden Lake spots a smoke; he hardly gets an azimuth in to Marblemount but I've got it too & send my reading in. Then all the other Lookouts in the North Cascades catch it—a big column in the Baker River District, between Noisy and Hidden Creeks.

So Phil on Sauk Mountain is busy calling Darrington and Marblemount for the suppression crews, and then the patrol plane comes to look at it and says it's about six acres of alpine timber. And the trucks are off, and Willey the cook has to go too, and the plane flies over to drop supplies at a fire-fighter's camp.

ℰ

Don't be a mountaineer, be a mountain.
    And shrug off a few with avalanches.

Sourdough Mountain at the hub of six valleys: Skagit,
Thunder, Ruby, Upper Skagit, Pierce Creek, Stetattle creek.

ℰ

20 August

  Skirt blown against her hips, thighs, knees
        hair over her ears
    climbing the steep hill in high-heeled shoes

(the Deer come for salt, not affection)

—Government Confucianism, as in the *Hsiao-ching* / Filial Piety—a devilish sort of liberalism. Allowing you should give enough justice and
food to prevent a revolution, yet surely keeping the people under the
thumb. "If you keep the taxes just low enough, the people will not
revolt, and you'll get rich." Movements against this psychology—the
Legalistic rule of Ch'in; Wang An-shih perhaps?
         This is Chinese; plus Blake's collected,
Walden and sumi painting, pass the time.

        ℭ

Nature a vast set of conventions, totally arbitrary, patterns and stresses
that come into being each instant; could disappear totally anytime; and
continues only as a form of play: the cosmic / comic   delight.
        "For in this period the Poet's work is done and all
the great events of time start forth and are conceived in such a period,
within a moment, a Pulsation of the artery."
        —True insight a love-making hovering
between the void & the immense worlds of creation. To symbolically represent Prajña as female is right. The Prajña girl statue from Java.

        ℭ

22 August

Old Roy Raymond hike up and see me. About noon I'm chopping
wood. We spend the afternoon playing horseshoes with mule-shoes; this
morning playing poker.
    "My Missus died a few years ago so I sold the house
    and the furniture 'til I got it down now to where I can get
    everything into a footlocker. My friends'd ask me
    What you sell that for, & hell, what use did I have for it?
    I'll never marry again."
So he spends his time in the mountains—construction jobs, forestry,
mining. Winters in Aberdeen.
    Kim on Desolation radios over (evenings) to read bits of picturesque
speech and patter from antique *Reader's Digests* he's found chez Lookout.

        ℭ

Ross Lake Guard Station   31 August

Friday morning with snow coming in and storms all across the North
Cascades, straight down from Canada, Blackie radios to come down. Work
all morning with inventory; put the shutters down & had to pack an enormous load of crap off the mountain. About 85 pounds.

Forest Service float on Ross Lake: all on a big raft; corrugated walls and
roofing. Porch with woodpile. A floating dock with crosscuts, falling saws,
spikes, wood, in't. At one end the green landing barge moored alongside.
The main raft, with a boat-size wood door; inside a tangle of tools, beds,
groceries. A vast Diesel marine engine-block in the middle of the deck
with a chainsaw beside it. Kim on a cot next to that. Shelves on the unpainted wall with rice, coffee, pancake syrup. Cords, vises, wires on the
workbench. A screen cooler full of bacon and ham. And this enters, under
the same roof, into another dock-room in which the patrol boat floats, full
of green light from the water. Around the edge bales of hay and drums of
Diesel. Moored alongside outside, the horse raft. Covered with straw and
manure. A sunny windy day, lapping the logs.

ɕ

Trail crew work up Big Beaver Creek   4 September

Crosscutting a very large down cedar across the trail and then wedging,
Kim gets below Andy bellers out
"Get your goddamn ass out of there you fuckin squarehead you wanna get
killed?"
We make an extra big pot of chocolate pudding at the shelter that
night, make Kim feel better.

Surge Milkers: "This man had a good little brown heifer that gave lots
of milk, and one morning he put the milker on her and went back inside
and fell asleep and slept an hour. And that little heifer had mastitis in two
days."

ɕ

Hitching south   ca. 21 Sept

Down from Skykomish, evening light,
back of a convertible wind whipping the blanket
clear sky darkening, the road winding along the river

willow and alder on the bank, a flat stretch of
green field; fir-covered hills beyond, dark
new barns and old barns—silvery shake barns—
    the new barns with tall round roofs.

ℭ

In Berkeley: 1 October 53

    "I am here to handle some of the preliminary
            arrangements for the Apocalypse.
    Sand in pockets, sand in hair,
    Cigarettes that fell in seawater
    Set out to dry in the sun.
    Swimming in out of the way places
    In very cold water, creek or surf
    Is a great pleasure."
Under the Canary Island Pine
zazen and eating lunch.   We are all immortals
       & the ground is damp.

Japan First
Time Around

"Arita Maru"   at sea   7: V: 56

Red ooze of the North Pacific—only sharks' teeth and the earbones of whales.   An endless mist of skeletons, settling to the ocean floor.
Marine limestone in the Himalaya at 20,000 feet
breadfruit, laurel, cinnamon and figtree grew in Greenland—cretaceous. "Length of fetch" the distance a batch of waves has run without obstruction.
salts—diatoms—copepods—herring—fishermen—us. eating.

❦

A sudden picture of Warm Springs Camp A loggers making flower arrangements in the yellow-pine tokonomas of their plank camp cabins. I'd work hard all day for that.
any single thing or complex of things *literally* as great as the whole.
wild lilac and lizards / blowing seafog down the hill.
A square is: because the world is round.

❦

At sea   16: V: 56

Moon in the first quarter sinking a path of light on the sea; Jupiter by the sickle of Leo in the west, Cygnus and Lyra in the east, Delphinus just over the haze of the night horizon. The tail of Scorpio in the water.

POETRY is to give access to persons—cutting away the fear and reserve and camping of social life: thus for Chinese poetry. Nature poetry too: "this is what I've seen." Playing with the tools—language, myth, symbolism, intellect—fair enough but childish to abuse.

just where am I in this food-chain?

❧

Red-tailed Tropic birds, and fields of plankton. Lawrence, in *Aaron's Rod:* "The American races—and the South Sea islanders—the Marquesans, the Maori blood. That was the true blood. It wasn't frightened."

". . . Why don't you be more like the Japanese you talk about? Quiet, aloof little devils. They don't bother about being loved. They keep themselves taut in their own selves—there, at the bottom of the spine, the devil's own power they've got there."

Lawrence and his fantastic, accurate, lopsided intuitions. The American Indians and Polynesians developed great cultures and almost deliberately kept their populations down.   and again,

"Love is a process of the incomprehensible human soul: love also incomprehensible but still only a process. The process should work to a completion, not to some horror of intensification and extremity wherein the soul and body ultimately perish. The completion of the process of love is the arrival at a state of simple, pure self-possession, for man and woman. Only that."

❧

At sea   21: V   and into Kobe

Coasting along Wakayama: the sharp cut steep green haze hills, boats about, high-prowed dip slop in wave wash and new white-bellied birds following wave-lick over, then, morning passing—sitting under a lifeboat watching land slip by. Beyond Awaji Isle—jokes about Genji. Into the long smoggy Osaka Bay leading finally up to Kobe—ship upon ship—rusty Korean tiny freighters—and to the pier.

A truckload of Seals on the road by Customs snaking their small heads about. And train, and thousands of crowded tile-roof houses along the track, patches of tended ground; O man—poorness and small houses.

❧

. . . some Americans here make reference to short hours of sleep and simple food—good Xrist you'd think Zen was just a roundabout way for the rich to live like the workingman—there are friends in America who are humble about their interest in the Dharma and ashamed of their profligacy while living on salvaged vegetables and broken rice—sleep six hours a night so as to study books and think, and so to work, to keep the wife and kids: what foppery is this—and it turns out you got to spend $30 for a special meditation cushion. The center in this world is quietly moving to San Francisco where it's most alive—these Japanese folks may be left behind and they won't (in the words of Fêng Kuan) recognize it when they see it.

ɕ

25: V

Today up Hiei-zan. Jodo-in, young bonze named Somon; the tomb of Dengyo Daishi. Vast cool wooden temple in the mountain shade—it smells good. A monk in white came with lunch on trays: pickles and rice and peas. Then W. and I went to the main room and picture of Dengyo Daishi, and a small shrine room to Kwannon that looked like a peyote dream.

(the only superstitions that are really dangerous to peasant Buddhist types are the superstitions of nationalism and the state)

Then: in fog-rain and frog-croak climbed up and along by a Cryptomeria sawmill (they fall trees same method we do judging by the butt cuts) to another temple; finally below that an even larger temple recently repainted—went in and lit candles. Uguisu don't sing, they shout.

ɕ

7: VI

. . . one begins to see the connecting truths hidden in Zen, Avatamsaka and Tantra. The giving of a love relationship is a Bodhisattva relaxation of personal fearful defenses and self-interest strivings—which communicates unverbal to the other and leaves *them* do the same. "Enlightenment" is this interior ease and freedom carried not only to persons but to all the universe, such-such-and void—which is in essence and always, freely changing and interacting. The emptiness of "both self and things"—only a Bodhisattva has no Buddha-nature. (*Lankavatara-sōtra.*)

So, Zen being founded on Avatamsaka, and the net-network of things; and Tantra being the application of the "interaction with no obstacles" vision on a personal-human level—the "other" becomes the lover, through whom the various links in the net can be perceived. As Zen goes to *anything* direct—rocks or bushes or people—the Zen Master's presence is to help one keep attention undivided, to always look one step farther along, to simplify the mind: like a blade which sharpens to nothing.

Tantra, Avatamsaka and Zen really closely historically related: and these aspects of philosophy and practice were done all at once, years ago, up on Hiei-zan.   Knit old dharma-trails.

❧

An ant is dragging a near-dead fly through the mosswoods by the tongue.

　　　—dreamed of a new industrial-age dark ages: filthy narrow streets and dirty buildings with rickety walks over the streets from building to building—unwashed illiterate brutal cops—a motorcycle cop and sidecar drove up and over a fat workingman who got knocked down in a fight—tin cans and garbage and drooping electric wires everywhere—

❧

15: VI

Leaving the temple this morning walked by a small fox shrine where a Zen monk was chanting: there I heard the subtle steady single-beat of oldest American-Asian shamanism. The basic song.   "Buddhist lectures on Shoshone texts" or *Shastra* / commentaries   on Navajo creation myth.

❧

Koen-ji　　28: VI

Key to evolution adaptability: the organism alters itself rather than continue fruitless competition.
　　　　　. . . logging camp morning, high clouds moving east, birds, morning light on the pine and sugi; everyone getting up to go to work.   Chao-chou: "Wal I been trainin horses for thirty yars and now I git kicked by a dunkey."

—the brain and nervous system all infolded ectoderm: thought but a kind of skin perception.

And now there are too many human beings.   Let's be animals or buddhas instead.

❦

The altar figure is Manjusri, in gold-lacquered wood. Not only can you tell "enlightenment" from the face, but you can tell how it was achieved. The old Zen Master statues in the meditation hall show them as human beings who made it through will, effort, years of struggle and intensity. Manjusri has the face of a man who did it with cool intellect and comprehension, cynicism and long historical views. Another made it by poverty, wandering, and simple-minded self-sufficient detachment.

Poking about in the abandoned monks' rooms—smell of an old unused mining cabin or logging shanty—a cupboard of bindles the boys left behind, a drawer full of letters, notebooks, seals; like magazines and coffee cups full of dust and mouseshit.

The old dark smoky kitchen where Han Shan might have worked. Now making udon noodles out of wheat flour batter with a pressing-and-cutting machine you crank by hand.

❦

Kyoto   30: IX

Nō play Yang Kuei Fei/Yōkihi—the episode of the Shaman's visit to Hōrai (Jade nowhere Island place)—he receives a hairpin, then she dances. The headdress gold-jewelled triangles and floral danglers: quiver although the dancer is immobile. A seismograph of imperceptible within. American Nō stage: background painting a desert and distant mountains? chorus on a long low bench.   Maybe one large real boulder.

❦

Eternal crouching ancient women in dark smoky temple kitchens, fanning the thornwood fire and dusting the hard black dirt floor—once the virgin of what ritual? And gold glittering temple hall?—

self-discipline is bad for the character.
THY HAND, GREAT ANARCH

"wisdom and berries grow on the same bush, but only one could ever be plucked at one time"—Emerson's Journals   (but I knew a packer could chew copenhagen snoose while eating huckleberries on opposite sides of the mouth and never did mix em up). "The profoundly secret pass that leads from fate to freedom."

𝔮*

6: X

W. the tender secret sensitive square artist, all in himself, a tiny smile, walks out and makes a clean bow, his head all curly blond, and sits down at black piano, him in black. Against the gold zigzag screen: and plays Haydn—as I could hear him for weeks on, practicing in his corner of Rinko temple; bluejeans and coffee in his double-sized cup through hot days and between naps.   Decorous passionate music of Old Europe out his Zen fingers, to the hall full of culture-thirsty student boys and girls in blackwhite uniform, fierce-eyed and full of orderly resentment, making their heart's Europe out of thousandfold paperback translations, Aesop to Sartre—digging this lush music. All in a land of rice paddy and green hills and rains where still deep-hatted Dharma-hobos try to roam.

𝔮*

24: X

Leaves begin very gradually to fall—what crazy communion of the birds wheeling and circling back and forth in calling flock, above the pine and against sunset cold white-and-blue clouds—a bunch of birds being one—

Breaking the aspected realms into names—the "Three Realms" or the Trikaya or the "Three Worlds"—done a step farther, as mythology, and seeing the powers and aspects in terms of personalities and relationships archetypally expressed. As the three worlds are one, but seen as three from different angles, so the Goddess is mother, daughter, and wife at the same time. Indra's net is not merely two-dimensional. The movements of the triad of mother, father and child can be made to express any device of mythological or metaphysical thought.

(Beware of anything that promises freedom or enlightenment—traps for eager and clever fools—a dog has a keener nose—every creature in a cave can justify himself. Three-fourths of philosophy and literature is the talk of people trying to convince themselves that they really like the cage they were tricked into entering.)

> My love thoughts these days
> Come thick like the summer grass
> Which soon as cut and raked

                            Grows wild again
                                          Yakamochi

—two days contemplating ecology, food chains and sex. Looking at
girls as mothers or daughters or sisters for a change of view. Curious
switch.

                                 ❦

13: XI

  And dreamed that the Egyptian god Set appeared to me & delivered a
long prophetic poem, which I forgot.
  O Muse who comes in a fiery cart wearing a skirt of revolving swords,
trumpeting and insistent; O Muse who comes through the hedge wearing
a gray coat, to stand under the ash-tree beckoning . . .
  Comes a time when the poet must choose: either to step deep in the
stream of his people, history, tradition, folding and folding himself in
wealth of persons and pasts; philosophy, humanity, to become richly foun-
dationed and great and sane and ordered. Or, to step beyond the bound
onto the way out, into horrors and angels, possible madness or silly Faus-
tian doom, possible utter transcendence, possible enlightened return, possible ignominious wormish perishing.

                                 ❦

22: XI   Founder's day at Daitoku-ji

  A ringing bell starts it all—a few "cloud and water" monks in traveling
clothes, in a cluster, chatting under the pines at the corner of the Dharma
Hall.   Colored banners.   Priests in purple and gold and Chinese high-
toed slippers with raven-beak hats on.
  A black-and-white dragon splashed across the ceiling glaring down,
body a circle in cloud and lightning—six burning two-foot candles, and
two four-foot pine boughs.   Priests walk in file scuffing the boat shoes.
Sunshine comes in through tree-beams; inside the hall here it's like a
grove of Redwood, or under a mountain. Oda Rōshi made eighteen bows.

                                 ❦

26: XI   Rinko-in

Barefoot down cold halls.

Maple red now glows, the high limbs first. Venus the morning star—at daybreak and evening, sparrows hurtle in thousands. Five men in jikatabi work shoes slouching across the baseball diamond by the Kamo river.   A woman under the bridge nursing her baby at noon hour, shovel and rake parked by. Faint windy mists in the hills north—smoke and charcoal and straw—at night hot soup "kasujiru" made of saké squeezings. Little girls in long tan cotton stockings, red garters, still the skimpy skirts. College boys cynically amble around in their worn-flat geta clogs and shiny black uniforms looking raw, cold and helpless. Big man on a motorcycle with a load of noodles.

"It is unspeakably wonderful to see a large volume of water falling with a thunderous noise."

"Sparrows entertained me singing and dancing, I've never had such a good time as today."

Japanese lesson.

☙

21: I: 57   Daikan, period of Great Cold

Thick frost and a few flakes of dry cold snow; ice thick in the stone hole water bowl boulder where the doves drink, frost keen lines on all the twigs of the naked plum and each small leaf of a tree.

EROTICISM of China and Japan a dark shadowy thing—a perfumed cunt in a cave of brocades; Greek eroticism is nakedness in full blast of sunlight; fucking on high sunny hills. India is hips and breasts, agile limbs on stone floors with intricate design.

Depth is the body.   How does one perceive internal physical states— yoga systems I guess—well well.   soil conservation / reforestation / birth control / spelling reform: "love the body."

☙

15: II: 57   Rinko-in

Fine clear morning sun melts frost—plum trees soon bloom—Dove early to the stone water bowl (froze hard, so it walked and pecked on it, no drink). Full moon last night—home from zazen—flying eaves of the Dharma Hall silvery slate tile against Orion—icy air slamming into the mouth. Stupid self dragging its feet while I sit fooling with recall and fantasy—where the sound or sight HITS and is transformed by the mental, at THAT razoredge is the gate. MU is the wedge to chock it up with, that very crack.

*

12: III: 57   Tōdai-ji's "Water-gathering" ceremony

Tōdai-ji's enormous Chinese-Indian Gate of Power. Mangy saw-horn bucks walking around. Mizutori, "water-gathering" at Second Month temple. Grandaddy of all sugi trees in front. Complex beaming and gabling—iron lanterns hanging, ornate, faintly glowing. Far off dream lamps of former birth, exotic and familiar. At seven p.m. monks run up the long stairway with twenty-foot torches and wave and shake them at the crowd, which delights to have the luck of standing under falling clouds of sparks. Inside the hall, priests run clack-clack around and around the central shrine in white wood shoes; stop, sit, and blow conch-shells. They recite the names of all the Gods of Japan, and all the thousands of Buddhas and Bodhisattvas. It takes most of the night. Finally a group comes out and goes down the steps to the well, makes two trips with decked-and-garlanded buckets of water to be blessed by Kwannon. Last, a bit more chanting and then the biggest torch of all is lit and danced INSIDE the hall by masked and head-dressed man—like a raven-beak—the bell bonging. Three A.M.

Later had breakfast with priests at a branch temple—came back on the early train to Kyoto watching the fresh snow-powdered hills and rising chill March sun, the last morning of the spring to wake up snowy. All those little houses, some smoking faint wispy blue in the long blue valley, and pure air.

*

21: III

Kyoto City Hospital: Nurse girls in starch white scud through the halls in flocks—teal over the mountains—Nurse girls play ball in the yard, patients watching. In the next walled yard puppies on chains wait queer medical fates; a dead one belly up, strange tubes in his throat and intestines, beside two dull cowering dogs in filth.

*

14: IV

Cherries, cherries—and over the hills from Pete's school—up past Hideyoshi's tomb and down and through a tunnel, out by a lake—on—air dry and dusty wind blowing—just rambling—drank saké on top of Higashiyama under a white petal-scattering tree. Down, almost trapped by the Miyako Hotel, on along the canal past drunk dancing grandmothers, and over brush hills, blue wild bushes blooming—again canal—to Pete's friend's house, a mycologist who does Nō and writes haiku and paints—days gone thus, spring rambles and flowers; beyond there lies—

C*

9: V: 57

In the monastery sesshin / intensive meditation week: from May Day on. One night I dreamt I was with Miura Rōshi, or maybe an unheard-of Polish revolutionary poet with a bald head—looking at Berkeley. But a new Berkeley—of the future—the Bay beach clean and white, the bay blue and pure; white buildings and a lovely boulevard of tall Monterey pines that stretched way back to the hills. We saw a girl from some ways off walking toward us, long-legged, her hair bound loosely in back.

Spring Sesshin
at Shokoku-ji

Shokoku Temple is in northern Kyoto, on level ground, with a Christian college just south of it and many blocks of crowded little houses and stone-edged dirt roads north. It is the mother-temple of many branch temples scattered throughout Japan, and one of the several great temple-systems of the Rinzai Sect of Zen. Shokoku-ji is actually a compound: behind the big wood gate and tile-topped crumbling old mud walls are a number of temples each with its own gate and walls, gardens, and acres of wild bamboo grove. In the center of the compound is the soaring double-gabled Lecture Hall, silent and airy, an enormous dragon painted on the high ceiling, his eye burning down on the very center of the cut-slate floor. Except at infrequent rituals the hall is unused, and the gold-gilt Buddha sits on its high platform at the rear untroubled by drums and chanting. In front of the Lecture Hall is a long grove of fine young pines and a large square lotus-pond. To the east is a wooden bell tower and the unpretentious gate of the Sodo, the training school for Zen monks, or unsui.[1] They will become priests of Shokoku-ji temples. A few, after years of zazen (medita-

[1]*Unsui.* The term is literally "cloud, water"—taken from a line of an old Chinese poem, "To drift like clouds and flow like water." It is strictly a Zen term. The Japanese word for Buddhist monks and priests of all sects is *bozu* (bonze). One takes no formal vows upon becoming an Unsui, although the head is shaved and a long Chinese-style robe called koromo is worn within Sodo walls. Unsui are free to quit the Zen community at any time. During the six months of the year in which the Sodo is in session (spring and fall) they eat no meat, but during the summer and winter off-periods they eat, drink and wear what they will. After becoming temple priests (Osho, Chinese Ho-shang), the great majority of Zen monks marry and raise families. The present generation of young Unsui is largely from temple families.

tion), koan study,[2] and final mastery of the Avatamsaka (Kegon) philosophy, become Roshi[3] (Zen Masters), qualified to head Sodos, teach lay groups, or do what they will. Laymen are also permitted to join the Unsui in evening Zendo (meditation hall) sessions, and some, like the Unsui, are given a koan by the Roshi and receive regular sanzen—the fierce face-to-face moment where you spit forth truth or perish—from him. Thus being driven, through time and much zazen, to the very end of the problem.

In the routine of Sodo life, there are special weeks during the year in which gardening, carpentry, reading and such are suspended, and the time given over almost entirely to zazen. During these weeks, called *sesshin,* "concentrating the mind"—sanzen is received two to four times a day, and hours of zazen in the Zendo are much extended. Laymen who will observe the customs of Sodo life and are able to sit still are allowed to join in the sesshin. At Shokoku-ji, the spring sesshin is held the first week of May.

The sesshin starts in the evening. The participants circle in single file into the mat-floored Central Hall of the Sodo and sit in a double row in dim light. The Roshi silently enters, sits at the head, and everyone drinks tea, each fishing his own teacup out of the deep-sleeved black robe. Then the Jikijitsu—head Unsui of the Zendo (a position which revolves among the older men, changing every six months)—reads in formal voice the rules of Zendo and sesshin, written in Sung Dynasty Sino-Japanese. The roshi says you all must work very hard; all bow and go out, returning to the Zendo for short meditation and early sleep.

At three A.M. the Fusu (another older zenbo who is in charge of finances and meeting people) appears in the Zendo ringing a hand-bell. Lights go on—ten-watt things tacked under the beams of a building lit for centuries by oil lamps—and everyone wordlessly and swiftly rolls up his single quilt and stuffs it in a small cupboard at the rear of his mat, leaps off the raised platform that rings the hall, to the stone floor, and scuffs out in straw sandals to dash icy water on the face from a stone bowl. They come back quickly and sit crosslegged on their zazen cushions, on the same mat

---

[2] Koans are usually short anecdotes concerning the incomprehensible and illogical behavior and language of certain key Chinese Zen Masters of the T'ang Dynasty. The koan assigned to the student is the subject of his meditation, and his understanding of it is the subject of sanzen, an interview with the Zen Master. Very advanced students are also required to relate koan-understanding to the intellectual concepts of Buddhist philosophy.

[3] roshi. Literally, "old master"—Chinese Lao-shih. A Roshi is not simply a person who "understands" Zen, but specifically a person who has received the seal of approval from his own Zen Master and is his "Dharma heir." A person may comprehend Zen to the point that his roshi will say he has no more to teach him, but if the Roshi does not feel the student is intellectually and scholastically equipped to transmit Zen as well, he will not permit him to be his heir. Most Roshi are Zen monks, but laymen and women have also achieved this title.

used for sleeping. The Jikijitsu stalks in and sits at his place, lighting a stick of incense and beginning the day with the rifleshot crack of a pair of hardwood blocks whacked together and a ding on a small bronze bell. Several minutes of silence, and another whack is heard from the Central Hall. Standing up and slipping on the sandals, the group files out of the Zendo, trailing the Jikijitsu—who hits his bell as he walks—and goes down the roofed stone path, fifty yards long, that joins the Zendo and the Central Hall. Forming two lines and sitting on the mats, they begin to chant sutras. The choppy Sino-Japanese words follow the rhythm of a fish-shaped wooden drum and a deep-throated bell. They roar loud and chant fast. The roshi enters and between the two lines makes deep bows to the Buddha-image before him, lights incense, and retires. The hard-thumping drum and sutra-songs last an hour, then suddenly stop and all return to the Zendo. Each man standing before his place, they chant the *Prajña-paramita-hridaya Sõtra*, the Jikijitsu going so fast now no one can follow him. Then hoisting themselves onto the mats, they meditate. After half an hour a harsh bell-clang is heard from the Roshi's quarters. The Jikijitsu bellows "Getout!" and the zenbos dash out racing, feet slapping the cold stones and robes flying, to kneel in line whatever order they make it before the sanzen room. A ring of the bell marks each new entrance before the roshi. All one hears from outside is an occasional growl and sometimes the whack of a stick. The men return singly and subdued from sanzen to their places.

Not all return. Some go to the kitchen, to light brushwood fires in the brick stoves and cook rice in giant black pots. When they are ready they signal with a clack of wood blocks, and those in the Zendo answer by a ring on the bell. Carrying little nested sets of bowls and extra-large chopsticks, they come down the covered walk. It is getting light, and at this time of year the azalea are blooming. The moss-floored garden on both sides of the walk is thick with them, banks under pine and maple, white flowers glowing through mist. Even the meal, nothing but salty radish pickles and thin rice gruel, is begun and ended by whacks of wood and chanting of short verses. After breakfast the zenbos scatter: some to wash pots, others to mop the long wood verandas of the central hall and sweep and mop the Roshi's rooms or rake leaves and paths in the garden. The younger unsui and the outsiders dust, sweep, and mop the Zendo.

The Shokoku-ji Zendo is one of the largest and finest in Japan. It is on a raised terrace of stone and encircled by a stone walk. Outside a long overhang roof and dark unpainted wood—inside round log posts set on granite footings—it is always cool and dark and very still. The floor is square slate laid diagonal. The raised wood platform that runs around the edge has mats for forty men. Sitting in a three-walled box that hangs from the center of the ceiling, like an overhead-crane operator, is a life-size wood statue of the Buddha's disciple Kasyapa, his eyes real and piercing anyone who enters the main door. In an attached room to the rear of the Zendo is a shrine to the founder of Shokoku-ji, his statue in wood, eyes peering out of a dark alcove.

By seven A.M. the routine chores are done and the Jikijitsu invites those cleaning up the Zendo into his room for tea. The Jikijitsu and the Fusu both have private quarters, the Fusu lodging in the Central Hall and the Jikijitsu in a small building adjoining the Zendo. The chill is leaving the air, and he slides open the paper screens, opening a wall of his room to the outside. Sitting on mats and drinking tea they relax and smoke and quietly kid a little, and the Jikijitsu—a tigerish terror during the zazen sessions—is very gentle. "You'll be a roshi one of these days" a medical student staying the week said to him. "Not me, I can't grasp koans," he laughs, rubbing his shaved head where the roshi has knocked him recently. Then they talk of work to be done around the Sodo. During sesshin periods work is kept to a minimum, but some must be done. Taking off robes and putting on ragged old dungarees everyone spreads out, some to the endless task of weeding grass from the moss garden, others to the vegetable plots. The Jikijitsu takes a big mattock and heads for the bamboo-grove to chop out a few bamboo shoots for the kitchen. Nobody works very hard, and several times during the morning they find a warm place in the sun and smoke.

At ten-thirty they quit work and straggle to the kitchen for lunch, the main meal. Miso soup full of vegetables, plenty of rice, and several sorts of pickles. The crunch of bicycles and shouts of children playing around the bell tower can be heard just beyond the wall. After lunch the laymen and younger unsui return to the Zendo. More experienced men have the greater responsibilities of running the Sodo, and they keep busy at accounts, shopping and looking after the needs of the roshi. Afternoon sitting in the Zendo is informal—newcomers take plenty of time getting comfortable, and occasionally go out to walk and smoke a bit. Conversation is not actually forbidden, but no one wants to talk.

Shortly before three, things tighten up and the Jikijitsu comes in. When everyone is gathered, and a bell heard from the Central Hall, they march out for afternoon sutra-chanting. The sutras recited vary from day to day, and as the leader announces new titles some men produce books from their sleeves to read by, for not all have yet memorized them completely. Returning to the Zendo, they again recite the *Prajña-paramita-hridaya Sōtra,* and the Jikijitsu chants a piece alone, his voice filling the hall, head tilted up to the statue of Kasyapa, hand cupped to his mouth as though calling across miles.

After they sit a few minutes the signal is heard for evening meal, and all file into the kitchen, stand, chant, sit, and lay out their bowls. No one speaks. Food is served with a gesture of "giving," and one stops the server with a gesture of "enough." At the end of the meal—rice and pickles—a pot of hot water is passed and each man pours some into his bowls, swashes it around and drinks it, wipes out his bowls with a little cloth. Then they are nested again, wrapped in their cover, and everyone stands and leaves.

It is dusk and the Zendo is getting dark inside. All the zenbos begin to assemble now, some with their cushions tucked under arm, each bowing before Kasyapa as he enters. Each man, right hand held up before the chest flat like a knife and cutting the air, walks straight to his place, bows toward the center of the room, arranges the cushions, and assumes the cross-legged "half-lotus" posture. Other arrive too—teachers, several college professors and half a dozen university students wearing the black uniforms that serve for classrooms, bars and temples equally well—being all they own. Some enter uncertainly and bow with hesitation, afraid of making mistakes, curious to try zazen and overwhelmed by the historical weight of Zen, something very "Japanese" and very "high class." One student, most threadbare of all, had a head shaved like an Unsui and entered with knowledge and precision every night, sitting perfectly still on his cushions and acknowledging no one. By seven-thirty the hall is half full—a sizable number of people for present-day Zen sessions—and the great bell in the bell tower booms. As it booms, the man ringing it, swinging a long wood-beam ram, sings out a sutra over the shops and homes of the neighborhood. When he has finished, the faint lights in the Zendo go on and evening zazen has begun.

The Jikijitsu sits at the head of the hall, marking the half-hour periods with wood clackers and bell. He keeps a stick of incense burning beside him, atop a small wood box that says "not yet" on it in Chinese. At the end of the first half-hour he claps the blocks once and grunts "kinhin." This is "walking zazen," and the group stands—the Unsui tying up sleeves and tucking up robes—and at another signal they start marching single file around the inside of the hall. They walk fast and unconsciously in step, the Jikijitsu leading with a long samurai stride. They circle and circle, through shadow and under the light, ducking below Kasyapa's roost, until suddenly the Jikijitsu claps his blocks and yells "Getout!"—the circle broken and everyone dashing for the door. Night sanzen. Through the next twenty minutes they return to resume meditation—not preparing an answer now, but considering the roshi's response.

Zazen is a very tight thing. The whole room feels it. The Jikijitsu gets up, grasps a long flat stick and begins to slowly prowl the hall, stick on shoulder, walking before the rows of sitting men, each motionless with eyes half-closed and looking straight ahead downward. An inexperienced man sitting out of balance will be lightly tapped and prodded into easier posture. An unsui sitting poorly will be without warning roughly knocked off his cushions. He gets up and sits down again. Nothing is said. Anyone showing signs of drowsiness will feel a light tap of the stick on the shoulder. He and the Jikijitsu then bow to each other, and the man leans forward to receive four blows on each side of his back. These are not particularly painful—though the loud whack of them can be terrifying to a newcomer—and serve to wake one well. One's legs may hurt during long sitting, but there is no relief until the Jikijitsu rings his bell. The mind must simply be placed elsewhere. At the end of an hour the bell does ring and the second kinhin begins—a welcome twenty minutes of silent rhythmic walking. The walking ends abruptly and anyone not seated and settled when the Jikijitsu whips around the hall is knocked off his cushion. Zen aims at freedom but its practice is disciplined.

Several unsui slip out during kinhin. At ten they return—they can be heard coming, running full speed down the walk. They enter carrying big trays of hot noodles, udon, in large lacquer bowls. They bow to the Jikijitsu and circle the room setting a bowl before each man; giving two or even three bowls to those who want them. Each man bows, takes up chopsticks, and eats the noodles as fast as he can. Zenbos are famous for fast noodle-eating and no one wants to be last done. As the empty bowls are set down they are gathered up and one server follows, wiping the beam that fronts the mats with a rag, at a run. At the door the servers stop and bow to the group. It bows in return. Then one server announces the person—usually a friend or patron of the Sodo—who footed the bill for the sesshin noodles that night. The group bows again. Meditation is resumed. At ten-thirty there is another rest period and men gather to smoke and chat a little in back. "Are there really some Americans interested in Zen?" they ask with astonishment—for their own countrymen pay them scant attention.

At eleven bells ring and wood clacks, and final sutras are chanted. The hall is suddenly filled with huge voices. The evening visitors take their cushions and leave, each bowing to the Jikijitsu and Kasyapa as he goes. The others flip themselves into their sleeping quilts immediately and lie dead still. The Jikijitsu pads once around, says, "Take counsel of your pillow," and walks out. The hall goes black. But this is not the end, for as soon as the lights go out, everyone gets up again and takes his sitting cushion, slips outside, and practices zazen alone wherever he likes for another two hours. The next day begins at three A.M.

This is the daily schedule of the sesshin. On several mornings during the week, the roshi gives a lecture (*teisho*) based on some anecdote in the

Zen textbooks—usually from *Mumonkan* or *Hekiganroku*. As the group sits in the Central Hall awaiting his entrance, one Zenbo stands twirling a stick around the edge-tacks of a big drum, filling the air with a deep reverberation. The Roshi sits cross-legged on a very high chair, receives a cup of tea, and delivers lectures that might drive some mad—for he tells these poor souls beating their brains out night after night that "the Perfect Way is without difficulty" and he means it and they know he's right.

In the middle of the week everyone gets a bath and a new head-shave. There is a Zen saying that "while studying koans you should not relax even in the bath," but this one is never heeded. The bathhouse contains two deep iron tubs, heated by brushwood fires stoked below from outside. The blue smoke and sweet smell of crackling hinoki and sugi twigs, stuffed in by a fire-tender, and the men taking a long time and getting really clean. Even in the bathhouse you bow—to a small shrine high on the wall—both before and after bathing. The Jikijitsu whets up his razor and shaves heads, but shaves his own alone and without mirror. He never nicks himself anymore.

On the day after bath they go begging (*takuhatsu*). It rained this day, but putting on oiled-paper slickers over their robes and wearing straw sandals they splashed out. The face of the begging zenbo can scarcely be seen, for he wears a deep bowl-shaped woven straw hat. They walk slowly, paced far apart, making a weird wailing sound as they go, never stopping. Sometimes they walk for miles, crisscrossing the little lanes and streets of Kyoto. They came back soaked, chanting a sutra as they entered the Sodo gate, and added up a meager take. The rain sluiced down all that afternoon, making a green twilight inside the Zendo and a rush of sound.

The next morning during tea with the Jikijitsu, a college professor who rents rooms in one of the Sodo buildings came in and talked of koans. "When you understand Zen, you know that the tree is really *there*."—The only time anyone said anything of Zen philosophy or experience the whole week. Zenbos never discuss koans or sanzen experience with each other.

The sesshin ends at dawn on the eighth day. All who have participated gather in the Jikijitsu's room and drink powdered green tea and eat cakes. They talk easily, it's over. The Jikijitsu, who has whacked or knocked them all during the week, is their great friend now—compassion takes many forms.

Buddhism and the Possibilities of a Planetary Culture

Buddhism holds that the universe and all creatures in it are intrinsically in a state of complete wisdom, love, and compassion, acting in natural response and mutual interdependence. The personal realization of this from-the-beginning state cannot be had for and by one-"self," because it is not fully realized unless one has given the self up and away.

In the Buddhist view, what obstructs the effortless manifestation of this realization is ignorance, which projects into fear and needless craving. Historically, Buddhist philosophers have failed to analyze out the degree to which ignorance and suffering are caused or encouraged by social factors, considering fear and desire to be given facts of the human condition. Consequently the major concern of Buddhist philosophy is epistemology and "psychology," with no attention paid to historical or sociological problems. Although Mahayana Buddhism has a grand vision of universal salvation, the actual achievement of Buddhism has been the development of practical systems of meditation toward the end of liberating a few dedicated individuals from psychological hang-ups and cultural conditionings. Institutional Buddhism has been conspicuously ready to accept or ignore the inequalities and tyrannies of whatever political system it found itself under. This can be death to Buddhism, because it is death to any meaningful function of compassion. Wisdom without compassion feels no pain.

No one today can afford to be innocent, or to indulge themselves in ignorance of the nature of contemporary governments, politics, and social orders. The national polities of the modern world are "states" that maintain their existence by deliberately fostered craving and fear: monstrous protection rackets. The "free world" has become economically dependent on a fantastic system of stimulation of greed that cannot be fulfilled, sexual desire that cannot be satiated, and hatred that has no outlet except against oneself, the persons one is supposed to love, or the revolutionary aspirations of pitiful, poverty-stricken marginal societies. The conditions of the Cold War have fumed most modern societies—both communist and capitalist—into vicious distorters of true human potential. They try to create populations of *preta*—hungry ghosts, with giant appetites and throats no bigger than needles. The soil, the forests, and all animal life are being consumed by these cancerous collectivities; the air and water of the planet is being fouled by them.

There is nothing in human nature or the requirements of human social organization that requires a society to be contradictory, repressive, and productive of violent and frustrated personalities. Findings in anthropology and psychology make this more and more evident. One can prove it for oneself by taking a good look at Original Nature through meditation. Once a person has this much faith and insight, one will be led to a deep concern for the need for radical social change through a variety of nonviolent means.

The joyous and voluntary poverty of Buddhism becomes a positive force. The traditional harmlessness and avoidance of taking life in any form has nation-shaking implications. The practice of meditation, for which one needs only "the ground beneath one's feet," wipes out mountains of junk being pumped into the mind by the mass media and supermarket universities. The belief in a serene and generous fulfillment of natural loving desires destroys ideologies that blind, maim, and repress—and points the way to a kind of community which would amaze "moralists" and transform armies of men who are fighters because they cannot be lovers.

Avatamsaka (Kegon or Hua-yen) Buddhist philosophy sees the world as a vast, interrelated network in which all objects and creatures are necessary and illuminated. From one standpoint, governments, wars, or all that we consider "evil" are uncompromisingly contained in this totalistic realm. The hawk, the swoop, and the hare are one. From the "human" standpoint we cannot live in those terms unless all beings see with the same enlightened eye. The Bodhisattva lives by the sufferer's standard, and must be effective in aiding those who suffer.

The mercy of the West has been social revolution; the mercy of the East has been individual insight into the basic self/void. We need both.

They are both contained in the traditional three aspects of the Dharma path: wisdom *(prajña)*, meditation *(dhyana)*, and morality *(shila)*. Wisdom is intuitive knowledge of the mind of love and clarity that lies beneath one's ego-driven anxieties and aggressions. Meditation is going into the mind to see this for yourself—over and over again, until it becomes the mind you live in. Morality is bringing it back out in the way you live, through personal example and responsible action, ultimately toward the true community *(sangha)* of "all beings." This last aspect means, for me, supporting any cultural and economic revolution that moves clearly toward a truly free world. It means using such means as civil disobedience, outspoken criticism, protest, pacifism, voluntary poverty, and even gentle violence if it comes to a matter of restraining some impetuous crazy. It means affirming the widest possible spectrum of nonharmful individual behavior—defending the right of individuals to smoke hemp, eat peyote, be polygamous, polyandrous, or homosexual. Worlds of behavior and custom long banned by the Judaeo-Capitalist-Christian-Marxist West. It means respecting intelligence and learning, but not as greed or means to personal power. Working on one's own responsibility, but willing to work with a group. "Forming the new society within the shell of the old"—the I.W.W. slogan of 70 years ago.

The traditional, vernacular, primitive, and village cultures may appear to be doomed. We must defend and support them as we would the diversity of ecosystems; they are all manifestations of Mind. Some of the elder societies accomplished a condition of Sangha, with not a little of Buddha and Dharma as well. We touch base with the deep mind of peoples of all times and places in our meditation practice, and this is an amazing revolutionary aspect of the Buddhadharma. By a "planetary culture" I mean the kind of societies that would follow on a new understanding of that relatively recent institution, the national state, an understanding that might enable us to leave it behind. The state is greed made legal, with a monopoly on violence; a natural society is familial and cautionary. A natural society is one that "follows the way," imperfectly but authentically.

Such an understanding will close the circle and link us in many ways with the most creative aspects of our archaic past. If we are lucky, we may eventually arrive at a world of relatively mutually tolerant small societies attuned to their local natural region and united overall by a profound respect and love for the mind and nature of the universe.

I can imagine further virtues in a world sponsoring societies with matrilineal descent, free-form marriage, "natural credit" economics, far less population, and much more wilderness.

Passage to
More Than India

*"It will be a revival, in higher form, of the liberty,
equality, and fraternity of the ancient gentes."*
LEWIS HENRY MORGAN

The Tribe

The celebrated human Be-In in San Francisco, January of 1967, was called
"A Gathering of the Tribes." The two posters: one based on a photograph
of a Shaivite sadhu with his long matted hair, ashes, and beard; the other
based on an old etching of a Plains Indian approaching a powwow on his
horse—the carbine that had been cradled in his left arm replaced by a gui-
tar. The Indians, and the Indian. The tribes were Berkeley, North Beach,
Big Sur, Marin County, Los Angeles, and the host, Haight-Ashbury. Out-
riders were present from New York, London, and Amsterdam. Out on the
polo field that day the splendidly clad ab/originals often fell into clusters,
with children, a few even under banners. These were the clans.

Large old houses are rented communally by a group, occupied by couples and singles (or whatever combinations) and their children. In some
cases, especially in the rock-and-roll business and with light-show groups,
they are all working together on the same creative job. They might even
be a legal corporation. Some are subsistence farmers out in the country,
some are contractors and carpenters in small coast towns. One woman can
stay home and look after all the children while the other women hold jobs.
They will all be cooking and eating together and they may well be brown-

rice vegetarians. There might not be much alcohol or tobacco around the house, but there will certainly be a stash of marijuana and probably some LSD. If the group has been together for some time it may be known by some informal name, magical and natural. These households provide centers in the city and also out in the country for loners and rangers; gathering places for the scattered smaller hip families and havens for the questing adolescent children of the neighborhood. The clan sachems will sometimes gather to talk about larger issues—police or sheriff department harassments, busts, anti-Vietnam projects, dances, and gatherings.

All this is known fact. The number of committed total tribesmen is not so great, but there is a large population of crypto-members who move through many walks of life undetected and only put on their beads and feathers for special occasions. Some are in the academies, others in the legal or psychiatric professions—useful friends indeed. The number of people who use marijuana regularly and have experienced LSD is (considering it's all illegal) staggering. The impact of all this on the cultural and imaginative life of the nation—even the politics—is enormous.

And yet, there's nothing very new about it, in spite of young hippies just in from the suburbs for whom the "beat generation" is a kalpa away. For several centuries now Western Man has been ponderously preparing himself for a new look at the inner world and the spiritual realms. Even in the centers of nineteenth-century materialism there were dedicated seekers—some within Christianity, some in the arts, some within the occult circles. Witness William Butler Yeats. My own opinion is that we are now experiencing a surfacing (in a specifically "American" incarnation) of the Great Subculture which goes back as far perhaps as the late Paleolithic.

This subculture of illuminati has been a powerful undercurrent in all higher civilizations. In China it manifested as Taoism—not only Lao-tzu but the later Yellow Turban revolt and medieval Taoist secret societies—and the Zen Buddhists up till early Sung. Within Islam the Sufis. In India the various threads converged to produce Tantrism. In the West it has been represented largely by a string of heresies starting with the Gnostics, and on the folk level by "witchcraft."

Buddhist Tantrism, or *Vajrayana* as it's also known, is probably the finest and most modern statement of this ancient shamanistic-yogic-gnostic-socioeconomic view: that mankind's mother is Nature and Nature should be tenderly respected; that man's life and destiny are growth and enlightenment in self-disciplined freedom; that the divine has been made flesh and that flesh is divine; that we not only should but *do* love one another. This view has been harshly suppressed in the past as threatening to both Church and State. Today, on the contrary, these values seem almost biologically essential to the survival of humanity.

The Family

Lewis Henry Morgan (d. 1881) was a New York lawyer. He was asked by his club to reorganize it "after the pattern of the Iroquois confederacy." His research converted him into a defender of tribal rights and started him on his career as an amateur anthropologist. His major contribution was a broad theory of social evolution which is still useful. Morgan's *Ancient Society* inspired Engels to write *Origins of the Family, Private Property and the State* (1884, and still in print in both Russia and China), in which the relations between the rights of women, sexuality and the family, and attitudes toward property and power are tentatively explored. The pivot is the revolutionary implications of the custom of matrilineal descent, which Engels learned from Morgan; the Iroquois are matrilineal.

A schematic history of the family:

Hunters and gatherers—a loose monogamy within communal clans usually reckoning descent in the female line (matrilineal).

Early agriculturalists—a tendency toward group and polyandrous marriage, continued matrilineal descent and smaller-sized clans.

Pastoral nomads—a tendency toward stricter monogamy and patrilineal descent; but much premarital sexual freedom.

Iron-Age agriculturalists—property begins to accumulate and the family system changes to monogamy or polygyny with patrilineal descent. Concern with the legitimacy of heirs.

Civilization so far has implied a patriarchal, patrilineal family. Any other system allows too much creative sexual energy to be released into channels that are "unproductive." In the West, the clan, or gens, disappeared gradually, and social organization was ultimately replaced by political organization, within which separate male-oriented families compete: the modern state.

Engels' Marxian classic implies that the revolution cannot be completely achieved in merely political terms. Monogamy and patrilineal descent may well be great obstructions to the inner changes required for a people to truly live by "communism." Marxists after Engels let these questions lie. Russia and China today are among the world's staunchest supporters of monogamous, sexually turned-off families. Yet Engels' insights were not entirely ignored. The Anarcho-Syndicalists showed a sense for experimental social reorganization. American anarchists and the I.W.W. lived a kind of communalism, with some lovely stories handed down of free love—their slogan was more than just words: "Forming the new society within the shell of the old." San Francisco poets and gurus were attending meetings of the "Anarchist Circle"—old Italians and Finns—in the 1940s.

The Redskins

In many American Indian cultures it is obligatory for every member to get out of the society, out of the human nexus, and "out of his head," at least once in his life. He returns from his solitary vision quest with a secret name, a protective animal spirit, a secret song. It is his "power." The culture honors the man who has visited other realms.

Peyote, the mushroom, morning glory seeds, and jimsonweed are some of the best-known herbal aids used by Indian cultures to assist in the quest. Most tribes apparently achieved these results simply through yogic-type disciplines: including sweat-baths, hours of dancing, fasting, and total isolation. After the decline of the apocalyptic fervor of Wovoka's Ghost Dance religion (a pan-Indian movement of the 1880s and 1890s that believed that if all the Indians would dance the Ghost Dance with their Ghost shirts on, the Buffalo would rise from the ground, trample the white men to death in their dreams, and all the dead game would return; America would be restored to the Indians), the peyote cult spread and established itself in most of the western American tribes. Although the peyote religion conflicts with preexisting tribal religions in a few cases (notably with the Pueblo), there is no doubt that the cult has been a positive force, helping the Indians maintain a reverence for their traditions and land through their period of greatest weakness—which is now over. European scholars were investigating peyote in the twenties. It is rumored that Dr. Carl Jung was experimenting with peyote then. A small band of white peyote users emerged, and peyote was easily available in San Francisco by the late 1940s. In Europe some researchers on these alkaloid compounds were beginning to synthesize them. There is a karmic connection between the peyote cult of the Indians and the discovery of lysergic acid in Switzerland.

Peyote and acid have a curious way of tuning some people in to the local soil. The strains and stresses deep beneath one in the rock, the flow and fabric of wildlife around, the human history of Indians on this continent. Older powers become evident: west of the Rockies, the ancient creator-trickster, Coyote. Jaime de Angulo, a now-legendary departed Spanish shaman and anthropologist, was an authentic Coyote-medium. One of the most relevant poetry magazines is called *Coyote's Journal*. For many, the invisible presence of the Indian, and the heartbreaking beauty of America work without fasting or herbs. We make these contacts simply by walking the Sierra or Mohave, learning the old edibles, singing and watching.

The Jewel in the Lotus

At the Congress of World Religions in Chicago in the 1890s, two of the most striking figures were Swami Vivekananda (Shri Ramakrishna's disciple) and Shaku Soyen, the Zen Master and Abbot of Engaku-ji, representing Japanese Rinzai Zen. Shaku Soyen's interpreter was a college student named Teitaro Suzuki. The Ramakrishna-Vivekananda line produced scores of books and established Vedanta centers all through the Western world. A small band of Zen monks under Shaku Sokatsu (disciple of Shaku Soyen) was raising strawberries in Hayward, California, in 1907. Shigetsu Sasaki, later to be known as the Zen Master Sokei-an, was roaming the timberlands of the Pacific Northwest just before World War I, and living on a Puget Sound Island with Indians for neighbors. D. T. Suzuki's books are to be found today in the libraries of biochemists and on stone ledges under laurel trees in the open-air camps of Big Sur gypsies.

A Californian named Walter Y. Evans-Wentz, who sensed that the mountains on his family's vast grazing lands really did have spirits in them, went to Oxford to study the Celtic belief in fairies and then to Sikkim to study Vajrayana under a lama. His best-known book is *The Tibetan Book of the Dead*.

Those who do not have the money or time to go to India or Japan, but who think a great deal about the wisdom traditions, have remarkable results when they take LSD. The *Bhagavad-Gita,* the Hindu mythologies, *The Serpent Power,* the *Lankavatara-sōtra,* the *Upanishads,* the *Hevajra-tantra,* the *Mahanirvana-tantra*—to name a few texts—become, they say, finally clear to them. They often feel they must radically reorganize their lives to harmonize with such insights.

In several American cities traditional meditation halls of both Rinzai and Soto Zen are flourishing. Many of the newcomers turned to traditional meditation after initial acid experience. The two types of experience seem to inform each other.

The Heretics

"When Adam delved and Eve span,
Who was then a gentleman?"

The memories of a Golden Age—the Garden of Eden—the Age of the Yellow Ancestor—were genuine expressions of civilization and its discontents. Harking back to societies where women and men were more free with each other; where there was more singing and dancing; where there were no serfs and priests and kings.

Projected into future time in Christian culture, this dream of the Millennium became the soil of many heresies. It is a dream handed down right to our own time—of ecological balance, classless society, social and economic freedom. It is actually one of the possible futures open to us. To those who stubbornly argue "it's against human nature," we can only patiently reply that you must know your own nature before you can say this. Those who have gone into their own natures deeply have, for several thousand years now, been reporting that we have nothing to fear if we are willing to train ourselves, to open up, explore and grow.

One of the most significant medieval heresies was the Brotherhood of the Free Spirit, of which Hieronymus Bosch was probably a member. The Brotherhood believed that God was immanent in everything, and that once one had experienced this God-presence in himself he became a Free Spirit; he was again living in the Garden of Eden. The brothers and sisters held their meetings naked, and practiced much sharing. They "confounded clerics with the subtlety of their arguments." It was complained that "they have no uniform . . . sometimes they dress in a costly and dissolute fashion, sometimes most miserably, all according to time and place." The Free Spirits had communal houses in secret all through Germany and the Lowlands, and wandered freely among them. Their main supporters were the well-organized and affluent weavers.

When brought before the Inquisition they were not charged with witchcraft, but with believing that man was divine, and with making love too freely, with orgies. Thousands were burned. There are some who have as much hostility to the adepts of the subculture today. This may be caused not so much by the outlandish clothes and dope, as by the nutty insistence on "love." The West and Christian culture on one level deeply wants love to win—and having decided (after several sad tries) that love can't, people who still say it will are like ghosts from an old dream.

Love begins with the family and its network of erotic and responsible relationships. A slight alteration of family structure will project a different love-and-property outlook through a whole culture . . . thus the communism and free love of the Christian heresies. This is a real razor's edge. Shall the lion lie down with the lamb? And make love even? The Garden of Eden.

White Indians

The modern American family is the smallest and most barren family that has ever existed. Each newly married couple moves to a new house or apartment—no uncles or grandmothers come to live with them. There are seldom more than two or three children. The children live with their peers and leave home early. Many have never had the least sense of family.

I remember sitting down to Christmas dinner eighteen years ago in a communal house in Portland, Oregon, with about twelve others my own age, all of whom had no place they wished to go home to. That house was my first discovery of harmony and community with fellow beings. This has been the experience of hundreds of thousands of men and women all over America since the end of World War II. Hence the talk about the growth of a "new society." But more; these gatherings have been people spending time with each other—talking, delving, making love. Because of the sheer amount of time "wasted" together (without TV) they know each other better than most Americans know their own family. Add to this the mind-opening and personality-revealing effects of grass and acid, and it becomes possible to predict the emergence of groups who live by mutual illumination—have seen themselves as of one mind and one flesh— the "single eye" of the heretical English Ranters; the meaning of sahajiya, "born together"—the name of the latest flower of the Tantric community tradition in Bengal.

Industrial society indeed appears to be finished. Many of us are, again, hunters and gatherers. Poets, musicians, nomadic engineers, and scholars; fact-diggers, searchers, and re-searchers scoring in rich foundation territory. Horse-traders in lore and magic. The super hunting-bands of mercenaries like RAND or CIA may in some ways belong to the future, if they can be transformed by the ecological conscience, or acid, to which they are very vulnerable. A few of us are literally hunters and gatherers, playfully studying the old techniques of acorn flour, seaweed-gathering, yucca-fiber, rabbit snaring, and bow hunting. The densest Indian population in pre-Columbian America north of Mexico was in Marin, Sonoma, and Napa Counties, California.

And finally, to go back to Morgan and Engels, sexual mores and the family are changing in the same direction. Rather than the "breakdown of the family" we should see this as the transition to a new form of family. In the near future, I think it likely that the freedom of women and the tribal spirit will make it possible for us to formalize our marriage relationships in any way we please—as groups, or polygynously or polyandrously, as well as monogamously. I use the word "formalize" only in the sense of make public and open the relationships, and to sacramentalize them; to see family as part of the divine ecology. Because it is simpler, more natural, and breaks up tendencies toward property accumulation by individual families, matrilineal descent seems ultimately indicated. Such families already exist. Their children are different in personality structure and outlook from anybody in the history of Western culture since the destruction of Knossos.

The American Indian is the vengeful ghost lurking in the back of the troubled American mind. Which is why we lash out with such ferocity and passion, so muddied a heart, at the black-haired young peasants and soldiers who are the "Viet Cong." That ghost will claim the next generation as its own. When this has happened, citizens of the USA will at last begin to be Americans, truly at home on the continent, in love with their land. The chorus of a Cheyenne Indian Ghost dance song—*hi-niswa' vita'ki'ni*—"We shall live again."

> "Passage to more than India!
> Are thy wings plumed indeed for such far flights?
> O soul, voyagest thou indeed on voyages like those?"

Poetry and
the Primitive

*Notes on Poetry as an Ecological
Survival Technique*

Bilateral Symmetry

"Poetry" as the skilled and inspired use of the voice and language to embody rare and powerful states of mind that are in immediate origin personal to the singer, but at deep levels common to all who listen. "Primitive" as those societies that have remained nonliterate and nonpolitical while necessarily exploring and developing in directions that civilized societies have tended to ignore. Having fewer tools, no concern with history, a living oral tradition rather than an accumulated library, no overriding social goals, and considerable freedom of sexual and inner life, such people live vastly in the present. Their daily reality is a fabric of friends and family, the field of feeling and energy that one's own body is, the earth they stand on and the wind that wraps around it; and various areas of consciousness.

At this point some might be tempted to say that the primitive's real life is no different from anybody else's. I think this is not so. To live in the "mythological present" in close relation to nature and in basic but disciplined body/mind states suggests a wider-ranging imagination and a closer subjective knowledge of one's own physical properties than is usually available to men living (as they themselves describe it) impotently and inadequately in "history"—their mind-content programmed, and their caressing of nature complicated by the extensions and abstractions which elaborate tools are. A hand pushing a button may wield great power, but that hand will never learn what a hand can do. Unused capacities go sour.

Poetry must sing or speak from authentic experience. Of all the streams of civilized tradition with roots in the paleolithic, poetry is one of the few that can realistically claim an unchanged function and a relevance which will outlast most of the activities that surround us today. Poets, as few others, must live close to the world that primitive men are in: the world, in its nakedness, that is fundamental for all of us—birth, love, death; the sheer fact of being alive.

Music, dance, religion, and philosophy of course have archaic roots—a shared origin with poetry. Religion has tended to become the social justifier, a lackey to power, instead of the vehicle of hair-raising liberating and healing realizations. Dance has mostly lost its connection with ritual drama, the miming of animals, or tracing the maze of the spiritual journey. Most music takes too many tools. The poet can make it on his own voice and mother tongue, while steering a course between crystal clouds of utterly incommunicable nonverbal states—and the gleaming daggers and glittering nets of language.

In one school of Mahayana Buddhism, they talk about the "Three Mysteries." These are Body, Voice, and Mind. The things that are what living *is* for us, in life. Poetry is the vehicle of the mystery of voice. The universe, as they sometimes say, is a vast breathing body.

With artists, certain kinds of scientists, yogins, and poets, a kind of mind-sense is not only surviving but modestly flourishing in the twentieth century. Claude Lévi-Strauss (*The Savage Mind*) sees no problem in the continuity: "It is neither the mind of savages nor that of primitive or archaic humanity, but rather mind in its untamed state as distinct from mind cultivated or domesticated for yielding a return. . . . We are better able to understand today that it is possible for the two to coexist and interpenetrate in the same way that (in theory at least) it is possible for natural species, of which some are in their savage state and others transformed by agriculture and domestication, to coexist and cross . . . whether one deplores or rejoices in the fact, there are still zones in which savage thought, like savage species, is relatively protected. This is the case of art, to which our civilization accords the status of a national park."

Making Love with Animals

By civilized times, hunting was a sport of kings. The early Chinese emperors had vast fenced hunting reserves; peasants were not allowed to shoot deer. Millennia of experience, the proud knowledges of hunting magic—

animal habits—and the skills of wild plant and herb gathering were all but scrubbed away. Much has been said about the frontier in American history, but overlooking perhaps some key points: the American confrontation with a vast wild ecology, an earthly paradise of grass, water, and game—was mind-shaking. Americans lived next to vigorous primitives whom they could not help but respect and even envy, for three hundred years. Finally, as ordinary men supporting their families, they often hunted for food. Although marginal peasants in Europe and Asia did remain part-time hunters at the bottom of the social scale, these Americans were the vanguard of an expanding culture. For Americans, *nature* means wilderness, the untamed realm of total freedom—not brutish and nasty, but beautiful and terrible. Something is always eating at the American heart like acid: it is the knowledge of what we have done to our continent, and to the American Indian.

Other civilizations have done the same, but at a pace too slow to be remembered. One finds evidence in T'ang and Sung poetry that the barren hills of central and northern China were once richly forested. The Far Eastern love of nature has become fear of nature: gardens and pine trees are tormented and controlled. Chinese nature poets were too often retired bureaucrats living on two or three acres of trees trimmed by hired gardeners. The professional nature-aesthetes of modern Japan, tea-teachers and flower-arrangers, are amazed to hear that only a century ago dozens of species of birds passed through Kyoto where today only swallows and sparrows can be seen; and the aesthetes can scarcely distinguish those. "Wild" in the Far East means uncontrollable, objectionable, crude, sexually unrestrained, violent; actually ritually polluting. China cast off mythology, which means its own dreams, with hairy cocks and gaping pudenda, millennia ago; and modern Japanese families participating in an "economic miracle" can have daughters in college who are not sure which hole babies come out of. One of the most remarkable intuitions in Western thought was Rousseau's Noble Savage: the idea that perhaps civilization has something to learn from the primitive.

Man is a beautiful animal. We know this because other animals admire us and love us. Almost all animals are beautiful and paleolithic hunters were deeply moved by it. To hunt means to use your body and senses to the fullest: to strain your consciousness to feel what the deer are thinking today, this moment; to sit still and let your self go into the birds and wind while waiting by a game trail. Hunting magic is designed to bring the game to you—the creature who has heard your song, witnessed your sincerity, and out of compassion comes within your range. Hunting magic is not only aimed at bringing beasts to their death, but to assist in their birth—to promote their fertility. Thus the great Iberian cave paintings are not of hunting alone—but of animals mating and giving birth. A Spanish farmer who saw some reproductions from Altamira is reported to have said, "How beautifully this cow gives birth to a calf!" Breuil has said, "The religion of those days did *not* elevate the animal to the position of a god . . . but it was *humbly entreated* to be fertile." A Haida incantation goes:

> The Great One coming up against the current
> > begins thinking of it.
> The Great One coming putting gravel in his mouth
> > thinks of it
> You look at it with white stone eyes—
> > Great Eater begins thinking of it.

People of primitive cultures appreciate animals as other people off on various trips. Snakes move without limbs, and are like free penises. Birds fly, sing, and dance; they gather food for their babies; they disappear for months and then come back. Fish can breathe water and are brilliant colors. Mammals are like us, they fuck and give birth to babies while panting and purring; their young suck their mothers' breasts; they know terror and delight, they play.

Lévi-Strauss quotes Swanton's report on the Chickasaw, the tribe's own amusing game of seeing the different clans as acting out the lives of their totemic emblems: "The Raccoon people were said to live on fish and wild fruit, those of the Puma lived in the mountains, avoided water of which they were very frightened and lived principally on game. The Wild Cat clan slept in the daytime and hunted at night, for they had keen eyes; they were indifferent to women. Members of the Bird clan were up before daybreak: 'They were like real birds in that they would not bother anybody . . . the people of this clan have different sorts of minds, just as there are different species of birds.' They were said to live well, to be polygamous, disinclined to work, and prolific . . . the inhabitants of the 'bending-post-oak' house group lived in the woods . . . the High Corncrib house people were respected in spite of their arrogance: they were good gardeners, very industrious but poor hunters; they bartered their maize for game. They were said to be truthful and stubborn, and skilled at forecasting the weather. As for the Redskunk house group: they lived in dugouts underground."

We all know what primitive cultures don't have. What they *do* have is this knowledge of connection and responsibility that amounts to a spiritual ascesis for the whole community. Monks of Christianity or Buddhism, "leaving the world" (which means the games of society), are trying, in a decadent way, to achieve what whole primitive communities—men, women, and children—live by daily; and with more wholeness. The shaman-poet is simply the man whose mind reaches easily out into all manners of shapes and other lives, and gives song to dreams. Poets have carried this function forward all through civilized times: poets don't sing about society, they sing about nature—even if the closest they ever get to nature is their lady's queynt. Class-structured civilized society is a kind of mass ego. To transcend the ego is to go beyond society as well. "Beyond" there lies, inwardly, the unconscious. Outwardly, the equivalent of the unconscious is the wilderness: both of these terms meet, one step even farther on, as *one*.

One religious tradition of this communion with nature which has survived into historic Western times is what has been called witchcraft. The antlered and pelted figure painted on the cave wall of Trois Frères, a shaman-dancer-poet, is a prototype of both Shiva and the Devil.

Animal marriages (and supernatural marriages) are a common motif of folklore the world around. A recent article by Lynn White puts the blame for the present ecological crisis on the Judaeo-Christian tradition—animals don't have souls and can't be saved; nature is merely a ground for us to exploit while working out our drama of free will and salvation under the watch of Jehovah. The Devil? "The Deivill apeired vnto her in the liknes of ane prettie boy in grein clothes . . . and at that tyme the Deivil gaive hir his markis; and went away from her in the liknes of ane blak dowg." "He wold haw carnall dealling with ws in the shap of a deir, or in any vther shap, now and then, somtyme he vold be lyk a stirk, a bull, a deir, a rae, or a dowg, etc, and haw dealling with us."

The archaic and primitive ritual dramas, which acknowledged all the sides of human nature, including the destructive, demonic, and ambivalent, were liberating and harmonizing. Freud said *he* didn't discover the unconscious, poets had centuries before. The purpose of California shamanism was "to heal disease and resist death, with a power acquired from dreams." An Arapaho dancer of the Ghost Dance came back from his trance to sing:

> I circle around, I circle around
>
> The boundaries of the earth,
> The boundaries of the earth
>
> Wearing the long wing feathers as I fly
> Wearing the long wing feathers as I fly.

The Voice as a Woman

"Everything was alive—the trees, grasses, and winds were dancing with me, talking with me; I could understand the songs of the birds." This ancient experience is not so much—in spite of later commentators—"religious" as it is a pure perception of beauty. The phenomenal world experienced at certain pitches is totally living, exciting, mysterious, filling one with a trembling awe, leaving one grateful and humble. The wonder of the mystery returns direct to one's own senses and consciousness: inside and outside; the voice breathes, "Ah!"

Breath is the outer world coming into one's body. With pulse—the two always harmonizing—the source of our inward sense of rhythm. Breath is spirit, "inspiration." Expiration, "voiced," makes the signals by which the species connects. Certain emotions and states occasionally seize the body; one becomes a whole tube of air vibrating—all voice. In mantra chanting, the magic utterances, built of seed-syllables such as OM and AYNG and AH, repeated over and over, fold and curl on the breath until—when most weary and bored—a new voice enters, a voice speaks through you clearer and stronger than what you know of yourself; with a sureness and melody of its own, singing out the inner song of the self, and of the planet.

Poetry, it should not have to be said, is not writing or books. Nonliterate cultures with their traditional training methods of hearing and reciting, carry thousands of poems—death, war, love, dream, work, and spirit-power songs—through time. The voice of inspiration as an "other" has long been known in the West as the Muse. Widely speaking, the muse is anything other that touches you and moves you. Be it a mountain range, a band of people, the morning star, or a diesel generator. Breaks through the ego-barrier. But this touching-deep is as a mirror, and man in his sexual nature has found the clearest mirror to be his human lover. As the West moved into increasing complexities and hierarchies with civilization, Woman as nature, beauty, and the Other came to be an all-dominating symbol; secretly striving through the last three millennia with the Jehovah or Imperator God-figure, a projection of the gathered power of anti-nature social forces. Thus in the Western tradition the Muse and Romantic Love became part of the same energy, and woman as nature the field for experiencing the universe as sacramental. The lovers' bed was the sole place to enact the dances and ritual dramas that link primitive people to their geology and the Milky Way. The contemporary decline of the cult of romance is linked to the rise of the sense of the primitive, and the knowledge of the variety of spiritual practices and paths to beauty that cultural anthropology has brought us. We begin to move away now, in this interesting historical spiral, from monogamy and monotheism.

Yet the muse remains a woman. Poetry is voice, and according to Indian tradition, voice, vāk (vox)—is a Goddess. Vāk is also called Sarasvati, she is the lover of Brahma and his actual creative energy; she rides a peacock, wears white, carries a book-scroll and a vīna. The name Sarasvati means "the flowing one." "She is again the Divine in the aspect of wisdom and learning, for she is the Mother of Veda; that is of all knowledge touching Brahman and the universe. She is the Word of which it was born and She is that which is the issue of her great womb, Mahāyoni. Not therefore idly have men worshipped Vāk, or Sarasvati, as the Supreme Power."

As Vāk is wife to Brahma ("wife" means "wave" means "vibrator" in Indo-European etymology) so the voice, in everyone, is a mirror of his own deepest self. The voice rises to answer an inner need; or as BusTon says, "The voice of the Buddha arises, being called forth by the thought of the living beings." In esoteric Buddhism this becomes the basis of a mandala meditation practice: "In their midst is Nayika, the essence of *Ali,* the vowel series—she possesses the true nature of Vajrasattva, and is Queen of the Vajra-realm. She is known as the Lady, as Suchness, as Void, as Perfection of Wisdom, as limit of Reality, as Absence of Self."

The conch shell is an ancient symbol of the sense of hearing, and of the female; the vulva and the fruitful womb. At Koptos there is a bas-relief of a four-point buck, on the statue of the god Min, licking his tongue out toward two conches. There are many Magdalenian bone and horn engravings of bear, bison, and deer licking abstract penises and vulvas. At this point (and from our most archaic past transmitted) the mystery of voice becomes one with the mystery of body.

How does this work among primitive peoples in practice? James Mooney, discussing the Ghost Dance religion, says, "There is no limit to the number of these [Ghost Dance] songs, as every trance at every dance produces a new one, the trance subject after regaining consciousness embodying his experience in the spirit world in the form of a song, which is sung at the next dance and succeeding performances until superseded by other songs originating in the same way. Thus a single dance may easily result in twenty or thirty new songs. While songs are thus born and die, certain ones which appeal especially to the Indian heart, on account of their mythology, pathos, or peculiar sweetness, live and are perpetuated."

Modern poets in America, Europe, and Japan are discovering the breath, the voice, and trance. It is also for some a discovery to realize that the universe is not a dead thing but a continual creation, the song of Sarasvati springing from the trance of Brahma. "Reverence to Her who is eternal, Raudrī, Gaurī, Dhātri, reverence and again reverence, to Her who is the Consciousness in all beings, reverence and again reverence. . . . Candī says."

Hopscotch and Cats Cradles

The clouds are "Shining Heaven" with his
different bird-blankets on
HAIDA

The human race, as it immediately concerns us, has a vertical axis of about 40,000 years and as of A.D. 1900 a horizontal spread of roughly 3000 different languages and 1000 different cultures. Every living culture and language is the result of countless cross-fertilizations—not a "rise and fall" of civilizations, but more like a flowerlike periodic absorbing—blooming—bursting and scattering of seed. Today we are aware as never before of the plurality of human life-styles and possibilities, while at the same time we are tied, like in an old silent movie, to a runaway locomotive rushing headlong toward a singular catastrophe. Science, as far as it is capable of looking "on beauty bare," is on our side. Part of our being modern is the fact of our awareness that we are one with our beginnings—contemporary with all periods—members of all cultures. The seeds of every social structure or custom are in the mind.

The anthropologist Stanley Diamond has said, "The sickness of civilization consists in its failure to incorporate (and only then) to move beyond the limits of the primitive." Civilization is so to speak a lack of faith, a human laziness, a willingness to accept the perceptions and decisions of others in place of one's own—to be less than a full man. Plus, perhaps, a primate inheritance of excessive socializing; and surviving submission/dominance traits (as can be observed in monkey or baboon bands) closely related to exploitative sexuality. If evolution has any meaning at all we must hope to slowly move away from such biological limitations, just as it is within our power to move away from the self-imposed limitations of small-minded social systems. We all live within skin, ego, society, and species boundaries. Consciousness has boundaries of a different order—"the mind is free." College students trying something different because "they do it in New Guinea" are part of the real work of modern man: to uncover the inner structure and actual boundaries of the mind. The third Mystery. The charts and maps of this realm are called mandalas in Sanskrit. (A poem by the Sixth Dalai Lama runs "Drawing diagrams I measured / Movement of the stars / Though her tender flesh is near / Her mind I cannot measure.") Buddhist and Hindu philosophers have gone deeper into this than almost anyone else but the work is just beginning. We are now gathering all the threads of history together and linking modern science to the primitive and archaic sources.

The stability of certain folklore motifs and themes, while showing evidences of linguistic borrowing and offering examples of the deeper meaning of linguistic drift, finally prove that the laws which styles and structures (art-forms and grammars, songs and ways of courting) attend all relate and reflect each other as mirrors of the self. Even the uses of the word *nature,* as in the seventeenth-century witch Isobel Gowdie's testimony about what it was like to make love to the Devil—"I found his nature cold within me as spring-well-water"—throw light on human nature.

Thus nature leads into nature—the wilderness—and the reciprocities and balances by which man lives on earth. Ecology: "eco" (*oikos*) meaning "house" (cf. "ecumenical"): Housekeeping on Earth. Economics, which is merely the housekeeping of various social orders—taking out more than it puts back—must learn the rules of the greater realm. Ancient and primitive cultures had this knowledge more surely and with almost as much empirical precision (see H. C. Conklin's work on Hanunoo plant-knowledge, for example) as the most concerned biologist today. Inner and outer: the *Brihadāranyaka Upanishad* says, "Now this Self is the state of being of all contingent beings. In so far as a man pours libations and offers sacrifice, he is in the sphere of the gods; in so far as he recites the Veda he is in the sphere of the seers; in so far as he offers cakes and water to the ancestors, in so far as he gives food and lodging to men, he is of the sphere of men. In so far as he finds grass and water for domestic animals, he is in the sphere of domestic animals; in so far as wild beasts and birds, even down to ants, find something to live on in his house, he is of their sphere."

The primitive world view, far-out scientific knowledge, and the poetic imagination are related forces which may help if not to save the world or humanity, at least to save the Redwoods. The goal of Revolution is Transformation. Mystical traditions within the great religions of civilized times have taught a doctrine of Great Effort for the achievement of Transcendence. This must have been their necessary compromise with civilization, which needed for its period to turn man's vision away from nature, to nourish the growth of the social energy. The archaic, the esoteric, and the primitive traditions alike all teach that beyond transcendence is Great Play, and Transformation. After the mind-breaking Void, the emptiness of a million universes appearing and disappearing, all created things rushing into Krishna's devouring mouth; beyond the enlightenment that can say "these beings are dead already; go ahead and kill them, Arjuna" is a loving, simple awareness of the absolute beauty and preciousness of mice and weeds.

Tsong-kha-pa tells us of a transformed universe:

1. This is a Buddha-realm of infinite beauty
2. All men are divine, are subjects
3. Whatever we use or own are vehicles of worship
4. All acts are authentic, not escapes.

Such authenticity is at the heart of many a primitive world view. For the Anaguta of the Jos plateau, Northern Nigeria, North is called "up"; South is called "down." East is called "morning" and West is called "evening." Hence (according to Dr. Stanley Diamond in his *Anaguta Cosmography*), "Time flows past the permanent central position . . . they live at a place called noon, at the center of the world, the only place where space and time intersect." The Australian aborigines live in a world of ongoing recurrence—comradeship with the landscape and continual exchanges of being and form and position; every person, animals, forces, all are related via a web of reincarnation—or rather, they are "interborn." It may well be that rebirth (or interbirth, for we are actually mutually creating each other and all things while living) is the objective fact of existence which we have not yet brought into conscious knowledge and practice.

It is clear that the empirically observable interconnectedness of nature is but a corner of the vast "jewelled net" that moves from without to within. The spiral (think of nebulae) and spiral conch (vulva/womb) is a symbol of the Great Goddess. It is charming to note that physical properties of spiral conches approximate the Indian notion of the world-creating dance, "expanding form"—"We see that the successive chambers of a spiral Nautilus or of a straight Orthoceras, each whorl or part of a whorl of a periwinkle or other gastropod, each additional increment of an elephant's tusk, or each new chamber of a spiral foraminifer, has its leading characteristic at once described and its form so far described by the simple statement that it constitutes a *gnomon* to the whole previously existing structure" (D'Arcy Thompson).

The maze dances, spiral processions, cats cradles, Micronesian string star-charts, mandalas, and symbolic journeys of the old wild world are with us still in the universally distributed children's game. Let poetry and Bushmen lead the way in a great hop forward:

> In the following game of long hopscotch, the part marked H is for Heaven: it is played in the usual way except that when you are finishing the first part, on the way up, you throw your tor into Heaven. Then you hop to 11, pick up your tor,
> jump to the very spot where your tor landed in Heaven,
> and say, as fast as you can,
> the alphabet forwards and backwards,
> your name, address and telephone number (if you have one),
> your age,
> and the name of your boyfriend or girl-friend (if you have one of those).

PATRICIA EVANS, *Hopscotch*

Suwa-no-se Island
and the
Banyan Ashram

Several years ago Nanao Sakaki, the wanderer and poet, was traveling on
a small interisland freighter between Kyushu and Amami Oshima and
got into a conversation with a fellow passenger, an islander, who casually
invited Nanao to come visit his island. Nanao did, another year, and just
when a typhoon came; so he was holed up for over a week in a farmhouse
waiting for the storm to blow over.

The island has only eight households—forty people—and, though the
major part of the island is volcano and lavaflow, there is plenty of unoccu-
pied land that is livable. Hence the islanders told Nanao that if he or his
friends wished to come camp or live there, they'd be welcome.

Nanao's old circle of friends in Tokyo, the "Emerald Breeze" branch of
the "Harijan" (formerly known as the Bum Academy), had already started
a farm in the highlands of Nagano prefecture. They decided to add Suwa-
no-se Island to their plans: In May, Nanao, Miko and Shinkai went down;
Pon in June with several others; Franco, Naga, Masa, and me in July. You
have to go to Kagoshima, the southernmost town of size in Kyushu. A boat
leaves for the "Ten Islands" once a week. Unpredictably. So that we were
hung up for five days in Kagoshima, a cheap waterfront inn, while the
ship waited out a typhoon scare. Did our grocery shopping and walked
out to the ends of breakwaters waiting.

The "Toshima Maru" left at six in the evening. A little diesel freighter
of 250 tons. At daybreak coming in on Kuchi-no-erabu Island—silvery

rainsqualls, green cliffs, flashings of seabirds. The ship called at three islands through the day—anchoring beyond the edge of the coral reef, loading and unloading from tossing little unpainted island boats.

Late in the afternoon the ship was approaching Suwa-no-se, a violet mountain from afar, with cloudcaps and banners of mist. (The fishermen who come down from Miyazaki on Kyushu in their seaworthy little 3 ton fishing boats call it "Yake-jima"—Burning Island. Because much of the time the volcano is smoking.)

Anchoring offshore, the *Toshima Maru* blows its whistle and finally, down a steep trail through bamboo, a few men running. After half an hour a small boat puts out from behind a big boulder and cement breakwater at the base of the cliffs—steers through a path in the coral reef and comes alongside the freighter. The islanders bring out watermelons and wild goats. The goats go down to Amami Oshima where people like to eat them. Then, us, with our rucksacks and provisions, aboard the little boat, ashore through rough waves and getting wet, up on the rocky beach. Stepping over and through the lines and cables of several small fishing boats, nets, cables of the winch system for handling the boats in and out. Everybody waiting for us, almost black from being always in the sun. Packed all our groceries and rucksacks up the switchbacks and across a mile or so of trail through semijungle to the abandoned house and clearing they were using. Nanao and Shinkai had just finished a small extra shelter of bamboo; dome-shaped, with a thatch roof—so there was sleeping space for everyone. Fourteen people, almost half of them women.

Suwa-no-se is latitude 29° 36', which puts it on a level roughly with the Canary Islands, Cairo, Chihuahua, Persepolis, and Lhasa. Almost halfway from Kyushu to Amami Oshima. The Amami group of islands continue into the Ryukyus and the culture is quite similar to the Okinawan but there are dialect differences. From Yoron Island you can see Okinawa they say. Yoron is part of Japan. Suwa-no-se was probably populated off and on for several thousand years, depending on the activity of the volcano. The "Ten Islands" are part of a steppingstone system of islands all the way from Taiwan to Kyushu, by which paleolithic voyagers worked their way up to Japan. So they must have stopped off. Suwa-no-se was abandoned after the great eruption of the 15th century, and nobody returned until a century ago when some settlers came up from Amami to try again. Our villagers are thus of the Amami line, and speak Amami dialect; play the snake-head "jabisen" instead of the catskin-head "shamisen." They keep pigs, which is also an Amami custom. Mainland Japanese have never much taken to pigs. Also, they drink distilled sweet-potato liquor instead of sake; and sweet potatoes make a main part of the year's food—cheaper and easier to raise on the windy islands than rice.

The main part of the island is mountainous and uninhabited, but there is a kind of plateau about 400 feet above sea level that makes a southern extension, with several good streams running through it—an arable plateau maybe two miles by three miles, and covered for the most part by bamboo and grasses. A great pasture of fifty or so acres toward the east, and some pine and *Tabu* forests on the flanks of the mountain. Banyan trees and other large subtropical plants follow in the watercourses.

Sweet-potato and watermelon fields are cut-out squares in the bamboo here and there. The houses are clustered toward the west, which is closest to the little harbor; each house separate and enclosed in a wall of bamboo. Even the trails are shadowy corridors through the bamboo jungle and under the limbs of the banyan.

In the open pasture twenty-three head of black beef cattle at large, and on the edge of the pasture the abandoned farmhouse that became our headquarters. Up the meadow a way toward the mountain is a magnificent banyan on the edge of a ravine—we cleared out a meditation ground within its hanging roots—finally called our whole place "Banyan Ashram," or Pon calls it "Banyan Dream."

Daily work was clearing a new field for sweet-potato planting. We had to get all the bamboo root runners out, turning it over with hoes and grubbing the roots. Backbreaking work, and very slow. Because of midday heat it could only be done before ten-thirty or after four. In midday we napped in the shade of the banyan, or in the Bamboo House. Other work was fuel-gathering (dead pine underbranches; dead bamboo; or driftwood from the beaches loaded in a carrying basket and toted with a tumpline on the forehead) and cooking; done by turn in pairs in an open kitchen-shed with a thatch roof on an old brick campfire stove. Chinese style. (Our diet was basically brown rice and miso soup with potatoes and sweet potatoes and occasional watermelons or local bananas.) Also a lot of carpentry and construction work was continually going on, and a few hands every few days down to the village to join in on a village project, community trail-repair, or helping gut and flay an extra-large flying fish catch before it could spoil.

The ocean: every day except when the wind was too strong (fringe of a typhoon somewhere) most of us made it to the beach. There are three places to go: the eastern beach, forty minutes by trail, is wide and rough, with a good view of the volcano. The waves are very heavy. It looks across the Pacific toward Mexico. The coral reef goes out a long way, so it's not suitable for skindiving except when the weather is exceptionally calm. The beach has splendid driftwood and drift-lumber, and lots of seashells to gather. There's a cave toward one end within which thirty-six cows can stand in a rainstorm without getting wet. The southern beach is reached by a brushy trail also forty minutes—steep descent down the cliff but possible no-hands; it has a shorter coral ledge and a lovely natural cove within the coral which is deep and affords a passage into deep water under the breakers (you swim out to the gate and dive and glide underwater for thirty or forty feet and surface beyond the heavy pounding). There are strong tidal currents here, and we decided it was dangerous for anyone not an excellent swimmer and diver.

The western beach is the most sheltered and the best for fishing. We had vague ideas about spearfishing from the beginning and I brought a pocketful of steel harpoon heads (the smallest ones) with me—but it wasn't until Arikawa-san, the youngest family man of the islanders, showed us how to make a long bamboo spear with an iron rod in the end on which the spearhead sockets (attached to the main bamboo by leader) that we seriously began to think about adding fish to our diet. The spear is powered by inner-tube rubber, and is about nine feet long. Ito and I made three of these. With flippers and goggles, spent two fruitless days in the water till we began to understand the habits and feelings of the different species. Then we began to take them regularly. It became noticeably easier to do heavy work with more protein in the diet.

Most of us would be vegetarians by choice, but this was a real case of necessity and ecology. The volcanic soil of the island (and the volcanic ash fallout) makes it hard to raise many vegetables there; but the waters are rich in fish. We offered our respects and gratitude to the fish and the Sea Gods daily, and ate them with real love, admiring their extraordinarily beautiful, perfect little bodies.

Hundreds of varieties and thousands of individuals, all edible. Cobalt blue, shades of yellow and orange seemed the most common. None of the fish are really "tropical" and strange—but they are clearly subtropical with more variety than you'd find in colder waters. I became absorbed in the life of the sea. Without a fish book I came to recognize dozens of species and gradually came to know their habits and peculiarities and territories and emotions.

There is a great truth in the relationship established by hunting: as in love or art, you must become one with the other. (Which is why Paleolithic hunting magic is so important historically: the necessities of identity, intuition, stillness, that go with hunting make it seem as though shamanism and yoga and meditation may have their roots in the requirements of the hunter—where a man learns to be motionless for a day, putting his mind in an open state so that his consciousness won't spook creatures that he knows will soon be approaching.)

In spearfishing we learned you must never choose a specific fish for a quarry: you must let the fish choose you, and be prepared to shoot the fish that will come into range. For some fish you must be one with the sea and consider yourself a fish among fish. But there was one large and unpredictable variety (cobalt with a crescent-shaped tail) that digs the strange. When one of those was around I would change my mind and consider myself a freak and be out of place; in which case he will come to look at you out of curiosity.

When you go down with the fishes minus your spear they treat you differently too. I got so I could go down to twenty-five or thirty feet fairly comfortably. An old man originally from Okinawa, Uaji-san, dives sixty feet. He's seventy years old, and has a wise, tough, beautiful young wife. He caught a sea turtle and gave most of it to the Ashram once.

Sometimes the islanders had special catches on their little boats; once we had all the shark meat we could eat; another time a giant feast of raw sawara; once a whole bucket of flying-fish eggs. A few times went on shellfish-gathering expeditions together. By next summer the Ashram plans to have a small boat, which will make fishing a regular and efficient operation.

The weather is breezy, the sun hot. The ocean sends up great squalls and sudden rainstorms which dry up in twenty minutes. The volcano goes grummmmmmmm and lots of purple smoke comes up, into the sky, to 15,000 feet.

Meals were served on the mat-floor of the farmhouse, everybody cross-legged, with Taku-chan the Gotos' two-year-old boy wandering stark naked through it all. After supper at night we generally sat almost totally silent around our two or three candles, sometimes humming mantras or folksongs; or went out in the cow pasture with a bottle of shochu and played the jew's-harp (which the Harijan all call a bigigi, the New Guinea name for it) and the Kenya drum (a present from Ginzap four years ago) to our patron star, Antares.

Those who rose very early went to meditate under the banyan—a lovely thing especially because of the song of the Akahige ("Redbeard" Temminck's Robin) which sings in the early-morning canyons with a remarkable trilling, falling song that drops three octaves and echoes across hills and meadows. Also the songs of the Hototo-gisu (Himalayan Cuckoo) and Blue Doves—filling up the whole morning world with song. While morning mists blow and curl around and the grass is all dewy and the Rising Sun of Japan comes up through the ocean and the fog like a big red rising sun flag.

After breakfast every morning there would be a quiet, natural discussion of the day's work; people would volunteer for various tasks—never any pressuring—somebody might say, "Let's be sure and put the tools back where we got them, I couldn't find the file yesterday" or something—but without acrimony; Westerners have much to learn from this easy cooperativeness and sense of getting the work done without fuss. The Banyan people had less ego-friction (none!) and difficulty over chores than any group I've ever seen.

Masa Uehara and I were married on the island on August 6, the new moon. The whole ashram stayed up late the night before, packing a breakfast for the morrow—and broiling a splendid pink tai that was a present from the village. (No marriage is complete if you don't eat tai afterwards, the noble, calm AUSPICIOUS FISH of Japan.) We got up at 4:30 and started up the brush trail in the dark. First dipping into a ravine and then winding up a jungly knife-edge ridge. By five we were out of the jungle and onto a bare lava slope. Following the long ridge to an older, extinct crater, and on to the crest of the main crater and the summit shortly after sunrise. The lip of the crater drops off into cloud; and out of the cloud comes a roaring like an airport full of jets: a billowing of steam upwards. The cloud and mist broke, and we could see 800 feet or so down into the crater—at least a mile across—and fumaroles and steam-jets; at the very center red molten lava in a little bubbly pond. The noise, according to the switch of the wind, sometimes deafening.

Standing on the edge of the crater, blowing the conch horn and chanting a mantra; offering shochu to the gods of the volcano, the ocean, and the sky; then Masa and I exchanged the traditional three sips—Pon and Nanao said a few words; Masa and I spoke; we recited the Four Vows together, and ended with three blasts on the conch. Got out of the wind and opened the rucksacks to eat the food made the night before, and drink the rest of the shochu. We descended from the summit and were down to the Banyan tree by eleven—went direct on out to the ocean and into the water; so that within one morning we passed from the windy volcanic summit to the warm coral waters. At four in the afternoon all the villagers came to the Ashram—we served saké and shochu—pretty soon everyone was singing Amami folksongs and doing traditional dances.

The sweet-potato field got cleared and planted; Franco left a bit early to be in San Luis Obispo by mid-September; we started clearing another patch of land and built a big outdoor table of driftwood; went around to the north side of the island in a small boat to investigate other possibilities of settlements and fishing.

Masa and I caught the *Toshima Maru* heading on south at the end of August and visited Cho in Koniya; with Shinkai checked on boatbuilders' prices; took another ship up to Kagoshima (all night on the deck sitting on matting watching the full moon).

And hitchhiked to Miyazaki for a three-day Harijan gathering and a look at the neolithic tumuli in the region; and back to Kyoto. Miko and

Akibananda and others will be on the island all year; Pon and Nanao are back up in Nagano at the mountain Ashram now.

It is possible at last for Masa and me to imagine a little of what the ancient—archaic—mind and life of Japan were. And to see what could be restored to the life today. A lot of it is

simply in being aware of clouds and wind.

He Who Hunted Birds in His Father's Village

The Myth

He Who Hunted Birds in His Father's Village
(Told by Walter McGregor of the Sealion-town people)

He was a chief's son. He wore two marten-skin blankets, one over the other. After he had shot birds for some time he went along among some bull pines, which stood in an open space behind the town, and presently heard geese calling. Then he went thither. Two women were bathing in a lake. On the shore opposite two goose skins hung over a stick. The roots of their tails were spotted with white.

After he had looked a while he ran quickly (to them). He sat down on the two skins. Then they asked him for their (skins). He asked the best looking to marry him. The other said to him: "Do not marry my younger sister. I am smarter. Marry me." "No; I am going to marry your younger sister." Now she agreed. "Even so, marry my younger sister. You caught us swimming in the lake our father owns. Come, give me my skin." Then he gave it to her. She put her head into it as she swam in the lake. Lo, a goose swam about in the lake. It swam about in it making a noise.

Then she flew. She was unwilling to fly away from her younger sister. After she had flown about above her for a while, she flew up. She vanished through the sky. Then he gave her (the other) one marten-skin blanket and went home with her. He put his wife's skin between two heads of a cedar standing at one end of the town. He entered his father's house with her.

The chief's son had a wife. So his father called the people together for the marriage feast. They gave her food. Instead (of eating it) she merely smelled it. She ate no kind of human food.

By and by her mother-in-law steamed some *tcal*. But she liked that. While her mother-in-law was yet cooking them she told her husband to tell her to hurry. They put some before her. She ate it all. Then they began giving her that only to eat.

One day, when he was asleep, he was surprised to find that his wife's

---

71

skin, after she came in and lay down, was cold. And, when the same thing happened again, he began watching her. He lay as if asleep. He felt her get up quietly. Then she went out, and he also went out just after her. She passed in front of the town. She went to the place where her skin was kept. Thence she flew away. She alighted on the farther side of a point at one end of the town.

Then he went thither quickly. She was eating the stalks of the sea grass that grew there. As the waves broke in they moved her shoreward. He saw it. Then she flew up to the place where her (feather) skin had been kept. And he entered the house before her. Then he lay down where they had their bed, after which his wife lay down cold beside him.

They became nearly starved in the town. One day the woman said to him from the place where she was sitting: "Now my father has sent down food to me." Behind the town geese were coming down making a great noise, and she went thither. They went with her. All kinds of good food lay there such as *tcal* and wild clover roots. They brought them away. For this her father-in-law called in the people.

When this was gone she said the same thing again: "Now my father is bringing food down to me." Geese again made a great noise coming down behind the town and she went thither. Again heaps of food of all kinds lay around, and they carried that also out. For that, too, her father-in-law called together the people.

At that time someone in the town said: "They think a great deal of goose food." The woman heard it. Immediately she went off. Her husband in vain tried to stop her. She went off as one of a strange family would. In the same way he tried to stop her in front of the town. She went to the place where her skin was. She flew up. She flew around above the town for a while. Her heart was not strong to fly away from her husband. By and by she vanished through the sky.

Then her husband began to walk about the town wailing. By and by he entered the house of an old man at one end of the town and asked him: "Do you know the trail that leads to my wife?" "Why, brave man, you married the daughter of a supernatural being too great for people even to think of." At once he began bringing over all sorts of things to him. After he had given him twisted cedar limbs, a gimlet, and bones, he said to him: "Now, brave man, take oil. Take two wooden wedges also. Take as well, a comb, thongs, boxes of salmon eggs, the skin of a silver salmon, the point of a salmon spear." After he had got all these he came to him. "Old man, here are all the things you told me to take." "Now, brave man, go on. The trail runs inland behind my house."

Then he started in on it. After he had gone on for a while he came to someone who was looking upon himself for lice. Every time he turned around the lice fell off from him. After he had looked at him unobserved for a while he said to him: "Now brave man, do not tickle me by looking at me. It was in my mind that you were coming." Then he came out to him and combed his head. He also put oil on it. He cleared him of lice. He gave the comb and the hair oil to him. Then he said to him: "This trail leads to the place where your wife is."

He started along the trail. After he had gone on for a while (he saw) a mouse with cranberries in its mouth going along before him. She came to a fallen tree. She could not get over it. Then he took her by the back with his fingers and put her across. Her tail was bent up between her ears (for joy), and she went on before him. Presently she went among the stalks of a clump of ferns.

Now he rested himself there. Something said to him: "The chief-woman asks you to come in." Then he raised the ferns. He stood in front of a big house. He entered. The chief-woman was steaming cranberries. She talked as she did so. Her voice sounded sharp. And, after she had given him something to eat, Mouse Woman said to him: "You helped me when I went to get some poor cranberries from a patch I own. I will lend you what I wore when I went hunting when I was young."

Then she brought out a box. After she had opened a nest of five boxes, she took out of the inmost a mouse skin with small, bent claws. And she said to him: "Practice wearing this." And, although it was so small, he entered it. It went on easily. Then he climbed around upon the roof of the house inside. And Mouse Woman said to him again: "You know how to use it. Now go on."

Again he set out upon the trail. After he had gone along for a while he heard someone grunting under a heavy burden. Then he came to the place. A woman was trying to carry off a pile of large, flat stones upon her back. The twisted cedar limbs she had kept breaking. After he had looked at her for a while he went out to her. "Say, what are you doing?" Then the woman said: "They got me to carry the mountains of the Haida Island. I am doing it."

Then he took out his thongs and said to her: "Let me fix it." And he bound the thongs around it. He said to her, "Now carry it on your back," and she carried it. It did not break. Then the woman said to him, "Now brave man, thank you for helping me. The trail to your wife's place runs here."

Then he set out upon it. After he had gone on for a while he came to a hill in an open place on top of which rose something red. Then he went to it. Around the bottom of this something lay human bones. There was no way in which one could go up. Then he entered the mouse skin and rubbed salmon eggs before him (on the pole). He went up after it. When he stood on top of this he clambered up on the sky.

There, too, there ran a trail, and he started off upon it. After he had gone on for a while he heard the noise of laughter and singing. After he had gone on a while longer (he came to where) a big stream flowed down. Near it sat Eagle. On the other side also sat Heron. Above sat Kingfisher. On the other side sat Black Bear. He (Black Bear) had no claws. He said to Eagle: "Grandfather, lend me some claws." Then he lent him some. At that time he came to have claws.

After he had sat there for a while a half-man came vaulting along. He had only one leg and one arm. He had but half a head. He speared silver salmon in the river and pulled them in. Then he entered his silver salmon skin and swam up to meet him. When he speared him he could not pull him down. Then he cut his string. And the half-man said: "What did it is like a human being."

Now he came to him. "Say, did something pull off your spearpoint?" "Yes," he said to him. Then he gave him the one he had. That was Master Hopper, they say. After he had gone up (he came upon) two large old men who had come after firewood. They were cutting at the trunks of rotten trees and throwing the chips into the water, when silver salmon went down in a shoal.

He went behind and put stones in from behind, and their wedges were broken off. Then he (one) said: "Alas, they will make trouble for us." Then he went and gave them his two wedges. They were glad and said to him: "This house is your wife's."

Then he went out (to it). He went and stood in front of the house. His wife came out to him. Then he went in with her. She was glad to see her husband. And all the things they gathered he, too, gathered along with them.

After he had been there for some time he came to dislike the place. And his wife told her father. Then his father-in-law called the people. In the house he asked them: "Who will take my son-in-law down?" And Loon said: "I will put him near my tail, dive into the water right in front with him, come up at the end of his father's village, and let him off." Then they thought he was not strong enough for it.

Then he asked again. Grebe said the same thing. Him, too, they thought not strong enough to do it. Then Raven said that he would take him down. And they asked him: "How are you going to do it?" "I will put him into my armpit and fly down with him from the end of the town. When I get tired I will fall over and over with him." Then they thought he could do it.

They stood in a crowd at the end of the town looking at him. He did with him as he had said. When he became very tired and was nearly down he threw him off upon a reef which lay there. "Yuwaiya, what a heavy thing I am taking down." Shortly he (the man) was making a noise there as a seagull.

Function of the Myth

Introductory

Contemporary theory of the function of mythology almost inevitably involves theory of the function of language, ritual, religion, and art—either as similar but separate modes of psychocultural activity, or as ultimately identical aspects of the same thing, sometimes termed "Myth" in the broader sense of all symbolic cognition. The philosophical substructures implied in most of these theories include everything from metaphysics to theory of knowledge. In utilizing concepts from them it will be impossible to take into account the possible criticisms of their basic assumptions. My intention is to present the possible extent of the cultural function of the Haida Swan-Maiden myth, through a description and discussion of general statements by individuals of philosophical, literary, psychological, and anthropological persuasions. In doing so it may be argued that I am misinterpreting a theory or ignoring some underlying assumptions. I can only answer that the total view achieved by this method is my own doing, created by the selection of relevant concepts and implying no criticism of or assent to, any one point of view. It may appear, through my manner of presentation, that the scholars quoted are all in essential agreement. This is, to the best of my knowledge, only occasionally true, and under the peaceful surface of this discussion rage a number of minor controversies with which I am but superficially acquainted.

Anthropological studies dealing with oral literature as a functional element in culture are rare; and they are, with few exceptions, restricted to generalizing on the subject of mythology. Functionally oriented ethnology has never been practiced on the Haida. The concluding definition of the Haida Swan-Maiden myth will be the product of the most speculative approach in this thesis. Its verification would require residence in the culture, which for me is not possible.

The basic assumption of this chapter is that mythology has a function in culture. This may seem too obvious a fact to require statement, but many past theories of mythology have operated as if myths were irrational diseases from which savage minds suffered, or the result of idle, mistaken savage speculation in which elaborate stories were constructed to describe the phases of the moon or processes of sunrise and sunset. Much of the modern interest in mythology stems from the recognition of its social function, as does the even more recent attitude of some scholars and poets that the function mythology serves in primitive culture is desperately needed by contemporary society. The progress-minded nineteenth-century anthropologists, for whom mythology seemed curious, irrational, and "wrong," could never have discovered the world-shaking significance in irrational and (to Andrew Lang's continual dismay) sometimes bestial little stories which today are seen as descriptions of man's inmost needs. For example, take the modern associations attached to the Oedipus myth.

This chapter will first present statements of the function and nature of mythology, then clarify the sociopsychological processes as studied by Abram Kardiner, link together a number of other views on the function of mythology in his terms, and conclude with a summary of the entire thesis and the dimensions of mythology as indicated by this study.

Description of the Function

Recognition of the social function of mythology may be traced, in terms of the first influential, articulate public statement on the subject, to Bronislaw Malinowski's "Myth in Primitive Psychology," published in 1926. His essay was based on field observation among the Trobriand Islanders. He wrote:

> Myth as it exists in a savage community, that is, in its living primitive form, is not merely a story told but a reality lived. It is not of the nature of fiction, such as we read today in a novel, but it is a living reality, believed to have once happened in primeval times, and continuing ever since to influence the world and human destinies. This myth is to the savage what, to a fully believing Christian, is the Biblical story of Creation, of the Fall, of the Redemption by Christ's Sacrifice on the Cross. As our sacred story lives in our ritual, in our morality, as it governs our faith and controls our conduct, even so does his myth for the savage.

> . . . Myth fulfills in primitive culture an indispensable function: it expresses, enhances, and codifies belief; it safeguards and enforces morality; it vouches for the efficiency of ritual and contains practical rules for the guidance of man. Myth is thus a vital ingredient of

human civilization; it is not an idle tale, but a hard-worked active force; it is not an intellectual explanation or an artistic imagery, but a pragmatic character of primitive faith and moral wisdom.

Although Malinowski's essay, which was limited to primitive culture, emphasized the necessity of studying mythology in the cultural context, he has been cited by later writers with divergent and much more inclusive views of myth. Mark Schorer, for example:

> Myths are the instruments by which we continually struggle to make our experience intelligible to ourselves. A myth is a large, controlling image that gives philosophical meaning to the facts of ordinary life; that is, which has organizing value for experience.
>
> . . . Literature ceases to be perceptual and tends to degenerate into mere description without adequate myth; for, to cite Malinowski, myth, continually modified and renewed by the modification of history, is in some form an "indispensable ingredient of all culture."

On the same page Schorer quotes Jung, and shows indebtedness to Jung's view of myth by the statement "Myth is fundamental, the dramatic representation of our deepest instinctual life."

The same essay provoked an objection from Robert Lowie:

> . . . What if myth is "not merely a story but a reality lived?" We cannot relive the reality, but we can study that textual rendering which Malinowski disdains as merely the "intellectual" aspect of the tales divorced from their mystic aura.

C. Kerenyi made the complete marriage of Malinowski's view and Jungian theory, while setting out to show that we *can* relive the reality. He quotes the entire "reality lived" passage and writes:

> The myth, he (Malinowski) says, is not an explanation put forward to satisfy scientific curiosity; it is the re-arising of a primordial reality in narrative form.
>
> Mythology gives a ground, lays a foundation. It does not answer the question "why," but "whence?" In Greek we can put this difference very nicely. Mythology does not actually indicate "causes," *aitia*. It does this (is "aetiological") only to the extent that . . . the *aitia* are *archai* or first principles . . . (happenings in mythology) are the *archai* to which everything individual and particular goes back and out of which it is made, whilst they remain ageless, inexhaustible, invincible in timeless primordiality, in a past that proves imperishable because of its eternally repeated rebirths.

Kerenyi suggests the possibility of the archetypal "mythologems" being present—literally—in the physical beginnings of man:

> He experiences it (the mythologem) as his own absolute *archai,* a beginning since when he was a unity fusing in itself all the contradictions of his nature and life to be. To this origin, understood as the beginning of a new world-unity, the mythologem of the *divine child* points. The mythologem of the *maiden goddess* points to yet another *archai,* also experienced as one's own origin but which is at the same time the *archai* of countless beings before and after oneself, and by virtue of which the individual is endowed with infinity already in the germ.

Another scholar who is well aware of Malinowski's work is I. A. Richards. He wrote of the "greater and saner mythologies"—

> They are no amusement or diversion to be sought as a relaxation and an escape from the hard realities of life. They are these hard realities in projection, their symbolic recognition, coordination and acceptance. Through such mythologies our will is collected, our powers unified, our growth controlled. . . . Without his mythologies man is only a cruel animal without a soul—for a soul is a central part of his governing mythology—he is a congeries of possibilities without order and without aim.

Kerenyi's theory remains so problematical as to render no heuristic service. Of Schorer's and Richards' views—if they are to prove of value— we must ask: how and why are hard realities projected, and how, once projected, do they serve as "controlling images"—and what do they control? The two key words "projection" and "control" have been used before in this essay in connection with the cultural content of mythology, and the operation of magic and ritual. The investigation of these words will show them to mean essentially the same thing in the various contexts cited, and demonstrate what Malinowski probably had in mind when he said that a myth is a reality lived.

Kardiner's Use of the Term "Projection"

Abram Kardiner uses the term "projection" in a fairly specific sense, and in doing so describes what he conceives the process to be psychologically—and how values get into myths. His psychology is a socially-oriented neo-Freudianism. In *The Individual and His Society* and *The Psychological Frontiers of Society* he has presented a method of study and interpretation of culture that he believes will enable the student to determine the formative institutions (those institutions which regulate the formative experiences of childhood) and the influences of these institutions on the individual personality and total cultural configuration. The analysis of the mythology of the culture under observation plays an important part in Kardiner's analysis:

> We have had up to this point a series of inferences about the probable effects of certain formative institutions. How can this guess be substantiated or contradicted? If your hypothesis is correct, namely that these conditions in childhood become consolidated and form a basis for subsequent projective use, then we can expect to find some evidence of it in all projective systems . . . religious, folklore, and perhaps other institutions. In other words, if we know how the basic personality is established, we can make certain predictions about the institutions this personality is likely to invent. If we follow the particular personality created by the above mentioned conditions (sporadic minimal parental care, teasing of and deliberate misrepresentation to, children by parents) we expect to find folk tales dealing with parental hatred, with desertion by parents. . . .

Kardiner's assumption is that as the individual personality is shaped by the primary institutions, the oral prose-narrative, possessed and transmitted by the group, will mirror a group-personality derived from childhood experience. In reversing the process, he believes the culture's basic personality will reflect the psychologically relevant elements to be found in the tales. Kardiner's technique in both books is to cite ethnographic material on a culture, including a selection of abstracted tales, then to analyze the culture on the basis of the ethnographer's report and his own psychological assumptions, and finally, to cite the folktales as corroborative evidence of the truth of his analysis. In doing so, he avoids any discussion of the world distribution of types and motifs involved. The primary institutions center in the family structure—maternal care, induction of affectivity, maternal attitudes, early disciplines, sexual disciplines and institutionalized sibling attitudes. He lists these and a number of other institutions as the "Key Integrative Systems," which he ranks in terms of their manifestation in the basic personality structure as follows:

1. Projective systems based on experience with the aid of rationaliza tions, generalizations, systematization and elaboration. To this category belong the security system of the individual and the superego systems, that is, those dealing with conscience and ideals.
2. Learned systems connected with drives.
3. Learned systems in which no drives are involved but ideas associated with activities. Groups 2 and 3 lay the basis for specific psychosomatic tension release routes.

4. Taboo systems, all learned as part of reality.
5. Pure empirical reality systems, subject to demonstrations.
6. Value systems and ideologies (which cut across all previous systems.)

Projective systems are schematically represented by Kardiner as being created in the following manner:

Nuclear experiences which define apperceptions and emotionally directed interests, e.g., punishments for delinquency.

(resulting in:)

Abstraction and generalization: e.g., "If I am obedient I will suffer no pain."

(resulting in:)

Projection and systematization: e.g., "I am ill, therefore I have wronged."

(resulting in:)

Rationalization (equals) ideology (equals) a system to overcome tensions:
    "There is a supreme being who observes my behavior. He has the attributes of omnipotence and omniscience, etc. If I do wrong I will be punished. If I suffer I will be reinstated." Once this system is accepted as reality, any number of rational systems can be devised to "prove" it, to modify it, or to render it workable.

By the same process a body of mythology is created, although the projected attitudes are contained in narrative form. In his analysis of Comanche folklore, for instance, Kardiner finds these underlying projections:

The story of the faithless wife who sides with the Ute against her husband and is punished by him is another evidence of the underlying distrust of women, undoubtedly a projection of their (the Comanches') own anxiety about loss of power for war and sex alike.

A magic-flight story of children (Hansel and Gretel type):

It belittles the importance of parental care, and in sour-grapes fashion indicates that they (the children) don't need the parents anyway, they can look after themselves. This seems very like a protest against the unusual burdens placed on the child to emulate the parents and to become prematurely independent.

Kardiner divides the integrational systems into the major categories of "reality" and "projective" systems. He writes:

> In every society studied we found evidence of these two systems. The empirical reality systems were found in the manipulation and making of tools, the knowledge of planting, and so forth; the projective systems in religion, folklore, and many other systems.
>
> These two types of mental process depend upon different orders of experience. . . . Both have emotional components . . . the experiential base of a projective system is generally forgotten; its only remains in the personality are to be found in the conditioned perceptions. . . . Projective systems are . . . excrescences developed from nuclear traumatic experiences within the growth pattern of the individual.

He terms the latter system the "projective screen"—and in his discussion of its operation, becomes so annoyed with it as to ignore its functional value:

> The fantasy or projective screen hides social realities, and one cannot come to grips with them because the fantasy screen itself becomes the chief object of preoccupation and is mistaken for the reality to be dealt with.

In the same chapter, he admits "there is no difference between the actual logical or ratiocinative processes in the two (reality and projective) systems." The projective screen appears to be identical with what writers term "myth" in its broadest sense: the myth that reflects projected values, and in doing so reinforces the social fabric individual by individual, making it possible for the culture to survive. In admitting the identity of mental processes in the two systems, Kardiner lays himself open to the charge of projecting Western values in assuming that there are any "social realities" actually masked by the projective screen. For the culture in question, mythological and social realities are identical, and the function of mythology is to enforce this fusion—even though, to use Richards' term, the projections are of "hard realities." An even more extreme attack on Kardiner's dichotomy between projective and reality systems could be made from the philosophical stand denying the dualism of subject and object: the whole world is a projection, and mythology a particularly ordered projection that enables the more chaotic aspects of the world to be classified and comprehended.

Whether one agrees with Kardiner's projective-reality dichotomy or not, the careful scholarship and documented arguments of the two books, particularly the later one, are extremely convincing. Kardiner's description of the nature of projection undoubtedly covers a number of its most basic aspects and provides, if one accepts the Freudian tenets, a very workable theory of the interrelations of culture, personality, and mythology.

Projection and Control

The ideas, attitudes, or situations projected into a myth—those derived from everyday experience as well as the less obvious ones based on childhood experience—have a peculiar relationship with the symbolic units representing them in narrative. The social value and the values expressed in myth are somehow connected, and in the myth's function, the projected unit appears to control and shape the experiences it was derived from, rather than remaining a subsidiary reflection of experience. Wherever mythology functions as a living part of culture, this may generally be said to be true. It is a fact of great significance about the human mind, and it has puzzled and annoyed rational-minded thinkers from the beginnings of Western philosophy right up to Kardiner. The myth unit does not control by any physical means, however, but by a metaphorical similarity to experience: by a process of sympathetic magic.

The identification of the operation of mythical narrative for the group with the principles of sympathetic magic—through the association of images with acts, causing the culture to take the image as primary to the act, and then to organize the acts in accordance with the myth, seems less farfetched when the close relationships between ritual and myths are recalled. Ritual is a conscious, community-enacted drama—often based on mythical plots and portraying characters from mythology—designed to control certain natural forces by enacting metaphorically similar situations in which the desired results are symbolically attained. Ritual unites the group and individual consciousness in a sense of community that not only breaks down the distinction between the two psychologically, but enforces the identity of projective and physical reality so as to make the whole universe become an aspect of the human community. Individual acts of magic operate in a similar fashion, taking place within the larger framework of belief. The whole "religious control of the universe" derives its potency from sympathetic, not physical actions on things. Sympathetic magic is, as Frazer points out, based on "mistaken" associations, and never actually shapes physical events. Functionally, however, it is a real force, and literally controls human affairs. It never controls them according to principles that run counter to physical fact in nature—part of the efficacy of the projective screen is its close integration with physical laws which concern the economic survival of the group. On the basis of this fact, Campbell writes,

It has been customary to describe the seasonal festivals of so-called native peoples as efforts to control nature. This is a misrepresentation. There is much of the will to control in every act of man . . . (but) . . . the dominant motive in all truly religious (as opposed to black-magical) ceremonial is that of submission to the inevitables of destiny—and in the seasonal festivals this motive is particularly apparent.

No tribal rite has yet been recorded which attempts to keep winter from descending; on the contrary, all rites prepare the community to endure, together with the rest of nature, the season of the terrible cold. And in the spring, the rites do not seek to compel nature to pour forth immediately corn, beans, and squash for the lean community; on the contrary: the rites dedicate the whole people to the work of nature's season.

Myth is, functionally, the verbal equivalent of ritual, magically operating with words, images, and situations in narrative form as ritual operates with symbolic acts.

Each of the narrative levels in a myth is capable of working as sympathetic magic, so that the complex of symbol-referent equivalences that may be found in any one myth in principle is a hierarchy (proceeding from particulars to wholes) of symbolic modes which is, at its farthest extent, culture itself. To clarify this, Frazer's description of the magical function of words must be recalled:

Unable to discriminate clearly between words and things, the savage commonly fancies that the link between a name and the person or thing denominated by it is not a mere arbitrary and ideal association, but a real and substantial bond which unites the two in such a way that magic may be wrought on a man just as easily through his name as through his hair, his nails, or any other material part of his person.

This is elaborated by Malinowski, who based his discussion on field observation:

. . . we are made to realize how deeply rooted is the belief that a word has some power over a thing, that it is akin or even identical in its contained "meaning" with the thing or with its prototype. . . . The word gives power, allows one to exercise an influence over an object or an action. . . . The word acts on the thing and the thing releases the word in the human mind. This indeed is nothing more or less than the essence of the theory which underlies the use of verbal magic.

Language and myth both derive from these principles, and although they become divergent at later "stages," the underlying relationship may always be seen, according to Ernst Cassirer:

> . . . for, no matter how widely the contents of myth and language may differ, yet the same form of mental conception is operative in both. It is the form which one may denote as *metaphorical thinking*.

Metaphorical thinking is the subjective identification of symbols and referents—on the basis of the control of symbol over referent—in Cassirer's view; another way of saying sympathetic magic.

Language, it is sometimes argued, is a fundamental prerequisite of ideation. Although this point cannot be adequately proved or refuted, it is certain A. L. Kroeber is right in assuming the necessity of language for the existence of culture:

> Cultural activity, even of the simplest kind, inevitably rests on ideas or generalizations; and such or any ideas, in turn, human minds seem to be able to formulate and operate with and transmit only through speech. Nature consists of an endless array of particular phenomena. To combine these particulars into a generalization or an abstraction, such as passing from potential awareness of the thousands of stones along a river bed into the idea of stone as a distinctive material— this synthesis appears to require production of some kind of symbol, perhaps as a sort of psychological catalyzing agent: a symbol such as the sounds that make up the word *stone*. In short, culture can probably function only on the basis of abstractions, and these in turn seem to be possible only through speech.

As the single word abstracts and controls for the user the essence of its referent; the image, metaphor, and myth abstract, organize, and symbolically represent larger blocks of experience—patterns of experience—which can be psychologically controlled by the individual because of their essential compact form. Actual experience is too disorganized and chaotic to allow the individual or group any feeling of security and order without the myth mechanism. In culture, language is a learned function that almost always communicates over any length of time within patterns of verbal significance larger than particular words. Mythology is the central patterning force of that verbal organization which survives through generations, containing the cosmology and value-system of the group. Even if the mythology is, as Kardiner says, ultimately the product of certain human institutions—the survival of the institutions in culture depends on the continuation of the mythological function. Myth is a "reality lived" because for every individual it contains, at the moment of telling, the projected content of both his unarticulated and conscious values: simultaneously ordering, organizing, and making comprehensible the world within which the values exist. One might even reformulate the statement to say "Reality is a myth lived."

The mythological symbolizing of experience, and the subsequent control of experience, has been seen by some writers as the principle of any organization of value and knowledge. A comparatively early statement of this view was that of George Santayana:

> Mythology and theology are the most striking illustrations of this human method of incorporating much diffuse experience into graphic and picturesque ideas; but steady reflection will hardly allow us to see anything else in the theories of science and philosophy.

This attitude toward the projective screen of "Myth" is common today among literary critics and a few philosophers. Susanne Langer's *Philosophy in a New Key* relates the nature and function of mythology and ritual to a fundamental symbol-making activity of man, basic to his nature. She states the relation of this theory to modern science:

> The problem of observation is all but eclipsed by the problem of *meaning.* And the truth of empiricism in science is jeopardized by the surprising truth that our sense-data are primarily symbols.

Individuals create their private symbolisms, and as the private symbolisms become articulately expressed in some cultures—particularly those with writing-complicated interactions of individual and group mythologies

> . . . in a never ending interplay of symbolic gestures, built up the pyramided structure called civilization. In this structure very few bricks touch the ground.

The function of mythology may then be summarized: it provides a symbolic representation of projected values and empirical knowledge within a framework of belief which relates individual, group, and physical environment, to the end of integration and survival. The implication of this function for modern literary theory has been seized by many critics. In *Theory of Literature,* René Wellek and Austin Warren say:

> Our view . . . sees the meaning and function of literature as centrally present in metaphor and myth.

Or T. S. Eliot's discussion of the use of the *Odyssey* by James Joyce as an ordering framework for his novel *Ulysses:*

In using the myth, in manipulating a continuous parallel between contemporaneity and antiquity, Mr. Joyce is pursuing a method which others must pursue after him. They will not be imitators, any more than the scientist who uses the discoveries of an Einstein in pursuing his own, independent, further investigations. It is simply a way of controlling, of ordering, of giving a shape and a significance to the immense panorama of futility and anarchy which is contemporary history. . . . Psychology (such as it is, and whether our reaction to it be comic or serious), ethnology, and *The Golden Bough* have concurred to make what was impossible even a few years ago. Instead of narrative method, we may now use the mythical method.

One of the most extreme statements by a contemporary literary critic is that of Philip Wheelwright, who sees the community myth-consciousness as essential for good literature—

The poetry of our time doesn't matter much, it is a last echo of something important that was alive long ago. What matters is the myth-consciousness of the next generations, the spiritual seed that we plant in our children; their loves and insights and incubating sense of significant community. On that depend the possibilities of future greatness—in poetry and everything else.

A number of contemporary poets are not giving up yet, however. Some, like Robert Graves and Peter Viereck, have taken to speaking of the "magical" nature of poetry. Viereck sees no contradiction in his insistence on both "classicism" in poetry and its "holy dread"—the two formulate a

. . . dualism of what Nietzsche called the Dionysian and Apollonian; also the "dark gods" of the unconscious and the more rational, civilized conscious mind. The creative tension of these antitheses is in the shiver of holy dread, the tragic exaltation which makes the hair stand on end and is the difference between poetry and verse.

He refers to the "all-important night-side of art, its magic" much as Graves claims,

Poetry began in the matriarchal age, and derives its magic from the moon, not from the sun. No poet can hope to understand the nature of poetry unless he has had a vision of the Naked King crucified to the lopped oak, and watched the dancers, red-eyed from the acrid smoke of the sacrificial fires, stamping out the measure of the dance, their bodies bent uncouthly forward, with a monotonous chant of:

"Kill! kill! kill!" and "Blood! blood! blood!"

The literary interest in magic derives from three sources: Frazer's *The Golden Bough*, Malinowski's *Myth in Primitive Psychology,* and Jung's *Psychology of the Unconscious.* Frazer presented the theory of magic and the concrete symbols attached to the strangely memorable myths of the dying god; Malinowski described the function of myth, and Jung suggested the possibility that it might be possible to write literature using symbols from Frazer which would function in modern civilization—for individuals—as myth functions in primitive culture for the group. In doing so, the poet would not only be creating workable private mythologies for his readers, but moving toward the formation of a new social mythology. This is the duty of the modern artist, according to Campbell, who believes that only in the "storehouse of recorded values"—literature—can this be accomplished:

> It is not society that is to guide and save the creative hero, but precisely the reverse. And so every one of us shares the supreme ordeal—carries the cross of the redeemer—not in the bright moments of his tribe's great victories, but in the silences of his personal despair.

It is impossible to test the function of the Haida Swan-Maiden myth against such inclusive theorizing. It is important to repeat, nonetheless, that the Swan-Maiden story was a myth, not a tale, among the Haida. An element of belief was present. The myth undoubtedly had some function—not very important, perhaps, since it is merely a very short myth and not the whole mythology. It played an inconspicuous role among the longer, more important myths of the Raven cycle, probably serving as entertainment during potlatches and the long winter ceremonials. It must be remembered that this is no mean role: the potlatch, as described in chapter two, was one of the key institutions of the Haida, enabling the prestige and class system to reassert itself periodically, and providing a social situation in which the reciting of myths was required. As one of these myths, the Swan-Maiden story was at the center of Haida life. It reinforced the Haida conception of the universe, of the nature of supernatural beings and animals, and of the nature of human intercourse with the supernatural sphere. Many large, important works of literature in the Western canon do proportionately less in relation to the values of their culture.

Conclusion

The dimensions of the myth: The myth has been seen as social document, as the product of historical diffusion and compounded from motifs distributed all over the world, as metaphysical and psychological truth in symbolic form, as literature, and as a vital functioning aspect of a culture. The fact that a myth is many things at once is obvious, but the specialists in each of the many realms of knowledge I have drawn from do not communicate much with each other. For that reason, in almost any single-approach study of mythology it is always possible to find statements which a specialist from another field could easily refute.

The dimensions of the approaches: The problems of mythology cut across the boundaries of scholarly disciplines—and no one approach can hope to do justice to the many ways in which any myth is related to (1) its culture, (2) the body of world mythology, (3) culture as an abstract universal, (4) the working of the human mind and the values it sets up. In its totality the study of a myth is the study of "man and his works."

The thorough investigation: such inclusiveness is neither possible nor desirable in the work of individual scholars. One can ask which aspect of the study of mythology should the student concerned with oral literature consider central to an investigation which would take into account the many factors suggested in this thesis, yet not lose itself in theoretical ramifications which do not illuminate oral literature itself. The answer, I believe, must be the individual version. Working with a single version, complete with language and culture attached, will keep one continually referring back to the social existence of the myth or tale, even while pursuing the fascinating but occasionally fanciful possibilities it may possess. Within any single version, as this study has suggested, there is a richness of process and significance that remains important—no matter how slight the version and how marginal the culture—to all human activity. Concrete insights derived from the study of individual versions, rare as they are in present-day studies, will surely prove useful to the understanding of the imaginative and social life of man. I have not unearthed any particular insights of this order, but perhaps I have shown why one may validly point to even "He Who Hunted Birds in His Father's Village" and say, "There digge!"

FROM

The Real Work

The "East West" Interview

Peter Barry Chowka interviewed Snyder in New York City over a five-day period in April of 1977. The interview was conducted in Allen Ginsberg's apartment, on the subway, while walking the New York City streets. Snyder was in New York to give a series of readings and to participate in a conference sponsored by the American Academy of Poets on "Chinese Poetry and the American Imagination."

    Chowka is a free-lance writer and researcher whose detailed, in-depth studies of subjects ranging from fast-food chains to the politics of cancer have been widely published. The interview first appeared in the summer, 1977, issues of East West Journal.

CHOWKA: You have said that you left graduate school "to pursue the Dharma which had become more interesting to me." In some detail, could you recount the context—influences, people, books—of those years that led you to Buddhism?

SNYDER: When I was young, I had an immediate, intuitive, deep sympathy with the natural world, which was not taught me by anyone. In that sense, nature is my "guru" and life is my sadhana. That sense of the authenticity, completeness, and reality of the natural world itself made me aware even as a child of the contradictions that I could see going on around me in the state of Washington, in the way of exploitation, logging, development, pollution. I lived on the edge of logging country, and the trees were rolling by on the tops of trucks, just as they are still. My father was born and raised on the Kitsap County farm that my grandfather had homesteaded; he was a smart man, a very handy man, but he only knew about fifteen different trees and after that he was lost. I wanted more precision; I wanted to look deeper into the underbrush.

I perceived, also without it being taught to me, that there were such things as native people who were still around. In particular, one of them was an old man who came by about once a month to our little farm north of Seattle selling salmon that his people had smoked. They were Salish people who lived in a little Indian settlement on the shores of Puget Sound a few miles from us. My childhood perception of the world was white people, a few old Salish Indians, and this whole natural world that was half-intact and half-destroyed before my eyes.

At that age I had no idea of European culture or of politics. The realities were my mind, my self, and my place. My sympathies were entirely with my place—being able to see Mount Rainier far off to the east on a clear day or to climb the bluff of the hill to the west and look out over Puget Sound and the islands and see the Olympic Mountains. That was far more real to me than the city of Seattle, about ten miles south, which seemed like a ghost on the landscape.

(Peter Orlovsky joins us at this point.)

ORLOVSKY: What kind of a farm did your father have?

SNYDER: It was a little dairy farm, only two acres in pasture, surrounded by woods. As early as I was allowed, at age nine or ten, I went off and slept in the woods at night alone. I had a secret camp back in the woods that nobody knew about; I had hidden the trail to it. As soon as my father figured I knew how to put out a campfire, he let me go off and cook for myself and stay a day or two.

CHOWKA: This interest was mainly self-taught?

SNYDER: Very much self-taught. As soon as I was permitted, from the time I was thirteen, I went into the Cascade Mountains, the high country, and got into real wilderness. At that age I found very little in the civilized human realm that interested me. When I was eleven or twelve, I went into the Chinese room at the Seattle art museum and saw Chinese landscape paintings; they blew my mind. My shock of recognition was very simple: "It looks just like the Cascades." The waterfalls, the pines, the clouds, the mist looked a lot like the northwest United States. The Chinese had an eye for the world that I saw as real. In the next room were the English and European landscapes, and they meant nothing. It was no great lesson except for an instantaneous, deep respect for something in Chinese culture that always stuck in my mind and that I would come back to again years later.

When I went into college I was bedeviled already by the question of these contradictions of living in and supposedly being a member of a society that was destroying its own ground. I felt the split between two realms that seemed equally real, leading me into a long process of political thought, analysis, and study, and—of course—the discovery of Marxist thought. For a long time I thought it was only capitalism that went wrong. Then I got into American Indian studies and at school majored predominantly in anthropology and got close to some American Indian elders. I began to perceive that maybe it was all of Western culture that was off the track and not just capitalism—that there were certain self-destructive tendencies in our cultural tradition. To simplify a long tale, I also saw that American Indian spiritual practice is very remote and extremely difficult to enter, even though in one sense right next door, because it is a practice one has to be born into. Its intent is not cosmopolitan. Its content, perhaps, is universal, but you must be a Hopi to follow the Hopi way.

By this time I was also studying Far Eastern culture at Reed College. I read Ezra Pound's and Arthur Waley's translations of Chinese poetry, a translation of the *Tao Te Ching,* and some texts of Confucius. Within a year or so I went through the *Upanishads, Vedas, Bhagavad-Gita,* and most of the classics of Chinese and Indian Buddhist literature. The convergence that I found really exciting was the Mahayana Buddhist wisdom-oriented line as it developed in China and assimilated the older Taoist tradition. It was that very precise cultural meeting that also coincided with the highest period of Chinese poetry—the early and middle T'ang Dynasty Zen masters and the poets who were their contemporaries and in many cases friends—that was fascinating. Then I learned that this tradition is still alive and well in Japan. That convinced me that I should go and study in Japan.

CHOWKA: How did you discover that it was still alive?

SNYDER: By reading books and also by writing letters. It's obvious that Buddhism presents itself as cosmopolitan and open to everyone, at least if male. I knew that Zen monasteries in Japan would be more open to me than the old Paiute or Shoshone Indians in eastern Oregon, because they *have* to be open—that's what Mahayana Buddhism is all about. At that point, spring 1952, I quit graduate school in linguistics and anthropology at Indiana University and hitchhiked back to Berkeley to enroll in the Oriental languages department at the University of California so I could prepare myself to go to Asia. I spent my summers working in the Northwest in lookouts and trail crews and logging and forest service jobs, like a migratory bird going north in summer and returning south in winter.

CHOWKA: You have said that you taught yourself zazen from books although you then decided a teacher was necessary.

SNYDER: I decided that quite clearly when I was twenty-one or twenty-two.

CHOWKA: And after that, then, you grounded yourself in the languages and philosophy to prepare to go to Japan?

SNYDER: Right, although sitting, you know, isn't that hard a thing to learn, if you understand what posture is.

ORLOVSKY: In what year did you first sit in meditation?

SNYDER: It must have been in '49 that I taught myself to sit.

CHOWKA: Is there a particular book which gave you the direction?

SNYDER: Several translations of various texts from India and China told how to sit. And looking at a good statue and seeing that it has good posture and how the legs are crossed—it's not hard. I soon corrected my errors because you cannot sustain sitting for very long if your posture is off; it becomes painful, breath doesn't feel right, et cetera.

ORLOVSKY: Did you sit regularly from '51 on?

SNYDER: Pretty much. Not a whole lot—though maybe a half an hour every morning when I was going to graduate school. When I was working in the mountains in the summers, I was able to sit a lot.

ORLOVSKY: By '55 was your sitting practice different from when you began?

SNYDER: I didn't feel self-conscious about it anymore. When I first sat, I recall how very strange, how very un-Western, it felt. I remember at Indiana University I was doing zazen in the apartment that I shared with the anthropologist Dell Hymes. Somebody walked in and caught me sitting there and I felt strange, they felt strange, and then it got all around the university: "That graduate student from Oregon does weird things." But that's the way it was, twenty years ago! It's nice now that people can sit cross-legged and nobody pays much attention.

ORLOVSKY: When did you first sit ten hours a day?

SNYDER: I never started sitting like that until I went to Japan and was forced to. I still wouldn't sit ten hours a day unless somebody forced me, because there's too much other work in the world to be done. Somebody's got to grow the tomatoes. There's not going to be that much meditation in the world if we're going to have a democratic world that isn't fueled with nuclear energy, because there isn't that much spare energy. We damn well better learn that our meditation is primarily going to be our work with our hands. We can't have twenty-five percent of the population going off and becoming monks at the expense of the rest, like in Tibet; that's a class structure thing, a byproduct of exploitation—sitting an hour a day is not. Sitting ten hours a day means that somebody else is growing your food for you; for special shots, okay, but people can't do it for a whole lifetime without somebody else having to give up their meditation so that *you* can meditate.

CHOWKA: When you first began sitting, how did it change your life? Did it immediately affect the poetry you were writing, or was the effect more gradual?

SNYDER: It was gradual.

CHOWKA: But you knew when you began sitting that you liked it and wanted to continue it.

SNYDER: I had a pretty fair grasp of what the basic value of meditation is—an intellectual grasp, at least—even then. It wasn't alien to my respect for primitive people and animals, all of whom/which are capable of simply just *being* for long hours of time. I saw it in that light as a completely natural act. To the contrary, it's odd that we don't do it more, that we don't, simply like a cat, *be* there for a while, experiencing ourselves as whatever we are, without any extra thing added to that. I approached meditation on that level; I wasn't expecting anything to happen. I wasn't expecting instantaneous satori to hit me just because I got my legs right. I found it a good way to be. There are other ways to be taught about that state of mind than reading philosophical texts: the underlying tone in good Chinese poetry, or what is glimmering behind the surface in a Chinese Sung Dynasty landscape painting, or what's behind a haiku, is that same message about a way to *be,* that is not explicatable by philosophy. Zen meditation—zazen—is simply, literally, a way to be, and when you get up, you see if you can't be that way even when you're not sitting: just *be,* while you're doing other things. I got that much sense of sitting to make me feel that it was right and natural even though it seemed unnatural for a while.

CHOWKA: Could you tell us about your teacher, Oda Sesso?

SNYDER: I spent my first year in Japan living in Shokoku-ji, learning Japanese and serving as personal attendant to Miura Isshu Rōshi. As my first teacher, he instructed me to continue my studies with Oda Sesso Rōshi, who was the head abbot of Daitoku-ji at that time. So I went up to Daitoku-ji, was accepted as a disciple by Oda Sesso, and started going to sesshins and living periodically in the monastery.

I still think a lot about Oda Sesso Rōshi. You know, we have an image of Zen masters: Rinzai masters are supposed to shout and hit you; Soto Zen masters are supposed to do something else—I'm not sure what. In actual fact, they're all very human and very different from one another. Oda Rōshi was an especially gentle and quiet man—an extremely subtle man, by far the subtlest mind I've ever been in contact with, and a marvelous teacher whose teaching capacity I would never have recognized if I hadn't stayed with it, because it was only after five or six years that I began to realize that he had been teaching me all along. I guess that's what all the roshis are doing: teaching even when they're not "teaching." One of the reasons that you have to be very patient and very committed is that the way the transmission works is that you don't *see* how it works for a long time. It begins to come clear later. Oda Rōshi delivered *teisho* lectures in so soft a voice nobody could hear him. Year after year, we would sit at lectures—lectures that only roshis can give, spontaneous commentaries on classical texts—and not hear what he was saying. Several years after Oda Rōshi had died, one of the head monks, with whom I became very close, said to me, "You know those lectures that Oda Rōshi gave that we couldn't hear? I'm beginning to hear them now."

CHOWKA: How did you come to choose Rinzai over Soto Zen, or was it a function of the contacts you had made?

SNYDER: It was partly a function of contacts. But if I'd had a choice I would have chosen Rinzai Zen. As William Butler Yeats says, "The fascination of what's difficult / has dried the sap out of my veins. . . ." The challenge of koan study—the warrior's path, almost—and maybe some inner need to do battle ("Dharma combat") were what drew me to it. By the time I went to Japan, I had the language capacity to handle the texts enough to be able to do it. Another reason: the koans are a mine of Chinese cultural information. Not only do they deal with fundamental riddles and knots of the psyche and ways of unraveling the Dharma, it's done in the elegant and pithy language of Chinese at its best, in which poetry (a couplet, a line, or even an entire poem) is employed often as part of the koan.

CHOWKA: You wrote in *Earth House Hold*: "Zen aims at freedom through practice of discipline," and the hardest discipline is "always following your own desires." Within that context, how is the "original mind" or "no mind" of Zen different from the so-called unenlightened normal consciousness of a non-Buddhist?

SNYDER: Unenlightened consciousness is very complicated—it's not simple. It's already overlaid with many washes of conditioning and opinion, likes and dislikes. In that sense, enlightened, original mind is just simpler, like the old image of the mirror without any dust on it, which in some ways is useful. My own personal discovery in the Zen monastery in Kyoto was that even with the extraordinary uniformity of behavior, practice, dress, gesture, every movement from dawn till dark, in a Zen monastery everybody was really quite different. In America everybody dresses and looks as though they are all different, but maybe inside they're all really the same. In the Far East, everybody dresses and looks the same, but I suspect inside they're all different. The dialectic of Rinzai Zen practice is that you live a totally ruled life, but when you go into the sanzen room, you have absolute freedom. The roshi wouldn't say this, but if you forced him to, he might say, "You think our life is too rigid? You have complete freedom here. Express yourself. What have you got to show me? Show me your freedom!" This really puts you on the line—"Okay, I've *got* my freedom; what do I want to do with it?" That's part of how koan practice works.

CHOWKA: Why did you not take formal vows of a monk?

SNYDER: Well, I actually did at one time; my hair is long now simply because I haven't shaved it lately. There is no role for a monk in the U.S.

CHOWKA: While you were studying in Japan for most of ten years, you always knew that you'd return to the U.S.?

SNYDER: Oh, yes.

CHOWKA: Was your return hastened by the death of your teacher?

SNYDER: Probably. At a certain point I realized that, for the time, I'd been in Japan enough. I began to feel the need to put my shoulder to the wheel on this continent. It wasn't just returning—the next step of my own practice was to be here.

CHOWKA: When you were interviewed in 1967 for *Conversations: Christian and Buddhist* you were studying at Daitoku-ji but not actually living in the monastery.

SNYDER: I was living in a small house that was ten minutes' walk from the monastery. It was really necessary to spend most of the time at the house, because in a monastery you have no access to texts or dictionaries. All of the other monks had already memorized everything, literally. As an outsider-novice-foreigner, you are continually wrestling with problems of translation and terminology—you have to go look things up.

ORLOVSKY: Was there a library at the monastery?

SNYDER: No. There are no books and no reading at a monastery. There was also the economic consideration of having to make a living. So part-time I taught conversational English to the engineers of various electronics companies to make enough money to rent a little house, buy my food, ride a bicycle.

CHOWKA: A decade ago, or even earlier, you prophesied a great development of interest in Buddhism in the West. In 1967 you said, "The 'truth' in Buddhism is not dependent in any sense on Indian or Chinese culture." Could you comment on your view now that ten years have passed?

SNYDER: What I felt at the time and what I think all of us feel is that we're talking about the Dharma without any particular cultural trapping. If a teaching comes from a given place, it's a matter of courtesy and also necessity to accept it in the form that it's brought. Things take forms of their own; we don't *know* what's going to happen in the future. The Buddhadharma, which is the Dharma as taught by a line of enlightened human beings (rather than the Dharma as received from deities via trance, revelation, or *bhakta,* which is what Hinduism is) is *nirmanakaya*-oriented—it goes by changeable bodies. Right now it goes primarily through human bodies. Already it is all over the globe, and it has no name and needs no name.

CHOWKA: In a 1961 essay, "Buddhist Anarchism," revised in *Earth House Hold* as "Buddhism and the Coming Revolution," you criticize institutional Buddhism in the East as "conspicuously ready to accept or ignore the inequalities/tyrannies of whatever political system it found itself under." In your 1967 conversation with Aelred Graham in Kyoto, you spoke of the other organized faiths as "degenerations that come with complex civilized social systems," although you added that "In the Christian world there is much more serious thought about the modern age and what to do with it than in the Buddhist world." Now, ten years later, Buddhism, especially the Tibetan and Zen varieties, is much more widely available in North America. Has the coming of the Buddhadharma to the West altered your view about its complicity with degenerate, oppressive political systems?

SNYDER: Not particularly. It has to be understood that in Asia—India, China, and Japan—the overwhelming fact of life for three millennia has been the existence of large, centralized, powerful states. Much as in Europe until the Renaissance, it was assumed that the government was a reflection of natural order and that if there were inequalities or tyrannies that came from the government, although one might dislike them, there was no more use in complaining about them than there would be use in complaining about a typhoon. The better part was to *accept*. One of the most interesting things that has ever happened in the world was the Western discovery that history is arbitrary and that societies are human, and not divine, or natural, creations—that we actually have the capacity of making choices in regard to our social systems. This is a discovery that came to Asia only in this century. We in the West have an older history of dealing with it.

The organizations of Buddhism, Taoism, and Hinduism made the essential compromises they had to make to be tolerated by something that was far more powerful than themselves, especially in the imperial state of China. One of those compromises was to not criticize the state. You can't blame them for it, because they had no sense of there being an alternative. Even so, an interesting set of historical moves occurred in Chinese Buddhism. During the early period of Zen an essay was written that said Buddhist monks do not have to bow to the emperor since they are outside the concerns of the state. Later, in the thirteenth century, in Zen monasteries, sutras were chanted on behalf of the long life of the emperor; the monasteries supported and aided the regime. What it came to most strikingly was the almost complete cooperation of the Buddhist establishment in Japan (with some notable exceptions) with the military effort of World War II.

We don't have to go into how passionately nationalistic the Hindu Party of India is. The fact is that all of the world religions—Hindu, Buddhist, Islamic, Christian—share certain characteristics because they are all underneath the umbrella of civilization. As it turns out, one of the "World Religions'" main functions is to more or less support or reinforce the societies they are within. Even those who define their mission as liberating human beings from illusion have found it necessary to make compromises so that their little subculture wouldn't lose its tax-free buildings and landholdings and would be permitted to have a corner of existence in the society. This is also why monastic institutions are celibate. If they gave birth to their own children, they would become a tribe; as a tribe, they would have a deeper investment in the transformation of society and would *really* be a thorn in the flesh. As it is, if they simply are replenished by getting, in every generation, individuals from outside, they will never have that much investment in social transformation. If it's not a celibate sangha, then it's an alternative to society, an alternative that might be too threatening.

CHOWKA: You wrote in *Earth House Hold:* "Beware of anything that promises freedom or enlightenment—traps for eager and clever fools— three-quarters of philosophy and literature is the talk of people trying to convince themselves that they really like the cage they were tricked into entering." In an interview in the August *East West Journal,* Robert Bly agrees with Gurdjieff, who said it is important that true teachings be somewhat hard to find—there is only so much "knowledge" available at any one time and one's psyche can be changed only if a lot of knowledge comes at once; if offered to too many people via mass movements, the knowledge is dissipated. Bly goes on to say that there has been an infantilization of humanity, citing a book on the subject by Kline and Jonas, whose thesis is that each generation following the Industrial Revolution is more infantile than the previous, thus, for example, needing many more supportive devices merely to survive.

Would you comment on these observations in terms of your own view of the spiritual movements which have proliferated during this decade?

SNYDER: There is a very fine spiritual line that has to be walked between being unquestioning/passive on the one hand and obnoxiously individualistic/ultimately-trusting-no-one's-ideas-but-your-own on the other. I don't think it's uniquely American; I think that all people have these problems on one level or another. Maybe that's one meaning of the Middle Way: to walk right down the center of that. In one of the Theravada scriptures the Buddha says, "Be a light unto yourself. In this six-foot-long body is birth and death and the key to the liberation from birth and death." There is one side of Buddhism that clearly throws it back on the individual—each person's own work, practice, and life. Nobody else can do it for you; the Buddha is only the teacher.

Americans have a supermarket of adulterated ideas available to them, thinned out and sweetened, just like their food. They don't have the apparatus for critical discernment either. So that the term "infantilization" is something I can relate to. I think there's a lot of truth in it. The primary quality of that truth is the lack of self-reliance, personal hardiness—self-sufficiency. This lack can also be described as the alienation people experience in their lives and work. If there is any one thing that's unhealthy in America, it's that it is a whole civilization trying to get out of work—the young, especially, get caught in that. There is a triple alienation when you try to avoid work: first, you're trying to get outside energy sources/resources to do it for you; second, you no longer know what your own body can do, where your food or water come from; third, you lose the capacity to discover the unity of mind and body via your work.

The overwhelming problem of Americans following the spiritual path is that they are doing it with their heads and not with their bodies. Even if they're doing it with their heads *and* bodies, their heads and bodies are in a nice supportive situation where the food is brought in on a tray. The next step, doing their own janitorial work and growing their own food, is missing, except in a few places.

CHOWKA: Would you like to comment on those few places where people are provided with teaching which requires work, too?

SNYDER: The San Francisco Zen Center is a good example. In both the mountain and city centers they are striving conscientiously to find meaningful work for everybody—work that, in the city center, is not foppish or artificial but is relevant to the immediate needs of that neighborhood, which is predominantly black, with lots of crime. Zen Center opened a grocery store and a bakery; they sell vegetables from their garden in Green Gulch in the grocery store. It's an effort in the right direction—that which is "spiritual" and that which is sweeping the floor are not so separated. This is one of the legacies of Zen, Soto or Rinzai—to steadily pursue the unity of daily life and spiritual practice.

CHOWKA: Does that relate to a difference between the Chinese and Indian legacies as they've been applied to North American spiritual disciplines?

SNYDER: The spiritual legacy of Chinese culture is essentially Zen (or Ch'an) Buddhism. The secondary spiritual legacy of China is in the aesthetics—the poetry and painting (Confucius, Lao-tzu, and Chuang-tzu are included in that; also Mencius, whose work will be appreciated more in time for its great human sanity, although it's deliberately modest in its spiritual claims). Ch'an Buddhism added to Indian Buddhism the requirement that everybody work: "a day without work, a day without food." The cultural attitude toward begging in China was totally different from that in India; the Chinese public wouldn't stand for beggars. Long before, in India, giving money to beggars was considered praiseworthy and merit-creating, which created an ecological reinforcing niche for people to live by begging. You can see it in the strictly yogic or sadhu approach, which separates lay society from people who follow a religious path. When the society is so strictly split, lay people have no access to spirituality except to gain merit by giving money to those who follow a spiritual path. This is true today in Theravadin countries like Thailand and Ceylon.

In India, although the word *bhikkhu* means beggar, it also meant that these people were aristocrats; they wouldn't pick up a hoe, they certainly wouldn't touch shit, they wouldn't even touch money, because that's demeaning and low-caste. This is a tendency that possibly is imbibed from Brahminism and caste structure. So although Buddhism starts out with no caste, with the concept of bhikkhu, nonetheless, the bhikkhu becomes rated so highly socially that, in a certain way, he's like a Brahmin—he's "pure" and shouldn't become defiled in any way. This lays the groundwork for the later extraordinary hierarchization of the Buddhist orders of India and Tibet. The Chinese culture wouldn't tolerate that. Po-chang, in his monastic rules written during the T'ang Dynasty, makes clear that begging is not a main part of our way of self-support. Our way of self-support is to grow our own food, build our own buildings, and make everybody, including the teacher, work. As long as he's physically able, the teacher must go out and labor with his hands along with his students. For all of the later elegance and elitism that crept into Ch'an and Zen, this is a custom that has not broken down. Roshis in Japan do physical work alongside their monks, still. That has been for them a source of abiding health.

There are other things within the Ch'an administrative structures, within the monasteries, that are quite amazingly democratic when it comes to certain kinds of choices. All of the monks—whether novices or elders—have an equal vote. That is a Chinese quality in that spiritual legacy. Another development that is Chinese, as far as I can tell, is group meditation. In India and Tibet, meditation is practiced primarily in a solitary form. The Chinese and Japanese made group sitting a major part of their practice. There is a communalization of practice in China, a de-emphasis of individual, goofy, yogic wandering around. For the Chinese monk there is a phase of wandering, but it's after many years of group practice/labor. I love both India and China; I love the contradictions. I can identify with both—see the beauty of both ways of going at it.

CHOWKA: Buddhism as practiced in the East is criticized often for being dominated by males. Is this situation improving?

SNYDER: The single most revolutionary aspect of Buddhist practice in the United States is the fact that women are participating in it. This is the one vast sociological shift in the entire history of Buddhism. From the beginning, women essentially had been excluded. But in America, fully fifty percent of the followers everywhere are women. What that will do to some of these inherited teaching methods and attitudes is going to be quite interesting.

One of the things I learned from being in Japan and have come to understand with age is the importance of a healthy family. The family is the Practice Hall. I have a certain resistance to artificially created territories to do practice in, when we don't realize how much territory for practice we have right at hand always.

CHOWKA: In the later draft of your essay "Buddhist Anarchism" you added the qualifier "gentle" to the "violence" you felt was occasionally permissible in dealing with the system. I'm curious if this word change means your view was tempered during the eight years that separated the two versions; perhaps oddly, too, the adjective "gentle" appeared at the end of the sixties, when talking about "violence," at least, had become quite acceptable.

SNYDER: If I were to write it now, I would use far greater caution. I probably wouldn't use the word "violence" at all. I would say now that the time comes when you set yourself against something, rather than flow with it; that's also called for. The very use of the word "violence" has implications—we know what they are. I was trying to say that, to be true to Mahayana, you have to act in the world. To act responsibly in the world doesn't mean that you always stand back and let things happen: you play an active part, which means making choices, running risks, and karmically dirtying your hands to some extent. That's what the Bodhisattva ideal is all about.

CHOWKA: You once mentioned an intuitive feeling that hunting might be the origin of zazen or samadhi.

SNYDER: I understand even more clearly now than when I wrote that, that our earlier ways of self-support, our earlier traditions of life prior to agriculture, required literally thousands of years of great attention and awareness, and long hours of stillness. An anthropologist, William Laughlin, has written a useful article on hunting as education for children. His first point is to ask why primitive hunters didn't have better tools than they did. The bow of the American Indians didn't draw more than forty pounds; it looked like a toy. The technology was really very simple—piddling! They did lots of other things extremely well, like building houses forty feet in diameter, raising big totem poles, making very fine boats. Why, then, does there seem to be a weakness in their hunting technology? The answer is simple: they didn't hunt with tools, they hunted with their minds. They did things—learning an animal's behavior—that rendered elaborate tools unnecessary.

You learn animal behavior by becoming an acute observer—by entering the mind—of animals. That's why in rituals and ceremonies that are found throughout the world from ancient times, the key component of the ceremony is animal *miming*. The miming is a spontaneous expression of the capacity of becoming physically and psychically one with the animal, showing the people know just what the animal does. (*Snyder mimics a lizard.*) Even more interesting: in a hunting and gathering society you learn the landscape as a field, multidimensionally, rather than as a straight line. We Americans go everywhere on a road; we have points A and B to get from here to there. Whenever we want something, we define it as being at the end of this or that line. In Neolithic village society, that was already becoming the case, with villages linked by lines. In a society in which everything comes from the field, however, the landscape with all its wrinkles and dimensions is memorized. You know that over there is milkweed from which come glue and string, over the hill beyond that is where the antelopes water. . . . That's a field sensing of the world. All of it partakes of the quality of samadhi.

More precisely, certain kinds of hunting are an entering into the movement-consciousness-mind-presence of animals. As the Indians say, "Hunt for the animal that comes to you." When I was a boy I saw old Wishram Indians spearing salmon on the Columbia River, standing on a little plank out over a rushing waterfall. They could stand motionless for twenty to thirty minutes with a spear in their hands and suddenly—they'd have a salmon. That kind of patience!

I am speculating simply on what are the biophysical, evolutionary roots of meditation and of spiritual practice. We know a lot more about it than people think. We know that the practices of fasting and going off into solitude—stillness—as part of the shaman's training are universal. All of these possibilities undoubtedly have been exploited for tens of thousands of years—have been a part of the way people learned what they are doing.

CHOWKA: In a 1975 interview you said, "The danger *and* hope politically is that Western civilization has reached the end of its ecological rope. Right now there is the potential for the growth of a real people's consciousness." In *Turtle Island* you identify the "nub of the problem" as "how to flip over, as in jujitsu, the magnificent growth-energy of modern civilization into a nonacquisitive search for deeper knowledge of self and nature." You hint that "the 'revolution of consciousness' [can] be won not by guns but by seizing key images, myths, archetypes . . . so that life won't seem worth living unless one is on the transforming energy's side." What specific suggestions and encouragement can you offer today so that this "jujitsu flip" can be hastened, practically, by individuals?

SNYDER: It cannot even be begun without the first of the steps on the Eightfold Path, namely Right View. I'll tell you how I came to hold Right View in this regard, in a really useful way. I'm a fairly practical and handy person; I was brought up on a farm where we learned how to figure things out and fix them. During the first year or two that I was at Daitoku-ji Sodo, out back working in the garden, helping put in a little firewood, or firing up the bath, I noticed a number of times little improvements that could be made. Ultimately I ventured to suggest to the head monks some labor- and time-saving techniques. They were tolerant of me for a while. Finally, one day one of them took me aside and said, "We don't want to do things any better or any faster, because that's not the point—the point is that you live the whole life. If we speed up the work in the garden, you'll just have to spend that much more time sitting in the zendo, and your legs will hurt more." It's all one meditation. The importance is in the right balance, and not how to save time in one place or another. I've turned that insight over and over ever since.

What it comes down to simply is this: If what the Hindus, the Buddhists, the Shoshone, the Hopi, the Christians are suggesting is true, then all of industrial/technological civilization is really on the wrong track, because its drive and energy are purely mechanical and self-serving—*real* values are someplace else. The real values are within nature, family, mind, and into liberation. Implicit are the possibilities of a way of living and being which is dialectically harmonious and complexly simple, because that's the Way. Right Practice, then, is doing the details. And how do we make the choices in our national economic policy that take into account *that* kind of cost accounting—that ask, "What is the natural-spiritual price we pay for this particular piece of affluence, comfort, pleasure, or labor saving?" "Spiritual price" means the time at home, time with your family, time that you can meditate, the difference between what comes to your body and mind by walking a mile as against driving (plus the cost of the gas). There's an accounting that no one has figured out how to do.

The only hope for a society ultimately hell-bent on self-destructive growth is not to deny growth as a mode of being, but to translate it to another level, another dimension. The literalness of that other dimension is indeed going to have to be taught to us by some of these other ways. There are these wonderfully pure, straightforward, simple, Amish, won't-have-anything-to-do-with-the-government, plain folk schools of spiritual practice that are already in our own background.

The change can be hastened, but there are preconditions to doing that which I recognize more clearly now. Nobody can move from Right View to Right Occupation in a vacuum as a solitary individual with any ease at all. The three treasures are Buddha, Dharma, and Sangha. In a way the one that we pay least attention to and have least understanding of is sangha—community. What have to be built are community networks— not necessarily communes or anything fancy. When people, in a very modest way, are able to define a certain unity of being together, a commitment to staying together for a while, they can begin to correct their use of energy and find a way to be mutually employed. And this, of course, brings a commitment to the place, which means right relation to nature.

CHOWKA: In a letter to the editor in a recent issue of *East West Journal,* a reader wondered if the editor and other people who share so-called new consciousness occupations (jobs that might be more independent and rewarding, or less alienating than the norm), in interacting primarily with other like-minded or similarly engaged people, tend to become isolated from ordinary mainstream humanity. In talking with Aelred Graham ten years ago, you touched on this: "I almost can't escape from a society of turned-on people, which amounts to ten or fifteen thousand. . . . This is my drawback . . . I never meet those people (bourgeois, puritanical) in America." In his *Southern Review* article on your work in 1968, Thomas Parkinson notes (although he does not agree with) one criticism of your writing, thus: "Snyder does not face problems of modern life. . . . His poetry doesn't answer to the tensions of modern life and depends on a life no longer accessible or even desirable for man." There is also the danger that Herbert Marcuse sees in *One Dimensional Man,* that "the peculiar strength of the technological culture [is] to be able to make tame commodities out of potentially revolutionary states of consciousness." Would you comment on these points—isolation, irrelevance, and cooptation?

SNYDER: Taking the first point: At the time I talked to Graham, I was living in Kyoto and I hadn't lived in America in any serious way for many years; that was a very special statement I made to Graham at that point. In actual fact, I've lived more in the flux of society on more levels than practically anybody I know. I've held employment on all levels of society. I can pride myself on the fact that I worked nine months on a tanker at sea and nobody once ever guessed I had been to college.

I grew up with a sense of identification with the working class. I have lots of experience with this society—always have had and still do. I realize the danger of getting locked into a self-justifying group, which we see all around us. Since I've come back to the U.S.—and for the last seven years I've lived in rural California—I've been able to live and move with all kinds of people, which has been very good for me. A lot of my friends are doing the same. The whole "back to the land" movement, at least in California, at first had the quality of people going off into little enclaves. But the enclaves broke down rapidly as people discovered not only that they would *have to* but that they would *enjoy* interacting with their back-woods neighbors. A wonderful exchange of information and pleasure came out of what originally was hostile; each side discovered that they had something to learn from the other. Certain things that at first were taboo have become understood and acceptable.

The interesting point is the criticism of my poetry as invoking essentially outmoded values or situations that are not relevant or desirable. It's complicated to try to defend that. The answer lies in a critique of contemporary society and the clarification of lots of misunderstandings people have about what "primitive" constitutes, and even simpler clarifications about what your grandmother's life was like. It isn't really a main thrust in my argument or anyone else's I know that we should go backward. Whenever you get into this kind of discussion, one of the first things you are charged with from some corner is that "Well, you want to go backwards." So you have to answer it over and over again, but still people keep raising it. I remember a journalist once told David Brower of Friends of the Earth, "You want us to go back to the Stone Age!" and David replied, "Well, I'd be quite content to go back to the twenties, when the population was half of what it is now." Jerry Brown asked me the same question in a discussion about three weeks ago; he said, "You're going against the grain of things all the time, aren't you?" I said, "It's only a temporary turbulence I'm setting myself against. I'm in line with the big flow." (*Snyder laughs.*)

When we talk about a "norm" or a "Dharma," we're talking about the grain of things in the larger picture. Living close to earth, living more simply, living more responsibly, are all quite literally in the grain of things. It's coming back to us one way or another, like it or not—when the excessive energy supplies are gone. I will stress, and keep stressing, these things, because one of the messages I feel I have to convey—not as a preaching but as a demonstration hidden within poetry—is of deeper harmonies and deeper simplicities, which are essentially sanities, even though they appear irrelevant, impossible, behind us, ahead of us, or right now. "Right now" is an illusion, too.

The point by Marcuse that you raised is a real danger. I'm conscious enough of it, but I'm not sure about how one handles it except by being really careful and wary; that's one of the reasons why I stay out of the media pretty much—maybe a simpleminded way of keeping myself from being preempted or made into a commodity.

CHOWKA: You studied anthropology in school and it's remained one of your main interests. Some time ago you said, "We won't be white men 1,000 years from now . . . or fifty years from now. Our whole culture is going someplace else." More recently, you told a Montana newspaper,

"We may be the slight degeneration of what was really a fine form," as you cited a recent study of a Stone Age habitation in southern France which showed the people to have had larger brains, much leisure time, and an aesthetic or religious orientation. Would you give your anthropologically grounded innate/intuitive assessment in this larger "Dharma" view of where we're at now?

SNYDER: We have to develop a much larger perspective on the historical human experience. Much of that perspective is simply knowing the facts — facts that are available but simply haven't entered into people's thinking. This is the new, larger humanism, and it helps us to understand our spiritual strivings, too. On the average, the human brain was larger 40,000 years ago than it is now. Even the Neanderthal had a brain larger than modern man. This information is from a study of skull casts. Whether or not it's terribly relevant, we don't know, but it's a very interesting point. Marshall Sahlins, an economic anthropologist at the University of Chicago, in *Stone Age Economics,* offers the research, methodology, and conclusion that upper Paleolithic people worked about fifteen hours a week and devoted the rest of their time to cultural activities. That period and shortly thereafter coincides with the emergence of the great cave art — for example, in the Pyrenees in southern France. We can only speculate about who those people were; however, we do know that they were fully intelligent, that their physical appearance was no different from people you see today (except their stature — at least that of the Cro-Magnon — was a little larger), and that they ate extremely well.

Not only are there thousands of caves and thousands of paintings in the caves, but paintings occur in caves two miles deep where you have to crawl through pools of cold water and traverse narrow passages in the dark, which open up on chambers that have great paintings in them. This is one of our primary koans: What have human beings been up to? The cave tradition of painting, which runs from 35,000 to 10,000 years ago, is the world's longest single art tradition. It completely overwhelms anything else. In that perspective, civilization is like a tiny thing that occurs very late.

The point that many contemporary anthropologists, like Sahlins and Stanley Diamond, are making is that our human experience and all our cultures have not been formed within a context of civilization in cities or large numbers of people. Our self — biophysically, biopsychically, as an animal of great complexity — was already well formed and shaped by the experience of bands of people living in relatively small populations in a world in which there was lots of company: other life forms, such as whales, birds, animals. We can judge from the paintings, from the beauty and accuracy of the drawings, and also from the little Magdalenian stone carvings, the existence of a tremendous interest, exchange, and sympathy between people and animals. The most accurate animal drawings that have been done until modern scientific animal drawings are these cave drawings: right perspective, right attention.

To come a step farther: in certain areas of the world, the Neolithic period was long a stable part of human experience. It represented 8,000 to 10,000 years of relative affluence, stability, a high degree of democracy, equality of men and women—a period during which all of our vegetables and animals were domesticated, and weaving and ceramics came into being. Most of the arts that civilization is founded on, the crafts and skills, are the legacy of the Neolithic. You might say that the ground-work for all the contemporary spiritual disciplines was well done by then. The world body of myth and folklore—the motifs of folklore and the main myths and myth themes distributed universally around the globe— is evidence of the depth of the tradition. So, in that perspective, civiliza-tion is new, writing is even newer, and writing as something that has an influence on many people's lives came only during the last three or four centuries. Libraries and academies are very recent developments, and world religions—Buddhism among them—are quite new. Behind them are millennia of human beings sharpening, developing, and getting to know themselves.

The last eighty years have been like an explosion. Several billion bar-rels of oil have been burned up. The rate of population growth, resource extraction, destruction of species, is unparalleled. We live in a totally anomalous time. It's actually quite impossible to make any generaliza-tions about history, the past or the future, human nature, or anything else, on the basis of our present experience. It stands outside of the mainstream. It's an anomaly. People say, "We've got to be realistic, we have to talk about the way things *are*." But the way things for now *are* aren't real. It's a temporary situation.

CHOWKA: In *Earth House Hold* you wrote of Native Americans, "Their period of greatest weakness is over."

SNYDER: I hope that wasn't wishful thinking.

CHOWKA: You're not sure now?

SNYDER: Ah, it's touch and go. In a sense, they're in the same boat with all of us. Maybe a few of the peoples can hold something together because they have a population of sufficient size. But it's going to be very tricky. Diamond says the major theme of civilization is the slow but steady de-struction or absorption of local, kin-based, or tribal populations by the Metropole. That process is still at work. The other side of it is the amaz-ing resistance that some cultures show to being worn away, like the Hopi and the other Pueblos. They're incredibly strong and may well survive.

I've often wondered what makes these societies so tough. And it may well be that they are close to an original source of integrity and health. Erasing all negative associations for the word "primitive," it means *primus* or "first," like "original mind," original human society, original way of being. Another curious thing about the relationship between "primitive" and "civilized" is that no primitive society ever became civilized of its own free will; if it had the choice, it stayed itself.

In India today, three or four miles as the crow flies away from a 3,000-year-old agricultural civilization using Sanskrit, having temples and Brahmins—three miles up into the hills are original tribal societies that have lived that close to civilization for 3,000 years, and still they are the same people; they just can't be bothered. There is a reason why some of them are really strong; it's a systems/ecology reason, which I hit on finally after reading Margalef's book *Perspectives in Ecological Theory* and Eugene Odum.

Every given natural region has a potential top situation where all of the plants that will grow there have grown up now and all of those that will push out something else have pushed out something else, and it reaches a point of stability. If you cut all the forests and you wait many hundreds of years, it'll come to something again.

CHOWKA: It's an optimum condition.

SNYDER: This condition, called "climax," is an optimum condition of diversity—optimum stability. When a system reaches climax, it levels out for centuries or millennia. By virtue of its diversity it has the capacity to absorb all sorts of impacts. Insects, fungi, weather conditions come and go; it's the opposite of monoculture. If you plant a forest back into all white pine, one of these days the white pine blister rust comes along and kills all the white pine. If you have a natural mixed forest, the white pine will be hit a little by blister rust but they won't be in a solid stand, they'll be broken up. Another aspect of a climax situation is that almost half of the energy that flows in the system does not come from annual growth, it comes from the recycling of dead growth. In a brand-new system—for instance, after a piece of ground has been scraped with a bulldozer, when weeds and grass come up—the annual energy production is all new growth production; there is very little to be recycled. But with a 40 percent recycling situation, there is a rich population of fungi, and beetles, and birds that feed on bugs, and predators that feed on birds that feed on bugs that eat the rotten wood; you've then achieved the maximum optimal biomass (actual quantity of living beings) in one place. This is also what is called "maturity." By some oddity in the language it's also what we call a virgin forest, although it's actually very experienced, wise, and mature. Margalef, a Spanish ecologist, theoretician, genius, has suggested that the evolution of species flows in line with the tendency of systems to reach climax. Many species exist in relation to the possibility of climax and to its reinforcement.

Certain human societies have demonstrated the capacity to become mature in the same way. Once they have achieved maturity, they are almost indestructible. But this kind of maturity has nothing to do with the maturity of civilization. (The only societies that are mature are primitive societies—they actually are that old, too: 30,000 years here, 10,000 years there.) "Civilization" is analogous to a piece of scraped-back ground that is kept perpetually scraped back so that you always get a lot of grass quickly every year—monoculture, rapid production, a few species, lots of energy produced, but no recycling to fall back on. So, civilization is a new kind of system rather than an old or mature one.

CHOWKA: An essay in *Turtle Island* tells us to "Find your place on the planet and dig in." Could you speak about your attempt to "dig in" in northern California, and the local political action you have found to be necessary?

SNYDER: To say "we must dig in" or "here we must draw our line" is a far more universal application than growing your own food or living in the country. One of the key problems in American society now, it seems to me, is people's lack of commitment to any given place—which, again, is totally unnatural and outside of history.

Neighborhoods are allowed to deteriorate, landscapes are allowed to be strip-mined, because there is nobody who will live there and take responsibility; they'll just move on. The reconstruction of a people and of a life in the United States depends in part on people, neighborhood by neighborhood, county by county, deciding to stick it out and make it work where they are, rather than flee. Zen Center has certainly demonstrated this with their tenacity in San Francisco, where, instead of being overwhelmed by the deterioration processes at work around them, they've reversed the flow by refusing to leave and by, against all odds, putting in a park—turning things around just by being there. Any group of people (not just Zen Center) who have that consciousness can do that. A corollary to that is my own experience in rural California: I have never learned so much about politics or been so involved in day-to-day social problems. I've spent years arguing the dialectic, but it's another thing to go to supervisors' meetings and deal with the establishment, to be right in the middle of whatever is happening right here, rather than waiting for a theoretical alternative government to come along.

I'll say this real clearly, because it seems that it has to be said over and over again: There is no place to flee to in the U.S. There is no "country" that you can go and lay back in. There is no quiet place in the woods where you can take it easy and be a stoned-out hippie. The surveyors are there with their orange plastic tape, the bulldozers are down the road warming up their engines, the real estate developers have got it all on the wall with pins on it, the county supervisors are in the back room drinking coffee with the real estate subdividers, the sheriff's department is figuring to get a new deputy for your area soon, and the forest service is just about to let out a big logging contract to some company. That's the way it is everywhere, right up to the north slope of Alaska, all through Canada, too. It's the final gold rush mentality. The rush right now is on for the last of the resources that are left standing. And that means that the impact is hitting the so-called country and wilderness. In that sense, we're on the front lines. I perceived that when I wrote the poem; that's why I called it "Front Lines." I also figured that we were going to have to stay and hold the line for our place.

A friend of mine came to where I live five years ago, and he could see what was going to come down. He said, "I'm not going to settle here, I'm going to British Columbia." So with his wife and baby he drove two hundred and fifty miles north of Vancouver, B.C., and then seventy miles on a dirt road to the end of the road, and then walked two miles to a cabin that they knew about, and bought a piece of land only a few miles south of the St. Elias range. That summer there they discovered they were surrounded by chain saws that were clear-cutting the forest, and that there were giant off-the-road logging trucks running up and down the seventy miles of dirt road, so that it was to take your life in your hands to try to go into town to get something. "Town" was a cluster of laundromats, discarded oil drums, and mobile homes that had been flown in. That's the world. My friends came back down to California; it was too industrial up there.

I would take this all the way back down to what it means to get inside your belly and cross your legs and sit—to sit down on the ground of your mind, of your original nature, your place, your people's history. Right Action, then, means sweeping the garden. To quote my teacher, Oda Sesso: "In Zen there are only two things: you sit, and you sweep the garden. It doesn't matter how big the garden is." That is not a new discovery; it's what people have been trying to do for a long time. That's why there are such beautiful little farms in the hills of Italy, people did that.

CHOWKA: Could you give examples of some issues that have arisen in your county and that you've addressed—the kinds of action required and support you received?

SNYDER: One issue was building codes: housing and toilets. A number of people had their houses tagged as illegal, because they hadn't gotten a building permit, the construction used did not conform to the code, or they substituted outhouses for septic tanks.

CHOWKA: This happened where you live. What is it like there?

SNYDER: Genuinely rural and remote. A lot of time and work on the part of hundreds of people all over California, ultimately, went into fighting a tactic whose purpose was to try to get them out as an undesirable minority population who had moved in and lowered real estate values. Such things were reversed by intelligence and research, and the very clear argument that it's obviously unfair to impose suburban housing development standards in a rural area. Now some changes have been made in the code of California to permit rural people to build their homes in a simpler way. A small victory—to have an outhouse! Some other changes have been made in the code to make it legal not to have electricity and legal to have a wood stove. The codes were actually getting to the point where you *had* to have electricity to be legal. It's a small issue but one in which people's lives and homes are at stake.

More interesting is the question of schools, school boards, and the degree of autonomy you can practice with education if you have a school board with some kind of vision and a unity of purpose behind it. We went through quite a number building a public school locally—it was clearly the will of the people to build it in a beautiful, careful, and craftly way, not making it into an interchangeable-pod schoolhouse. Because the architects, Zach Stewart and Dan Osborne, who were hired by the school board also were visionary men with great patience, it was possible, at the cost of two extra years of work, to get the state to approve it. It was also possible because hundreds of people donated thousands of hours of free time to the building of it; it became a work of art. That's what a community can do for its children. It's also possible to keep on top of the local forest service and their timber policies in a way that the conservationists in the big city can't. They can do a lot—they have lobbyists with a lot of clout in Washington. But there are certain things that are effectively accomplished when local people say, "We don't like the way this is being handled here on public land." If you have both local people and people with a lobbyist in Washington coming with the same message, then you have something working on these public land managers, who tend to be rather arrogant.

Where I live, the greater proportion of the land in the county is public land; we find ourselves in the position of being the only ombudsman for the use of that land. Nobody else is watching but us. At the same time we can't be too unrealistic or idealistic about it, because we know what those jobs mean to our neighbors. If you want to say that there should be no more logging in this section, you also have to ask what the alternative employment will be. Many people where I live are interested in developing crafts, skills, industries, co-ops that give the whole population a long-range economic viability. So throughout California—which is my main area of experience—I know of both rural and urban enclaves that are trying to develop, on every level, appropriate technologies, both material and spiritual. And I guess it's going on all over the country.

ᛰ

CHOWKA: I wonder about the value given to poetry in our society. *Turtle Island,* which won for you a Pulitzer Prize and is by contemporary standards a successful poetry book (selling almost 70,000 copies), when compared to mass market novels, for example, has sold very little.

SNYDER: For a book of formal poetry, *Turtle Island* sold quite a bit. But it's only one kind of poetry. Actually, Americans love poetry, pay huge sums of money for it, and listen to it constantly. Of course, I'm talking about song, because poetry is really song. Rock 'n' roll, ballad, and all other forms of song are really part of the sphere that, since ancient times, has been what poetry is. If you accept poetry as song, then there are plenty of songs already that are doing most of the work that poetry is supposed to do for people.

CHOWKA: You're using song a lot more now in your own poetry, as in "California Water Plan."

SNYDER: Yes, I'm using literal song-voice, singing voice or chanting voice, in poetry and probably will be doing it more. But even the way I read the other poems has the element of song in it, because the intensification of language and the compression of the already existing sound-system musicality of the spoken language itself is manifested by the reading of the poem. Part of the work of the poet is to intensify and clarify the existing musical sound-possibilities in the spoken language.

CHOWKA: You speak a lot about the "old ways" and the fact that song comes from a prehistoric tradition. Is the fact that song is so popular today, in poetry and popular song, proof that these "old ways" cannot be lost, that they are with us still?

SNYDER: One of the things that little children do first is to sing and chant to themselves. People spontaneously sing out of themselves—a different use of voice. By "song" we don't have to limit ourselves to the idea of lyric and melody, but should understand it as a joyous, rhythmic, outpouring voice, the voice *as* voice, which is the Sanskrit goddess Vāk— goddess of speech, music, language, and intelligence. Voice itself is a manifestation of our inner being.

CHOWKA: We know that poetry shares its roots with religion, music, dance. Why isn't poetry as compromised or diluted as you've said these other things—religion, music, et cetera—tend to be?

SNYDER: None of them is functioning with the wholeness that we can guess that they had once. That wholeness, in part, was a function of the fact that they all worked together: poetry didn't exist apart from song, song didn't exist apart from dance, dance didn't exist apart from ritual, ritual didn't exist apart from vision and meditation. Nonetheless, all of these forms have their own intrinsic validity. I wouldn't say that poetry today is any more valid than dance or drama.

CHOWKA: But you did say that in *Earth House Hold.*

SNYDER: Okay, I did say that, didn't I? What I meant was that poetry has maintained itself with more of its original simplicity perhaps than some of these other forms—it has taken on less technology in support of it. But then I would have to qualify that as to allow how the music which is popular song—which I think is a fascinating phenomenon apart from the fact that it's being used as a commodity—as it stands now is backed by a very complex technology; however, you can remove most of that technology and go back to an acoustic situation and it still has the power in a live setting.

CHOWKA: In *Earth House Hold* you write that "there comes a time when the poet must choose" between the "traditional-great-sane-ordered stream" and one that's "beyond the bound onto the way out, into . . . possible madness . . . possible enlightened return." Did you have yourself in mind when writing that? It's not completely clear if you've chosen one way or the other—I can see elements of both in your work.

SNYDER: I wrote that a long time ago, and I was able to say it because I could see both sides in myself and say, maybe somewhat artificially, that you have to be one way or the other. I'll rephrase it in terms of how I see it now: We have a sense that great artists and geniuses have to be crazy, or that genius and creativity are functions somehow of a certain kind of brilliant craziness, alienation, disorder, disassociation.

CHOWKA: Like Baudelaire, Rimbaud.

SNYDER: The model of a romantic, self-destructive, crazy genius that they and others provide us is understandable as part of the alienation of people from the cancerous and explosive growth of Western nations during the last one hundred and fifty years. Zen and Chinese poetry demonstrate that a truly creative person is more truly sane; that this romantic view of crazy genius is just another reflection of the craziness of our times. In a utopian, hoped-for, postrevolutionary world, obviously, poets are not going to have to be crazy and everybody, if they like, can get along with their parents; that would be the way it is. So I aspire to and admire a sanity from which, as in a climax ecosystem, one has spare energy to go on to even more challenging—which is to say more spiritual and more deeply physical—things. Which is not to disallow the fact that crazy, goofy, clowning, backwards behavior isn't fun and useful. In mature primitive societies the irrational goofy element is there and well accounted for.

CHOWKA: I want to return to this idea later in discussing the fifties. But first, who are some of the people you feel personify the "beyond the bound onto the way out" tradition today?

SNYDER: I don't know if I want to say anybody personifies it.

CHOWKA: You didn't have individuals in mind when you wrote it?

SNYDER: I can think of parts of individuals. I would say that maybe we can discriminate between poets who have fed on a certain kind of destructiveness for their creative glow (and some of those are no longer with us, consequently) as against those who have "composted" themselves and turned part of themselves back in on themselves to become richer and stronger, like Wendell Berry, whose poetry lacks glamour but is really full of nutrients.

CHOWKA: You mention Berry frequently; I gather he's one of your favorite poets. Could you talk about some other contemporary poets whom you read and enjoy?

SNYDER: I have a special regard for Robert Duncan because of his composting techniques and also because of his care, scholarship, acquaintance with the Western tradition and its lore, knowledge, and wisdom (which I have neglected)—I'm glad that he's doing it and I can learn from him. I'm glad that Robert Bly is looking at the Western tradition. I'm also a close reader of Michael McClure's poetry, for his long, careful, intense dedication to developing a specific biological/wild/unconscious/fairytale/new/scientific/imagination form. Maybe he's closer to Blake than anybody else writing. I can think of poets who are little known—like Robert Sund, who has only one book out—who have cultivated a fine observation and ear and tuned it to daily life, work, people, scenes of the West or wherever they are, who are unpretentious in the presentation of themselves, but who have very high-quality work. Wendell Berry is a man who does very high-quality work and is also a working farmer and a working thinker, who draws on the best of American roots and traditional mindfulness, like his Kentucky farming forebears, to teach us something that we're not going to learn by studying Oriental texts.

CHOWKA: He's grounded himself in this country.

SNYDER: He's grounded here, but at the same time opening it out so that we can say, "There was something like the Oriental wisdom here all along, wasn't there?"

CHOWKA: That wisdom tradition is universal.

SNYDER: It is universal, as good farming, and attention to how to treat things, are universal.

CHOWKA: The poets you've mentioned so far are all personal acquaintances to some degree. How much does knowing a poet personally, knowing how he/she writes, affect your appreciation of the poet's work?

SNYDER: I've run into poems by poets I haven't known in the least that have excited me instantaneously, like Lillian Robinson, who lives in up-state New York, whose work (a poem called "In the Night Kitchen") I saw in a little magazine. (I got her address and asked her to send me a couple more poems.) I watch for those things—for the growth of people who are our peers and contemporaries—and hopefully, too, I try to see something of what's coming in from other places.

I've been responding to your question about who I read and what I think of poets; I've been answering in a conventional modern American poet mold. I'd like to explain how I *really* do things, because it's part of my view and my practice. I no longer feel the necessity to identify myself as a member of the whole society.

CHOWKA: North American society?

SNYDER: Yes. It's too large and too populous to have any reasonable hope of keeping your fingers on it, except by the obviously artificial mode of mass media television, which I don't see anyway, and which presents only a very highly specialized surface from that society. What I realistically aspire to do is to keep up with and stimulate what I think is really strong and creative in my own viable region, my actual nation: northern California/southern Oregon, which we might call Kuksu country, subdivision of Turtle Island continent. Within that, I do know what's happening and I do read and follow and go to readings with and read poems with the poets who are beginning to develop a depth and a grounding out of it. We also have our own way of keeping touch in terms of our local drainage (which is the North Pacific) across the North Pacific rim, with companion poets in Japan, like Nanao Sakaki and his circle—great Japanese bioregional poets who, analogously to us calling North America "Turtle Island," call Japan "Jomonia" and have an island-Pacific-bioregion sense of it. I don't see anything provincial or parochial in it because it implies a stimulus to others to locate themselves equally well. Having done so, we will see a mosaic of natural regions which then can talk across the boundaries and share specifics with each other. Southwest specifics, like I get from the rancher-writer Drummond Hadley, teach me ecosystems and mind-understandings that are different from ours in the sense of how you relate to the blue sky and to turquoise. I can talk about how we relate to heavy winter rains and large conifers.

CHOWKA: But you retain still a global consciousness to the extent that you've identified nuclear power as the greatest danger to the planet, which is not purely a local issue.

SNYDER: There are two kinds of earth consciousness: one is called global, the other we call planetary. The two are 180 degrees apart from each other, although on the surface they appear similar. "Global consciousness" is world-engineering-technocratic-utopian-centralization men in business suits who play world games in systems theory; they include the environ-mentalists who are employed at the backdoor of the Trilateral Commis-sion. "Planetary thinking" is decentralist, seeks biological rather than technological solutions, and finds its teachers for its alternative possibili-ties as much in the transmitted skills of natural peoples of Papua and the headwaters of the Amazon as in the libraries of the high Occidental civi-lizations. It's useful to make this distinction between a planetary and a global mind. "Planetary mind" is old-ways internationalism which rec-ognizes the possibility of one earth with all of its diversity; "global con-sciousness" ultimately would impose a not-so-benevolent technocracy on everything via a centralized system.

CHOWKA: I'd like to return the discussion to your career, and how you began to have your work published. At one point you said that very early you decided, in effect, that "there was nothing more to be done vis-à-vis seeking a poetic career." Did publishing your first poems and books require some exertion or did it literally all fall into place without any effort?

SNYDER: I had sent poems around a little bit for a while. I think maybe only one or two things were published. It was partly a Buddhist decision. I was working for the forest, fixing trails up in the high country of Yose-mite, I was getting more into meditation—walking or mountain medita-tion—by myself. I finished off the trail crew season and went on a long mountain meditation walk for ten days across some wilderness. During that process-thinking about things and my life—I just dropped poetry. I don't want to sound precious, but in some sense I did drop it. Then I started writing poems that were better. From that time forward I always looked on the poems I wrote as gifts that were not essential to my life; if I never wrote another one, it wouldn't be a great tragedy. Ever since, every poem I've written has been like a surprise. I've never expected or counted on writing another one. What I really got to work on at that time was studying Chinese and preparing myself to go to Japan and study. But I guess I really didn't give up poetry enough because while I was in Japan I was always what is described as the lowest type of Zen student—the type who concerns himself once in a while with literature. So, I confess I did go on writing poems from time to time, which is inexcusable! I couldn't help myself.

CHOWKA: You mentioned China positively in *Turtle Island* ("I lost my remaining doubts about China") and in a letter about Suwa-no-se Island ("People's China has many inspiring examples"). You also published a poem in *The Back Country* titled "To the Chinese Comrades." What are your feelings about China now?

SNYDER: I guess I probably spoke too soon in saying I've lost my remaining doubts; I still have doubts about China—certainly doubts about China as a model for the rest of the industrial world. Many lessons, though, can be learned but they cannot be applied wholesale—people wouldn't stand for it. But, yes, China is filled with inspiring examples of cooperation, reforestation, and less inspiring examples like the campaign to kill sparrows some years ago.

CHOWKA: What about their disaffiliation with their spiritual lineage?

SNYDER: That doesn't trouble me too much. I believe the Chinese had been pretty well disaffiliated from that already for some time. But, in a sense, the primary values already had sunk in so deeply that they didn't have to articulate them much anymore. Also, as a student of Chinese history, I perceive a little about the cycles that it moves in. If the rest of the world holds together, I would bet that a century and a half from now China again will be deeply back into meditation, as part of the pendulum swing of things. In a way, People's China is a manifestation of wonderful qualities of cooperation and selfless endeavor toward a common goal that were there all along. The negative side, though, is that China has been the most centralized, bureaucratic, civilized culture on earth for the longest time; unquestionably because of that, much was lost within and without. Much diversity was lost. The Chinese in the past, and probably still, don't have an appreciation for the ethnic or the primitive. For centuries, they have been looking down on their own border people or on the small aboriginal enclaves—tiny cultures in the hills of which there are still hundreds within China. So I feel ambivalent about China. Without doubt one can recognize the greatness of its achievement on all levels and think of it as a model of what a civilization can be; but then I can just as soon say, "But I wish there *weren't* any civilization!"

Sir Joseph Needham is very impressed by the Chinese revolution; in his book *Science and Civilization in China* he says that Taoism foreshadows the Revolution, and that's true. Taoism is a Neolithic world view and a matrilineal, if not matriarchal, Chinese world view that somehow went through the sound barrier of early civilization and came out the other side halfway intact, and continued to be the underlying theme of Chinese culture all through history up until modern times—antifeudalistic; appreciative of the female principle, women's powers, intuition, nature, spontaneity, and freedom. So Needham says that Taoism through history has been a 2,000-year-long holding action for China to arrive at socialism. That's how positively *he* looks at it. The contemporary Chinese look back on Taoism a heritage in their past that as socialists they can respond to. Buddhism is a foreign religion—it came from India! But the Taoist component in Chinese culture will surely return again to the surface.

(Peter Orlovsky enters the conversation.)

ORLOVSKY: Are there any tribes in China still that have been left alone?
SNYDER: There are some. You can't communalize certain kinds of production in certain areas—you can't improve on what they're doing already. If a group has a good communal village agriculture—a hill situation not susceptible to use of tractors—it might as well be left alone.

The present Chinese regime, like every regime in the world, has been guilty of some very harsh and ethnocentric treatment of people, especially the Tibetans, which is inexcusable. At the same time they hold out a certain measure of hope, especially to people of the Third World underdeveloped countries, who are offered only two models of what to do. One model is to plug into the nearest fossil fuel source and become a satellite country of the United States or some other industrial nation; the other option is the Chinese: get the landlords off your back, straighten out the tax structure, and then do better agriculture with the tools you have available. The Chinese are perhaps on the verge of becoming more industrialized, and this good opinion of them may soon evaporate; as a strategy for what they consider to be their own survival, they may go the same route we have. The other point I want to make is that although it's true that China is the world's most centralized and bureaucratic, the oldest, and in some ways the most autocratic civilization, at the same time it has been filled with a rich mix of humanity from north to south, east to west: dialects, subcultures, of all sorts, of great vigor—many of them in one way or another amazingly still around. But it isn't something we would want to be, we would never want to be as populated as China.
CHOWKA: One of the more interesting points to arise during the "Chinese Poetry and the American Imagination" conference this week is a question that you raised. We had assumed that there was a tone of intimacy, of cooperation, of communality in a lot of the Chinese poetry that was discussed. You wondered if the new, wider, Occidental interest in classical Chinese poetry presaged the development of similar qualities here.
SNYDER: I think it's inevitable that American society move farther and farther away from certain kinds of extreme individualism, for no reason other than that the frontier is gone and the population has grown; partially, it may be the social dynamics of crowding. (Although, of course, many societies that are not crowded are nonetheless highly cooperative.) But I didn't raise this point as a prophecy, but as a question. The negative side of the spirit of individualism—the "everybody get their own" exploitative side—certainly is no longer appropriate. It can be said to have been in some ways productive when there were enormous quantities of resources available; but it's counterproductive in a postfrontier society. It's counterproductive when the important insight for everyone is how to interact

appropriately and understand the reciprocity of things, which is the actual model of life on earth—a reciprocal, rather than a competitive, network. The ecological and anthropological sciences are in the forefront of making models for our new value systems and philosophies. We are moving away from social Darwinism. As the evolutionary model dominated nineteenth- and early twentieth-century thinking, henceforth the ecological model will dominate our model of how the world is—reciprocal and interacting rather than competitive.

*

CHOWKA: Many of the ideas you've expressed are certainly as radical as those of Allen Ginsberg and the other writers who were part of the Beat literary group. You share a similar, unequivocal vision of where and how society went wrong, which unsettles many people. Compared to Allen and the others, however, relatively little has been written about you in a negative way. Why the difference?

SNYDER: Allen became extremely famous! He got a lot of negative criticism, but he also got an enormous amount of positive criticism. The proof of the pudding is in the eating: he sold hundreds of thousands of copies of *Howl*. It's great not to have had much negative criticism, but there are some people who never have had a negative word said about them, and nobody's read their books either. The point is to enter the dialogue of the times. Certainly, some of the things I have to say strike at the root. Until recently, most people, including Marxists, have been unable to bring themselves to think of the natural world as part of the dialectic of exploitation; they have been human-centered—drawing the line at exploitation of the working class. My small contribution to radical dialectic is to extend it to animals, plants: indeed, to the whole of life.

CHOWKA: I'd like to talk about your work in Governor Jerry Brown's administration as a member of the Arts Council. What does that job entail?

SNYDER: As a member of the Arts Council, I attend monthly meetings and committee meetings, answer a lot of mail, talk to many people and check things out, so to speak, all of which is connected with some policies and ideas that we as a council of nine members are beginning to formulate on the thorny question of how to use the people's money—how to feed it back to the people for the support of art and culture.

CHOWKA: Are the members of the Council working artists?

SNYDER: With one exception they are all working artists, which was Brown's idea.

CHOWKA: The Council is new under his administration?

SNYDER: Yes. It's a departure from the usual arts commission being peopled by essentially wealthy patrons of the arts for whom being on a state's arts council is a social plum—perpetuating the idea that there are "good people" who have made a lot of money and also love the arts who then decide how to give money to artists. It was Brown's idea to change that, which has made a small ripple across the country; it demonstrates that artists can read, write, administer, and do things that a lot of people said they couldn't. (It takes me away from my own work, though.)

CHOWKA: When I met Robert Bly this week he told me he has strong objections to your being on the Arts Council; he sees a danger in the state trying to deal with and fund the arts in a centralized way.

SNYDER: This is a dialogue that goes on now across the U.S., in England, and in other places where the state uses public money to support art. When Governor Brown first took office, he had strong reservations about whether there should be a state arts council at all, from several standpoints, ranging from the question of "Is this a proper use of tax money?" to whether government involvement in the arts would result in implicit censorship or ultimately thought or aesthetic control. Those of us he talked to at that time shared those fears and worries, and were ourselves ambivalent about being on an arts council. But, it was with a strong experimental hope that there might be a way to use people's money to benefit creativity, avoiding these pitfalls, that we got involved.

There is no question that art meets real needs of the people. For artists—whether full-time professionals or part-time amateurs—ecologically, economically, their niche is there. But within the complexities of our present industrialized, civilized world, you have to come to grips with the problem in a new way. An economic subsidy of a very special order accounts for so much of the energy, affluence, craziness, and speed of the last eighty years. Fossil fuel subsidy is underwriting mass production. Fossil fuel energy is a subsidy from nature; we do not have to pay for the BTUs in oil what we would have to pay if it were not already concentrated and available in an easily usable form in the ground. Put simply, the arts—with the exception of certain modern media arts—are labor-intensive. Labor-intensive activities of any sort cannot compete with fossil-fueled ones—hand-thrown as against mass-produced pots, for example. As it happens, art cannot mass produce. To produce an opera requires hours of rehearsal; there is no way of automating that.

CHOWKA: And study, too—the preparation of an individual artist.

SNYDER: Yes. If we value art and higher cultural forms (and they should be valued, because they are preserves of the human spirit—as Lévi-Strauss says, "national parks of the mind"), then the people themselves are going to have to keep them going, until the time when the fossil fuel subsidy is withdrawn and the arts can compete in the free market economy like the family farm (when labor-intensive agriculture can be economically competitive once again). My view is that public support is necessary to carry the arts through, in the same way that we are trying to carry endangered species through.

Since we have taken on this task, we in California have been considered populists, because we have tried to adjust the balances of where money goes and what deserves support. We've put a stress on thinking of art in terms of creativity and process rather than commodity and product. We look on creativity as a birthright of everybody; we're trying to play down the sense of artist as special genius or talent, and be more sensitive to the community roles and possibilities of artists working on many levels of professionalism.

The local craftsperson or artist down the street is as valuable in being the yeast of social change and direction as anyone else. In terms of quality, we in California are concerned with recognizing and rewarding excellence, but we don't want to impose standards of excellence that derive simply from the Western European high cultural tradition. So our Arts Council is a very diverse group.

You raised the question of centralization. Actually, the Arts Council is less centralized than it would appear. The actual selection of who gets grants is decided by panelists—other artists or teachers—chosen from around the state who donate time to read applications. We translate their opinions into actions. Further, the state is divided demographically into five areas of racial, cultural, and economic spread, so that without compromising quality we make a point of affirmative action. We make sure that folks from the back country and the inner city know what's happening so that they can participate.

CHOWKA: You don't see any conflict between having a state job administering money to artists and writers and being a poet and writer yourself?

SNYDER: Arts Council members don't get paid. The time I give to it is public service time; and it takes a lot of my time. You have to trust that the people whom the governor appoints are going to be fair. The fact that we're artists should be seen as a plus, because we're in a position to know from inside with our own hearts how things can and should be. The knowledge of what kind of work it takes to be an artist is also one of our strengths. Concerning other conflicts of interest, we members of the Arts Council are the only artists in the state who cannot apply for grants!

CHOWKA: Can you say more about your own evolving practice?

SNYDER: You're asking me what is my Buddhist practice? I'll ask you, "What do you mean by 'practice'?"

CHOWKA: The realization that there is something to be done.

SNYDER: What about the realization that there is nothing to be done?

CHOWKA: Then why would one go to Japan to study?

SNYDER: But what is "practice"?

CHOWKA: Sitting, for one thing.

SNYDER: Sitting—okay. So you're defining "practice" essentially as a concrete, periodic activity.

CHOWKA: Partially.

SNYDER: It might be mantra chanting, too; it might be doing a certain number of prostrations everyday.

Periodic, repetitive behavior, to create, re-create, enforce, reinforce certain tendencies, certain potentialities, in the biopsyche. There is another kind of practice, which also is habitual and periodic, but not necessarily as easily or clearly directed by the will: that's the practice of necessity. We are six-foot-long vertebrates, standing on our hind legs, who have to breathe so many breaths per minute, eat so many BTUs of plant-transformed solar energy per hour, et cetera. I wouldn't like to separate our mindfulness into two categories, one of which is your forty-minute daily ritual, which is "practice," and the other not practice. Practice simply is one intensification of what is natural and around us all of the time. Practice is to life as poetry is to spoken language. So as poetry is the practice of language, "practice" is the practice of life. But from the enlightened standpoint, all of language is poetry, all of life is practice. At any time when the attention is there fully, then all of the Bodhisattva's acts are being done.

I've had many teachers who have taught me good practices, good habits. One of the first practices I learned is that when you're working with another person on a two-person crosscut saw, you never push, you only pull; my father taught me that when I was eight. Another practice I learned early was safety: where to put your feet when you split wood so that the ax won't glance off and hurt your feet. We all have to learn to change oil on time or we burn out our engines. We all have to learn how to cook. By trial and error, but also by attention, it gets better. Another great teaching that I had came from some older men, all of whom were practitioners of a little-known esoteric indigenous Occidental school of mystical practice called mountaineering. It has its own rituals and initiations, which can be very severe. The intention of mountaineering is very detached—it's not necessarily to get to the top of a mountain or to be a solitary star. Mountaineering is done with teamwork. Part of its joy and delight is in working with two other people on a rope, maybe several ropes together, in great harmony and with great care for each other, your motions related to what everyone else has to do and can do to the point of ascending. The real mysticism of mountaineering is the body/mind practice of moving on a vertical plane in a realm that is totally inhospitable to human beings.

From many people I learned the practice of how to handle your tools, clean them, put them back; how to work together with other men and women; how to work as hard as you can when it's time for you to work, and how to play together afterwards. I learned this from the people to whom I dedicated my first book, *Riprap*. I came also to a specific spiritual practice, Buddhism, which has some extraordinary teachings within it. The whole world is practicing together; it is not rare or uncommon for people who are living their lives in the world, doing the things they must do, if they have not been degraded or oppressed, to be fully conscious of the dignity and pride of their life and their work. It's largely the fellaheen oppression and alienation that is laid down on people by certain civilized societies throughout history that breaks up people's original mind, original wisdom, the sense and sanity of their work and life. From that standpoint Buddhism, like Christianity, is responding to the alienation of a fragmented society. In doing this, Buddhism developed a sangha, which is celibate as a strategy to maintain a certain kind of teaching that in a sense goes against the grain of the contemporary civilization, but will not go *too* much against the grain because it's a survival matter.

The larger picture is the possibility that humanity has more original mind from the beginning than we think. Part of our practice is not just sitting down and forming useful little groups within the society but, in a real Mahayana way, expanding our sense of what has happened to us all into a realization that natural societies are in themselves communities of practice. The community of practice that is right at the center of Buddhism, and Hinduism also, is the Neolithic cattle-herding proto-Brahmin family that sang the Vedas together, morning and night. The singing of the Vedas by a group of people, in the family/household, is what lies behind all of the mantras, chants, sutras, and ceremonies that go on all over the Hindu-Buddhist world today. It all goes back to nine thousand years ago, when families sat down and sang together. The yogic practices and meditation come through a line of teaching concerned with life, death, and healing.

To me, the natural unit of practice is the family. The natural unit of the play of practice is the community. A sangha should mean the community, just as the real Mahayana includes all living beings. There is cause and consequence. On one level, Theravadin Buddhism says, "Life is suffering, and we must get out of the Wheel"—that's position of cause. But from position of consequence we can say, "The life cycle of creation is endless. We watch the seasons come and go, life into life forever. The child becomes parent, who then becomes our respected elder. Life, so sacred; it is good to be a part of it all." That's an American Indian statement that also happens to be the most illuminated statement from the far end of Buddhism, which does not see an alienated world that we must strive to get out of, but a realized world, in which we know that all plays a part.

Still, so far I've been making my points on practice and original mind from the standpoint of culture and history. That must be done as a corrective, because almost no one understands what civilization is, what it has done, and what the alternatives could be. But I'm not saying an "ideal society" would mean no more work, no more practice, all enlightened play. We still have to get at something called the *kleshas*—obstacles, poisons, mixed-up feelings, mean notions, angriness, sneaky exploitations. Buddhism evolved to deal with these. We're born with them; I guess they come with the large brain super-survival ego sense this primate climaxes with. Maybe all that ego-survival savvy was evolutionary once; now it's counterrevolutionary. But whether we say "Meditate and follow the Buddhadharma" or "Work well and have gratitude to Mother Earth," we're getting at these poisons; that's what the shaman's healing song is all about.

CHOWKA: The place where you've settled—your home in the northern California Sierras—is important to your practice.

SNYDER: Where I live, there is a friendly number of people, diverse as they are, who have a lot of the same spirit. Because we are together in the same part of the world and expect to be together there for the next two or three thousand years, we hope to coevolve our strengths and help each other learn. That cooperation and commitment is in itself practice. In addition, many of the people there have a background in one or another school of Buddhism or Hinduism (although the constellation by which we playfully describe the possibilities is Zen/Hopi/Jew).

Some people don't have to do a hundred thousand prostrations, because they do them day by day in work with their hands and bodies. All over the world there are people who are doing their sitting while they fix the machinery, while they plant the grain, or while they tend the horses. And they *know* it; it's not unconscious. Everybody is equally smart and equally alive.

Where I am, we love occasions to come together. We have a little more time now that we've gotten some of our main water system, fence building, and house building done; we now have the chance to sit together, dance together, and sing together more often.

FROM

Passage Through India

The "Cambodge"

We left Kyoto on a cold frosty morning—tenth of December 1961, I think it was—just two days after the end of the big Rohatsu Osesshin at the Daitoku-ji monastery, clear and blue sky—with our rucksacks, but Joanne in high heels because we were going on one of the classier express trains, and she still didn't believe me when I said travel in India would be like camping out. In Tokyo we stayed two days with a young couple I'd known only by correspondence—Clayton Eshleman, a new poet, and his new wife. On the twelfth we took the interurban electric from Tokyo down to Yokohama, cleared through immigration and customs, and walked down this long dock to the *Cambodge* where it was moored along-side—a pretty big ship, all painted white. Up the gangplank, and imme-diately were transported into a new non-Japanese world. Here was a sud-den warm perfumy smell, and perfumy stewards, all talking French, and women stewards with sharp permanent hairdos and thin eyebrow lines like older French women seem to go for. I recollect Joanne getting kind of tangled up with her rucksack and the narrow doors and passageways and becoming sort of rattled—I was immediately uncomfortable because of the warmth of the heated ship when we had just come from unheated Japan, and were wearing heavy winter underwear, and sweaters. A steward led us to our cabins, way forward into cabin class. The change is abrupt, because in tourist class they have wooden doors and trim, and a few car-pets, but in cabin class it's all steel doors and steel lockers and steel bunks and rubbertile flooring. But nice and clean. Showed us the dining room, which is all bright yellow and red, recently redone, with bright red plas-tic-covered chairs and couches along the wall, very cheery and happy, with portholes to look out and a music system playing popular music con-stantly. We unpacked and put our stuff in our lockers—at the last minute in Kyoto I decided to buy a camera and be sure of getting good photos in

India, so I bought an Asahi Pentax single-lens reflex 35 mm with f2 lens, and was paranoid about it, hiding it in the back of the locker and putting padlocks where I could and locking the cabin. We were given the freedom of the forward deck so there we stood in the late afternoon as the ship pulled away from the dock and we saw the last of the low glare of Yokohama neon (it's a real port town) turning on as it got dark and we sailed away—not really knowing if we'd ever get back to Japan again, India seeming so remote and scary still.

The first few days on the ship were chilly and rough, lots of people stayed in their cabins. A young couple we knew from Kyoto was also on board. Jack Craig had come originally from Cupertino, California, to study Zen, then through a friend of Al Klyce (who is probably back in San Francisco now with his Japanese wife) met a girl working in a bar, whom he fell for, and after several months of tedious hassling they got married and six months later or so left Japan bound for Hong Kong, and thence India by plane, Europe, and New York, where they are now. Jack's lovely wife Ginko was so miserably seasick she thought she'd perish.

Just before Hong Kong the weather cleared and the water smoothed, and we got a chance to talk to some of our fellow cabin-class tween-deck passengers. One was Helmut Kugl, a German who had gone off to Australia and worked as a carpenter, then went to Japan for four months, and was now off to India to "find Krishnamurti" because he had picked up a book by Krishnamurti and decided this was what he wanted. Anti-German, and totally against any kind of discipline or authority, but he was only about twenty-four, red-haired and freckly—a perpetual frown of doubt on his brow and constant deep and contradictory philosophical questions—he claimed not to have even finished high school. Hilda Hunt was about sixty, divorcée, dressed up in lavender, always having her drink before dinner and always talking about her days on the New Orleans *Time-Picayune* (she "knew Hemingway" when he was living in New Orleans)—wrote verse—and had numerous fantastic stories to tell, but was withal quite sweet—had been visiting some younger relatives who were with the armed services in Japan, and was now on the long trip round to Europe, to visit some more young relatives stationed in Germany.

An Australian named Neale Hunter had done French, Chinese, and Japanese literature at the University of Melbourne, then went to work in the bush for a year or so, took the money and went to Japan, Tokyo—lived for about four months in Shinjuku, Tokyo (a kind of bar and underworld hangout zone of enormous dimensions) then took off for India—fellow who knows about literature, wild life, and for some reason became a converted Catholic and is now trying to reconcile Catholicism and Buddhism to suit himself. Among others were a French couple, early-middle-aged anarchists who live in New Caledonia; a pair of nineteen-year-old American boys from Los Angeles off on a world tour, and a couple of gentle Ceylonese school teachers who played chess all the time and argued their respective religions, Catholic and Buddhist.

Hong Kong: we first off headed for the Japanese Consul and presented our papers, applying for a new visa to Japan. Then walked around on the hillside back of town—Joanne went shopping for a raincoat, and Neale and I went into an old-style wineshop and talked to the old men in broken Chinese, sampling from various crocks and getting a little drunk—wandered up and down through the crowded alleys, people hanging all their laundry out the apartment balcony windows, old stained concrete and plaster. New buildings don't seem to last long. Hong Kong so crowded—and barbed wire machine-gun emplacements set up all around. Lively, shopping is a major activity, stores are filled with every conceivable thing, especially luxury. Joanne got a French raincoat—we met back at the ship. The next day Joanne, Neale, and I took a bus out to the border—about a thirty-mile ride. This is on the mainland side. We got up on a hill and gazed out through pine trees at the Chinese Peoples' Republic—spread out before us, a watery plain with houses here and there—a barbed-wire fence along a river at the foot of the hill showing where the actual line is. We could see men far off in China loading a little boat on the river, and hear the geese and chickens and water buffaloes from far away. It was warmish, gray cloudy, soft. Went back on the train to Kowloon (nine dragons) where our ship was—the seamen out handling rigging, sheaves, and cables. Joanne is wearing her fine yellow raincoat. The villages in mainland Hong Kong have a very different feeling from those in Japan. The rows in the gardens aren't so straight, the buildings not so neat—and the building material is brick instead of wood (though roofs are thatch); the people all wear the wide trousers and jackets, men and women alike, and the coolie hats in the field. But Hong Kong has food in a way no Japanese town could. The Japanese simply don't have the Chinese sense for cooking and eating (and a Japanese meal out, dinner party, say, is always a drag until people are finally drunk enough on sake to loosen up; whereas the Chinese have glorious multi-course banquets as a matter of course). In Hong Kong it's like walking along the market sections of Grant Avenue, Chinatown, only better, the wineshops and herb shops in between. That evening to an Australian-run bar for a while, then back to the end of the pier, looking across to the Victoria (Island) side, the celebrated lights going up the steep hill, drinking beer in the dark—a freighter comes in, blotting out the neon, the bridge decks alight, and a junk in full sail, batwing taut membrane over bones—goes out darkly and silent, a single yellow kerosene lamp dim in the stern.

The houses on the New Territory are all thatched, dry brown colors as the parched winter brown of the long plain stretching north—fallow paddies, with water buffalo, cows, pigs, and flocks of geese here and there browsing.

> The dried out winter ricefields
> men far off loading junks in the river
> bales of rice on their shoulders
> a little boat poles out
>   —roosters and geese—
>   —looking at China

Bought $347 worth of rupees in Hong Kong at 7 RS to $1 US, where official rate in India is 4.75 to $1. Ship sailed at midnight and we were bound for Saigon.

Out of Hong Kong they moved Joanne and me from our cabin-class cabins and put us together in one tiny two-man cabin in the tourist-class section. Food was still to be taken deck-class, but our living quarters had been altered. I never understood why except they did get a large number of additional cabin-class passengers, Indians and Chinese, and perhaps were overcrowded. So now in the messhall, besides our previous friends, there were women in saris and pigtailed old Chinese women in silk trousers—and the waters were warm, we were sunbathing on deck. At night took up the star map and a flashlight, and identified the southern stars, Canopus and Achernar, and the Southern Cross, until one of the seamen came down from the bridge and said our little flashing of the flashlight was hard on the bridge lookout, so we stopped. Always in motion.

Coasting South Vietnam—come into muddy waters, the smell from ashore—go in a bay and up the river. Both banks jungle swamps, a bird or a fishing canoe now and then. A thick almost-comfortable warmth over it all. Turns and twists in the river. A freighter comes sailing over the jungle. One P.M. land in Saigon—surrounded by shaggy ricefield delta plains, a few thatched houses in clumps of palm. Long bridge and double-spire church visible . . . Saigon is really French. They sell French bread everywhere, right along with funny-looking broiled animal innards, fruits, and kinds of fish and vegetables, which knowing the name wouldn't help you. The women are all beautiful and wear silk pajamas with a silk tunic and long loose hair, and apparently brassieres that make them all come to sharp points in front. Walked a bit in the afternoon, and then out in the night street stalls—fruit juices, caged birds, crushed sugarcane with ice and lime. Next day went to the botanical gardens and zoo and museum compound, dug most of all the gibbon, which has no tail and a maniac laugh while running on the ground with his arms, which are longer than his whole body, sort of crossed behind his neck up. Tall trees, shuttered, colored houses, white or yellow walls. The architecture seems to be colonial Franco-Spanish. We fed the elephant's trunk nose finger some apples from the ship. Then she curtseyed.

Vietnam women fluttering and trailing high-collared, tight-waisted, loose floppy ankles and thin silk swish legs—high small sharp breasts, waves of black heavy clean hair. Always a gold ring in the right ear. Sidewalk cafes and cheap beer, so later in the day we sit and watch, eat ham sandwich and French pastries. Sail back down the river at 1:30 in the afternoon. You'd never guess there was any kind of war going on around here, but for a very rare truck going through with soldiers in jungle outfits, but no weapons visible, no guards with submachine guns on the corners or guys in tanks parked at intersections. Yet we read in the newspapers of ambushes and kidnappings just 15 miles out of town. Government of South Vietnam is bunch of Catholic elite westernized prudes anyhow, completely out of touch with "the people."

Next was Singapore. As we approached it the weather became muggy and the ocean surface heavy and oily, the water changed from blue to green. Also I got dysentery about then, terrible cramps. So I went ashore for only five hours in Singapore, feeling miserable, and remember little from that time. Our new passengers included a lot of adolescent Sikh boys with their fuzzed young faces and girlish wisps of hair sticking out from under their turbans. Indian women and children all over the deck, squabbling— and a tall white-haired fine-featured Swiss lady with her Chinese husband. They had just recently left mainland China—had been traders in Shanghai for many many years. With them was their son who looked in his mid-twenties. They were on their way to Switzerland. They claimed no good had come out of communism in China; the peasants were worse off than before on account of bad agricultural practices, everyone miserable and resigned—no bars or lights at night, everybody the same dull clothes, blue suit; but they were freely allowed to leave China and were never in any way molested. I think they just found life getting dull there, and they had no love for Chiang Kai-shek.

Now we were crossing the Bay of Bengal, bound for Ceylon. The Indians out on the deck all day listening to Indian radio on their Singapore or Hong Kong transistors. Saris blowing and swirling about the deck—several hours spent reexamining our loads and lightening our packs—give away the long underwear (which was scratchy old army surplus stuff full of holes anyhow)—and Joanne planning to leave her heavy coat and high heels behind in Colombo to pick up later—even so we have about forty pounds each, with sleeping bags, cooking pots, etc. We knew the jig was up when I went up on deck and saw our two Ceylonese teacher friends had mysteriously changed from Western dress and were now in Ceylonese sarongs—and weren't bothering to speak much English anymore—they were in their own waters. That night we passed the light on the southern end of Ceylon, and at dawn we were in Colombo harbor, to be thrust off the security of the ship and into the "world."

Pondicherry

That evening caught a third-class sleeping car on northbound for Pondicherry. Third-class sleeping means cars with huge ledges overhead, and a
ledge that folds up and hooks on chains where the back was, above the
usual bench seat, making in all a triple-tiered bunk arrangement for each
seat. Luggage goes under the bottom seat or just on the aisle between the
two facing benches (compartment style). We got into one of these and
slept in our board bunks, like Chinamen being sent back to China to die,
until early morning, transferred to another train, and by seven A.M. were
nearing the coast.

Train we transferred to was a small, deserted local engine, and when
we climbed into the third-class car it looked like the compartment I got
into was empty. Actually a couple of people were huddled across from us,
under a big handspun shawl. I started to put my rucksack under the seat,
and found a man sleeping there, so put it on the seat beside me. Joanne
huddled up and slept some more, while I watched the pair across from us.
They stirred and moved around some; it was a man with long hair, earrings, and a girl about twelve . . . when they threw back the shawl I saw
both were dressed only in skimpy loincloths under the single shawl . . .
she had large gold hoops in her ears, bangles on her wrists and ankles, and
wild brownish hair down over her shoulders, looked as if it had never
been combed . . . both were barefoot, and covered with dust, looked at
Joanne and me with kind of vague wild curiosity . . . at the next stop they
both got off on the wrong side of the train and walked off across the tracks
and into a grove . . . They had been riding free, and were (as I came to
know later) probably "tribal people," still thinking of themselves as
members of a certain tribe, not necessarily Hindus, in fact still living
rather primitive lives . . . they both had lovely faces.

Pondicherry was formerly a French enclave and when we got there, sure enough the policemen and train officials were speaking French. We took a bicycle rickshaw to the head office of the Sri Aurobindo Ashram where we planned to stay. An ashram is a unique Indian institution, it is a religious community based around some teacher and branch of Hinduism; the person of the teacher being very important. Not all ashrams are actually religious—the Gandhi ashrams and Vinoba Bhave ashrams are primarily aimed at combining a kind of spiritual communism with community service and social work. The Aurobindo ashram was founded sometime after World War I (I think) by Sri Aurobindo Ghose, a Bengali who had been educated from childhood on in England, returned to India and became a rabid nationalist, and then switched to yoga. He claimed to have founded a new type of yoga, "Integral Yoga," and heralded a new "Divine Life" on earth. From the mid-twenties on he was assisted in his work by a woman known only as the Mother. I have been told she was a French lady to begin with, who left her husband to live in Pondicherry. She came gradually to be the person actually running the ashram, and Sri Aurobindo spent the last years of his life in virtual seclusion. He died in 1950. The Mother runs it all now. I had heard of Aurobindo some years ago around the Academy of Asian Studies. Frederick Spiegelberg was an Aurobindo fan, and they had a few copies of Aurobindo's huge book, *The Life Divine,* around. I don't want to go into his philosophy here, but it is a rather eclectic spirit-oriented system, which has affinities with neo-Platonism, Gnosticism, as well as Vedanta, and it is not truly monistic, as Vedanta is, but rather belongs, it seems to me, in the class with antimatter dualisms like Manichaeism, Nestorian Xtianity, some sorts of Gnosticism, and Catharites. I rather doubt that it is a truly Indian philosophy. Maybe if I read more on it I'll change my mind.

The ashram is considered to be the best organized in India. It has supposedly 1300 members, all under the direct control of the Mother. They live in various buildings and houses owned by the ashram (i.e., owned by the Mother) scattered through the old French section of Pondicherry. ". . . a few things are strictly forbidden: they are—(1) politics, (2) smoking, (3) alcoholic drink and (4) sex enjoyment"—this applies only to actual inmates of the ashram, not guests (thank god!).

Now the funny thing is, to digress, that this absurd list of prohibitions, once you are within India, seems less and less outrageous. The prohibition of politics is probably the one that would hurt most Indians most. But the rest of us might give up politics. As for smoking, Indian tobacco was so bad I quit smoking in India anyway, and haven't taken it up again yet. Alcohol is almost impossible to buy in India, rather expensive if you find it, and absolutely foul to drink. Actually illegal in many states. As for "sex enjoyment" (and they mean this to apply to married inmates of the ashram along with everyone else), practically all Indian semireligious or religious traditional thought is in agreement on the notion that sexual activity of any sort is deleterious to Spiritual Progress. Brahmacharya is considered a very Good Thing. One who practices continence, usually a married man who has taken a vow of continence, is called a Brahmacharin. Gandhi was a Brahmacharin, from something like 1914 on never slept with his wife, and urged all his followers to adopt similar practice. Somebody once taxed Gandhi with this saying, "you became a Brahmacharin after you were all dried up anyway"—to which he replied, "my wife never looked so attractive to me, nor was my sexual potency ever as strong, as when I took the vow." Of course, a family man isn't supposed to do this until he's at least had a son.

The only exception to this view in religious circles is amongst the Shaivite-Shakti-Tantric circles (which people say still flourish in Orissa and Bengal) where sexual intercourse is practiced as a ritual designed, after long preparation, to hook everyday orgasm into the Cosmic Orgasm. But nobody (except the millions of peasants and untouchables) takes sex simply as sex, and leaves it at that. Anyway, anything that Gandhi urged is tantamount to an *order* to the semi-intelligentsia (except get along with Muslims).

To get back to Pondicherry, it is a lovely French-looking town, deserted almost—really dead but for the ashram, facing on a long white beach, with warm gentle surf. On side alleys you notice the bristly long-snouted black pigs rooting about, eating horrible garbage, and the hovels of the Scheduled Castes (untouchables) that make up a major portion of the population of South India.

Two little girls squatting on the cement rim of a canal, stark naked, taking craps, talking to each other all the while, the yellow shit sort of dribbling down the edge of the cement, then up they jump and run off playing.

Secretary at the ashram headquarters sent us in a bike rick to a place called Parc-a-charbon, right by the sea, where we were to stay a few nights. We got a little room with two wooden cots, actually sort of boxes with drawers underneath to put your gear in, and hasps for padlocking, a thin mattress on top, and a wood frame over it with a mosquito netting. A table, a chair, a big earthenware waterpot in the corner, damp all over, the water inside cool from the constant evaporation.

We were the only people living here but for a Cambodian Buddhist monk, some lay Yogins, and the man who was caretaker for the building (a converted godown from French merchant days) who was a large good-natured fellow with elephantiasis of one leg and hence had smelly wet bandages wrapped around it all the time and couldn't go far because it was so hard to walk. His room was covered with pictures of the Mother.

We got to see the Mother the next morning early, at her *darshan.* Darshan is another big Indian thing, it simply means appearance, or presence. Underlying it is a belief that you don't need to be instructed or led by a holy person, just by proximity or seeing them you are immeasurably benefited. So the Mother appears every morning about 6:15 A.M. on the balcony of her house, and three or four hundred people gather on the street below. She comes out, looks at everybody slowly in big circles, then looks up and out and goes into "a meditative trance"—eyes open, body shifting from time to time. Then, smiling a bit, she looks at everybody once more, and backs off the balcony. She has a gauzy silk scarf over her head and brow, and a kind of twenties-ish elegance. A real production. And she must be close to her eighties. Her age doesn't seem to worry the ashram people, though.

A woman from Canada named Beverly Siegerman, who has been at the ashram three years, told us that the Mother would never die, and that by a gradual process of physical-spiritual transformation some of the other people around the ashram would live forever too. The goal is that mankind becomes, in time, entirely transmuted, lives immortally and sexlessly.

Some of the people there are quite intelligent, but for their acceptance of some of these doctrines. That's India for you. There is a staggering amount of Aurobindo literature in English, all published right in Pondicherry by ashram workers. The POINT is, though, from my standpoint, that there was no practice of any kind—study, meditation, etc., to be seen. And this is what I am always looking for. No matter how ridiculous a theory or doctrine may be, it may have associated meditation exercises that are pragmatically quite good. Aurobindo ashramites seem to exist entirely on a devotion-and-faith basis, "open yourself to the influence of the Mother." This also can be a valid path (devotion and submission) but it requires a very critical study of doctrine.

Khajuraho

Next day, February 17, left Banaras on the Kashi Express, 1:15 P.M., bound for the little town of Satna. At Satna detrained 11:30 P.M. No retiring room here, so prepared to sleep in the waiting rooms. I went into the men's waiting room, spread my sleeping-bag cover out on a couch and washed up. Joanne came in and said she had gone into the women's waiting room and went right on into the washroom and started cleaning up, wearing her slacks. An old woman in there started talking to her in some language but Joanne couldn't understand so didn't pay much attention. Finally the old lady left and came back a few minutes later leading some RR station-men. One asked Joanne in English, "Are you a woman?" She said, "Last time I looked I was," and the men laughed nervously and told the old lady Joanne was a woman all right, and then scolded her for being such a stupid old country lady, and left laughing.

Railway station life—going to the refreshment stand and getting cupfuls of boiled tea in our tin cups; buying *pera* (a kind of candy made of boiled down milk) or *puri* from venders.

Following morning caught a 6 A.M. bus, bound cross country for the ancient erotic temple, Khajuraho. A fine rolling drive through a flat landscape of occasional twisty deciduous trees, boulders, distant New Mexico-type bluffs. This is in the state of Madhya Pradesh, a somewhat backward area, with the aboriginal Bhil and Gond tribes still around, and center of Thuggee activities in the eighteenth–nineteenth centuries. Indian highways are pretty good. At 11 A.M. were at Khajuraho and marched off with our packs to the circuit house, where we got a room. Circuit houses were originally built to accommodate civil servants and traveling British parties—there is a network of them all over India. Now some of them, as at Khajuraho, have been cleaned up, enlarged, and developed into government-run tourist hostels, at very reasonable prices. We spent the afternoon of the eighteenth and all day the nineteenth closely studying the ten or so temples, set a mile apart in two groups. These also were built in the eleventh–twelfth centuries, during the high period of Tantric Hinduism, when at the courts of several rulers, as in Madhya Pradesh and Orissa both, the people in control became adepts at sexual yoga and devotees of the Goddess. Hence this great flowering of incredibly elegant soaring stone buildings, carved in intricate detail both inside and out with the forms of beautiful women and men, often embracing and frequently making love in a variety of postures. They are so moving, and true, that under their spell one wonders what's wrong with the world that everyone simply doesn't make love with everyone else, it seems the naturalest and most beautiful thing to do. I took as many photographs as I could, actually cliff-climbing the temple walls. These are Archeological Survey controlled, hence you are allowed to make rubbings and take photographs without hindrance; kept up beautifully with grass- and flower-lined lawns.

The great Shiva temple is a model of Mt. Kailash, where Shiva is supposed to live; hence it is a model of a mountain, hollow, with Shiva inside—and the structure of the towers reproduces a feeling of ridges, gendarmes, subpeaks; the horizontal molding lines reproduced from the base of the plinth up in a variety of variations are a kind of geological-paleontological system of strata, moving up through animal friezes to the "human" level—fossils of dancers, lovers, fighters with leogriffs—temple wall like a human paleontology laid bare—rising; to the Divine Couples seated in shrines on sub-pinnacles—vegetable, mineral, and animal universes—complete—to the mountain summit, spire of pure geometry, a rock crown like the sun. And also, the lingam—inside, in the center of the hill in a small dark room—the main figure of it all; damp gloom—holding it all, lovers and animals, in history, vertically, to the brilliant light and heat of the outside sun. The north walls of temples mossier, darker, with lichen.

Dharamshala

After an all-night ride, we arrived at Pathankot, in northwest Punjab, at
five in the morning March 28. This is the jumping-off point for the two-
day bus trip to Kashmir. It is not far from the Pakistan border. We turned
east, however, toward the mountains. There is a valley system about a hundred and fifty miles deep into the Punjab Himalaya. The first section is
the Manali and the second the Kulu valley. They are very beautiful. We
wanted to go to the Kulu and walk over a 14,000-foot pass to visit the
Tibetan-culture, barren, and mountainous Lahoul valley, but didn't have
time. So we went up the hillside in the Manali valley, to the 6,000-foot
town of Dharamshala, where the Dalai Lama has his permanent headquarters (courtesy of the Indian government) and a sizeable settlement of
Tibetan refugees. Lodged in a tourist bungalow. A long gentle slope below
us, of green wheatfields, orchards, running water creeks, and cascades
everywhere. The richest-feeling, cleanest, and airiest region we'd seen in
India. Above Dharamshala white-capped ridges rise to 14,000 feet and
there are fine deodar forests around. We had dinner at the Lhasa Hotel—a
meal of Tibetan noodles with meat in it. (First meat in months, as we had
gone all-out vegetarian for a while.) In the evening we all smoked opium,
since Allen and Peter had picked some up in Delhi and gotten a pipe as
well. It was a funny kind of opium, mixed with charcoal in a little ball to
make it burn better. Usual opium is a sticky ball you have to warm in a
spoon over a candle or stove and then lay a burning coal next to it in the
bowl to make it smoke when you inhale. It tasted OK, and after a few balls
Joanne and I retired. An interesting feeling—all night a sensation of being
not awake and not asleep, just sort of floating, with pleasant thoughts but
nothing of consequence—quite different from the heavy content of peyote with all its visual kicks and bad-take possibilities. In the morning we
were all nauseated, another effect of opium. Next morning tried to reach

the Dalai Lama's ashram, two miles farther up the hill, but the phone was out of order. So we make arrangements to stay a night in the Triund Forest bungalow, which is a seven-mile hike up the hill at 10,000 feet, and go off at the invitation of a young Sikh to a local fair. Walked about two miles along the hillside, through little tributary valleys full of thundering creeks, and above wheatfields with neat channels and ditches leading the clear running water. It was a beautiful day, with just a few banner clouds above us on the snowpeaks.

It was a fair of the local hillpeople, called Gaddis, who are big sheepherders. The men wore robelike tan wool coats hitched up in the belt so that they only hung down to midthigh. The belt is a coil of woven wool rope, which they can unwind and use if they need it. The men wear small gold earrings and little woven caps. The women have a complicated costume and pounds of jewelry, at least on fair days. It was held on a wide, high, grassy plateau. Hand-run ferris wheels, goat carcasses hung in trees being skinned out; a bank of drums and drummers, long-haired sheep standing on top of boulders. "Shakespearean," Allen said—it was indeed anciently and idyllically pastoral.

A series of amateur wrestling matches: an older-looking man, light of build, with one weak polio-affected leg, matched against a heavier, more muscular, younger man. Gurdip the Sikh said the old man would win, but we couldn't see how. They wore tiny jockstraps, and fought in a dirt pit in the middle of the grass. The old man was underneath all the time, but he couldn't seem to be put on his back. At one point he was on his hands and knees, and the big fellow was on his back. The old man reached up and caught him back of the neck, and threw him clean over his shoulder and laid him out flat, then got up and did a limpy little victory dance while the other man got up rubbing his neck and looking sheepish and bewildered—the old guy joined with a little orchestra band marching around the perimeter of the wrestling ground, dancing and hopping along.

Morning of March 30 we set out climbing with our rucksacks. Passing the Dalai Lama's ashram we made arrangements to meet him the following afternoon, then went on climbing up the trail. A long steady climb. Eat lunch by a snowbank. Behind us finally comes the *chowkidar* (caretaker) of the bungalow, who doesn't live in it full time. He could speak no English, and was kind of a problem for us. The Triund house is on a ridge that climbs up higher toward the main mountains, and drops off steeply on both sides. Spectacular view. This house is really for the Forest Service, but non-civil-servants can use it if it's not officially occupied. We have a terrible time getting firewood, water (by melting snow), and kerosene lamps. This chowkidar is the most useless creature, just sort of hanging around watching us, and doing nothing himself. Part of the trouble was that it was well before the usual season when people use the place. In the logbook, we noticed that the Dalai Lama had come, with two or three others, seven times up here, often for three or four days at a time. He is always referred to in English as "His Holiness."

In the evening we built a cozy fire in the fireplace. Next morning I got up quite early and left the others sleeping, and pushed up the ridge. It was blowing mist, and pretty soon started to snow lightly. I climbed to timberline and a little beyond, until finally I was on a great snowfield leading up toward the actual peak of the mountain, Dhaulagiri. Instead of an iceaxe I was using a steel-tipped cane I had got at the village below. The wind became extremely strong and I was getting covered with snow on one side, and there was no view whatsoever. So I turned reluctantly back, from my highest elevation in the Himalayas, about 12,500 feet. That wouldn't even get you to the base of Everest. On the way down, in a little nook at the base of two cliffs, I saw a stone platform with splashes of faded orange color on it, and some rusty steel tridents stuck in the boulders beside it. The meditation-platform and living quarters of a Shiva-ascetic, at some time. Back at the Forest House the smoke was coming out the chimney and there was a hot breakfast. Around noon we started down.

Dalai Lama

The Dalai Lama's ashram has fences around it, and a few armed Indian army
guards. Between the tops of the deodars are strung long ribbons of prayer
flags. After getting cleared through the guardhouse (and washing up at a
pump, right in front of the guards) we were led to a group of low wooden
buildings and given a waiting room to wait in. I guess the Indians are
afraid the Chinese might come and kidnap the Dalai if they're not careful.
A few minutes later the Dalai Lama's interpreter came in, a neatly Western-dressed man in his thirties with a Tibetan cast, who spoke perfect
English. His name is Sonam Topgay. He immediately started to ask me
about Zen Buddhism. It seems he had found a book on Zen (if I understood him right) in a public toilet in Calcutta, and was immediately struck
by its resemblance to the school of Tibetan Buddhism he followed. After
that we didn't talk about Zen much, but he told me about the Zok-chen
branch of Rnin ma-pa (Red Hat), which is a Tantric meditation school.
He said it was by far the highest and greatest of all schools of Buddhism,
including the Yellow Hat (which happens to be the sect his employer, the
Dalai Lama, is head of). (Don't tell the Dalai Lama I said this.) He is originally from Sikkim, went to college in Delhi majoring in psychology. Got
fits of depression and figured out a method of "introspection" to see what
was the mind that felt depressed. Then he went to Lhasa and met a saintly
old woman age 122 who told him to go see Dudjon Rimpoche of the Rnin
ma-pa, which he did, becoming that man's disciple. He also married a
girl in Lhasa. He said that one of the good things about his school of Buddhism was that you could marry, and you and your wife could meditate
together while making love. Then they came out, when the Chinese moved
in, with their baby girl. (A book by Evans-Wentz called *The Tibetan Book
of Liberation,* I believe, is of this sect. *Book of the Dead,* also.) They also say,

perfect total enlightenment can come: 1) at the moment of dying, 2) by eating proper sacramental food, 3) through dance and drama, and 4) at the moment of orgasm.

Then he told us the Dalai Lama was busy talking to the Maharajah of Sikkim, who had just dropped in, and that's why it had been such a long wait. So we went into the Dalai Lama's chamber. It has colorful *tankas* hanging all around and some big couches in a semicircle. We shake hands with him except that I do a proper Buddhist deep bow. The Dalai Lama is big and rather handsome. He looks like he needs more exercise. Although he understands a lot of English, always keeps an interpreter by when talking to guests. Allen and Peter asked him at some length about drugs and drug experiences, and their relationship to the spiritual states of meditation. The Dalai Lama gave the same answer everyone else did: drug states are real psychic states, but they aren't ultimately useful to you because you didn't get them on your own will and effort. For a few glimpses into the unconscious mind and other realms, they may be of use in loosening you up. After that, you can too easily come to rely on them, rather than undertaking such a discipline as will actually alter the structure of the personality in line with these insights. It isn't much help to just glimpse them with no ultimate basic alteration in the ego that is the source of lots of the psychic-spiritual ignorance that troubles one. But he said he'd be interested in trying psilocybin, the mushroom derivative, just to see what Westerners are so excited about. Allen promised to try and put Harvard onto it, and have this professor Dr. Tim Leary send him some.

Then the Dalai Lama and I talked about Zen sect meditation, him asking "how do you sit? how do you put your hands? how do you put your tongue? where do you look?"—as I told or showed him. Then he said, yes, that's just how we do it. Joanne asked him if there couldn't be another posture of meditation for Westerners, rather than crosslegged. He said, "It's not a matter of national custom," which I think is about as good an answer as you could get.

The Dalai doesn't spend all his time in his ashram; in fact he had just returned from a tour of south India, Mysore, where a few Tibetan refugee resettlements are. And last thing I've heard (since I got back to Japan) is that he's going to set out and do some real Buddhist preaching over India, and maybe Europe and America eventually, spinning the wheel of the Dharma. He is at the least a very keen-minded well-read man, and probably lots more than that. Also, he himself is still in training—there are the "Senior Gurus of the Dalai Lama," the most learned of Tibetans, who keep him on a hard study schedule and are constantly testing and debating with him.

Walked back down the hill, two miles in the dark, illuminated by occasional lightning flash, to our bungalow. To sleep late, some Englishman shouting under our windows.

On April 1, two in the afternoon, we took the bus back out of Dharamshala, our last look at the mountains; hardly had the bus got started and I said "my God I've forgot the cameras!" Joanne turned white and Allen and Peter looked serious. So I said April Fools. Little Tibetan kids running down the street in the black-and-red boots, little robes flying, long braided hair. By evening we were in Pathan-kot, and took a railway retiring room. I went out and bought some eggs, some bananas, and some orange gin (the Punjab isn't dry). It was hotter than it had been up at Dharamshala. We got one of the sweepers to promise to wake us at 4:30 A.M., because we were going to catch the Pathankot Express, which leaves at 5:00, the next morning.

Letters

To Philip Whalen

from Gary Snyder, Friday 17 Sept 1954

Dear Pausanius—

Am un-mashed only by failure of natural law and percentages to wreak expected damage, as I (and all other chokersetters) am/are daily subject to falling pecker-poles, snapped jill-pokes, toppling snags, rolling logs, giant caterpillars which the driver cannot see over the hood of (to know and avoid you), tripping cables, swinging butter hooks, the idiocy of man running the show, and other horrors too numerous to mention . . .

. . . The Volume II of Creel's *Analects* is a Joy to own and use, I proclaim its worth. Afraid some acquaintance with Vol I is in order, nonetheless. May have to return to the Winter Palace in mid-October, if it keeps reigning on us

Ascetically, Tiger . . .

To Philip Whalen, from Gary Snyder, March 1954

I finally dropped by Patchen's & picked up my poncho. He is very gentle & pleasant, & looks terribly worn—understandable, since he has to go to the hospital every week & get his back shot full of novocain while they do things to it in hopes of cure.

Rexroth has stomach trouble and his wife Marthe is pregnant again. But he still happily holds forth on KPFA & has managed to insult virtually everyone in the Bay Area now; he has the university here positively frothing. & a recent flaying of Huxley's Vedanta business & southern California orientalists has won him packs of new enemies. He said, roughly, "The only living member of the Huxley family who can think with even moderate clarity is Julian."

Genji [the author's cat] is getting to be a total idiot. His behaviour is less and less predictable.

Weather is lovely & clear here; winter plums blossoming.

Yes: everything you say about Pound, Williams, Eliot & Joyce is true. It really IS a problem; what use to put Joyce to now. I have comforted myself with the notion that *Finnegans Wake* is to be approached best as a big Mahayana sutra; something like the Gandavyuha, & really outside any known occidental literary tradition . . .

I come to think more & more, poetry is a PROCESS & shd be, in a Buddhist sort of way, didactic & sensual.

which makes Williams, for me, rise in value considerable.

But the concern with Merkhn lit critics seeking out absolute standards for literature (conceiving of this as the only alternative to a Philistine relativism) is another reflection of Aristotle & the Xtians; there is probably a more useful aesthetic in oriental thought. (sic)

Well. let an old dog lie. You ought to pay us all a visit.

Greetings to Clarence. Foreward the arts.

Gary

To Philip Whalen, from Gary Snyder, Spring 1955

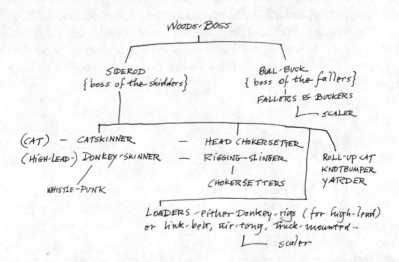

1) skidding-in high-lead, the donkey skinner can't see the logs or the position of the carriage for the chokers. The whistle-punk, in a view-position, toots stop-go—drop the rigging—pick it up signals. The rigging-slinger selects the loads & points them out to the choker-setters. when the rigging drops they run in & set chokers, then get out of the way.

in cat-logging the skinner drives out & gets the loads as selected by the head chokersetter. at the landing, the knotbumpers trim up the logs & then roll-up cat make them into decks (piles)

on high lead, a man is at the Donkey engine & unhooks the chokers. The logs are dropped in Cold-Decks to be loaded later—called yarding.

2) Falling The bull-buck selects & lays out the strips to be given each set of fallers—usually 2 men, one to fall & measure the tree into lengths, the other to limb and buck. The scaler comes behind & keeps the scale for each set.

3) loading—highly skilled job, especially running an air-tongs. Sets the logs on flatcars or trucks. When trucks, a scaler is present to check the loads soaz not to get too big

To Philip Whalen, from Gary Snyder, September 1955

Cher Maître

Here we are back from the Sierras, which proved, finally when I took a trip on my own, ten days by backpack & only partially on trail, to be possessed of a certain charm & isolation.

Old Harry Lamley wrote & said you are planning to come to the Bay Area to live this year. Now if this is true, and I hope it is, you must come as soon as possible, because you are scheduled to read some of your own poetry at a reading to be given at the Six Gallery on the first Friday in October.

There will also be poets Philip Lamantia, and a person named Allen Ginsberg whom I met recently, who is the person who wrote the letter about images of cloudy light to Williams in *Paterson,* others, & me, & Kenneth Rexroth will do introductions and such. I think it will be a poetickall bombshell.

I got you in on the deal on the basis of three poems *Martyrdom, K.W. Senex & If you're So Smart,* which have achieved a certain subterranean celebration via Rexroth & others. Rexroth got me in.

Otherwise, Berkeley is a pleasant place to be, my cabin is quiet & I study Japanese, I planted two pines & placed two granite rocks in a felicitous manner; Mrs. Lehman is full of spirit, Shandel in good health, & I have taken to baking my own bread on a recipe borrowed from Valery McCorkle. I gave my car to Mr. & Mrs. McCorkle, who live in Sausalito, to ease the task of running a family about. . . .

To Philip Whalen, from Gary Snyder, January 27, 1956

Dear Phil, a long snowy ride up 97 & through Warm Springs got us safely here, a night at Durham's a night at Bakers last night & tonight to be at Hoodlatch's. Everyone at Reed passed the idea of our reading on to some-one else so we made our own arrangements to be sponsored by Janus and read in Capehart Monday 8 pm the 13; lloyds class will sign. Almost a foot of new snow on the ground. I went skiing last night on Waverly golf course. Logging still going places, Ginsberg got a pair of cork boots at the goodwill for 2 bucks & wants to work in the woods. He is reconsidering rhetorical poetry, sez it makes him feel foolish to shout MOLOCH! at fir trees. the hardness & cleanness of Reed students I've talked to is gratify-ing to seeing and in a way still better than anything in the Bay area, devoid of self-pity & all camping, & certainly capable of some creative effort. Hoodlatch doesn't like the stuff I wrote this fall, too personal he says, but does like myths & texts & the berry feast; liked Kerouac's poems best of all. Everyone remembers you. We go to Seattle Sunday.

Hoodlatch has a quantity of blossoms, we mean to walk rainbows tonight.

Gary

To Philip Whalen, from Gary Snyder, 1957 26 Dec

All Xmas Eve & Day prowling Byzantium—Hagia Sophia the uttermost and beyond which O of religious interior building. Got drunk in Pera & caught a bus in Chalcedon; touched a marble pillar taken from the tem-ple of Diana at Ephasus; now at port in Sea of Marmara at Izmit, antiently Nicomedia. I can't bear it! Snow on the hills about; white spire minarets of isolated mountain Mosques.

GLEAM: wool, bread, mustaches.

To Philip Whalen, from Gary Snyder, 15 February 1958

Arabian Sea
Lat °90 Long. 75° E. Green

Got letter from you at Naha Okinawa; was too befuddled with shoreside amusements to compose an answer. Dockside bargirl & jukebox scenes, also more composed uptown Japanese coffeehouse & sake-shop alleyways talking nippongo & buying good green tea.

I have been: from Japan to Ceylon to Guam & Midway, back to Persian

Gulf, to Sicily & Italy, back to Persian Gulf, to Turkey (Iskenderun & Ismit) (The former town named after Isakander better known as Alexander), back to Persian Gulf, to Okinawa, & now en route to Persian Gulf one more time to take oil & then discharge in somewhere (the present orders are Pearl Harbor but that will doubtless be altered) & proceed full speed ahead both boilers burning on all 8 burners 90 rpm 420 lbs. steam pressure toward America.

I never got no other letters from you, like Thxgiving at Les Dalles: But lots of letters don't come.

At Napoli went out to Pompeii & mounted a bit up Vesuvio.

Seeing historical monuments first hand does have a bit of thrill in it. But Istanbul is more entertaining & Sophia is inexpressibly religious and vast.

Curiosity awakened now of Iranian Central-Asian world, Armenian backwaters, cypress-tree valleys of Karakorum, leather shoes & double-bend bows & spread of Islam.

Maybe I shall seek out & discover the original Amithaba.

Arabic art a great calligraphic shot like China; saw magnificent examples in museum in BYZ., huge mounted intricate script designs. Use broad-nib hand-carved bamboo tube-pen; ink apparently soot=ink like Far East.

Mediterranean countries & islands are deserted compared to Japan; barren, nothing but scrub & granite with scarcely any erosion.

Have got so I can make it with machinery; you ought to see me crawling around them tight places swinging wrenches and slapping in gaskets. The crew is all dingbats, some very original ones.

On & on, trip I can hardly remember when it starts & it seems like never end, time-flashes of two-day ports & all that load of strangeness & strange bodies & lingos so swiftly dream-like disappeared; one week tropics & dolphins, 2 weeks later bleak snow mountains & icy winds, what confusion.

Expect to be in U.S. around 1 April; full of devilish devices & rather wealthy.

Justinian says, running into his just-completed Sophia,

HO SOLOMON, I HAVE SURPASSED THEE

Drive that steel drill down. Poetry not as tension but as pressure & sudden vacuums when pressure surprisingly stops.

Keep me knowledged of where you are or will be. Harold's address is 340 Corte Madera—drop a card there if you make sudden shifts of place. How's for the mountain's this summer?

tiger

Dear Kabir

I DON:T KNOW if airmail or plain male is faster between here & your house, I don't suppose it could make much difference what with time lost revving up the props, greasing the ailerons, landing on beams, taxiing, getting clearance from the F.C.C., etc., on aeroplanes. In fact I will send this by steam-engine & see just how well it does.

I am living in the hermitage of Ma-rin now, with brand new Coleman lamp for reading light & spiffy coleman stove for quick cooking & wood stove for heat & cheer, & big cupboard full of Crystal Palace goodies like polenta, wheat flour, bulghur, rice, dates, etc. Mats on the floor & a fine black pot Shandel gave, & lots of books rescued from other people, & long crosscut saw & a broadaxe, galvanized washtub & washboard, a samurai sword my sis' longshoreman boyfriend gave me, cougar hide, sleeping bag, iron teapot japonaise, meditation hall in other room with big zendo bell & clackers, a goodwill leather jacket & denim railroad man's jacket & new pair levis, new pair tennis shoes, All in order. Also this typewriter I bought for $15.00.

Also, I may have said I bought a car '51 Austin, to run about in until I decide to roam again at which time it may be easily sold. Lew & Mary, & Greensfelders & McCorkle bros. were over here other night for house-warming. Everybody likes Lew & digs him & he comes on clearer and brighter all the time. I'm not saying this won't bug Mrs. Mary as I watch out of the corner of my eye; she feels (I fear) threatened. Also he got fired from his job & is now talking about going to work carpentering or construction etc.

Claude & I went Berkeley Buddhist bazaar & saw everybody; I'm to talk to them this Friday evening. Mr. Rev. Imamura is resigning his job as preacher come this fall'; he says he's been doing it for seventeen years & now wants time to study & think for a change.

Locke is here right now (4:20 p.m. Tuesday) figuring out a horoscope for his friend Mrs. Mary Somers. There is a wooden toad glaring at me & a sky chart spread out on the floor, I did it for Locke, but he refuses to look because he says he's only interested in the intellectual zodiac. . .

. . .this damned arctic climate
. . .I shiver all the time now

are you warm?

Gary

Thor's day

Dear Cunobelinus,

I just finished reading Count Belisarius after owning it unread for 8 years. Vita Brevis.

Darmmy Bums is quite a chronicle. I hope we all won't get arrested. I do wish Jack had taken more trouble to smooth out dialogues etc., transitions are rather abrupt sometimes.

I have stayed fearfully at home since I got back but for one brief foray into The Coffee Gallery. Everybody's reading it.

I started my Zendo going last week, from 8 to 10 every Tuesday Wednesday & Thursday evenings & people are coming in droves, & sitting very nicely & being very willing & apt pupils re the formalities of bows, entrances, exits, etc. . I am really astounded at the response.

Bob Greensfelder & I are going down to the Kaweahs (southrin Sierras) next week for a few days. He bought some new boots for the trip.

Rexroth has departed for Aix-en-Provence for about a year. I missed him. Nakagawa Soyen Roshi has returned to Japan already Wattsu Sensei says.

Alan came up yesterday to discuss his article beat zen, square zen, & zen: He says: Ferlinghetti wants him to write an enlarged version of it to be published as a pamphlet, & Tuttle do same in Nippon simultime. But Watts, having dug Dharmy Bums the most, wants to rewrite the whole thing treating the beat aspect entirely different, because he sees now, he says, that they aren't irresponsible or hostile at all but really serious people—like

II.

there are wildest looking types from Grant Ave. very energetically learning about zazen, & J.K. has told Truth Watts says about the holy golden-voiced spit spinning wheel of the law.

& so beat, square, etc. zen will come out in a very new light now under Mr. Watts' articulate pen. He is a very swinging person now, more time spent with family since he got kicked out of Academy, goes camping a lot and stays home writing and digs people more & in short is a great guy to be around.

Well come down come down, but don't look to see Kyogen Roshi. He am gone.

What about us assembling loony fragments J.K. of quick flip bonze poems, & whoever else has such, & put them all together in a miscellany to be called après le chinois, JACK MOUNTAIN ANTHOLOGY.

Please give my best to Ben & tell him I'm sorry I didn't get to see him again. Prod hoodlatch if you see him in Portland to type up his poems in a decent MS.

basta.   Keep clean and decent,

love

Gary

To Philip Whalen, from Gary Snyder, October 1958

They made me a fireman at first. because 12 men missed the ship in Yoko-hama—I never saw such drunks or brawls or loons on any ship or any-thing; guys eating snakes alive & tales of port before that, Sasebo, half the crew drunk ashore ten days running naked down streets & diving off piers, knocking over cabbage-strands & breaking bar windows, paying for it all, throwing ashtrays. But old ship got sort of straightened out after I came abroad, with new Captain & new Chief Engineer just arrived, only a few fights with wrenches all over the engineroom, etc. Went to Ceylon & saw snakecharmer, walked alone in the jungle by gray mother monkeys & hoped a cobra would scare me, climbed jungly tree to look on blue bay waters, sitting in a tree crotch with neat pile of dry monekyshit placed there, & drank beer in dingy dirtfloor place with print color pictures of the life of Gautama on the walls, little dirty children & shiftless men & chickens & white cows. From Ceylon back to Guam, discharged half our oil there, picked up new true firemen & demoted me to regular wiper's job & took on four Guamian boys to fill out our crew—they look like Indians, have Spanish names & speak some dialect of Malayo-Polynesian, Mariana Isles and Micronesian. Then went clear out to mid-Pacific to Midway to give up the rest of our oil, Albatross island & Navy base, a dis-mal scene but for contract Hawaiian workers with wood shed booze hall every night three days gambling & drinking beer, then brown tanned tat-tered & bearded guys the happiest, Chinamen, French, Polynesian, every-thing blood mixed and grownup there. We turned right around & sailed on 48 days to Bahrain Persia for more oil, green slick waters of Singapore & phosphorescent Indian Sea, Arabia Desert. That load of oil in, we arched around the southern coast of Araby a long scarp barren cliffs & splendid rockforms, though Suez full of thieves in bumboats, sneak alongside & steal whatever; out into Mediterranean choppy & cool now after Red Sea nights, one morning past Crete & then port in Sicily, a rocky fortress town called Augusta, also took train & walked a day around Catania, Europe & heavy Church of Italy, the streets deserted-looking after Japan, olive tree & cactus, somehow too tired for me.

To Philip Whalen, from Gary Snyder, 23.IX.1960

Dear Philip I have not yet gone down to seek a bell bowl for you but I soon will never fear. We were away the last half of August at beaches & islands in the Japan Sea & I learned how to wear a mask & swim under-water looking at fishes, also how to catch sea snails & eat them by boiling then unscrewing little soft snail from its shell by catching it with a pin & then using in deft twirling motion disengage its soft white (or green) corkscrew-shaped body from its shell in one deft motion without break-ing the flesh & then you can eat it just as it is. . .

What do you hear of reviews of Allen Grove Anthology?

How is Brother Jack K. doing down Big Sur or other wherever he is now days?

Also how is Lew? I owe him a letter

J. & me went to see *Black Orpheus* and *Jazz of a Summer's Day* last night & I swear I saw Greg Corso's face in the audience, a close up.

Progressive or what you call it jazz is just becoming the rage here & also a new cheaper, dryer, red wine is out, almost as cheap as happy's or Vista d'Oro. Only it isn't (!) nearly as good.

This long poem grows on me, the conception of it, only it's too intel-lectual still, apparently I work by getting a sort of overall intellectual structure & then sort of forgetting it a long time & then beginning to fairly spontaneously write into it.

Joanne keeps telling me to take my bath because we have to go to zazen soon & the fire is burning merrily under the iron tub & if I don't get in quick I won't be able to it will be too hot.

I will write you back quicker next time.

I study tea-ceremony with the old lady who lives upstairs here once in a while now but I haven't got to pick up a teabowl yet, I'm still practic-ing unfolding a purple napkin.

Persimmons on our tree getting ripe.

I feel we ought to do something to help change society for the better.

love,

Gary

To Philip Whalen, from Gary Snyder, 9.1.61

Dear Phillip, I send you a letter on this already ruined letter because it is the next to last air letter in the house & besides it shdn't go to waste.

It is the last day of the new years season & the town has returned to normal & I must return to work tomorrow. We spent almost the whole two weeks at home, excepting one day in Nara to look at the 8th century building Sangatsudo (only building that old surviving in Nara city proper) which is full of statuary, clay, wood & dry lacquer. & the museum at Kofukuji. All the Buddhas of that period have insufferably transcendent & blah faces, the exciting statues are the guardian kings, the "ten leading disciples of the Buddha" etc. The guardian kings are decked out in Persian armor & weird weapons & various mean looks, very lively. The ten disciples look like a roomful of old winos, junkies, Mexican fruitpickers, & invalid professors with all their distinct & unique expressions—all in rags. But not grotesque or thoroughly out of it, as some of the arhat figures. We saw the Big Daddy Buddha (first time for me) at Todaiji, which is truly enormous. Palm of the hand six feet long, etc. But it is not beautiful or moving. & one can't help wondering why they every wanted to put so much bronze in one pile, seeing as how bronze has other uses. Biggest wood building in the world (supposed) housing it—a magnificent structure—but somehow lacking, at least for me, Sancta Sophia is more a "Buddhist" temple. More presence of the Void. Maybe because of that great empty dome. The empty dome of the big bronze Buddha. Well. & we went to the Katsura detached villa (by special permission only) & were properly impressed by what is undoubtedly the best domestic architecture in Japan & an example for the world. Designed unfortunately to be used only in the summer Nobody cd make the winter through there. . .

    Gareth

To Philip Whalen, from Gary Snyder, {10.III.61}

Dear Phil, ain't nothing to get one writing a letter like the Wife away, a slug of ole Nikka whiskey, & some castrated Japanese pop singer whining on the radio to the bastardized chords of eurasian dance band fluff. (The Wife, to whom no disrespect intended, is out teaching her native tongue to the natives)

Well the question I had in mind, was the old theoretical problem that all modern politicians (sweet John Kennedy incl.) must face, ie. can one take the responsibility on himself of ordering the death of 1 or 20 or etc. people for the evident future good for larger numbers. *Any* social action aside from complete non-violence, is also faced with this, & what if you want action? Not that I'm saying I do. I agree with you completely. In fact, I just finished reading Camus' *Rebel* & he has a very interesting solution; i.e. that in a rebellion it is necessary sometimes to kill, but who has killed in rebellion, to protect the very reason for this revolt, must voluntarily sacrifice his own life to balance it.

Not with ideas. With rage is far better. & it's you that did it, no pencilpusher in the Capital. As Camus says, though, boil it down & murder is the essential moral problem of the time. An ex-Zen monk recently gave me the lovely information that during the recent disturbance, Zen Masters to a man let their monks go to war & told them to become one with "MU" and kill for the Emperor. One can learn a lot from tradition, but you can't count on it to provide you with decent values . . .

I pray that you develop patience, one of the *paramitas*—but too much p. is bad too. the radio is driving me mad

love,

Gary

To Will Petersen

just off Singapore

Dear Pete, I discover that I'm on a rusty tramp tanker. It seems I signed a thing called ship's articles which means I am supposed to stay on this ship until it goes back to America—which won't be for another five months, unless the engine breaks down or the crew goes totally mad, which it may well do.

. . . if I'm going to be on this tub for a long time I think I better lay in some reading matter. I rely on you . . .

To Will Petersen, from Gary Snyder, 8 September

Bay of Bengal

Forget all that shit about books for the time, we just got new orders to go to Trincomalee Ceylon and then to Colombo, & after that nobody knows

To Will Petersen, from Gary Snyder, 10 November

Red Sea in the narrow place
just South of Suez heading Northwest

. . . it sounds so beautiful & fragile & impossible & maybe when you get this something awful will have happened & everybody will be catapulted back into little lonely rooms again. But DON'T let it because you are the best scene in the whole gloomy world . . .

all the long way southwest the southern coast of Arabia never out of

sight of what is really an enormous straight cliff well over a thousand feet
high,

    not a sign of life not even one

    spit of a seed

    Crew madly talking Italy, world of quick fuck

    The Classical World

    hit me like bricks in Byzantium, to which I have

    journeyed & returned

    . . . Iranian & Turkic long-mustache & leather-stocking world: the real
bridge between east & west those people, minarets, desert capitals now
dust & ancient Buddha-days in Turkestan before Mahomet heard the dove;
& the terrible silence of Hagia Sophia that has been Christian & Moslem
& is now void, who knows what temple next?—its hanging lamps & tile
high figures that are any sacred couple

    in the world & any sacred baby be coyote jesus gautama or quetzal-
coatl . . .

    In the little poems & long epics back then there is the same wire twang-
ing that we hear in DHL.

    & old crackerbeard.

    Wow, an image; poetry like a guitar string—

    one end anchored to the void that makes it hum,

    the other to busy old finger world that picks a tune.

    I'm tired of images like that.

    Just went topside & saw the Southern Cross bummed a sip of vodka off
the cook.

To Will Petersen, from Gary Snyder, Aegean Sea: 22 December 1957

Dear Pete, well about 35 days ago it seems an age I did get two letters

    From my last letter-place, Bahrain Persia, went to Augusta Sicily—
through sandy old Suez & hashish-smoking Egyptian boatmen—Crete at
dawn one morning 10 miles north, & Sicily foggy & windy with white-
brown olive trees & rocky hills & pastel houses with red tile roofs, good
wine & good bread, a dreary whorehouse scene of nothing-but-blowjobs
& too much expense; & whole drunken crew barely finding its way back
to ship; then on through straits of Messina & up to Pozzuoli which is a
suburb of Naples & at Naples I stayed sober & spent a day in Pompeii &
journeying up to Vesuvius. Pompeii a most impressive town & images of
another life entirely—civilization is a matter of proceeding from one mass
kick to another, & when the kick is forgotten the civilization it was is as
unavailable to our minds as a half-forgotten dream & is as weird; as com-

plete and self-contained, & as transitory;—*not* an expression of Buddhist sentiments, but a comment on the nature of high culture to be a sort of obsession delusion so that those under its influence may stick to triangles never imagine circles, paint in red but never conceive of blue consider themselves (as we do) to be complete humans missing no possibilities— when another equally consistent, logical, self-contained little cosmos of thought & action which is utterly inconceivable to us lies just around some historical corner. From Italy back to Persian Gulf & then out around the Indian Ocean (enroute to Pearl Harbor our orders get changed & we alter course back to Red Sea & Suez) & again Mediterranean, this time Turkey.

This damned ship just goes on & on like the Flying Dutchman, I sort of begin to believe it will never go home or stay anywhere more than a day, until the last drop of deep-down Arabian oil is drawn & the last gear-box oiled & the ultimate airplane wrecked & all the paint gone & the Sappa Creek just floating around in its own rust & ruin with its Hoary white-bearded crew re-reading the ten thousandth time the same magazine & wondering when we'll ever get home

This is the sea where the heroes sail. & the goddesses came to shepherds on mountainstops, & the dawn is REALLY rosy-fingered, the sea wine-dark, & I intoxicate myself with Classical memories & look about for pagan deities & long-prowed galleys.

Wrote long poeme called "Tanker Blues".

Also this short piece amongst others:

> USNS SAPPA CREEK
> *. . . rags in bales,*
> *the final home for bathrobes*
> *little boy bluejeans & housewife dresses*
>
> *. . .*

On these long runs
after a certain time you flip & get happy & quit figuring how much you're making & how long till you get home & just amble about hollering & laughing covered with grease & loaded with silly wrenches & generally being a sort of Bodhisattva of machinery without any past or future, I got a full beard & wornout shorts & no shirt & old bandanna on my head which is shaggy.

To Will Petersen, from Gary Snyder, March 1958

near the
gilbert islands
in the rainy
dark
a heavy swell
ten p.m. drinking tea

this is the last time this hoss'll write from sea I suppose, unless we are mysteriously sent back to Arabia to go on and on—till the oil runs dry under the big shale hills and the sheiks go back to goats and mares and Aristotle Onassis is dry bones in greek richman's graveyard, when the oil is gone and ball bearings finally creak rusty & shuddering to a final stop and little boys with tallowpots have run alongside covered wagons greasing the axles by hand again, juice gone from the ground & the sap dried up in the machinery & we'll put cowbutter on our hands—& the only tankers will carry olive oil and wine

we are coming leisurely by way of the south seas home; passing south of mindanao through the sulu sea, through the celebes sea, over the equator and under the southern cross, we drew in 22 March to volcanic green flowery hills of steep pago pago bay, tutuila a little island in samoa, and for thirty hours lived in lotus-eater land, a buddha-realm of flowers and delight which is really like old captain cook and herman melville and everybody says, ravaging modern society seems a joke when you walk around where people nap in the daytime and make love at night and care for naught because nobody's jealous or scared, if babies get born they are raised up, when girls reach puberty they make love, when men feel energetic they take torches at night and go fishing—big thighed long-haired Samoan girls & our mad tight crazy rich crew; drinking can beer in bungalow screen-walled bar & dancing to samoan drum records, samoan men & women in flower-color lavalava skirts on happy haunches, or cadging beer from sappa creek crew, or talking away, the policemen says to me "I feel silly in this policemen shirt"—because he didn't like being the samoan policeman when everybody is having fun—so I took off my shirt and gave it to him; later a girl took my zoris too, so I was dancing in the bar shirtless and shoeless we all went to the seaside and had a bonfire and picnic and swimming and ate breadfruit—a robust girl attached on to me & said she was my girlfriend till the ship left, and wouldn't let me look at other girls, but she looked just fine, so we did it one time swimming in the water like seals or whales do I suppose—and when they get away from town they do like old times and villages, take off things above the waist and let bare breasts swing & smile in the light—all night at the beach— somebody took $20 out of my pocket while swimming & a lot of other guy's money too, but it's all so good-natured nobody even cared—there was a horse walking around too, eating flowers, just like a weird gauguin—the hills they say have wild pigs; there are some americans there too, maybe fifty, and they are all sleepy samoans now. Then in the afternoon we had to go & strolled back in couples to the ship which blasted go-away whistle, & up the gangplank to take in the mooring lines, the girls waving, & my girl Miss Afuvai whipping off her lavalava to wave it like a great flag in the wind, & then bending over to show her bare bottom to the crew, a great roar of laughter & approval, as we pull to the sea, & now 2 more days we get to Kwajalein to unload more oil, & then to Hawaii to finish off discharging, & we hope back to west coast.

To Will Petersen, from Gary Snyder, 22 April 1958

Ah, Pete, we came through.
Made it back to white clean sea-air San Francisco unrolled or robbed . . .

> Will Petersen wrote:
> *Can't find it*
> *It's in the dust, in dew, in*
> *moon, in shade of tree & flow of*
> *stream*
>
> > in my kitchen
> > in a jar
>
> *Tokonoma.*
> *Wherever. Anywhere.*
> *Staying overnight with Gary, 1969,*
> *in Midwest college town motel*
> *he makes of dresser top, a shrine*
>
> *places with casual precision a hand-hidden carved wooden*
> *bear; three, four other discrete objects, making*
> *of this careless space,*
> *his world.*
>
> *Open the sacred medicine bundle,*
> *unroll the sleeping bag*
>
> no one loves rock,
> but we are here
>
> *under stars*
> *at ease*

The Practice
of the Wild

The Etiquette
of Freedom

The Compact

One June afternoon in the early seventies I walked through the crackly gold grasses to a neat but unpainted cabin at the back end of a ranch near the drainage of the South Yuba in northern California. It had no glass in the windows, no door. It was shaded by a huge black oak. The house looked abandoned and my friend, a student of native California literature and languages, walked right in. Off to the side, at a bare wooden table, with a mug of coffee, sat a solid old gray-haired Indian man. He acknowledged us, greeted my friend, and gravely offered us instant coffee and canned milk. He was fine, he said, but he would never go back to a VA hospital again. From now on if he got sick he would stay where he was. He liked being home. We spoke for some time of people and places along the western slope of the northern Sierra Nevada, the territories of Concow and Nisenan people. Finally my friend broke his good news: "Louie, I have found another person who speaks Nisenan." There were perhaps no more than three people alive speaking Nisenan at that time, and Louie was one of them. "Who?" Louie asked. He told her name. "She lives back of Oroville. I can bring her here, and you two can speak." "I know her from way back," Louie said. "She wouldn't want to come over here. I don't think I should see her. Besides, her family and mine never did get along."

That took my breath away. Here was a man who would not let the mere threat of cultural extinction stand in the way of his (and her) values. To well-meaning sympathetic white people this response is almost incomprehensible. In the world of his people, never overpopulated, rich in acorn, deer, salmon, and flicker feathers, to cleave to such purity, to be perfectionists about matters of family or clan, were affordable luxuries. Louie and his fellow Nisenan had more important business with each other than conversations. I think he saw it as a matter of keeping their dignity, their pride, and their own ways—regardless of what straits they had fallen upon—until the end.

Coyote and Ground Squirrel do not break the compact they have with each other that one must play predator and the other play game. In the wild a baby black-tailed hare gets maybe one free chance to run across a meadow without looking up. There won't be a second. The sharper the knife, the cleaner the line of the carving. We can appreciate the elegance of the forces that shape life and the world, that have shaped every line of our bodies—teeth and nails, nipples and eyebrows. We also see that we must try to live without causing unnecessary harm, not just to fellow humans but to all beings. We must try not to be stingy, or to exploit others. There will be enough pain in the world as it is.

Such are the lessons of the wild. The school where these lessons can be learned, the realms of caribou and elk, elephant and rhinoceros, orca and walrus, are shrinking day by day. Creatures who have traveled with us through the ages are now apparently doomed, as their habitat—and the old, old habitat of humans—falls before the slow-motion explosion of expanding world economies. If the lad or lass is among us who knows where the secret heart of this Growth-Monster is hidden, let them please tell us where to shoot the arrow that will slow it down. And if the secret heart stays secret and our work is made no easier, I for one will keep working for wildness day by day.

"Wild and free." An American dream-phrase loosing images: a long-maned stallion racing across the grasslands, a V of Canada Geese high and honking, a squirrel chattering and leaping limb to limb overhead in an oak. It also sounds like an ad for a Harley-Davidson. Both words, profoundly political and sensitive as they are, have become consumer baubles. I hope to investigate the meaning of *wild* and how it connects with *free* and what one would want to do with these meanings. To be truly free one must take on the basic conditions as they are—painful, impermanent, open, imperfect—and then be grateful for impermanence and the freedom it grants us. For in a fixed universe there would be no freedom. With that freedom we improve the campsite, teach children, oust tyrants. The world is nature, and in the long run inevitably wild, because the wild, as the process and essence of nature, is also an ordering of impermanence.

Although *nature* is a term that is not of itself threatening, the idea of the "wild" in civilized societies—both European and Asian—is often associated with unruliness, disorder, and violence. The Chinese word for nature, *zi-ran* (Japanese *shizen*) means "self-thus." It is a bland and general word. The word for wild in Chinese, *ye* (Japanese *ya*), which basically means "open country," has a wide set of meanings: in various combinations the term becomes illicit connection, desert country, an illegitimate child (open-country child), prostitute (open-country flower), and such. In an interesting case, *ye-man zi-yu* ("open-country southern-tribal-person-freedom") means "wild license." In another context "open-country story" becomes "fiction and fictitious romance." Other associations are usually with the rustic and uncouth. In a way *ye* is taken to mean "nature at its worst." Although the Chinese and Japanese have long given lip service to nature, only the early Daoists might have thought that wisdom could come of wildness.

Thoreau says, "give me a wildness no civilization can endure." That's clearly not difficult to find. It is harder to imagine a civilization that wildness can endure, yet this is just what we must try to do. Wildness is not just the "preservation of the world," it *is* the world. Civilizations east and west have long been on a collision course with wild nature, and now the developed nations in particular have the witless power to destroy not only individual creatures but whole species, whole processes, of the earth. We need a civilization that can live fully and creatively together with wildness. We must start growing it right here, in the New World.

When we think of wilderness in America today, we think of remote and perhaps designated regions that are commonly alpine, desert, or swamp. Just a few centuries ago, when virtually *all* was wild in North America, wilderness was not something exceptionally severe. Pronghorn and bison trailed through the grasslands, creeks ran full of salmon, there were acres of clams, and grizzlies, cougar, and bighorn sheep were common in the lowlands. There were human beings, too: North America was *all populated.* One might say yes, but thinly—which raises the question of according to whom. The fact is, people were everywhere. When the Spanish foot soldier Alvar Núñez Cabeza de Vaca and his two companions (one of whom was African) were wrecked on the beach of what is now Galveston, and walked to the Rio Grande valley and then south back into present-day Mexico between 1528 and 1536, there were few times in the whole eight years that they were not staying at a native settlement or camp. They were always on trails.

It has always been part of basic human experience to live in a culture of wilderness. There has been no wilderness without some kind of human presence for several hundred thousand years. Nature is not a place to visit, it is *home*—and within that home territory there are more familiar and less familiar places. Often there are areas that are difficult and remote, but all are *known* and even named. One August I was at a pass in the Brooks Range of northern Alaska at the headwaters of the Koyukuk River, a green three-thousand-foot tundra pass between the broad ranges, open and gentle, dividing the waters that flow to the Arctic Sea from the Yukon. It is as remote a place as you could be in North America, no roads, and the trails are those made by migrating caribou. Yet this pass has been steadily used by Inupiaq people of the north slope and Athapaskan people of the Yukon as a steadily north-south trade route for at least seven thousand years.

All of the hills and lakes of Alaska have been named in one or another of the dozen or so languages spoken by the native people, as the researches of Jim Kari (1982; 1985) and others have shown. Euro-American map-makers name these places after transient exploiters, or their own girl-friends, or home towns in the Lower 48. The point is: it's all in the native story, yet only the tiniest trace of human presence through all that time shows. The place-based stories the people tell, and the naming they've done, is their archaeology, architecture, and *title* to the land. Talk about living lightly.

Cultures of wilderness live by the life and death lessons of subsistence economies. But what can we now mean by the words *wild* and for that matter *nature?* Languages meander like great rivers leaving oxbow traces over forgotten beds, to be seen only from the air or by scholars. Language is like some kind of infinitely interfertile family of species spreading or mysteriously declining over time, shamelessly and endlessly hybridizing, changing its own rules as it goes. Words are used as signs, as stand-ins, arbitrary and temporary, even as language reflects (and informs) the shift-ing values of the peoples whose minds it inhabits and glides through. We have faith in "meaning" the way we might believe in wolverines—put-ting trust in the occasional reports of others or on the authority of once seeing a pelt. But it is sometimes worth tracking these tricksters back.

The Words Nature, Wild, *and* Wilderness

Take *nature* first. The word *nature* is from Latin *natura,* "birth, constitu-tion, character, course of things"—ultimately from *nasci,* to be born. So we have *nation, natal, native, pregnant.* The probable Indo-European root (via Greek *gna*—hence cognate, agnate) is *gen* (Sanskrit *jan*), which provides *generate* and *genus,* as well as *kin* and *kind.*

The word gets two slightly different meanings. One is "the outdoors"— the physical world, including all living things. Nature by this definition is a norm of the world that is apart from the features or products of civi-lization and human will. The machine, the artifact, the devised, or the extraordinary (like a two-headed calf) is spoken of as "unnatural." The other meaning, which is broader, is "the material world or its collective objects and phenomena," including the products of human action and intention. As an agency nature is defined as "the creative and regulative physical power which is conceived of as operating in the material world and as the immediate cause of all its phenomena." Science and some sorts of mysticism rightly propose that *everything* is natural. By these lights there is nothing unnatural about New York City, or toxic wastes, or atomic energy, and nothing—by definition—that we do or experience in life is "unnatural."

(The "supernatural"? One way to deal with it is to say that "the supernatural" is a name for phenomena that are reported by so few people as to leave their reality in doubt. Nonetheless these events—ghosts, gods, magical transformations, and such—are described often enough to make them continue to be intriguing and, for some, credible.)

The physical universe and all its properties—I would prefer to use the word *nature* in this sense. But it will come up meaning "the outdoors" or "other-than-human" sometimes even here.

The word *wild* is like a Gray Fox trotting off through the forest, ducking behind bushes, going in and out of sight. Up close, first glance, it is "wild"—then farther into the woods next glance it's "wyld" and it recedes via Old Norse *villr* and Old Teutonic *wilthijaz* into a faint pre-Teutonic *ghweltijos* which means, still, wild and maybe wooded (*wald*) and lurks back there with possible connections to *will,* to Latin *silva* (forest, sauvage), and to the Indo-European root *ghwer,* base of Latin *ferus* (feral, fierce), which swings us around to Thoreau's "awful ferity" shared by virtuous people and lovers. The Oxford English Dictionary has it this way:

Of animals—not tame, undomesticated, unruly.
Of plants—not cultivated.
Of land—uninhabited, uncultivated.
Of foodcrops—produced or yielded without cultivation.
Of societies—uncivilized, rude, resisting constituted government.
Of individuals—unrestrained, insubordinare, licentious, dissolute, loose. "Wild and wanton widowes"—1614.
Of behavior—violent, destructive, cruel, unruly.
Of behavior—artless, free, spontaneous. "Warble his native woodnotes wild"—John Milton.

Wild is largely defined in our dictionaries by what—from a human standpoint—it is not. It cannot be seen by this approach for what it *is.* Turn it the other way:

Of animals—free agents, each with its own endowments, living within natural systems.

Of plants—self-propagating, self-maintaining, flourishing in accord with innate qualities.

Of land—a place where the original and potential vegetation and fauna are intact and in full interaction and the landforms are entirely the result of nonhuman forces. Pristine.

Of foodcrops—food supplies made available and sustainable by the natural excess and exuberance of wild plants in their growth and in the production of quantities of fruit or seeds.

Of societies—societies whose order has grown from within and is maintained by the force of consensus and custom rather than explicit legislation. Primary cultures, which consider themselves the original and eternal inhabitants of their territory. Societies which resist economic and political domination by civilization. Societies whose economic system is in a close and sustainable relation to the local ecosystem.

Of individuals—following local custom, style, and etiquette without concern for the standards of the metropolis or nearest trading post. Unintimidated, self-reliant, independent. "Proud and free."

Of behavior—fiercely resisting any oppression, confinement, or exploitation. Far-out, outrageous, "bad," admirable.

Of behavior—artless, free, spontaneous, unconditioned. Expressive, physical, openly sexual, ecstatic.

Most of the senses in this second set of definitions come very close to being how the Chinese define the term *Dao,* the *way* of Great Nature: eluding analysis, beyond categories, self-organizing, self-informing, playful, surprising, impermanent, insubstantial, independent, complete, orderly, unmediated, freely manifesting, self-authenticating, self-willed, complex, quite simple. Both empty and real at the same time. In some cases we might call it sacred. It is not far from the Buddhist term *Dharma* with its original senses of forming and firming.

The word *wilderness,* earlier *wyldernesse,* Old English *wildeornes,* possibly from "wild-deer-ness" (*deor,* deer and other forest animals) but more likely "wildern-ness," has the meanings:

A large area of wild land, with original vegetation and wildlife, ranging from dense jungle or rainforest to arctic or alpine "white wilderness."

A wasteland, as an area unused or useless for agriculture or pasture.

A space of sea or air, as in Shakespeare, "I stand as one upon a Rock, environ'd with a Wilderness of Sea" (*Titus Andronicus*). The oceans.

A place of danger and difficulty: where you take your own chances, depend on your own skills, and do not count on rescue.

This world as contrasted with heaven. "I walked through the wildernesse of this world" (*Pilgrim's Progress*).

A place of abundance, as in John Milton, "a wildernesse of sweets."

Milton's usage of wilderness catches the very real condition of energy and richness that is so often found in wild systems. "A wildernesse of sweets" is like the billions of herring or mackerel babies in the ocean, the cubic miles of krill, wild prairie grass seed (leading to the bread of this day, made from the germs of grasses)—all the incredible fecundity of small animals and plants, feeding the web. But from another side, wilderness has implied chaos, eros, the unknown, realms of taboo, the habitat of both the ecstatic and the demonic. In both senses it is a place of archetypal power, teaching, and challenge.

Wildness

So we can say that New York City and Tokyo are "natural" but not "wild." They do not deviate from the laws of nature, but they are habitat so exclusive in the matter of who and what they give shelter to, and so intolerant of other creatures, as to be truly odd. Wilderness is a *place* where the wild potential is fully expressed, a diversity of living and nonliving beings flourishing according to their own sorts of order. In ecology we speak of "wild systems." When an ecosystem is fully functioning, all the members are present at the assembly. To speak of wilderness is to speak of wholeness. Human beings came out of that wholeness, and to consider the possibility of reactivating membership in the Assembly of All Beings is in no way regressive.

By the sixteenth century the lands of the Occident, the countries of Asia, and all the civilizations and cities from the Indian subcontinent to the coast of North Africa were becoming ecologically impoverished. The people were rapidly becoming nature-illiterate. Much of the original vegetation had been destroyed by the expansion of grazing or agriculture, and the remaining land was of no great human economic use, "waste," mountain regions and deserts. The lingering larger animals—big cats, desert sheep, serows, and such—managed to survive by retreating to the harsher habitats. The leaders of these civilizations grew up with less and less personal knowledge of animal behavior and were no longer taught the intimate wide-ranging plant knowledge that had once been universal. By way of tradeoff they learned "human management," administration, rhetorical skills. Only the most marginal of the *paysan,* people of the land, kept up practical plant and animal lore and memories of the old ways. People who grew up in towns or cities, or on large estates, had less chance to learn how wild systems work. Then major blocks of citified mythology (Medieval Christianity and then the "Rise of Science") denied first soul, then consciousness, and finally even sentience to the natural world. Huge numbers of Europeans, in the climate of a nature-denying mechanistic ideology, were losing the opportunity for direct experience of nature.

A new sort of nature-traveler came into existence: men who went out as resource scouts, financed by companies or aristocratic families, penetrating the lightly populated lands of people who lived in and with the wilderness. Conquistadors and priests. Europe had killed off the wolves and bears, deforested vast areas, and overgrazed the hills. The search for slaves, fish, sugar, and precious metals ran over the edge of the horizon and into Asia, Africa, and the New World. These overrefined and warlike states once more came up against wild nature and natural societies: people who lived without Church or State. In return for gold or raw sugar, the white men had to give up something of themselves: they had to look into their own sense of what it meant to be a human being, wonder about the nature of hierarchy, ask if life was worth the honor of a king, or worth gold. (A lost and starving man stands and examines the nicked edge of his sword and his frayed Spanish cape in a Florida swamp.)

Some, like Nuño de Guzmán, became crazed and sadistic. "When he began to govern this province, it contained 25,000 Indians, subjugated and peaceful. Of these he has sold 10,000 as slaves, and the others, fearing the same fate, have abandoned their villages" (Todorov, 1985, 134). Cortés, the conqueror of Mexico, ended up a beaten, depressed beggar-to-the-throne. Alvar Núñez Cabeza de Vaca came out of his journey transformed into a person of the New World. He had rejoined the old ways and was never the same again. He gained a compassionate heart, a taste for self-sufficiency and simplicity, and a knack for healing. The types of both Guzmán and Núñez are still among us. Another person has also walked onto the Nō stage of Turtle Island history to hold hands with Alvar Núñez at the far end of the process—Ishi the Yahi, who walked into civilization with as much desperation as Núñez walked out of it. Núñez was among the first Europeans to encounter North America and its native myth-mind, and Ishi was the last Native American to fully know that mind—and he had to leave it behind. What lies between those two brackets is not dead and gone. It is perennially within us, dormant as a hardshelled seed, awaiting the fire or flood that awakes it again.

In those intervening centuries, tens of millions of North and South American Indians died early and violent deaths (as did countless Europeans), the world's largest mammal herd was extinguished (the bison), and fifteen million pronghorn disappeared. The grasslands and their soils are largely gone, and only remnants survive from the original old-growth eastern hardwood and western conifer forests. We all know more items for this list.

It is often said that the frontier gave a special turn to American history. A frontier is a burning edge, a frazzle, a strange market zone between two utterly different worlds. It is a strip where there are pelts and tongues and tits for the taking. There is an almost visible line that a person of the invading culture could walk across: out of history and into a perpetual present, a way of life attuned to the slower and steadier processes of nature. The possibility of passage into that myth-time world had been all but forgotten in Europe. Its rediscovery—the unsettling vision of a natural self—has haunted the Euro-American peoples as they continually cleared and roaded the many wild corners of the North American continent.

Wilderness is now—for much of North America—places that are formally set aside on public lands—Forest Service or Bureau of Land Management holdings or state and federal parks. Some tiny but critical tracts are held by private nonprofit groups like The Nature Conservancy or the Trust for Public Land. These are the shrines saved from all the land that was once known and lived on by the original people, the little bits left as they were, the last little places where intrinsic nature totally wails, blooms, nests, glints away. They make up only 2 percent of the land of the United States.

But wildness is not limited to the 2 percent formal wilderness areas. Shifting scales, it is everywhere: ineradicable populations of fungi, moss, mold, yeasts, and such that surround and inhabit us. Deer mice on the back porch, deer bounding across the freeway, pigeons in the park, spiders in the corners. There were crickets in the paint locker of the *Sappa Creek* oil tanker, as I worked as a wiper in the engine room out in mid-Pacific, cleaning brushes. Exquisite complex beings in their energy webs inhabiting the fertile corners of the urban world in accord with the rules of wild systems, the visible hardy stalks and stems of vacant lots and railroads, the persistent raccoon squads, bacteria in the loam and in our yogurt. The term *culture,* in its meaning of "a deliberately maintained aesthetic and intellectual life" and in its other meaning of "the totality of socially transmitted behavior patterns," is never far from a biological root meaning as in "yogurt culture"—a nourishing habitat. Civilization is permeable, and could be as inhabited as the wild is.

Wilderness may temporarily dwindle, but wildness won't go away. A ghost wilderness hovers around the entire planet: the millions of tiny seeds of the original vegetation are hiding in the mud on the foot of an arctic tern, in the dry desert sands, or in the wind. These seeds are each uniquely adapted to a specific soil or circumstance, each with its own little form and fluff, ready to float, freeze, or be swallowed, always preserving the germ. Wilderness will inevitably return, but it will not be as fine a world as the one that was glistening in the early morning of the Holocene. Much life will be lost in the wake of human agency on earth,

that of the twentieth and twenty-first centuries. Much is already lost—
the soils and waters unravel:

> "What's that dark thing in the water?
> Is it not an oil-soaked otter?"

Where do we start to resolve the dichotomy of the civilized and the wild?

Do you really believe you are an animal? We are now taught this in
school. It is a wonderful piece of information: I have been enjoying it all
my life and I come back to it over and over again, as something to investigate and test. I grew up on a small farm with cows and chickens, and
with a second-growth forest right at the back fence, so I had the good fortune of seeing the human and animal as in the same realm. But many people who have been hearing this since childhood have not absorbed the
implications of it, perhaps feel remote from the nonhuman world, are not
sure they are animals. They would like to feel they might be something
better than animals. That's understandable: other animals might feel they
are something different than "just animals" too. But we must contem-
plate the shared ground of our common biological being before emphasizing the differences.

Our bodies are wild. The involuntary quick turn of the head at a shout,
the vertigo at looking off a precipice, the heart-in-the-throat in a moment
of danger, the catch of the breath, the quiet moments relaxing, staring,
reflecting—all universal responses of this mammal body. They can be
seen throughout the class. The body does not require the intercession of
some conscious intellect to make it breathe, to keep the heart beating. It
is to a great extent self-regulating, it is a life of its own. Sensation and perception do not exactly come from outside, and the unremitting thought
and image-flow are not exactly inside. The world is our consciousness,
and it surrounds us. There are more things in mind, in the imagination, than "you" can keep track of—thoughts, memories, images, angers,
delights, rise unbidden. The depths of mind, the unconscious, are our
inner wilderness areas, and that is where a bobcat is *right now.* I do not mean
personal bobcats in personal psyches, but the bobcat that roams from
dream to dream. The conscious agenda-planning ego occupies a tiny territory, a little cubicle somewhere near the gate, keeping track of some of
what goes in and out (and sometimes making expansionistic plots), and
the rest takes care of itself. The body is, so to speak, in the mind. They are
both wild.

Some will say, so far so good. "We are mammal primates. But we have
language, and the animals don't." By some definitions perhaps they don't.
But they do communicate extensively, and by call systems we are just
beginning to grasp.

It would be a mistake to think that human beings got "smarter" at some point and invented first language and then society. Language and culture emerge from our biological-social natural existence, animals that we were/are. Language is a mind-body system that coevolved with our needs and nerves. Like imagination and the body, language rises unbidden. It is of a complexity that eludes our rational intellectual capacities. All attempts at scientific description of natural languages have fallen short of completeness, as the descriptive linguists readily confess, yet the child learns the mother tongue early and has virtually mastered it by six.

Language is learned in the house and in the fields, not at school. Without having ever been taught formal grammar we utter syntactically correct sentences, one after another, for all the waking hours of the years of our life. Without conscious device we constantly reach into the vast wordhoards in the depths of the wild unconscious. We cannot as individuals or even as a species take credit for this power. It came from someplace else: from the way clouds divide and mingle (and the arms of energy that coil first back and then forward), from the way the many flowerlets of a composite blossom divide and redivide, from the gleaming calligraphy of the ancient riverbeds under present riverbeds of the Yukon River streaming out the Yukon flats, from the wind in the pine needles, from the chuckles of grouse in the ceanothus bushes.

Language teaching in schools is a matter of corralling off a little of the language-behavior territory and cultivating a few favorite features—culturally defined elite forms that will help you apply for a job or give you social credibility at a party. One might even learn how to produce the byzantine artifact known as the professional paper. There are many excellent reasons to master these things, but the power, the *virtu*, remains on the side of the wild.

Social order is found throughout nature—long before the age of books and legal codes. It is inherently part of what we are, and its patterns follow the same foldings, checks and balances, as flesh or stone. What we call social organization and order in government is a set of forms that have been appropriated by the calculating mind from the operating principles in nature.

The World Is Watching

The world is as sharp as the edge of a knife—a Northwest Coast saying. Now how does it look from the standpoint of peoples for whom there is no great dichotomy between their culture and nature, those who live in societies whose economies draw on uncultivated systems? The pathless world of wild nature is a surpassing school and those who have lived through her can be tough and funny teachers. Out here one is in constant engagement with countless plants and animals. To be well educated is to have learned the songs, proverbs, stories, sayings, myths (and technologies) that come with this experiencing of the nonhuman members of the local ecological community. Practice in the field, "open country," is foremost. Walking is the great adventure, the first meditation, a practice of heartiness and soul primary to humankind. Walking is the exact balance of spirit and humility. Out walking, one notices where there is food. And there are firsthand true stories of "Your ass is somebody else's meal"—a blunt way of saying interdependence, interconnection, "ecology," on the level where it counts, also a teaching of mindfulness and preparedness. There is an extraordinary teaching of specific plants and animals and their uses, empirical and impeccable, that never reduces them to objects and commodities.

It seems that a short way back in the history of occidental ideas there was a fork in the trail. The line of thought that is signified by the names of Descartes, Newton, and Hobbes (saying that life in a primary society is "nasty, brutish, and short"—all of them city-dwellers) was a profound rejection of the organic world. For a reproductive universe they substituted a model of sterile mechanism and an economy of "production." These thinkers were as hysterical about "chaos" as their predecessors, the witch-hunt prosecutors of only a century before, were about "witches." They not only didn't enjoy the possibility that the world is as sharp as the edge of a knife, they wanted to take that edge away from nature. Instead of making the world safer for humankind, the foolish tinkering with the powers of life and death by the occidental scientist-engineer-ruler puts the whole planet on the brink of degradation. Most of humanity—foragers, peasants, or artisans—has always taken the other fork. That is to say, they have understood the play of the real world, with all its suffering, not in simple terms of "nature red in tooth and claw" but through the celebration of the gift-exchange quality of our give-and-take. "What a big potlatch we are all members of!" To acknowledge that each of us at the table will eventually be part of the meal is not just being "realistic." It is allowing the sacred to enter and accepting the sacramental aspect of our shaky temporary personal being.

The world is watching: one cannot walk through a meadow or forest without a ripple of report spreading out from one's passage. The thrush darts back, the jay squalls, a beetle scuttles under the grasses, and the signal is passed along. Every creature knows when a hawk is cruising or a human strolling. The information passed through the system is intelligence.

In Hindu and Buddhist iconography an animal trace is registered on the images of the Deities or Buddhas and Bodhisattvas. Manjusri, the

Bodhisattva of Discriminating Wisdom, rides a lion, Samantabhadra, the Bodhisattva of Kindness, rides an elephant, Sarasvati, the Goddess of Music and Learning, rides a peacock, Shiva relaxes in the company of a snake and a bull. Some wear tiny animals in their crowns or hair. In this ecumenical spiritual ecology it is suggested that the other animals occupy spiritual as well as "thermodynamic" niches. Whether or not their consciousness is identical with that of the humans is a moot point. Why should the peculiarities of human consciousness be the narrow standard by which other creatures are judged? "Whoever told people that 'Mind' means thoughts, opinions, ideas, and concepts? Mind means trees, fence posts, tiles, and grasses," says Dōgen (the philosopher and founder of the Soto school of Japanese Zen) in his funny cryptic way.

We are all capable of extraordinary transformations. In myth and story these changes are animal-to-human, human-to-animal, animal-to-animal, or even farther leaps. The essential nature remains clear and steady through these changes. So the animal icons of the Inupiaq people ("Eskimos") of the Bering Sea (here's the reverse!) have a tiny human face sewn into the fur, or under the feathers, or carved on the back or breast or even inside the eye, peeping out. This is the *inua,* which is often called "spirit" but could just as well be termed the "essential nature" of that creature. It remains the same face regardless of the playful temporary changes. Just as Buddhism has chosen to represent our condition by presenting an image of a steady, solid, gentle, meditating human figure seated in the midst of the world of phenomena, the Inupiaq would present a panoply of different creatures, each with a little hidden human face. This is not the same as anthropocentrism or human arrogance. It is a way of saying that each creature is a spirit with an intelligence as brilliant as our own. The Buddhist iconographers hide a little animal face in the hair of the human to remind us that we see with archetypal wilderness eyes as well.

The world is not only watching, it is listening too. A rude and thoughtless comment about a ground squirrel or a flicker or a porcupine will not go unnoticed. Other beings (the instructors from the old ways tell us) do not mind being killed and eaten as food, but they expect us to say please, and thank you, and they hate to see themselves wasted. The precept against needlessly taking life is inevitably the first and most difficult of commandments. In their practice of killing and eating with gentleness and thanks, the primary peoples are our teachers: the attitude toward animals, and their treatment, in twentieth-century American industrial meat production is literally sickening, unethical, and a source of boundless bad luck for this society.

An ethical life is one that is mindful, mannerly, and has style. Of all moral failings and flaws of character, the worst is stinginess of thought, which includes meanness in all its forms. Rudeness in thought or deed toward others, toward nature, reduces the chances of conviviality and interspecies communication, which are essential to physical and spiritual survival. Richard Nelson, a student of Indian ways, has said that an Athapaskan mother might tell her little girl, "Don't point at the mountain! It's rude!" One must not waste, or be careless, with the bodies or the parts of any creature one has hunted or gathered. One must not boast, or show much pride in accomplishment, and one must not take one's skill for granted. Wastefulness and carelessness are caused by stinginess of spirit, an ungracious unwillingness to complete the gift-exchange transaction. (These rules are also particularly true for healers, artists, and gamblers.)

Perhaps one should not talk (or write) too much about the wild world: it may be that it embarrasses other animals to have attention called to them. A sensibility of this sort might help explain why there is so little "landscape poetry" from the cultures of the old ways. Nature description is a kind of writing that comes with civilization and its habits of collection and classification. Chinese landscape poetry begins around the fifth century A.D. with the work of Xie Lingyun. There were fifteen hundred years of Chinese song and poetry before him (allowing as the *Shi-jing*—China's first collection of poems and songs, "The Book of Songs"—might register some five centuries of folksong prior to the writing down) and there is much nature, but no broad landscapes: it is about mulberry trees, wild edible greens, threshing, the forager and farmer's world up close. By Hsieh's time the Chinese had become removed enough from their own mountains and rivers to aestheticize them. This doesn't mean that people of the old ways don't appreciate the view, but they have a different point of view.

The same kind of cautions apply to the stories or songs one might tell about oneself. Malcolm Margolin, publisher of *News from Native California,* points out that the original people of California did not easily recount an "autobiography." The details of their individual lives, they said, were unexceptional: the only events that bore recounting were descriptions of a few of their outstanding dreams and their moments of encounter with the spirit world and its transformations. The telling of their life stories, then, was very brief. They told of dream, insight, and healing.

Back Home

The etiquette of the wild world requires not only generosity but a good-humored toughness that cheerfully tolerates discomfort, an appreciation of everyone's fragility, and a certain modesty. Good quick blueberry picking, the knack of tracking, getting to where the fishing's good ("an angry man cannot catch a fish"), reading the surface of the sea or sky—these are achievements not to be gained by mere effort. Mountaineering has the same quality. These moves take practice, which calls for a certain amount of self-abnegation, and intuition, which takes emptying of yourself. Great insights have come to some people only after they reached the point where they had nothing left. Alvar Núñez Cabeza de Vaca became unaccountably deepened after losing his way and spending several winter nights sleeping naked in a pit in the Texas desert under a north wind. He truly had reached the point where he had nothing. ("To have nothing, you must *have nothing!*" Lord Buckley says of this moment.) After that he found himself able to heal sick native people he met on his way westward. His fame spread ahead of him. Once he had made his way back to Mexico and was again a civilized Spaniard he found he had lost his power of healing—not just the ability to heal, but the *will* to heal, which is the will to be whole: for as he said, there were "real doctors" in the city, and he began to doubt his powers. To resolve the dichotomy of the civilized and the wild, we must first resolve to be whole.

One may reach such a place as Alvar Núñez by literally losing everything. Painful and dangerous experiences often transform the people who survive them. Human beings are audacious. They set out to have adventures and try to do more than perhaps they should. So by practicing yogic austerities or monastic disciplines, some people make a structured attempt at having nothing. Some of us have learned much from traveling day after day on foot over snowfields, rockslides, passes, torrents, and valley floor forests, by "putting ourselves out there." Another—and most sophisticated—way is that of Vimalakitti, the legendary Buddhist layman, who taught that by directly intuiting our condition in the actually existing world we realize that we have had nothing from the beginning. A Tibetan saying has it: "The experience of emptiness engenders compassion."

For those who would seek directly, by entering the primary temple, the wilderness can be a ferocious teacher, rapidly stripping down the inexperienced or the careless. It is easy to make the mistakes that will bring one to an extremity. Practically speaking, a life that is vowed to simplicity, appropriate boldness, good humor, gratitude, unstinting work and play, and lots of walking brings us close to the actually existing world and its wholeness.

People of wilderness cultures rarely seek out adventures. If they deliberately risk themselves, it is for spiritual rather than economic reasons. Ultimately all such journeys are done for the sake of the whole, not as some private quest. The quiet dignity that characterizes so many so-called primitives is a reflection of that. Florence Edenshaw, a contemporary Haida elder who has lived a long life of work and family, was asked by the young woman anthropologist who interviewed her and was impressed by her coherence, presence, and dignity, "What can I do for self-respect?" Mrs. Edenshaw said, "Dress up and stay home." The "home," of course, is as large as you make it.

The lessons we learn from the wild become the etiquette of freedom. We can enjoy our humanity with its flashy brains and sexual buzz, its social cravings and stubborn tantrums, and take ourselves as no more and no less than another being in the Big Watershed. We can accept each other all as barefoot equals sleeping on the same ground. We can give up hoping to be eternal and quit fighting dirt. We can chase off mosquitoes and fence out varmints without hating them. No expectations, alert and sufficient, grateful and careful, generous and direct. A calm and clarity attend us in the moment we are wiping the grease off our hands between tasks and glancing up at the passing clouds. Another joy is finally sitting down to have coffee with a friend. The wild requires that we learn the terrain, nod to all the plants and animals and birds, ford the streams and cross the ridges, and tell a good story when we get back home.

And when the children are safe in bed, at one of the great holidays like the Fourth of July, New Year's, or Halloween, we can bring out some spirits and turn on the music, and the men and the women who are still among the living can get loose and really wild. So that's the final meaning of "wild"—the esoteric meaning, the deepest and most scary. Those who are ready for it will come to it. Please do not repeat this to the uninitiated.

The Place, the Region, and the Commons

When you find your place where you are, practice occurs.
DŌGEN

The World Is Places

We experience slums, prairies, and wetlands all equally as "places." Like a mirror, a place can hold anything, on any scale. I want to talk about place as an experience and propose a model of what it meant to "live in place" for most of human time, presenting it initially in terms of the steps that a child takes growing into a natural community. (We have the terms *enculturation* and *acculturation,* but nothing to describe the process of becoming placed or re-placed.) In doing so we might get one more angle on what a "civilization of wildness" might require.

For most Americans, to reflect on "home place" would be an unfamiliar exercise. Few today can announce themselves as someone *from* somewhere. Almost nobody spends a lifetime in the same valley, working alongside the people they knew as children. Native people everywhere (the very term means "someone born there") and Old World farmers and city people share this experience of living in place. Still—and this is very important to remember—being inhabitory, being place-based, has never meant that one didn't travel from time to time, going on trading ventures or taking livestock to summer grazing. Such working wanderers have always known they had a home-base on earth, and could prove it at any campfire or party by singing their own songs.

The heart of a place is the home, and the heart of the home is the firepit, the hearth. All tentative explorations go outward from there, and it is back to the fireside that elders return. You grow up speaking a home language, a local vernacular. Your own household may have some specifics of phrase, of pronunciation, that are different from the *domus,* the *jia* or *ie* or *kum,* down the lane. You hear histories of the people who are your neighbors and tales involving rocks, streams, mountains, and trees that are all within your sight. The myths of world-creation tell you how *that mountain* was created and how *that peninsula* came to be there. As you grow bolder you explore your world outward from the firepit (which is the center of each universe) in little trips. The childhood landscape is learned on foot, and a map is inscribed in the mind—trails and pathways and groves—the mean dog, the cranky old man's house, the pasture with a bull in it—going out wider and farther. All of us carry within us a picture of the terrain that was learned roughly between the ages of six and nine. (It could as easily be an urban neighborhood as some rural scene.) You can almost totally recall the place you walked, played, biked, swam. Revisualizing that place with its smells and textures, walking through it again in your imagination, has a grounding and settling effect. But we might wonder how it is for those whose childhood landscape was being ripped up by bulldozers, or whose family moving about made it all a blur. I have a friend who still gets emotional when he recalls how the avocado orchards of his southern California youth landscape were transformed into hillside after hillside of suburbs.

Our place is part of what we are. Yet even a "place" has a kind of fluidity: it passes through space and time—"ceremonial time" in John Hanson Mitchell's phrase. A place will have been grasslands, then conifers, then beech and elm. It will have been half riverbed, it will have been scratched and plowed by ice. And then it will be cultivated, paved, sprayed, dammed, graded, built up. But each is only for a while, and that will be just another set of lines on the palimpsest. The whole earth is a great tablet holding the multiple overlaid new and ancient traces of the swirl of forces. Each place is its own place, forever (eventually) wild. A place on earth is a mosaic within larger mosaics—the land is all small places, all precise tiny realms replicating larger and smaller patterns. Children start out learning place by learning those little realms around the house, the settlement, and outward.

One's sense of the scale of a place expands as one learns the *region.* The young hear further stories and go for explorations that are also subsistence forays—firewood gathering, fishing, to fairs or to market. The outlines of the larger region become part of their awareness. (Thoreau says in "Walking" that an area twenty miles in diameter will be enough to occupy a lifetime of close exploration on foot—you will never exhaust its details.)

The total size of the region a group calls home depends on the land type. Every group is territorial, each moves within a given zone, even nomads stay within boundaries. A people living in a desert or grassland with great visible spaces that invite you to step forward and walk as far as you can see will range across tens of thousands of square miles. A deep old-growth forest may rarely be traveled at all. Foragers in gallery forests and grasslands will regularly move broadly, whereas people in a deep-soiled valley ideal for gardens might not go far beyond the top of the nearest ridge. The regional boundaries were roughly drawn by climate, which is what sets the plant-type zones—plus soil type and landforms. Desert wastes, mountain ridges, or big rivers set a broad edge to a region. We walk across or wade through the larger and smaller boundaries. Like children first learning our homeland we can stand at the edge of a big river, or on the crest of a major ridge, and observe that the other side is a different soil, a change of plants and animals, a new shape of barn roof, maybe less or more rain. The lines between natural regions are never simple or clear, but vary according to such criteria as biota, watersheds, landforms, elevation. (See Jim Dodge, 1981.) Still, we all know—at some point—that we are no longer in the Midwest, say, but in the West. Regions seen according to natural criteria are sometimes called bioregions.

(In pre-conquest America people covered great distances. It is said that the Mojave of the lower Colorado felt that everyone at least once in their lives should make foot journeys to the Hopi mesas to the east, the Gulf of California to the south, and to the Pacific.)

Every region has its wilderness. There is the fire in the kitchen, and there is the place less traveled. In most settled regions there used to be some combination of prime agricultural land, orchard and vine land, rough pasturage, woodlot, forest, and desert or mountain "waste." The de facto wilderness was the extreme backcountry part of all that. The parts less visited are "where the bears are." The wilderness is within walking distance—it may be three days or it may be ten. It is at the far high rough end, or the deep forest and swamp end, of the territory where most of you all live and work. People will go there for mountain herbs, for the trapline, or for solitude. They live between the poles of home and their own wild places.

Recollecting that we once lived in places is part of our contemporary self-rediscovery. It grounds what it means to be "human" (etymologically something like "earthling"). I have a friend who feels sometimes that the world is hostile to human life—he says it chills us and kills us. But how could we *be* were it not for this planet that provided our very shape? Two conditions—gravity and a livable temperature range between freezing and boiling—have given us fluids and flesh. The trees we climb and the ground we walk on have given us five fingers and toes. The "place" (from the root *plat,* broad, spreading, flat) gave us far-seeing eyes, the streams and breezes gave us versatile tongues and whorly ears. The land gave us a stride, and the lake a dive. The amazement gave us our kind of mind. We should be thankful for that, and take nature's stricter lessons with some grace.

Understanding the Commons

I stood with my climbing partner on the summit of Glacier Peak looking all ways round, ridge after ridge and peak after peak, as far as we could see. To the west across Puget Sound were the farther peaks of the Olympic Mountains. He said: "You mean there's a senator for all this?" As in the Great Basin, crossing desert after desert, range after range, it is easy to think there are vast spaces on earth yet unadministered, perhaps forgotten, or unknown (the endless sweep of spruce forest in Alaska and Canada)—but it is all mapped and placed in some domain. In North America there is a lot that is in public domain, which has its problems, but at least they are problems we are all enfranchised to work on. David Foreman, founder of the Earth First! movement, recently stated his radical provenance. Not out of Social Justice, Left Politics, or Feminism did I come—says David—but from the Public Lands Conservation movement—the solid stodgy movement that goes back to the thirties and before. Yet these land and wildlife issues were what politicized John Muir, John Wesley Powell, and Aldo Leopold—the abuses of public land.

American public lands are the twentieth-century incarnation of a much older institution known across Eurasia—in English called the "commons"—which was the ancient mode of both protecting and managing the wilds of the self-governing regions. It worked well enough until the age of market economies, colonialism, and imperialism. Let me give you a kind of model of how the commons worked.

Between the extremes of deep wilderness and the private plots of the farmstead lies a territory that is not suitable for crops. In earlier times it was used jointly by the members of a given tribe or village. This area, embracing both the wild and the semi-wild, is of critical importance. It is necessary for the health of the wilderness because it adds big habitat, overflow territory, and room for wildlife to fly and run. It is essential even to an agricultural village economy because its natural diversity provides the many necessities and amenities that the privately held plots cannot. It enriches the agrarian diet with game and fish. The shared land supplies firewood, poles and stone for building, clay for the kiln, herbs, dye plants, and much else, just as in a foraging economy. It is especially important as seasonal or full-time open range for cattle, horses, goats, pigs, and sheep.

In the abstract the sharing of a natural area might be thought of as a matter of access to "common pool resources" with no limits or controls on individual exploitation. The fact is that such sharing developed over millennia and always within territorial and social contexts. In the peasant societies of both Asia and Europe there were customary forms that gave direction to the joint use of land. They did not grant free access to outsiders, and there were controls over entry and use by member households. The commons has been defined as "the undivided land belonging to the members of a local community as a whole." This definition fails to make the point that the commons is both specific land *and* the traditional community institution that determines the carrying capacity for its various subunits and defines the rights and obligations of those who use it, with penalties for lapses. Because it is traditional and *local,* it is not identical with today's "public domain," which is land held and managed by a central government. Under a national state such management may be destructive (as it is becoming in Canada and the United States) or benign (as it often has been in the past)—but in no case is it locally managed. One of the ideas in the current debate on how to reform our public lands is that of returning them to regional control.

An example of traditional management: what would keep one household from bringing in more and more stock and tempting everyone toward overgrazing? In earlier England and in some contemporary Swiss villages (Netting, 1976), the commoner could only turn out to common range as many head of cattle as he could feed over the winter in his own corrals. This meant that no one was allowed to increase his herd from outside with a cattle drive just for summer grazing. (This was known in Norman legal language as the rule of *levancy and couchancy:* you could only run the stock that you actually had "standing and sleeping" within winter quarters.)

The commons is the contract a people make with their local natural system. The word has an instructive history: it is formed of *ko,* "together," with (Greek) *moin,* "held in common." But the Indo European root *mei* means basically to "move, to go, to change." This had an archaic special meaning of "exchange of goods and services within a society as regulated by custom or law." I think it might well refer back to the principle of gift economies: "the gift must always move." The root comes into Latin as *munus,* "service performed for the community" and hence "municipality."

There is a well-documented history of the commons in relation to the village economies of Europe and England. In England from the time of the Norman Conquest the enfeoffed knights and overlords began to gain control over the many local commons. Legislation (the Statute of Merton, 1235) came to their support. From the fifteenth century on, the landlord class, working with urban mercantile guilds and government offices, increasingly fenced off village-held land and turned it over to private interests. The enclosure movement was backed by the big wool corporations who found profit from sheep to be much greater than that from farming. The wool business, with its exports to the Continent, was an early agribusiness that had a destructive effect on the soils and dislodged peasants. The arguments for enclosure in England—efficiency, higher production— ignored social and ecological effects and served to cripple the sustainable agriculture of some districts. The enclosure movement was stepped up again in the eighteenth century: between 1709 and 1869 almost five million acres were transferred to private ownership, one acre in every seven. After 1869 there was a sudden reversal of sentiment, called the "open space movement," which ultimately halted enclosures and managed to preserve, via a spectacular lawsuit against the lords of fourteen manors, the Epping Forest.

Karl Polanyi (1975) says that the enclosures of the eighteenth century created a population of rural homeless who were forced in their desperation to become the world's first industrial working class. The enclosures were tragic both for the human community and for natural ecosystems. The fact that England now has the least forest and wildlife of all the nations of Europe has much to do with the enclosures. The takeover of commons land on the European plain also began about five hundred years ago, but one-third of Europe is still not privatized. A survival of commons practices in Swedish law allows anyone to enter private farmland to pick berries or mushrooms, to cross on foot, and to camp out of sight of the house. Most of the former commons land is now under the administration of government land agencies.

A commons model can still be seen in Japan, where there are farm villages tucked in shoestring valleys, rice growing in the *tanbo* on the bottoms, and the vegetable plots and horticulture located on the slightly higher ground. The forested hills rising high above the valleys are the commons—in Japanese called *iriai,* "joint entry." The boundary between one village and the next is often the very crests of the ridges. On the slopes of Mt. Hiei in Kyoto prefecture, north of the remote Tendai Buddhist training temples of Yokkawa, I came on men and women of Ohara village bundling up slender brush-cuttings for firewood. They were within the village land. In the innermost mountains of Japan there are forests that are beyond the reach of the use of any village. In early feudal times they were still occupied by remnant hunting peoples, perhaps Japanese-Ainu mixed-blood survivors. Later oms of these wildlands were appropriated by the government and declared "Imperial Forests." Bears became extinct in England by the thirteenth century, but they are still found throughout the more remote Japanese mountains, even occasionally just north of Kyoto.

In China the management of mountain lands was left largely to the village councils—all the central government wanted was taxes. Taxes were collected in kind, and local specialties were highly prized. The demands of the capital drew down Kingfisher feathers, Musk Deer glands, Rhinoceros hides, and other exotic products of the mountains and streams, as well as rice, timber, and silk. The village councils may have resisted overexploitation of their resources, but when the edge of spreading deforestation reached their zone (the fourteenth century seems to be a turning point for the forests of heartland China), village land management crumbled. Historically, the seizure of the commons—east or west—by either the central government or entrepreneurs from the central economy has resulted in degradation of wild lands and agricultural soils. There is sometimes good reason to kill the Golden Goose: the quick profits can be reinvested elsewhere at a higher return.

In the United States, as fast as the Euro-American invaders forcefully displaced the native inhabitants from their own sorts of traditional commons, the land was opened to the new settlers. In the arid West, however, much land was never even homesteaded, let alone patented. The native people who had known and loved the white deserts and blue mountains were now scattered or enclosed on reservations, and the new inhabitants (miners and a few ranchers) had neither the values nor the knowledge to take care of the land. An enormous area was de facto public domain, and the Forest Service, the Park Service, and the Bureau of Land Management were formed to manage it. (The same sorts of land in Canada and Australia are called "Crown Lands," a reflection of the history of English rulers trying to wrest the commons from the people.)

In the contemporary American West the people who talk about a "sagebrush rebellion" might sound as though they were working for a return of commons land to local control. The truth is the sagebrush rebels have a lot yet to learn about the place—they are still relative newcomers, and their motives are not stewardship but development. Some westerners are beginning to think in long-range terms, and these don't argue for privatization but for better range management and more wilderness preservation.

The environmental history of Europe and Asia seems to indicate that the best management of commons land was locally based. The ancient severe and often irreversible deforestation of the Mediterranean Basin was an extreme case of the misuse of the commons by the forces that had taken its management away from regional villages (Thirgood, 1981). The situation in America in the nineteenth and early twentieth centuries was the reverse. The truly local people, the Native Americans, were decimated and demoralized, and the new population was composed of adventurers and entrepreneurs. Without some federal presence the poachers, cattle grazers, and timber barons would have had a field day. Since about 1960 the situation has turned again: the agencies that were once charged with conservation are increasingly perceived as accomplices of the extractive industries, and local people—who are beginning to be actually local— seek help from environmental organizations and join in defense of the public lands.

Destruction extends worldwide and "encloses" local commons, local peoples. The village and tribal people who live in the tropical forests are literally bulldozed out of their homes by international logging interests in league with national governments. A well-worn fiction used in dispossessing inhabitory people is the declaration that the commonly owned tribal forests are either (1) private property or (2) public domain. When the commons are closed and the villagers must buy energy, lumber, and medicine at the company store, they are pauperized. This is one effect of what Ivan Illich calls "the 500-year war against subsistence."

So what about the so-called tragedy of the commons? This theory, as now popularly understood, seems to state that when there are open access rights to a resource, say pasturage, everyone will seek to maximize his take, and overgrazing will inevitably ensue. What Garrett Hardin and his associates are talking about should be called "the dilemma of common-pool resources." This is the problem of overexploitation of "unowned" resources by individuals or corporations that are caught in the bind of "If I don't do it the other guy will" (Hardin and Baden, 1977). Oceanic fisheries, global water cycles, the air, soil fertility—all fall into this class. When Hardin et al. try to apply their model to the historic commons it doesn't work, because they fail to note that the commons was a social institution, which, historically, was never without rules and did not allow unlimited access (Cox, 1985).

In Asia and parts of Europe, villages that in some cases date back to neolithic times still oversee the commons with some sort of council. Each commons is an entity with limits, and the effects of overuse will be clear to those who depend on it. There are three possible contemporary fates for common pool resources. One is privatization, one is administration by government authority, and the third is that—when possible—they become part of a true commons, of reasonable size, managed by local inhabitory people. The third choice may no longer be possible as stated here. Locally based community or tribal (as in Alaska) landholding corporations or cooperatives seem to be surviving here and there. But operating as it seems they must in the world marketplace, they are wrestling with how to balance tradition and sustainability against financial success. The Sealaska Corporation of the Tlingit people of southeast Alaska has been severely criticized (even from within) for some of the old-growth logging it let happen.

We need to make a world-scale "natural contract" with the oceans, the air, the birds in the sky. The challenge is to bring the whole victimized world of "common pool resources" into the Mind of the Commons. As it stands now, any resource on earth that is not nailed down will be seen as fair game to the timber buyers or petroleum geologists from Osaka, Rotterdam, or Boston. The pressures of growing populations and the powers of entrenched (but fragile, confused, and essentially leaderless) economic systems warp the likelihood of any of us seeing clearly. Our perception of how entrenched they are may also be something of a delusion.

Sometimes it seems unlikely that a society as a whole can make wise choices. Yet there is no choice but to call for the "recovery of the commons"—and this in a modern world that doesn't quite realize what it has lost. Take back, like the night, that which is shared by all of us, that which is our larger being. There will be no "tragedy of the commons" greater than this: if we do not recover the commons—regain personal, local, community, and peoples' direct involvement in sharing (in *being*) the web of the wild world—that world will keep slipping away. Eventually our complicated industrial capitalist/socialist mixes will bring down much of the living system that supports us. And, it is clear, the loss of a local commons heralds the end of self-sufficiency and signals the doom of the vernacular culture of the region. This is still happening in the far corners of the world.

The commons is a curious and elegant social institution within which human beings once lived free political lives while weaving through natural systems. The commons is a level of organization of human society that includes the nonhuman. The level above the local commons is the bioregion. Understanding the commons and its role within the larger regional culture is one more step toward integrating ecology with economy.

Bioregional Perspectives

The Region is the elsewhere of civilization.

MAX CAFARD

The little nations of the past lived within territories that conformed to some set of natural criteria. The culture areas of the major native groups of North America overlapped, as one would expect, almost exactly with broadly defined major bioregions (Kroeber, 1947). That older human experience of a fluid, indistinct, but genuine home region was gradually replaced—across Eurasia—by the arbitrary and often violently imposed boundaries of emerging national states. These imposed borders sometimes cut across biotic areas and ethnic zones alike. Inhabitants lost ecological knowledge and community solidarity. In the old ways, the flora and fauna and landforms are *part of the culture.* The world of culture and nature, which is actual, is almost a shadow world now, and the insubstantial world of political jurisdictions and rarefied economies is what passes for reality. We live in a backwards time. We can regain some small sense of that old membership by discovering the original lineaments of our land and steering—at least in the home territory and in the mind—by those rather than the borders of arbitrary nations, states, and counties.

Regions are "interpenetrating bodies in semi-simultaneous spaces" (Cafard, 1989). Biota, watersheds, landforms, and elevations are just a few of the facets that define a region. Culture areas, in the same way, have subsets such as dialects, religions, sorts of arrow-release, types of tools, myth motifs, musical scales, art styles. One sort of regional outline would be floristic. The coastal Douglas fir, as the definitive tree of the Pacific Northwest, is an example. (I knew it intimately as a boy growing up on a farm between Lake Washington and Puget Sound. The local people, the Snohomish, called it *lukta tciyats,* "wide needles.") Its northern limit is around the Skeena River in British Columbia. It is found west of the crest through Washington, Oregon, and northern California. The southern coastal limit of Douglas fir is about the same as that of salmon, which do not run south of the Big Sur River. Inland it grows down the west slope of the Sierra as far south as the north fork of the San Joaquin River. That outline describes the boundary of a larger natural region that runs across three states and one international border.

The presence of this tree signifies a rainfall and a temperature range and will indicate what your agriculture might be, how steep the pitch of your roof, what raincoats you'd need. You don't have to know such details to get by in the modern cities of Portland or Bellingham. But if you do know what is taught by plants and weather, you are in on the gossip and can truly feel more at home. The sum of a field's forces becomes what we call very loosely the "spirit of the place." To know the spirit of a place is to realize that you are a part of a part and that the whole is made of parts, each of which is whole. You start with the part you are whole in.

As quixotic as these ideas may seem, they have a reservoir of strength and possibility behind them. The spring of 1984, a month after equinox, Gary Holthaus and I drove down from Anchorage to Haines, Alaska. We went around the upper edge of the basin of the Copper River, skitted some tributaries of the Yukon, and went over Haines Summit. It was White and Black Spruce taiga all the way, still frozen up. Dropping down from the pass to saltwater at Chilkat inlet we were immediately in forests of large Sitka Spruce, Skunk Cabbage poking out in the swamps, it was spring. That's a bioregional border leap. I was honored the next day by an invitation to Raven House to have coffee with Austin Hammond and a circle of other Tlingit elders and to hear some long and deeply entwined discourses on the responsibilities of people to their places. As we looked out his front window to hanging glaciers on the peaks beyond the saltwater, Hammond spoke of empires and civilizations in metaphors of glaciers. He described how great alien forces—industrial civilization in this case—advance and retreat, and how settled people can wait it out.

Sometime in the mid-seventies at a conference of Native American leaders and activists in Bozeman, Montana, I heard a Crow elder say something similar: "You know, I think if people stay somewhere long enough—even white people—the spirits will begin to speak to them. It's the power of the spirits coming up from the land. The spirits and the old powers aren't lost, they just need people to be around long enough and the spirits will begin to influence them."

Bioregional awareness teaches us in *specific* ways. It is not enough just to "love nature" or to want to "be in harmony with Gaia." Our relation to the natural world takes place in a *place,* and it must be grounded in information and experience. For example: "real people" have an easy familiarity with the local plants. This is so unexceptional a kind of knowledge that everyone in Europe, Asia, and Africa used to take it for granted. Many contemporary Americans don't even *know* that they don't "know the plants," which is indeed a measure of alienation. Knowing a bit about the flora we could enjoy questions like: where do Alaska and Mexico meet? It would be somewhere on the north coast of California, where Canada Jay and Sitka Spruce lace together with manzanita and Blue Oak.

But instead of "northern California" let's call it Shasta Bioregion. The present state of California (the old Alta California territory) falls into at least three natural divisions, and the northern third looks, as the Douglas fir example shows, well to the north. The boundaries of this northern third would roughly run from the Klamath/Rogue River divide south to San Francisco Bay and up the delta where the Sacramento and San Joaquin rivers join. The line would then go east to the Sierra Crest and, taking that as a distinct border, follow it north to Susanville. The watershed divide then angles broadly northeastward along the edge of the Modoc Plateau to the Warner Range and Goose Lake.

East of the divide is the Great Basin, north of Shasta is the Cascadia/Columbia region, and then farther north is what we call Ish River country, the drainages of Puget Sound and the Straits of Georgia. Why should we do this kind of visualization? Again I will say: it prepares us to begin to be at home in this landscape. There are tens of millions of people in North America who were physically born here but who are not actually living here intellectually, imaginatively, or morally. Native Americans to be sure have a prior claim to the term "native." But as they love this land they will welcome the conversion of the millions of immigrant psyches into fellow "Native Americans." For the non-Native American to become at home on this continent, he or she must be *born again* in this hemisphere, on this continent, properly called Turtle Island.

That is to say, we must consciously, fully accept and recognize that this is where we live and grasp the fact that our descendants will be here for millennia to come. Then we must honor this land's great antiquity—its wildness—learn it—defend it—and work to hand it on to the children (of all beings) of the future with its biodiversity and health intact. Europe or Africa or Asia will then be seen as the place our ancestors came from, places we might want to know about and to visit, but not "home." Home— deeply, spiritually—must be here. Calling this place "America" is to name it after a stranger. "Turtle Island" is the name given this continent by Native Americans based on creation mythology (Snyder, 1974). The United States, Canada, Mexico, are passing political entities; they have their legitimacies, to be sure, but they will lose their mandate if they continue to abuse the land. "The State is destroyed, but the mountains and rivers remain."

But this work is not just for the newcomers of the Western Hemisphere, Australia, Africa, or Siberia. A worldwide purification of mind is called for: the exercise of seeing the surface of the planet for what it is— by nature. With this kind of consciousness people turn up at hearings and in front of trucks and bulldozers to defend the land or trees. Showing solidarity with a region! What an odd idea at first. Bioregionalism is the entry of place into the dialectic of history. Also we might say that there are "classes" that so far have been overlooked—the animals, rivers, rocks, and grasses—now entering history.

These ideas provoke predictable and usually uninformed reactions.

People fear the small society and the critique of the State. It is difficult to see, when one has been raised under it, that it is the State itself which is inherently greedy, destabilizing, entropic, disorderly, and illegitimate. They cite parochialism, regional strife, "unacceptable" expressions of cultural diversity, and so forth. Our philosophies, world religions, and histories are biased toward uniformity, universality, and centralization—in a word, the ideology of monotheism. Certainly under specific conditions neighboring groups have wrangled for centuries—interminable memories and hostilities cooking away like radioactive waste. It's still at work in the Middle East. The ongoing ethnic and political miseries of parts of Europe and the Middle East sometimes go back as far as the Roman Empire. This is not something that can be attributed to the combativeness of "human nature" per se. Before the expansion of early empires the occasional strife of tribes and natural nations was almost familial. With the rise of the State, the scale of the destructiveness and malevolence of warfare makes a huge leap.

In the times when people did not have much accumulated surplus, there was no big temptation to move in on other regions. I'll give an example from my own part of the world. (I describe my location as: on the western slope of the northern Sierra Nevada, in the Yuba River watershed, north of the south fork at the three-thousand-foot elevation, in a community of black oak, incense cedar, madrone, Douglas fir, and ponderosa pine.) The western slope of the Sierra Nevada has winter rain and snowfall and a different set of plants from the dry eastern slope. In pre-white times, the native people living across the range had little temptation to venture over, because their skills were specific to their own area, and they could go hungry in an unfamiliar biome. It takes a long education to know the edible plants, where to find them, and how to prepare them. So the Washo of the Sierra east side traded their pine nuts and obsidian for the acorns, yew bows, and abalone shells of the Miwok and Maidu to the west. The two sides met and camped together for weeks in the summer Sierra meadows, their joint commons. (Dedicated raiding cultures, "barbarians," evolve as a response to nearby civilizations and their riches. Genghis Khan, at an audience in his yurt near Lake Baikal, was reported to have said: "Heaven is exasperated with the decadence and luxury of China.")

There are numerous examples of relatively peaceful small-culture coexistence all over the world. There have always been multilingual persons peacefully trading and traveling across large areas. Differences were often eased by shared spiritual perspectives or ceremonial institutions and by the multitude of myths and tales that cross language barriers. What about the deep divisions caused by religion? It must be said that most religious exclusiveness is the odd specialty of the Judeo/Christian/Islamic faith, which is a recent and (overall) minority development in the world. Asian religion, and the whole world of folk religion, animism, and shamanism, appreciates or at least tolerates diversity. (It seems that the really serious cultural disputes are caused by different tastes in food. When I was choker-setting in eastern Oregon, one of my crew was a Wasco man whose wife was a Chehalis woman from the west side. He told me that when they got in fights she would call him a "goddamn grasshopper eater" and he'd shout back "fish eater"!)

Cultural pluralism and multilingualism are the planetary norm. We seek the balance between cosmopolitan pluralism and deep local consciousness. We are asking how the whole human race can regain self-determination in place after centuries of having been disenfranchised by hierarchy and/or centralized power. Do not confuse this exercise with "nationalism," which is exactly the opposite, the impostor, the puppet of the State, the grinning ghost of the lost community.

So this is one sort of start. The bioregional movement is not just a rural program: it is as much for the restoration of urban neighborhood life and the greening of the cities. All of us are fluently moving in multiple realms that include irrigation districts, solid-waste management jurisdictions, long-distance area code zones, and such. Planet Drum Foundation, based in the San Francisco Bay Area, works with many other local groups for the regeneration of the city as a living place, with projects like the identification and restoration of urban creeks (Berg and others, 1989). There are groups world-wide working with Third and Fourth World people revisualizing territories and playfully finding appropriate names for their newly realized old regions (*Raise the Stakes,* 1987). Four bioregional congresses have been held on Turtle Island.

As sure as impermanence, the nations of the world will eventually be more sensitively defined and the lineaments of the blue earth will begin to reshape the politics. The requirements of sustainable economies, ecologically sensitive agriculture, strong and vivid community life, wild habitat—and the second law of thermodynamics—all lead this way. I also realize that right now this is a kind of theater as much as it is ecological politics. Not just street theater, but visionary mountain, field, and stream theater. As Jim Dodge says: "The chances of bioregionalism succeeding . . . are beside the point. If one person, or a few, or a community of people, live more fulfilling lives from bioregional practice, then it's successful." May it all speed the further deconstruction of the superpowers. As "The Surre(gion)alist Manifesto" says:

> Regional politics do not take place in Washington, Moscow, and other "seats of power." Regional power does not "sit"; it flows every-

where. Through watersheds and bloodstreams. Through nervous systems and food chains. The regions are everywhere & nowhere. We are all illegals. We are natives and we are restless. We have no country; we live in the country. We are off the Inter-State. The Region is against the Regime—any Regime. Regions are anarchic.

(CAFARD, 1989)

Finding "Nisenan County"

This year Burt Hybart retired from driving dump truck, backhoe, grader, and Cat after many years. Roads, ponds, and pads are his sculpture, shapes that will be left on the land long after the houses have vanished. (How long for a pond to silt up?) Burt still witches wells, though. Last time I saw him he was complaining about his lungs: "Dust boiling up behind the Cat you couldn't see from here to there, those days. When I worked on the Coast. And the diesel fumes."

Some of us went for a walk in the Warner Range. It's in the far northeast corner of California, the real watershed boundary between the headwaters of the Pit River and the *nors* of the Great Basin. From the nine-thousand-foot scarp's high points you can see into Oregon, Goose Lake, and up the west side of the Warners to the north end of Surprise Valley. Dry desert hills to the east.

Desert mountain range. A touch of Rocky Montain flora here that leap-frogs over desert basins via the Steens Mountains of southeastern Oregon, the Blue Mountains, and maybe the Wallowas. Cattle are brought up from Eagleville on the east side, a town out of the 1880s. The proprietor of the Eagleville Bar told how the sheep-herders move their flocks from Lovelock, Nevada, in early March, heading toward the Warners, the ewes lambing as they go. In late June they arrive at the foot of the range and move the sheep up to the eight-thousand-foot meadows on the west side. In September the flocks go down to Madeline—the lambs right onto the meat trucks. Then the ewes' long truck ride back to Lovelock for the winter. We find the flock in the miles-long meadow heavens of Mule-ear flowers. The sheep business is Basque-run on all levels. Old aspen grove along the trail with sheepherder inscriptions and designs in the bark, some dated from the 1890s.

Patterson Lake is the gem of the Warners, filling an old cirque below the cliffs of the highest peak. The many little ledges of the cliffs are home to hawks. Young raptors sit solemnly by their nests. Mt. Shasta domi-nates the western view, a hub to these vast miles of Lodgepole and Jeffrey Pine, lava rock, hayfield ribbons, rivers that sink underground. Ha! This is the highest end of what we call "upriver"—and close to where it drains both ways, one side of the plateau tipping toward the Klamath River, the other to the Pit and the Sacramento. Mt. Shasta visible for so far—from the Coast Range, from Sierra Buttes down by Downieville—it gleams across the headwaters of all of northern California.

Old John Hold walks up a streambed, talking to it: "So that's what you've been up to!" Reading the geology, the wash and lay of the heavy metal that sinks below the sand, never tarnishing or rusting—gold. The new-style miners are here, too, St. Joseph Minerals, exploring the "diggings," the tertiary gravels. The county supervisors finally approved the EIR and the exploratory drilling begins. This isn't full-scale mining yet, and they'll come back in eighteen months with their big proposal (if they do). The drilling's not noticeable: a little tower and a trailer lost in the gravel canyons and ridges that were left from the days of hydraulicking.

There were early strong rains this fall, so the springs started up. Then the rain quit and the springs stopped. A warm December. Real rains started in January, with heavy snows above six thousand feet and not much below that. This year more kids go skiing. Resistance to it (as a decadent urban entertainment) crumbles family by family. Most adults here never were mountain people, didn't climb, ski, or backpack. They moved up from the city and like to think they're in a wilderness. A few are mountain types who moved down to be here, and are glad to be living where there are some neighbors. The kids go to Donner Pass to be sliding on the white crystals of future Yuba River waters. I get back to downhill skiing myself; it feels wonderful again. Downhill must have provided one of the fastest speeds human beings ever experienced before modern times. Cross-country ski trips in Sierra Buttes too. On the full moon night of April (the last night of the month) Bill Schell and I did a tour till 2 A.M. around Yuba Pass, snow shining bright in the moonlight, skis clattering on the icy slabs. Old mountain people turned settlers manage to finally start going back into the mountains after the house is built, the garden fenced, the drip-systems in. February brought ten inches of rain in six days. The ponds and springs stream over, the ground's all silvery with surface glitter of a skin of water. Fifteen feet of snow at Sugarbowl near Donner Pass.

Two old gents in the Sacramento Greyhound station. I'm next to an elder who swings his cane back and forth, lightly, the tip pivoting on the ground—and he looks about the room, back and forth, without much focus. He has egg on his chin. A smell of old urine comes from him, blows my way, time to time. Another elder walks past and out. He's very neat: a plastic-wrapped waterproof blanket-roll slung on his shoulder, a felt hat, a white chin beard like an Amish. Red bandanna tied round his neck, bib overalls. Under the overall bottoms peep out more trousers, maybe suit pants. So that's how he keeps warm, and keeps some clothes clean! Back in my traveling days men said, "Yeah, spend the winter in Sac."

I caught the bus on down to Oakland. In Berkeley, on the wall of the Lucas Books building, is a mural that shows a cross section of Alta California from the Northwest Coast to the Mojave Desert. I walked backward through the parking lot to get a look at it whole, sea lions, coyote, redtail hawk, creosote bush. Then noticed a man at one corner of it, touching it up. Talked to him, he is Lou Silva, who did the painting. He was redoing a mouse, and he said he comes back from time to time to put in more tiny fauna.

Spring is good to the apples, much fruit sets. Five male deer with antler velvet nubs walk about the meadow in the morning. High-country skiing barely ends and it's time to go fishing. Planting and building. This area is still growing, though not as rapidly as several years ago. The strong spirit of community of the early seventies has abated somewhat, but I like to think that when the going gets rough this population will stick together.

San Juan Ridge lies between the middle and south forks of the Yuba River in a political entity called Nevada County. New settlers have been coming in here since the late sixties. The Sierra counties are a mess: a string of them lap over the mountain crest, and the roads between the two sides are often closed in winter. A sensible redrawing of lines here would put eastern Sierra, eastern Nevada, and eastern Placer counties together in a new "Truckee River County" and the seat could be in Truckee. Western Placer and western Nevada counties south of the south fork of the Yuba would make a good new county. Western Sierra County plus a bit of Yuba County and northern Nevada County put together would fit into the watershed of the three forks of the Yuba. I would call it "Nisenan County" after the native people who lived here. Most of them were killed or driven away by the gold rush miners.

People live on the ridges because the valleys are rocky or brushy and have no level bottoms. In the Sierra Nevada a good human habitat is not a valley bottom, but a wide gentle *ridge* between canyons.

Blue Mountains Constantly Walking

Fudō and Kannon

> The mountains and rivers of this moment are the actualization of the way of the ancient Buddhas. Each, abiding in its own phenomenal expression, realizes completeness. Because mountains and waters have been active since before the eon of emptiness, they are alive at this moment. Because they have been the self since before form arose, they are liberated and realized.

This is the opening paragraph of Dōgen Kigen's astonishing essay *Sansuikyo*, "Mountains and Waters Sutra," written in the autumn of 1240, thirteen years after he returned from his visit to Songdynasty China. At the age of twelve he had left home in Kyoto to climb the well-worn trails through the dark hinoki and sugi (cedar-and-sequoia-like) forests of Mt. Hiei. This three-thousand-foot range at the northeast corner of the Kamo River basin, the broad valley now occupied by the huge city of Kyoto, was the Japanese headquarters mountain of the Tendai sect of Buddhism. He became a novice monk in one of the red-painted shadowy wooden temples along the ridges.

The blue mountains are constantly walking.

In those days travelers walked. The head monk at the Daitoku-ji Zen monks' hall in Kyoto once showed me the monastery's handwritten "Yearly Tasks" book from the nineteenth century. (It had been replaced by another handwritten volume with a few minor updates for the twentieth century.) These are the records that the leaders refer to through the year in keeping track of ceremonies, meditation sessions, and recipes. It listed the temples that were affiliated with this training school in order of the traveling time it took to get to them: from one day to four weeks' walk. Student monks from even those distant temples usually made a round trip home at least once a year.

Virtually all of Japan is steep hills and mountains dissected by fast shallow streams that open into shoestring valleys and a few wider river plains toward the sea. The hills are generally covered with small conifers and shrubs. Once they were densely forested with a cover of large hard woods as well as the irregular pines and the tall straight hinoki and sugi. Traces of a vast network of well-marked trails are still found throughout the land. They were tramped down by musicians, monks, merchants, porters, pilgrims, and periodic armies.

We learn a place and how to visualize spatial relationships, as children, on foot and with imagination. Place and the scale of space must be measured against our bodies and their capabilities. A "mile" was originally a Roman measure of one thousand paces. Automobile and airplane travel teaches us little that we can easily translate into a perception of space. To know that it takes six months to walk across Turtle Island/North America walking steadily but comfortably all day every day is to get some grasp of the distance. The Chinese spoke of the "four dignities"—Standing, Lying, Sitting, and Walking. They are "dignities" in that they are ways of being fully ourselves, at home in our bodies, in their fundamental modes. I think many of us would consider it quite marvelous if we could set out on foot again, with a little inn or a clean camp available every ten or so miles and no threat from traffic, to travel across a large landscape—all of China, all of Europe. That's the way to see the world: in our own bodies.

Sacred mountains and pilgrimage to them is a deeply established feature of the popular religions of Asia. When Dōgen speaks of mountains he is well aware of these prior traditions. There are hundreds of famous Daoist and Buddhist peaks in China and similar Buddhist and Shinto-associated mountains in Japan. There are several sorts of sacred mountains in Asia: a "sacred site" that is the residence of a spirit or deity is the simplest and possibly oldest. Then there are "sacred areas"—perhaps many dozens of square miles—that are special to the mythology and practice of a sect with its own set of Daoist or Buddhist deities—miles of paths—and dozens or hundreds of little temples and shrines. Pilgrims might climb thousands of feet, sleep in the plain board guesthouses, eat rice gruel and a few pickles, and circumambulate set routes burning incense and bowing at site after site.

Finally there are a few highly formalized sacred areas that have been deliberately modeled on a symbolic diagram (mandala) or a holy text. They too can be quite large. It is thought that to walk within the designated landscape is to enact specific moves on the spiritual plane (Grapard, 1982). Some friends and I once walked the ancient pilgrimage route of the Ōmine Yamabushi (mountain ascetics) in Nara prefecture from Yoshino to Kumano. In doing so we crossed the traditional center of the "Diamond-Realm Mandala" at the summit of Mt. Ōmine (close to six thousand feet) and four hiking days later descended to the center of the "Womb-Realm Mandala" at the Kumano ("Bear Field") Shrine, deep in a valley. It was the late-June rainy season, flowery and misty. There were little stone shrines the whole distance—miles of ridges—to which we sincerely bowed each time we came on them. This projection of complex teaching diagrams onto the landscape comes from the Japanese variety of Vajrayana Buddhism, the Shingon sect, in its interaction with the shamanistic tradition of the mountain brotherhood.

The regular pilgrimage up Mt. Ōmine from the Yoshino side is flourishing—hundreds of colorful Yamabushi in medieval mountain-gear scale cliffs, climb the peak, and blow conches while others chant sutras in the smoky dirt-floored temple on the summit. The long-distance practice has been abandoned in recent years, so the trail was so overgrown it was almost impossible to find. This four-thousand-foot-high direct ridge route makes excellent sense, and I suspect it was the regular way of traveling from the coast to the interior in paleolithic and neolithic times. It was the only place I ever came on wild deer and monkeys in Japan.

In East Asia "mountains" are often synonymous with wilderness. The agrarian states have long since drained, irrigated, and terraced the lowlands. Forest and wild habitat start at the very place the farming stops. The lowlands, with their villages, markets, cities, palaces, and wineshops, are thought of as the place of greed, lust, competition, commerce, and intoxication—the "dusty world." Those who would flee such a world and seek purity find caves or build hermitages in the hills—and take up the practices which will bring realization or at least a long healthy life. These hermitages in time became the centers of temple complexes and ultimately religious sects. Dōgen says:

> Many rulers have visited mountains to pay homage to wise people
> or ask for instructions from great sages. . . . At such time these
> rulers treat the sages as teachers, disregarding the protocol of the
> usual world. The imperial power has no authority over the wise
> people in the mountains.

So "mountains" are not only spiritually deepening but also (it is hoped) independent of the control of the central government. Joining the hermits and priests in the hills are people fleeing jail, taxes, or conscription. (Deeper into the ranges of southwestern China are the surviving hill tribes who worship dogs and tigers and have much equality between the sexes, but that belongs to another story.) Mountains (or wilderness) have served as a haven of spiritual and political freedom all over.

Mountains also have mythic associations of verticality, spirit, height, transcendence, hardness, resistance, and masculinity. For the Chinese they are exemplars of the "yang": dry, hard, male, and bright. Waters are feminine: wet, soft, dark "yin" with associations of fluid-but-strong, seeking (and carving) the lowest, soulful, life-giving, shape-shifting. Folk (and Vajrayana) Buddhist iconography personifies "mountains and waters" in the *rupas*—"images" of Fudō Myō-ō (Immovable Wisdom King) and Kannon Bosatsu (The Bodhisattva Who Watches the Waves). Fudō is almost comically ferocious-looking with a blind eye and a fang, seated or standing on a slab of rock and enveloped in flames. He is known as an ally of mountain ascetics. Kannon (Kuan-yin, Avalokitesvara) gracefully leans forward with her lotus and vase of water, a figure of compassion. The two are seen as buddha-work partners: ascetic discipline and relentless spirituality balanced by compassionate tolerance and detached forgiveness. Mountains and Waters are a dyad that together make wholeness possible: wisdom and compassion are the two components of realization. Dōgen says:

> Wenzi said, "The path of water is such that when it rises to the sky, it becomes raindrops; when it falls to the ground, it becomes rivers.". . . The path of water is not noticed by water, but is realized by water.

There is the obvious fact of the water-cycle and the fact that mountains and rivers indeed form each other: waters are precipitated by heights, carve or deposit landforms in their flowing descent, and weight the offshore continental shelves with sediment to ultimately tilt more uplifts. In common usage the compound "mountains and waters"—*shan-shui* in Chinese—is the straightforward term for landscape. Landscape painting is "mountains and waters pictures." (A mountain range is sometimes also termed *mai,* a "pulse" or "vein"—as a network of veins on the back of a hand.) One does not need to be a specialist to observe that landforms are a play of stream-cutting and ridge-resistance and that waters and hills interpenetrate in endlessly branching rhythms. The Chinese feel for land has always incorporated this sense of a dialectic of rock and water, of downward flow and rocky uplift, and of the dynamism and "slow flowing" of earth-forms. There are several surviving large Chinese horizontal handscrolls from premodern eras titled something like "Mountains and Rivers Without End." Some of them move through the four seasons and seem to picture the whole world.

"Mountains and waters" is a way to refer to the totality of the process

of nature. As such it goes well beyond dichotomies of purity and pollution, natural and artificial. The whole, with its rivers and valleys, obviously includes farms, fields, villages, cities, and the (once comparatively
small) dusty world of human affairs.

This

The blue mountains are constantly walking.

Dōgen is quoting the Chan master Furong. Dōgen was probably envi-
sioning those mountains of Asia whose trails he had walked over the
years—peaks in the three to nine-thousand-foot range, hazy blue or blue-
green, mostly tree-covered, maybe the steep jumbled mountains of coastal
South China where he had lived and practiced thirteen years earlier. (Timberline at these latitudes is close to nine thousand feet—none of these are
alpine mountains.) He had walked thousands of miles. ("The Mind studies the way running barefoot.")

If you doubt mountains walking you do not know your own walking.

Dōgen is not concerned with "sacred mountains"—or pilgrimages, or
spirit allies, or wilderness as some special quality. His mountains and
streams are the processes of this earth, all of existence, process, essence,
action, absence; they roll being and nonbeing together. They are what we
are, we are what they are. For those who would see directly into essential
nature, the idea of the sacred is a delusion and an obstruction: it diverts us
from seeing what is before our eyes: plain thusness. Roots, stems, and
branches are all equally scratchy. No hierarchy, no equality. No occult and
exoteric, no gifted kids and slow achievers. No wild and tame, no bound
or free, no natural and artificial. Each totally its own frail self. Even though
connected all which ways; even *because* connected all which ways.

This, *thusness,* is the nature of the nature of nature. The wild in wild.

So the blue mountains walk to the kitchen and back to the shop, to the
desk, to the stove. We sit on the park bench and let the wind and rain
drench us. The blue mountains walk out to put another coin in the parking meter, and go on down to the 7-Eleven. The blue mountains march
out of the sea, shoulder the sky for a while, and slip back into the waters.

Homeless

The Buddhists say "homeless" to mean a monk or priest. (In Japanese,
shukke—literally "out of the house.") It refers to a person who has supposedly left the householder's life and the temptations and obligations of the

secular world behind. Another phrase, "leaving the world," means getting away from the imperfections of human behavior—particularly as reinforced by urban life. It does not mean distancing yourself from the natural world. For some it has meant living as mountain hermits or members of religious communities. The "house" has been set against "mountains" or "purity." Enlarging the scale of the homeless world the fifth-century poet Zhiangyan said the proper hermit should "take the purple heavens to be his hut, the encircling sea to be his pond, roaring with laughter in his nakedness, walking along singing with his hair hanging down" (Warson, 1971, 82). The early Tang poet Han-shan is taken as the veritable model of a recluse—his spacious home reaches to the end of the universe:

> I settled at Cold Mountain long ago,
> Already it seems like years and years.
> Freely drifting, I prowl the woods and streams
> And linger watching things themselves.
> Men don't get this far into the mountains,
> White clouds gather and billow.
> Thin grass does for a mattress,
> The blue sky makes a good quilt.
> Happy with a stone underhead
> Let heaven and earth go about their changes.

"Homeless" is here coming to mean "being at home in the whole universe." In a similar way, self-determining people who have not lost the wholeness of their place can see their households and their regional mountains or woods as within the same sphere.

I attended the ceremonies at the shrine for the volcanic mountain of Suwa-no-se Island, in the East China Sea, one year. The path through the jungle needed brushing, so rarely did people go there. Two of us from the Banyan Ashram went as helpers to three elders. We spent the morning cutting overgrowth back, sweeping the ground, opening and wiping the unpainted wood altar-structure (about the size of a pigeon coop), and then placing some offerings of sweet potatoes, fruit, and *shochu* on the shelf before the blank space that in fact framed the mountain itself. One elder then faced the peak (which had been belching out ash clouds lately) and made a direct, perfunctory personal speech or prayer in dialect. We sat on the ground sweating and cut open watermelon with a sickle and drank some of the strong *shochu* then, while the old guys told stories of other days in the islands. Tall thick glossy green trees arched over us, roaring with cicada. It was not trivial. The domestic parallel is accomplished in each household with its photos of ancestors, offerings of rice and alcohol, and a vase with a few twigs of wild evergreen leaves. The house itself, with its funky tiny kitchen, bath, well, and entranceway altars, becomes a little shrine.

And then the literal "house," when seen as just another piece of the world, is itself impermanent and composite, a poor "homeless" thing in its own right. Houses are made up, heaped together, of pine boards, clay tiles, cedar battens, river boulder piers, windows scrounged from wrecking yards, knobs from K-Mart, mats from Cost Plus, kitchen floor of sandstone from some mountain ridge, doormat from Longs—made up of the same world as you and me and mice.

> Blue mountains are neither sentient nor insentient. You are neither sentient nor insentient. At this moment, you cannot doubt the blue mountains walking.

Not only plum blossoms and clouds, or Lecturers and roshis, but chisels, bent nails, wheelbarrows, and squeaky doors are all teaching the truth of the way things are. The condition of true "homelessness" is the maturity of relying on nothing and responding to whatever turns up on the doorstep. Dōgen encourages us with "A mountain always practices in every place."

Larger Than a Wolf, Smaller Than an Elk

All my life I have been in and around wild nature, working, exploring, studying, even while living in cities. Yet I realized a few years ago that I had never made myself into as good a botanist or zoologist or ornithologist as so many of the outdoor people I admire have done. Recalling where I had put my intellectual energies over the years it came to me that I had made my fellow human beings my study—that I had been a naturalist of my own species. I had been my own object-of-study too. I enjoy learning how different societies work out the details of subsistence and celebration in their different landscapes. Science, technology, and the economic uses of nature need not be antithetical to celebration. The line between use and misuse, between objectification and celebration, is fine indeed.

The line is in the details. I once attended the dedication of a Japanese temple building that had been broken down and transported across the Pacific to be resurrected on the West Coast. The dedication ceremony was in the Shinto style and included offerings of flowers and plants. The difficulty was that they were the plants that would have been used in a traditional Japanese dedication and had been sent from Japan—they were not plants of the new place. The ritualists had the forms right but clearly didn't grasp the substance. After everyone had gone home I tried to make brief introductions myself: "Japanese building of hinoki wood, meet manzanita and Ponderosa Pine . . . please take care of yourself in this dry climate. Manzanita, this building is used to damp air and lots of people. Please accept it in place of your dusty slopes." Humans provide their own sort of access to understanding nature and the wild.

The human diverseness of style and costume, and the constant transformations of popular culture, is a kind of symbolic speciation—as though humans chose to mimic the colors and patterns of birds. People from the high civilizations in particular have elaborate notions of separateness and difference and dozens of ways to declare themselves "out of nature." As a kind of game this might be harmless. (One could imagine the phylum Chordata declaring, "We are a qualitative leap in evolution representing something entirely transcendent entering what has hitherto been merely biology.") But at the very minimum this call to a special destiny on the part of human beings can be seen as a case of needlessly multiplying theories (Occam's razor). And the results—in the human treatment of the rest of nature—have been pernicious.

There is a large landscape handscroll called "Interminable Mountains and Streams" (attributed to Lu Yuan of the Ching dynasty; now in the Freer). We see, within this larger scope of rocks, trees, ridges, mountains, and watercourses, people and their works. There are peasants and thatched huts, priests and complexes of temples, scholars at their little windows, fishermen in their boats, traveling merchants with their loads, matrons, children. While the Buddhist tradition of North India and Tibet made the mandala—painted or drawn charts of the positions of consciousness and cause-and-effect chains—their visual teaching aids, the Chan tradition of China (especially the Southern Song) did something similar (I will venture to suggest) with landscape painting. If a scroll is taken as a kind of Chinese mandala, then all the characters in it are our various little selves, and the cliffs, trees, waterfalls, and clouds are our own changes and stations. (Swampy reedy thicket along a stream—what does *that* say?) Each type of ecological system is a different mandala, a different imagination. Again the Ainu term *iworu*, field-of-beings, comes to mind.

> All beings do not see mountains and waters in the same way. . . .
> Some see water as wondrous blossoms, hungry ghosts see water as
> raging fire or pus and blood. Dragons see water as a palace or a
> pavilion. . . . Some beings see water as a forest or a wall. Human
> beings see water as water. . . . Water's freedom depends only on
> water.

One July walking down from the headwaters of the Koyukuk River in the Brooks Range of Alaska I found myself able to look into the realm of Dall (mountain) Sheep. The green cloudy tundra summer alps—in which I was a frail visitor—were the most hospitable they would ever be to a hairless primate. The long dark winters do not daunt the Dall Sheep, though—they do not even migrate down. The winds blow the scant loose snow, and the dried forbs and grasses of arctic summer are nibbled through the year. The dozens of summer sheep stood out white against green: playing, napping, eating, butting, circling, sitting, dozing in their high smoothed out beds on ledges at the "cliff-edge of life and death." Dall Sheep (in Athapaskan called *dibee*) see mountains—Dōgen might say—"as a palace or pavilion." But that provisional phrase "palace or pavilion" is too high-class, urban, and human to really show how totally and uniquely *at home* each life-form must be in its own unique "buddha-field."

> Green mountain walls in blowing cloud
> white dots on far slopes, constellations,
> slowly changing, not stars, not rocks
> "by the midnight breezes strewn"
> cloud tatters, lavender arctic light
> on sedate wild sheep grazing
> tundra greens, held in the web of clan
> and kin by bleats and smells to the slow
> rotation of their Order living
> half in the sky—damp wind up from the
> whole North Slope and a taste of the icepack,
> the primus roaring now,
> here, have some tea.

And down in the little arctic river below the slopes the Grayling with their iridescent bodies are in their own (to us) icy paradise. Dōgen again:

Now when dragons and fish see water as a palace, it is just like human beings seeing a palace. They do not think it flows. If an outsider tells them, "What you see as a palace is running water," the dragons and fish will be astonished, just as we are when we hear the words, "Mountains flow."

We can begin to imagine, to visualize, the nested hierarchies and webs of the actual nondualistic world. Systems theory provides equations but few metaphors. In the "Mountains and Waters Sutra" we find:

It is not only that there is water in the world, but there is a world in water. It is not just in water. There is a world of sentient beings in clouds. There is a world of sentient beings in the air. There is a world of sentient beings in fire. . . . There is a world of sentient beings in a blade of grass.

It would appear that the common conception of evolution is that of competing species running a sort of race through time on planet earth, all on the same running field, some dropping out, some flagging, some victoriously in front. If the background and foreground are reversed, and we look at it from the side of the "conditions" and their creative possibilities, we can see these multitudes of interactions through hundreds of other eyes. We could say a food brings a form into existence. Huckleberries and salmon call for bears, the clouds of plankton of the North Pacific call for salmon, and salmon call for seals and thus orcas. The sperm whale is sucked into existence by the pulsing, fluctuating pastures of squid, and the open niches of the Galapagos Islands sucked a diversity of bird forms and functions out of one line of finch.

Conservation biologists speak of "indicator species"—animals or birds that are so typical of a natural area and its system that their condition is an indicator of the condition of the whole. The old conifer forests can be measured by "spotted owl," and the Great Plains once said (and would say it again) "bison." So the question I have been asking myself is: what says "humans"? What sucks *our* lineage into form? It is surely the "mountains and rivers without end"—the whole of this earth on which we find ourselves more or less competently at home. Berries, acorns, grass-seeds, apples, and yams call for dextrous creatures something like us to come forward. Larger than a wolf, smaller than an elk, human beings are not such huge figures in the landscape. From the air, the works of humanity are scratches and grids and ponds, and in fact most of the earth seems, from afar, to be open land. (We know now that our impact is far greater than it appears.)

As for towns and cities—they are (to those who can see) old tree trunks, riverbed gravels, oil seeps, landslide scrapes, blowdowns and burns, the leavings after floods, coral colonies, paper-wasp nests, beehives, rotting logs, watercourses, rock-cleavage lines, ledge strata layers, guano heaps, feeding frenzies, courting and strutting bowers, lookout rocks, and ground-squirrel apartments. And for a few people they are also palaces.

Decomposed

Hungry ghosts see water as raging fire or pus and blood . . .

Life in the wild is not just eating berries in the sunlight. I like to imagine a "depth ecology" that would go to the dark side of nature—the ball of crunched bones in a scat, the feathers in the snow, the tales of insatiable appetite. Wild systems are in one elevated sense above criticism, but they can also be seen as irrational, moldy, cruel, parasitic. Jim Dodge told me how he had watched—with fascinated horror—orcas methodically batter a gray whale to death in the Chukchi Sea. Life is not just a diurnal property of large interesting vertebrates; it is also nocturnal, anaerobic, cannibalistic, microscopic, digestive, fermentative: cooking away in the warm dark. Life is well maintained at a four-mile ocean depth, is waiting and sustained on a frozen rock wall, is clinging and nourished in hundred-degree desert temperatures. And there is a world of nature on the decay side, a world of beings who do rot and decay in the shade. Human beings have made much of purity and are repelled by blood, pollution, putrefaction. The other side of the "sacred" is the sight of your beloved in the underworld, dripping with maggots. Coyote, Orpheus, and Izanagi cannot help but look, and they lose her. Shame, grief, embarrassment, and fear are the anaerobic fuels of the dark imagination. The less familiar energies of the wild world, and their analogs in the imagination, have given us ecologies of the mind.

Here we encounter the peculiar habitat needs of the gods. They settle on the summits of mountains (as on Mt. Olympus), have chambers deep below the earth, or are invisibly all around us. (One major deity is rumored to be domiciled entirely off this earth.) The Yana said that Mt. Lassen of northern California—"Waganupa" in Ishi's tongue, a ten-thousand-foot volcano—is home to countless *kukini* who keep a fire going inside. (The smoke passes out through the smoke-hole.) They will enjoy their magical stick-game gambling until the time that human beings reform themselves and become "real people" that spirits might want to associate with once again.

The spirit world goes across and between species. It does not need to concern itself with reproduction, it is not afraid of death, it is not practical. But the spirits do seem to have an ambivalent, selective interest in cross-world communication. Young women in scarlet and white robes dance to call down the gods, to be possessed by them, to speak in their voices. The priests who employ them can only wait for the message. (I think it was D. H. Lawrence who said, "Drink and carouse with Bacchus, or eat dry bread with Jesus, but don't sit down without one of the gods.")

(The *personal* quality of mountain dreaming: I was half asleep on the rocky ground at Tower Lake in the Sierra. There are four horizontal bands of cream-colored rock wavering through the cliff face, and the dream said "those rock bands are your daughters.")

Where Dōgen and the Zen tradition would walk, chant a sutra, or do sitting meditation, the elder vernacular artisans of soul and spirit would play a flute, drum, dance, dream, listen for a song, go without food, and be available to communication with birds, animals, or rocks. There is a story of Coyote watching the yellow autumn cottonwood leaves float and eddy lightly down to the ground. It was so lovely to watch, he asked the cottonwood leaves if he might do it too. They warned him: "Coyote, you are too heavy and you have a body of bones and guts and muscle. We are light, we drift with the wind, but you would fall and be hurt." Coyote would hear none of it and insisted on climbing a cottonwood, edging far out onto a branch, and launching himself off. He fell and was killed. There's a caution here: do not be too hasty in setting out to "become one with." But, as we have heard, Coyote will roll over, reassemble his ribs, locate his paws, find a pebble with a dot of pitch on it to do for an eye, and trot off again.

Narratives are one sort of trace that we leave in the world. All our literatures are leavings—of the same order as the myths of wilderness peoples, who leave behind only stories and a few stone tools. Other orders of beings have their own literatures. Narrative in the deer world is a track of scents that is passed on from deer to deer with an art of interpretation that is instinctive. A literature of blood-stains, a bit of piss, a whiff of estrus, a hit of rut, a scrape on a sapling, and long gone. And there might be a "narrative theory" among these other beings—they might ruminate on "intersexuality" or "decomposition criticism."

I suspect that primary peoples all know that their myths are somehow "made up." They do not take them literally and at the same time they hold the stories very dear. Only upon being invaded by history and whipsawed by alien values do a people begin to declare that their myths are "literally true." This literalness in turn provokes skeptical questioning and the whole critical exercise. What a final refinement of confusion about the role of myths it is to declare that although they are not to be believed, they are nonetheless aesthetic and psychological constructs which bring order to an otherwise chaotic world and to which we should willfully commit ourselves! Dōgen's "You should know that even though all things are liberated and not tied to anything, they abide in their own phenomenal expression" is medicine for that. The "Mountains and Waters Sutra" is called a sutra not to assert that the "mountains and rivers of this moment" are a text, a system of symbols, a referential world of mirrors, but that this world in its actual existence is a complete presentation, an enactment— and that it stands for nothing.

Walking on Water

There's all sorts of walking—from heading out across the desert in a straight line to a sinuous weaving through undergrowth. Descending rocky ridges and talus slopes is a specialty in itself. It is an irregular dancing—always shifting—step of walk on slabs and scree. The breath and eye are always following this uneven rhythm. It is never paced or clocklike, but flexing—little jumps—sidesteps—going for the well-seen place to put a foot on a rock, hit flat, move on—zigzagging along and all deliberate. The alert eye looking ahead, picking the footholds to come, while never missing the step of the moment. The body-mind is so at one with this rough world that it makes these moves effortlessly once it has had a bit of practice. The mountain keeps up with the mountain.

In the year 1225 Dōgen was in his second year in South China. That year he walked out of the mountains and passed through the capital of the Southern Song dynasty, Hang-zhou, on his way north to the Wan-shou monastery at Mt. Jing. The only account of China left by Dōgen is notes on talks by the master Ru-jing (Kodera, 1980). I wonder what Dōgen would have said of city walking. Hang-zhou had level broad straight streets paralleling canals. He must have seen the many-storied houses, clean cobbled streets, theaters, markets, and innumerable restaurants. It had three thousand public baths. Marco Polo (who called it Quinsai) visited it twenty-five years later and estimated that it was probably the largest (at least a million people) and most affluent city in the world at that time (Gernet, 1962). Even today the people of Hang-zhou remember the lofty eleventh-century poet Su Shi, who built the causeway across West Lake when he was governor. At the time of Dōgen's walk North China was under the control of the Mongols, and Hang-zhou would fall to the Mongols in fifty-five more years.

The South China of that era sent landscape painting, calligraphy, both the Soto and Rinzai schools of Zen, and the vision of that great southern capital to Japan. The memory of Hang-zhou shaped both Osaka and Tokyo in their Tokugawa-era evolution. These two positions—one the austere Zen practice with its spare, clean halls, the other the possibility of a convivial urban life rich in festivals and theaters and restaurants—are two potent legacies of East Asia to the world. If Zen stands for the Far Eastern love of nature, Hang-zhou stands for the ideal of the city. Both are brimming with energy and life. Because most of the cities of the world are now mired in poverty, overpopulation, and pollution we have all the more reason to recover the dream. To neglect the city (in our hearts and minds for starters) is deadly, as James Hillman (1989, 169) says.

The "Mountains and Waters Sutra" goes on to say:

> All waters appear at the foot of the eastern mountains. Above all waters are all mountains. Walking beyond and walking within are both done on water. All mountains walk with their toes on all waters and splash there.

Dōgen finishes his meditation on mountains and waters with this: "When you investigate mountains thoroughly, this is the work of the mountains. Such mountains and waters of themselves become wise persons and sages"—become sidewalk vendors and noodle-cooks, become marmots, ravens, graylings, carp, rattlesnakes, mosquitoes. *All* beings are "said" by the mountains and waters—even the clanking tread of a Caterpillar tractor, the gleam of the keys of a clarinet.

Ancient Forests
of the Far West

But ye shall destroy their altars,
break their images, and cut down their groves.
EXODUS 34:13

After the Clearcut

We had a tiny dairy farm between Puget Sound and the north end of Lake Washington, out in the cut-over countryside. The bioregionalists call that part of northwestern Washington state "Ish" after the suffix that means "river" in Salish. Rivers flowing into Puget Sound are the Snohomish, Sky-komish, Samamish, Duwamish, Stillaguamish.

I remember my father dynamiting stumps and pulling the share out with a team. He cleared two acres and fenced it for three Guernseys. He built a two-story barn with stalls and storage for the cows below and chickens above. He and my mother planted fruit trees, kept geese, sold milk. Behind the back fence were the woods: a second-growth jungle of alder and cascara trees with native blackberry vines sprawling over the stumps. Some of the stumps were ten feet high and eight or ten feet in diameter at the ground. High up the sides were the notches the fallers had chopped in to support the steel-tipped planks, the springboards, they stood on while felling. This got them above the huge swell of girth at the bottom. Two or three of the old trees had survived—small ones by com-parison—and I climbed those, especially one western red cedar (*xelpai'its* in Snohomish) that I fancied became my advisor. Over the years I roamed the second-growth Douglas fir, western hemlock, and cedar forest beyond the cow pasture, across the swamp, up a long slope, and into a droughty stand of pines. The woods were more of a home than home. I had a permanent campsite where I would sometimes cook and spend the night.

When I was older I hiked into the old-growth stands of the foothill valleys of the Cascades and the Olympics where the shade-tolerant skunk cabbage and devil's club underbrush is higher than your head and the moss carpets are a foot thick. Here there is always a deep aroma of crumbled wet organisms—fungus—and red rotten logs and a few bushes of tart red thimbleberries. At the forest edges are the thickets of salal with their bland seedy berries, the yellow salmonberries, and the tangles of vine-maples. Standing in the shade you look out into the burns and the logged-off land and see the fireweed in bloom.

A bit older, I made it into the high mountains. The snowpeaks were visible from near our place: in particular Mt. Baker and Glacier Peak to the north and Mt. Rainier to the south. To the west, across Puget Sound, the Olympics. Those unearthly glowing floating snowy summits are a promise to the spirit. I first experienced one of those distant peaks up close at fifteen, when I climbed Mt. Saint Helens. Rising at 3 A.M. at timberline and breaking camp so as to be on glacier ice by six; standing in the rosy sunrise at nine thousand feet on a frozen slope to the crisp tinkle of crampon points on ice—these are some of the esoteric delights of mountaineering. To be immersed in ice and rock and cold and upper space is to undergo an eery, rigorous initiation and transformation. Being above all the clouds with only a few other high mountains also in the sunshine, the human world still asleep under its gray dawn cloud blanket, is one of the first small steps toward Aldo Leopold's "think like a mountain." I made my way to most of the summits of the Northwest—Mt. Hood, Mt. Baker, Mt. Rainier, Mt. Adams, Mt. Stuart, and more—in subsequent years.

At the same time, I became more aware of the lowlands. Trucks ceaselessly rolled down the river valleys out of the Cascades loaded with great logs. Walking the low hills around our place near Lake City I realized that I had grown up in the aftermath of a clearcut, and that it had been only thirty-five or forty years since all those hills had been logged. I know now that the area had been home to some of the largest and finest trees the world has ever seen, an ancient forest of hemlock and Douglas fir, a temperate-zone rainforest since before the glaciers. And I suspect that I was to some extent instructed by the ghosts of those ancient trees as they hovered near their stumps. I joined the Wilderness Society at seventeen, subscribed to *Living Wilderness,* and wrote letters to Congress about forestry issues in the Olympics.

But I was also instructed by the kind of work done by my uncles, our neighbors, the workers of the whole Pacific Northwest. My father put me on one end of a two-man crosscut saw when I was ten and gave me the classic instruction of "don't ride the saw"—don't push, only pull—and I loved the clean swish and ring of the blade, the rhythm, the comradeship, the white curl of the wood that came out with the rakers, the ritual of setting the handles, and the sprinkle of kerosene (to dissolve pitch) on the blade and into the kerf. We cut rounds out of down logs to split for firewood. (Unemployed men during the Depression felled the tall cedar stumps left from the first round of logging to buck them into blanks and split them with froes for the hand-split cedar shake trade.) We felled trees to clear pasture. We burned huge brush-piles.

People love to do hard work together and to feel that the work is real; that is to say primary, productive, needed. Knowing and enjoying the skills of our hands and our well-made tools is fundamental. It is a tragic dilemma that much of the best work men do together is no longer quite right. The fine information on the techniques of hand-whaling and all the steps of the flensing and rendering described in *Moby Dick* must now, we know, be measured against the terrible specter of the extinction of whales. Even the farmer or the carpenter is uneasy: pesticides, herbicides, creepy subsidies, welfare water, cheap materials, ugly subdivisions, walls that won't last. Who can be proud? And our conservationist-environmentalist-moral outrage is often (in its frustration) aimed at the logger or the rancher, when the real power is in the hands of people who make unimaginably larger sums of money, people impeccably groomed, excellently educated at the best universities—male and female alike—eating fine foods and reading classy literature, while orchestrating the investment and legislation that ruin the world. As I grew into young manhood in the Pacific Northwest, advised by a cedar tree, learning the history of my region, practicing mountaineering, studying the native cultures, and inventing the little rituals that kept my spirit sane, I was often supporting myself by the woodcutting skills I learned on the Depression stump-farm.

At Work in the Woods

In 1952 and '53 I worked for the Forest Service as a lookout in the northern Cascades. The following summer, wanting to see new mountains, I applied to a national forest in the Mt. Rainier area. I had already made my way to the Packwood Ranger Station and purchased my summer's supply of lookout groceries when the word came to the district (from Washington, D.C.) that I should be fired. That was the McCarthy era and the Velde Committee hearings were taking place in Portland. Many of my acquaintances were being named on TV. It was the end of my career as a seasonal forestry worker for the government.

I was totally broke, so I decided to go back to the logging industry. I hitched east of the Oregon Cascades to the Warm Springs Indian Reservation and checked in with the Warm Springs Lumber Company. I had scaled timber here the summer of '51, and now they hired me on as a chokersetter. This is the lava plateau country south of the Columbia River and in the drainage of the Deschutes, up to the headwaters of the Warm Springs River. We were cutting old-growth Ponderosa Pine on the middle slopes of the east side, a fragrant open forest of massive straight-trunked trees growing on volcanic soils. The upper edge verged into the alpine life-zone, and the lower edge—farther and farther out into the desert—became sagebrush by degrees. The logging was under contract with the tribal council. The proceeds were to benefit the people as a whole.

11 August '54
Chokersetting today. Madras in the evening for beer. Under the shadow of Mt. Jefferson. Long cinnamon-colored logs. This is "pine" and it belongs to "Indians"— what a curious knotting-up. That these Indians & these trees, that coexisted for centuries, should suddenly be possessor and possessed. Our concepts to be sure.

I had no great problem with that job. Unlike the thick-growing Douglas fir rainforests west of the Cascades, where there are arguments for clearcutting, the drier pine forests are perfect for selective cutting. Here the slopes were gentle and they were taking no more than 40 percent of the canopy. A number of healthy mid-sized seed trees were left standing. The D8 Cats could weave their way through without barking the standing trees.

Chokersetting is part of the skidding operation. First into the woods are the timber cruisers who estimate the standing board feet and mark the trees. Then come the road-building Cats and graders. Right on their heels are the gypo fallers—gypos get paid for quantity produced rather than a set wage—and then comes the skidding crew. West-of-the-mountains skidding is typically a high-lead or skyline cable operation where the logs are yarded in via a cable system strung out of a tall spar tree. In the east-side pine forest the skidding is done with top-size Caterpillar tractors. The Cat pulls a crawler-tread "arch" trailer behind it with a cable running from the Cat's aft winch up and over the pulley-wheel at the top of the arch, and then down where the cable divides into three massive chains that end in heavy steel hooks, the butt-hooks. I was on a team of two that worked behind one Cat. It was a two-Cat show.

Each Cat drags the felled and bucked logs to the landing—where they are loaded on trucks—from its own set of skid trails. While it is dragging a load of logs in, the chokersetters (who stay behind up the skid trails) are studying the next haul. You pick out the logs you'll give the Cat next trip, and determine the sequence in which you'll hook them so they will not cross each other, flip, twist over, snap live trees down, hang up on stumps, or make other dangerous and complicating moves. Chokersetters should be light and wiry. I wore White's caulked logger boots with steel points like tiny weasel-fangs set in the sole. I was thus enabled to run out and along a huge log or up its slope with perfect footing, while looking at the lay and guessing the physics of its mass in motion. The Cat would be coming back up the skid trail dragging the empty choker cables and would swing in where I signaled. I'd pluck two or three chokers off the butt-hooks and drag the sixteen-foot cables behind me into the logs and brush. The Cat would go on out to the other chokersetter who would take off his cables and do the same.

As the Cat swung out and was making its turnaround, the chokersetters would be down in dirt and duff, ramming the knobbed end of the choker under the log, bringing it up and around, and hooking it into the sliding steel catch called a "bell" that would noose up on the log when the choker pulled taut. The Cat would back its arch into where I stood, holding up chokers. I'd hook the first "D"—the ring on the free end of the choker—over the butt-hook and send the Cat to the next log. It could swing ahead and pull alongside while I leaped atop another load and hung the next choker onto the butt-hook. Then the winch on the rear of the Cat would wind in, and the butts of the logs would be lifted clear of the ground, hanging them up in the arch between the two crawler-tread wheels.

> Stood straight
> > holding the choker high
> As the Cat swung back the arch
> > piss-firs falling,
> Limbs snapping on the tin hat
> > bright D caught on
> Swinging butt-hooks
> > ringing against cold steel.
> > > from *Myths and Texts*

The next question was, how would they fan out? My Cat-skinner was Little Joe, nineteen and just recently married, chewing plug and always joking. I'd give him the highball sign and at the same time run back out the logs, even as he started pulling, to leap off the back end. Never stand between a fan of lying logs, they say. When the tractor hauls out they might swing in and snap together—"Chokersetters lose their legs that way." And don't stand anywhere near a snag when the load goes out. If the load even lightly brushes it, the top of the snag, or the whole thing, might come down. I saw a dead schoolmarm (a tree with a crotch in its top third) snap off and fall like that, grazing the tin hat of a chokersetter called Stubby. He was lucky.

> The D8 tears through piss-fir
> Scrapes the seed-pine
> > chipmunks flee,
> A black ant carries an egg
> Aimlessly from the battered ground.
> Yellowjackets swarm and circle
> Above the crushed dead log, their home.
> Pitch oozes from barked
> > trees still standing,
> Mashed bushes make strange smells.
> Lodgepole pines are brittle.
> Camprobbers flutter to watch.

I learned tricks, placements, pulls from the experienced chokersetters— ways to make a choker cable swing a log over, even to make it jump out from under. Ways and sequences of hooking on chokers that when first in place looked like a messy spiderweb, but when the Cat pulled out, the tangle of logs would right itself and the cables mysteriously fan out into a perfect pull with nothing crossed. We were getting an occasional eight-foot-diameter tree and many five and six footers: these were some of the most perfect ponderosa pine I have ever seen. We also had white fir, Douglas fir, and some larch.

I was soon used to the grinding squeaking roar and rattle of the Cat, the dust, and the rich smells that rose from the bruised and stirred-up soil and plant life. At lunchtime, when the machinery was silent, we'd see deer picking their way through the torn-up woods. A black bear kept breaking into the crummy truck to get at the lunches until someone shot him and the whole camp ate him for dinner. There was no rancor about the bear, and no sense of conquest about the logging work. The men were stoic, skillful, a bit overworked, and full of terrible (but funny!) jokes and expressions. Many of them were living on the Rez, which was shared by Wasco, Wishram, and Shoshone people. The lumber company gave priority to the Native American locals in hiring.

Ray Wells, a big Nisqually, and I
           each set a choker
On the butt-logs of two big Larch
In a thornapple thicket and a swamp.
           waiting for the Cat to come back,
"Yesterday we gelded some ponies
"My father-in-law cut the skin on the balls
"He's a Wasco and don't speak English
"He grabs a handful of tubes and somehow
           cuts the right ones.
"The ball jumps out, the horse screams
"But he's all tied up.
The Caterpillar clanked back down.
In the shadow of that racket
           diesel and iron tread
I thought of Ray Wells' tipi out on the sage flat
The gelded ponies
Healing and grazing in the dead white heat.

There were also old white guys who had worked in the lumber industry all their lives: one had been active in the Industrial Workers of the
World, the "Wobblies," and had no use for the later unions. I told him
about my grandfather, who had soapboxed for the Wobblies in Seattle's
Yesler Square, and my Uncle Roy, whose wife Anna was also the chief
cook at a huge logging camp at Gray's Harbor around World War I. I told
him of the revived interest in anarchosyndicalism among some circles in
Portland. He said he hadn't had anyone talk Wobbly talk with him in
twenty years, and he relished it. His job, knotbumper, kept him at the
landing where the skidding Cats dropped the logs off. Although the
buckers cut the limbs off, sometimes they left stubs which would make
the logs hard to load and stack. He chopped off stubs with a double-bitted axe. Ed had a circular wear-mark impressed in the rear pocket of his
stagged jeans: it was from his round axe-sharpening stone. Between loads
he constantly sharpened his axe, and he could shave a paper-thin slice off
a Day's Work plug, his chew, with the blade.

Ed McCullough, a logger for thirty-five years
Reduced by the advent of chainsaws
To chopping off knots at the landing:
"I don't have to take this kind of shit,
Another twenty years
           and I'll tell 'em to shove it"
          (he was sixty-five then)

In 1934 they lived in shanties
At Hooverville, Sullivan's Gulch.
When the Portland-bound train came through
The trainmen tossed off coal.

"Thousands of boys shot and beat up
For wanting a good bed, good pay,
                         decent food, in the woods—"
No one knew what it meant:
"Soldiers of Discontent."

On one occasion a Cat went to the landing pulling only one log, and not the usual 32-foot length but a 16. Even through it was only half-length the Cat could barely drag it. We had to rig two chokers to get around it, and there was not much pigtail left. I know now that the tree had been close to being of record size. The largest Ponderosa Pine in the world, near Mt. Adams, which I went out some miles of dust dirt roads to see, isn't much larger around than was that tree.

How could one not regret seeing such a massive tree go out for lumber? It was an elder, a being of great presence, a witness to the centuries. I saved a few of the tan free-form scales from the bark of that log and placed them on the tiny altar I kept on a box by my bunk at the logging camp. It and the other offerings (a flicker feather, a bit of broken bird's-egg, some obsidian, and a postcard picture of the Bodhisattva of Transcendent Intelligence, Manjusri) were not "my" offerings to the forest, but the forest's offerings to all of us. I guess I was just keeping some small note of it.

All of the trees in the Warm Springs forest were old growth. They were perfect for timber, too, most of them rot-free. I don't doubt that the many seed-trees and smaller trees left standing have flourished, and that the forest came back in good shape. A forester working for the Bureau of Indian Affairs and the tribal council had planned that cut.

Or did it come back in good shape? I don't know if the Warm Springs timber stands have already been logged again. They should not have been, but—

There was a comforting conservationist rhetoric in the world of forestry and lumber from the mid-thirties to the late fifties. The heavy clearcutting that has now devastated the whole Pacific slope from the Kern River to Sitka, Alaska, had not yet begun. In those days forestry professionals still believed in selective logging and actually practiced sustained yield. Those were, in hindsight, the last years of righteous forest management in the United States.

The raw dry country of the American West had an odd effect on American politics. It transformed and even radicalized some people. Once the West was closed to homesteading and the unclaimed lands became public domain, a few individuals realized that the future of these lands was open to public discussion. Some went from exploration and appreciation of wilderness to political activism.

Daoist philosophers tell us that surprise and subtle instruction might come forth from the Useless. So it was with the wastelands of the American West—inaccessible, inhospitable, arid, and forbidding to the eyes of most early Euro-Americans. The Useless Lands became the dreaming place of a few nineteenth- and early-twentieth-century men and women (John Wesley Powell on matters of water and public lands, Mary Austin on Native Americans, deserts, women) who went out into the space and loneliness and returned from their quests not only to criticize the policies and assumptions of the expanding United States but, in the name of wilderness and the commons, to hoist the sails that are filling with wind today. Some of the newly established public lands did have potential uses for lumber, grazing, and mining. But in the case of timber and grass, the best lands were already in private hands. What went into the public domain (or occasionally into Indian reservation status) was—by the standards of those days—marginal land. The off-limits bombing ranges and nuclear test sites of the Great Basin are public domain lands, too, borrowed by the military from the BLM.

So the forests that were set aside for the initial Forest Reserves were not at that time considered prime timber land. Early-day lumber interests in the Pacific Northwest went for the dense, low-elevation conifer forests like those around the house I grew up in or those forests right on saltwater or near rivers. This accessible land, once clearcut, became real estate, but the farther reaches were kept by the big companies as commercial forest. Much of the Olympic Peninsula forest land is privately held. Only by luck and chance did an occasional low-elevation stand such as the Hoh River forest in Olympic National Park, or Jedediah Smith redwoods in California, end up in public domain. It is by virtue of these islands of forest survivors that we can still see what the primeval forest of the West Coast—in its densest and most concentrated incarnation—was like. "Virgin forest" it was once called, a telling term. Then it was called "old growth" or in certain cases "climax." Now we begin to call it "ancient forest."

On the rainy Pacific slope there were million-acre stands that had been coevolving for millennia, possibly for over a million years. Such forests are the fullest examples of ecological process, containing as they do huge quantities of dead and decaying matter as well as the new green and preserving the energy pathways of both detritus and growth. An ancient forest will have many truly large old trees—some having craggy, broken-topped, mossy "dirty" crowns with much organic accumulation, most with holes and rot in them. There will be standing snags and tons of dead down logs. These characteristics, although not delightful to lumbermen ("overripe"), are what make an ancient forest more than a stand of timber: it is a palace of organisms, a heaven for many beings, a temple where life deeply investigates the puzzle of itself. Living activity goes right down to and under the "ground"—the litter, the duff. There are termites, larvae, millipedes, mites, earthworms, springtails, pillbugs, and the fine threads of fungus woven through. "There are as many as 5,500 individuals (not counting the earthworms and nematodes) per square foot of soil to a depth of 13 inches. As many as 70 different species have been collected from less than a square foot of rich forest soil. The total animal population of the soil and litter together probably approaches 10,000 animals per square foot" (Robinson, 1988, 87).

The dominant conifers in this forest, Douglas fir, western red cedar, western hemlock, noble fir, Sitka spruce, and coastal redwood, are all long-lived and grow to great size. They are often the longest-lived of their genera. The old forests of the western slopes support some of the highest per-acre biomass—total living matter—the world has seen, approached only by some of the Australian eucalyptus forests. An old-growth temperate hardwood forest, and also the tropical forests, average around 153 tons per acre. The west slope forests of the Oregon Cascades averaged 433 tons per acre. At the very top of the scale, the coastal redwood forests have been as high as 1,831 tons per acre (Waring and Franklin, 1979).

Forest ecologists and paleoecologists speculate on how such a massive forest came into existence. It seems the western forest of twenty or so million years ago was largely deciduous hardwoods—ash, maple, beech, oak, chestnut, elm, gingko—with conifers only at the highest elevations. Twelve to eighteen million years ago, the conifers began to occupy larger areas and then made continuous connection with each other along the uplands. By a million and a half years ago, in the early Pleistocene, the conifers had completely taken over and the forest was essentially as it is now. Forests of the type that had prevailed earlier, the hardwoods, survive today in the eastern United States and were also the original vegetation (before agriculture and early logging) of China and Japan. Visiting Great Smoky Mountains National Park today might give you an idea of what the mountain forests outside the old Chinese capital of Xian, known earlier as Ch'ang-an, looked like in the ninth century.

In the other temperate-zone forests of the world, conifers are a secondary and occasional presence. The success of the West Coast conifers can be attributed, it seems, to a combination of conditions: relatively cool and quite dry summers (which do not serve deciduous trees so well) combined with mild wet winters (during which the conifers continue to photosynthesize) and an almost total absence of typhoons. The enormous size of the trunks helps to store moisture and nutrients against drought years. The forests are steady-growing and productive (from a timber standpoint) while young, and these particular species keep growing and accumulating biomass long after most other temperate-zone trees have reached equilibrium.

Here we find the northern flying squirrel (which lives on truffles) and its sacred enemy the spotted owl. The Douglas squirrel (or chickaree) lives here, as does its sacred enemy the treetop-dashing pine marten that can run a squirrel down. Black bear seeks the grubs in long-dead logs in her steady ambling search. These and hosts of others occupy the deep shady stable halls—less wind, less swing of temperature, steady moisture—of the huge tree groves. There are treetop-dwelling red-backed voles who have been two hundred feet high in the canopy for hundreds of generations, some of whom have never descended to the ground (Maser, 1989). In a way the web that holds it all together is the mycelia, the fungus-threads that mediate between root-tips of plants and chemistry of soils, bringing nutrients in. This association is as old as plants with roots. The whole of the forest is supported by this buried network.

The forests of the maritime Pacific Northwest are the last remaining forests of any size left in the temperate zone. Plato's *Critias* passage (¶111) says: "In the primitive state of the country [Attica] its mountains were high hills covered with soil . . . and there was abundance of wood in the mountains. Of this last the traces still remain, for although some of the mountains now only afford sustenance to bees, not so very long ago there were still to be seen roofs of timber cut from trees growing there . . . and there were many other high trees. . . . Moreover the land reaped the benefit of the annual rainfall, not as now losing the water which flows off the bare earth into the sea." The cautionary history of the Mediterranean forests is well known. Much of this destruction has taken place in recent centuries, but it was already well under way, especially in the lowlands, during the classical period. In neolithic times the whole basin had perhaps 500 million acres of forest. The higher-elevation forests are all that survive, and even they occupy only 30 percent of the mountain zone—about 45 million acres. Some 100 million acres of land once densely covered with pine, oak, ash, laurel, and myrtle now have only traces of vegetation. There is a more sophisticated vocabulary in the Mediterranean for postforest or nonforest plant communities than we have in California (where everything scrubby is called chaparral). *Maquis* is the term for oak, olive, myrtle, and juniper scrub. An assembly of low waxy drought-resistant shrubs is called *garrigue*. *Batha* is open bare rock and eroding ground with scattered low shrubs and annuals.

People who live there today do not even know that their gray rocky hills were once rich in groves and wildlife. The intensified destruction was a function of the *type* of agriculture. The small self-sufficient peasant farms and their commons began to be replaced by the huge slave-run *latifundia* estates owned in absentia and planned according to central markets. What wildlife was left in the commons might then be hunted out by the new owners, the forest sold for cash, and field crops extended for what they were worth. "The cities of the Mediterranean littoral became deeply involved in an intensive region-wide trade, with cheap manufactured products, intensified markers and factory-like industrial production. . . . These developments in planned colonization, economic planning, world currencies and media for exchange had drastic consequences for the natural vegetation from Spain through to India" (Thirgood, 1981, 29).

China's lowland hardwood forests gradually disappeared as agriculture spread and were mostly gone by about thirty-five hundred years ago. (The Chinese philosopher Meng-zi commented on the risks of clearcutting in the fourth century B.C.) The composition of the Japanese forest has been altered by centuries of continuous logging. The Japanese sawmills are now geared down to about eight-inch logs. The original deciduous hardwoods are found only in the most remote mountains. The prized aromatic hinoki (the Japanese chamaecypress), which is essential to shrine and temple buildings, is now so rare that logs large enough for renovating traditional structures must be imported from the West Coast. Here it is known as Port Orford cedar, found only in southern Oregon and in the Siskiyou Mountains of northern California. It was used for years to make arrow shafts. Now Americans cannot afford it. No other softwood on earth commands such prices as the Japanese buyers are willing to pay for this species.

Commercial West Coast logging started around the 1870s. For decades it was all below the four-thousand-foot level. That was the era of the two-man saw, the double-bitted axe-cut undercuts, springboards, the kerosene bottle with a hook wired onto it stuck in the bark. Gypo handloggers felled into the saltwater bays of Puget Sound and rafted their logs to the mills. Then came steam donkey-engine yarders and ox teams, dragging the huge logs down corduroy skidroads or using immense wooden logging wheels that held the butt end aloft as the tail of the log dragged.

The ox teams were replaced by narrow-gauge trains, and the steam donkeys by diesel. The lower elevations of the West Coast were effectively totally clearcut.

Chris Maser (1989, xviii) says: "Every increase in the technology of logging and the utilization of wood fiber has expedited the exploitation of forests; thus from 1935 through 1980 the annual volume of timber cut has increased geometrically by 4.7% per year. . . . By the 1970s, 65% of the timber cut occurred above 4,000 feet in elevation, and because the average tree harvested has become progressively younger and smaller, the increase in annual acreage cut has been five times greater than the increase in volume cut during the last 40 years."

During these years the trains were replaced by trucks, and the high-lead yarders in many cases were replaced by the more mobile crawler-tread tractors we call Cats. From the late forties on, the graceful, musical Royal Chinook two-man falling saws were hung up on the walls of the barns, and the gasoline chainsaw became the faller's tool of choice. By the end of World War II the big logging companies had (with a few notable exceptions) managed to overexploit and mismanage their own timberlands and so they now turned to the federal lands, the people's forests, hoping for a bailout. So much for the virtues of private forest landowners—their history is abysmal—but there are still ill-informed privatization romantics who argue that the public lands should be sold to the highest bidders.

> San Francisco 2 × 4s
>   were the woods around Seattle:
> Someone killed and someone built, a house,
>   a forest, wrecked or raised
> All America hung on a hook
>   & burned by men in their own praise.

Before World War II the U.S. Forest Service played the role of a true conservation agency and spoke against the earlier era of clearcutting. It usually required its contractors to do selective logging to high standards. The allowable cut was much smaller. It went from 3.5 billion board feet in 1950 to 13.5 billion feet in 1970. After 1961 the new Forest Service leadership cosied up to the industry, and the older conservation-oriented personnel were washed out in waves through the sixties and seventies. The USFS now hires mostly road-building engineers. Their silviculturists think of themselves as fiber-growing engineers, and some profess to see no difference between a monoculture plantation of even-age seedlings and a wild forest (or so said Tahoe National Forest silviculturist Phil Aune at a public hearing on the management plan in 1986). The public relations people still cycle the conservation rhetoric of the thirties, as though the Forest Service had never permitted a questionable clearcut or sold old-growth timber at a financial loss.

The legislative mandate of the Forest Service leaves no doubt about its responsibility to manage the forest lands *as forests,* which means that lumber is only one of the values to be considered. It is clear that the forests must be managed in a way that makes them permanently sustainable. But Congress, the Department of Agriculture, and business combine to find ways around these restraints. *Renewable* is confused with *sustainable* (just because certain organisms keep renewing themselves does not mean they will do so—especially if abused—forever), and *forever*—the length of time a forest should continue to flourish—is changed to mean "about a hundred and fifty years." Despite the overwhelming evidence of mismanagement that environmental groups have brought against the Forest Service bureaucracy, it arrogantly and stubbornly resists what has become a clear public call for change. So much for the icon of "management" with its uncritical acceptance of the economic speed-trip of modern times (generating faster and faster logging rotations in the woods) as against: slow cycles.

We ask for slower rotations, genuine streamside protection, fewer roads, no cuts on steep slopes, only occasional shelterwood cuts, and only the most prudent application of the appropriate smaller clearcut. We call for a return to selective logging, and to all-age trees, and to serious heart and mind for the protection of endangered species. (The spotted owl, the fisher, and the pine marten are only part of the picture.) There should be *absolutely no more logging* in the remaining ancient forests. In addition we need the establishment of habitat corridors to keep the old-growth stands from becoming impoverished biological islands.

Many of the people in the U.S. Forest Service would agree that such practices are essential to genuine sustainability. They are constrained by the tight net of exploitative policies forced on them by Congress and industry. With good practices North America could maintain a lumber industry and protect a halfway decent amount of wild forest for ten thousand years. That is about the same number of years as the age of the continuously settled village culture of the Wei River valley in China, a span of time that is not excessive for humans to consider and plan by. As it is, the United States is suffering a net loss of 900,000 acres of forest per year (*Newsweek,* 2 October 1989). Of that loss, an estimated 60,000 acres is ancient forest (Wilson, 1989, 112).

The deep woods turn, turn, and turn again. The ancient forests of the West are still around us. All the houses of San Francisco, Eureka, Corvallis, Portland, Seattle, Longview, are built with those old bodies: the 2 × 4s and siding are from the logging of the 1910s and 1920s. Strip the paint in an old San Francisco apartment and you find prime-quality coastal redwood panels. We live out our daily lives in the shelter of ancient trees. Our great-grandchildren will more likely have to live in the shelter of riverbed-aggregate. Then the forests of the past will be truly entirely gone.

Out in the forest it takes about the same number of years as the tree lived for a fallen tree to totally return to the soil. If societies could learn to live by such a pace there would be no shortages, no extinctions. There would be clear streams, and the salmon would always return to spawn.

> A virgin
> Forest
> Is ancient; many-
> Breasted,
> Stable; at
> Climax.

Excursus: Sailor Meadow, Sierra Nevada

We were walking in mid-October down to Sailor Meadow (about 5,800 feet), to see an old stand on a broad bench above the north fork of the American River in the northern Sierra Nevada. At first we descended a ridge-crest through chinquapin and manzanita, looking north to the wide dome of Snow Mountain and the cliffs above Royal Gorge. The faint trail leveled out and we left it to go to the stony hills at the north edge of the hanging basin. Sitting beneath a cedar growing at the top of the rocks we ate lunch.

Then we headed southwest over rolls of forested stony formations and eventually more gentle slopes into a world of greater and greater trees. For hours we were in the company of elders.

Sugar pines predominate. There are properly mature symmetrical trees a hundred and fifty feet high that hold themselves upright and keep their branches neatly arranged. But then *beyond* them, *above* them, loom the *ancient trees:* huge, loopy, trashy, and irregular. Their bark is redder and the plates more spread, they have fewer branches, and those surviving branches are great in girth and curve wildly. Each one is unique and goofy. Mature incense cedar. Some large red fir. An odd Douglas fir. A few great Jeffrey pine. (Some of the cedars have catface burn marks from some far-back fire at their bases—all on the northwest side. None of the other trees show these burn marks.)

And many snags, in all conditions: some just recently expired with red or brown dead needles still clinging, some deader yet with plates of bark hanging from the trunk (where bats nest), some pure white smooth dead ones with hardly any limbs left, but with an occasional neat woodpecker hole; and finally the ancient dead: all soft and rotten while yet standing.

Many have fallen. There are freshly fallen snags (which often take a few trees with them) and the older fallen snags. Firm down logs you must climb over, or sometimes you can walk their length, and logs that crumble as you climb them. Logs of still another age have gotten soft and begun to fade, leaving just the pitchy heartwood core and some pitchy rot-proof limbs as signs. And then there are some long subtle hummocks that are the last trace of an old gone log. The straight line of mushrooms sprouting along a smooth ground surface is the final sign, the last ghost, of a tree that "died" centuries ago.

A carpet of young trees coming in—from six inches tall to twenty feet, all sizes—waiting down here on the forest floor for the big snags standing up there dead to keel over and make more canopy space. Sunny, breezy, warm, open, light—but the great trees are all around us. Their trunks fill the sky and reflect a warm golden light. The whole canopy has that sinewy look of ancient trees. Their needles are distinctive tiny patterns against the sky—the red fir most strict and fine.

The forests of the Sierra Nevada, like those farther up the West Coast, date from that time when the earlier deciduous hardwood forests were beginning to fade away before the spreading success of the conifers. It is a million years of "family" here, too, the particular composition of local forest falling and rising in elevation with the ice age temperature fluctuations, advancing or retreating from north and south slope positions, but keeping the several plant communities together even as the boundaries of their zones flowed uphill or down through the centuries. Absorbing fire, adapting to the summer drought, flowing through the beetle-kill years; always a web reweaving. Acorns feeding deer, manzanita feeding robins and raccoons, madrone feeding band-tailed pigeon, porcupine gnawing young cedar bark, bucks thrashing their antlers in the willows.

The middle-elevation Sierra forest is composed of sugar pine, ponderosa pine, incense cedar, Douglas fir, and at slightly higher elevations Jeffrey pine, white fir, and red fir. All of these trees are long-lived. The sugar pine and ponderosa are the largest of all pines. Black oak, live oak, tanbark oak, and madrone are the common hardwoods.

The Sierra forest is sunny-shady and dry for fully half the year. The loose litter, the crackliness, the dustiness of the duff, the curl of crisp madrone leaves on the ground, the little coins of fallen manzanita leaves.

The pine-needle floor is crunchy, the air is slightly resinous and aromatic, there is a delicate brushing of spiderwebs everywhere. Summer forest: intense play of sun and the vegetation in still steady presence—not giving up water, not wilting, not stressing, just quietly holding. Shrubs with small, aromatic, waxy, tough leaves. The shrub color is often blue-gray.

The forest was fire-adapted over the millennia and is extremely resistant to wildfire once the larger underbrush has burnt or died away. The early emigrants described driving their wagons through parklike forests of great trees as they descended the west slope of the range. The early logging was followed by devastating fires. Then came the suppression of fires by the forest agencies, and that led to the brushy understory that is so common to the Sierra now. The Sailor Meadow forest is a spacious, open, fireproof forest from the past.

At the south end of the small meadow the area is named for, beyond a thicket of aspen, standing within a grove of flourishing fir, is a remarkably advanced snag. It once was a pine over two hundred feet tall. Now around the base all the sapwood has peeled away, and what's holding the bulky trunk up is a thin column of heartwood, which is itself all punky, shedding, and frazzled. The great rotten thing has a lean as well! Any moment it might go.

How curious it would be to die and then remain standing for another century or two. To enjoy "dead verticality." If humans could do it we would hear news like, "Henry David Thoreau finally toppled over." The human community, when healthy, is like an ancient forest. The little ones are in the shade and shelter of the big ones, even rooted in their lost old bodies. All ages, and all together growing and dying. What some silviculturists call for—"even-age management," plantations of trees the same size growing up together—seems like rationalistic utopian totalitarianism. We wouldn't think of letting our children live in regimented institutions with no parental visits and all their thinking shaped by a corps of professionals who just follow official manuals (written by people who never raised kids). Why should we do it to our forests?

"All-age unmanaged"—that's a natural community, human or other. The industry prizes the younger and middle-aged trees that keep their symmetry, keep their branches even of length and angle. But let there also be really old trees who can give up all sense of propriety and begin throwing their limbs out in extravagant gestures, dancelike poses, displaying their insouciance in the face of mortality, holding themselves available to whatever the world and the weather might propose. I look up to them: they are like the Chinese Immortals, they are Han-shan and Shi-de sorts of characters—to have lived that long is to have permission to be eccentric, to be the poets and painters among trees, laughing, ragged, and fearless. They make me almost look forward to old age.

In the fir grove we can smell mushrooms, and then we spot them along the base of rotten logs. A cluster of elegant polypores, a cortinarius, and in the open, pushing up dry needles from below, lots of russula and boletus. Some scooped-out hollows where the deer have dug them out. Deer love mushrooms.

We tried to go straight across the southern end of the meadow but it was squishy wet beneath the dry-looking collapsed dead plants and grasses, so we went all the way around the south end through more aspen and found (and saved) more mushrooms. Clouds started blowing in from the south and the breeze filled the sky with dry pine needles raining down. It was late afternoon, so we angled up steep slopes cross-country following deer-paths for an hour and found the overgrown trail to an abandoned mine, and it led us back to the truck.

Us Yokels

This little account of the great forests of the West Coast can be taken as a model of what has been happening elsewhere on the planet. All the natural communities of the world have been, in their own way, "ancient" and every natural community, like a family, includes the infants, the adolescents, the mature adults, the elders. From the corner of the forest that has had a recent burn, with its fireweed and blackberries, to the elder moist dark groves—this is the range of the integrity of the whole. The old stands of hoary trees (or half-rotten saguaro in the Sonoran Desert or thick-boled well-established old manzanita in the Sierra foothills) are the grandparents and information-holders of their communities. A community needs its elders to continue. Just as you could not grow culture out of a population of kindergarten children, a forest cannot realize its own natural potential without the seed-reservoirs, root-fungus threads, birdcalls, and magical deposits of tiny feces that are the gift from the old to the young. Chris Maser says, "We need ancient forests for the survival of ancient forests."

When the moldboard plows of the early midwestern farmers "cut the grass roots—a sound that reminded one of a zipper being opened or closed—a new way of life opened, which simultaneously closed, probably forever, a long line of ecosystems stretching back thirty million years" (Jackson, 1987, 78). But the oldest continuous ecosystems on earth are the moist tropical forests, which in Southeast Asia are estimated to date back one hundred million years.

Thin arching buttressing boles of the white-barked tall
straight trees, Staghorn ferns leaning out from the limbs
and the crotches up high. Trees they call brushbox,
coachwood, crabapple, Australian red cedar (names
brought from Europe)—and Red carrabeen, Yellow
carrabeen, Stinging-trees, Deep blue openings leaning
onward.

Light of green arch of leaves far above
Drinking the water that flows through the roots
Of the forest, Terania creek, flowing out of Pangaia,
Down from Gondwanaland,
Stony soil, sky bottom shade

Long ago stone deep
Roots from the sky
Clear water down through the roots
Of the trees that reach high in the shade
Birdcalls bring us awake
Whiplash birdcalls laugh us awake—

Booyong, Carrabeen, Brushbox, Black butt, Wait-a-while
(Eucalypts dry land thin soil succeeders
Searching scrabbly ground for seventy million years—)

> But these older tribes of trees
> Travel always as a group.
> Looking out from the cliffs
> On the ridge above treetops,
> Sitting up in the dust ledge shelter
> Where we lived all those lives.

Queensland, 1981

A multitude of corporations are involved in the deforestation of the tropics. Some got their start logging in Michigan or the Pacific Northwest—
Georgia Pacific and Scott Paper are now in the Philippines, Southeast
Asia, or Latin America with the same bright-colored crawler tractors and
the buzzing yellow chainsaws. In the summer of 1987 in Brazil's western
territory of Rondonia—as part of the chaotic "conversion" of Amazonia to
other uses—an area of forest the size of Oregon was in flames. One sometimes hears the innocent opinion that everyone is a city-dweller now.
That time may be coming, but at the moment the largest single population in the world is people of several shades of color farming in the
warmer zones. Until recently a large part of that realm was in trees, and

the deep-forest dwelling cultures had diverse and successful ways to live there. In those times of smaller population, the long-rotation slash-and-burn style of farming mixed with foraging posed no ecological threat. Today a combination of large-scale logging, agribusiness development, and massive dam projects threatens every corner of the backcountry.

In Brazil there is a complex set of adversaries. On one side the national government with its plans for development is allied with multinationals, wealthy cattle interests, and impoverished mainstream peasants. On the other side, resisting deforestation, are the public and private foresters and scientists making cause with the small local lumber firms, the established jungle-edge peasants, environmental organizations, and the forest-dwelling tribes. The Third World governments usually deny "native title" and the validity of communal forest ownership histories, such as the *adat* system of the Penan of Sarawak, a sophisticated multidimensional type of commons. The Penan people must put their bodies in the road to protest logging trucks *in their own homeland* and then go to jail as criminals.

Third World policies in regard to wilderness all too often run a direction set by India in 1938 when it opened the tribal forest lands of Assam to outside settlement saying "indigenous people alone would be unable, without the aid of immigrant settlers, to develop the province's enormous wasteland resources within a reasonable period" (Richards and Tucker, 1988, 107). All too many people in power in the governments and universities of the world seem to carry a prejudice against the natural world— and also against the past, against history. It seems Americans would live by a Chamber-of-Commerce Creationism that declares itself satisfied with a divinely presented Shopping Mall. The integrity and character of our own ancestors is dismissed with "I couldn't live like that" by people who barely know how to live *at all.* An ancient forest is seen as a kind of over-ripe garbage, not unlike the embarrassing elderly.

Forestry. "How
Many people
Were harvested
In Viet-nam?"

Clear-cut. "Some
Were children,
Some were over-ripe."

The societies that live by the old ways (Snyder, 1977) had some remarkable skills. For those who live by foraging—the original forest botanists and zoologists—the jungle is a rich supply of fibers, poisons, medicines, intoxicants, detoxicants, containers, water-proofing, food, dyes, glues, incense, amusement, companionship, inspiration, and also stings, blows, and bites. These primary societies are like the ancient forests of our human history, with similar depths and diversities (and simultaneously "ancient" and "virgin"). The *lore* of wild nature is being lost along with the inhabitory human cultures. Each has its own humus of custom, myth, and lore that is now being swiftly lost—a tragedy for us all.

Brazil provides incentives for this kind of destructive development. Even as some mitigations are promised, there are policies in place that actively favor large corporations, displace natives, and at the same time do nothing for the mainstream poor. America disempowers Third World farmers by subsidizing overproduction at home. Capitalism plus big government often looks like welfare for the rich, providing breaks to companies that clearcut timber at a financial loss to the public. The largest single importer of tropical hardwoods is Japan (Mazda, Mitsubishi) and the second largest is the USA.

We must hammer on the capitalist economies to be at least capitalist enough to see to it that the corporations that buy timber off our public lands pay a fair market price for it. We must make the hard-boiled point that the world's trees are virtually worth more standing than they would be as lumber, because of such diverse results of deforestation as life-destroying flooding in Bangladesh and Thailand, the extinction of millions of species of animals and plants, and global warming. And, finally, we are not speaking only of forest-dwelling cultures or endangered species like voles or lemurs when we talk of ecological integrity and sustainability. We are looking at the future of our contemporary urban-industrial society as well. Not so long ago the forests were our depth, a sun-dappled underworld, an inexhaustible timeless source. Now they are vanishing. We are all endangered yokels. (*Yokel:* some English dialect, originally meaning "a green woodpecker or yellowhammer.")

Grace

There is a verse chanted by Zen Buddhists called the "Four Great Vows." The first line goes: "Sentient beings are numberless, I vow to save them." *Shujōmuhen seigando.* It's a bit daunting to announce this intention—aloud—to the universe daily. This vow stalked me for several years and finally pounced: I realized that I had vowed to let the sentient beings save *me.* In a similar way, the precept against taking life, against causing harm, doesn't stop in the negative. It is urging us to *give* life, to *undo* harm.

Those who attain some ultimate understanding of these things are called "buddhas," which means "awakened ones." The word is connected to the English verb "to bud." I once wrote a little parable:

Who the Buddhas Are
All the beings of the universe are already realized. That is, with the exception of one or two beings. In those rare cases the cities, villages, meadows, and forests, with all their birds, flowers, animals, rivers, trees, and humans, that surround such a person, all collaborate to educate, serve, challenge, and instruct such a one, until that person also becomes a New Beginner Enlightened Being. Recently realized beings are enthusiastic to teach and train and start schools and practices. Being able to do this develops their confidence and insight up to the point that they are fully ready to join the seamless world of interdependent play. Such new enlightened beginners are called "Buddhas" and they like to say things like "I am enlightened together with the whole universe" and so forth.

Boat in a Storm, 1987

Good luck! One might say. The test of the pudding is in the *eating.* It narrows down to a look at the conduct that is entwined with food. At mealtime (seated on the floor in lines) the Zen monks chant:

235

Porridge is effective in ten ways
To aid the student of Zen
No limit to the good result
Consummating eternal happiness

and

Oh, all you demons and spirits
We now offer this food to you
May all of you everywhere
Share it with us together

and

We wash our bowls in this water
It has the flavor of ambrosial dew
We offer it to all demons and spirits
May all be filled and satisfied
Om makula sai svaha

And several other verses. These superstitious-sounding old ritual formulas are never mentioned in lectures, but they are at the heart of the teaching. Their import is older than Buddhism or any of the world religions. They are part of the first and last practice of the wild: *Grace.*

Everyone who ever lived took the lives of other animals, pulled plants, plucked fruit, and ate. Primary people have had their own ways of trying to understand the precept of nonharming. They knew that taking life required gratitude and care. There is no death that is not somebody's food, no life that is not somebody's death. Some would take this as a sign that the universe is fundamentally flawed. This leads to a disgust with self, with humanity, and with nature. Otherworldly philosophies end up doing more damage to the planet (and human psyches) than the pain and suffering that is in the existential conditions they seek to transcend.

The archaic religion is to kill god and eat him. Or her. The shimmering food-chain, the food-web, is the scary, beautiful condition of the biosphere. Subsistence people live without excuses. The blood is on your own hands as you divide the liver from the gallbladder. You have watched the color fade on the glimmer of the trout. A subsistence economy is a sacramental economy because it has faced up to one of the critical problems of life and death: the taking of life for food. Contemporary people do not need to hunt, many cannot even afford meat, and in the developed world the variety of foods available to us makes the avoidance of meat an easy choice. Forests in the tropics are cut to make pasture to raise beef for the American market. Our distance from the source of our food enables us to be superficially more comfortable, and distinctly more ignorant.

Eating is a sacrament. The grace we say clears our hearts and guides the children and welcomes the guest, all at the same time. We look at eggs, apples, and stew. They are evidence of plenitude, excess, a great reproductive exuberance. Millions of grains of grass-seed that will become rice or flour, millions of codfish fry that will never, and *must* never, grow to maturity. Innumerable little seeds are sacrifices to the food-chain. A parsnip in the ground is a marvel of living chemistry, making sugars and flavors from earth, air, water. And if we do eat meat it is the life, the bounce, the swish, of a great alert being with keen ears and lovely eyes, with foursquare feet and a huge beating heart that we eat, let us not deceive ourselves.

We too will be offerings—we are all edible. And if we are not devoured quickly, we are big enough (like the old down trees) to provide a long slow meal to the smaller critters. Whale carcasses that sink several miles deep in the ocean feed organisms in the dark for fifteen years. (It seems to take about two thousand to exhaust the nutrients in a high civilization.)

At our house we say a Buddhist grace—

We venerate the Three Treasures [teachers, the wild, and friends]
And are thankful for this meal
The work of many people
And the sharing of other forms of life.

Anyone can use a grace from their own tradition (and really give it meaning)—or make up their own. Saying some sort of grace is never inappropriate, and speeches and announcements can be tacked onto it. It is a plain, ordinary, old-fashioned little thing to do that connects us with all our ancestors.

A monk asked Dong-shan: "Is there a practice for people to follow?"
Dong-shan answered: "When you become a real person, there is such a practice."

Sarvamangalam, Good Luck to All.

A Place in Space

Smokey the Bear Sutra

Once in the Jurassic, about 150 million years ago, the Great Sun Buddha in this corner of the Infinite Void gave a great Discourse to all the assembled elements and energies: to the standing beings, the walking beings, the flying beings, and the sitting beings—even the grasses, to the number of thirteen billion, each one born from a seed—assembled there: a Discourse concerning Enlightenment on the planet Earth.

"In some future time, there will be a continent called America. It will have great centers of power such as Pyramid Lake, Walden Pond, Mount Rainier, Big Sur, the Everglades, and so forth, and powerful nerves and channels such as the Columbia River, Mississippi River, and Grand Canyon. The human race in that era will get into troubles all over its head and practically wreck everything in spite of its own strong intelligent Buddha-nature.

"The twisting strata of the great mountains and the pulsings of great volcanoes are my love burning deep in the earth. My obstinate compassion is schist and basalt and granite, to be mountains, to bring down the rain. In that future American Era I shall enter a new form, to cure the world of loveless knowledge that seeks with blind hunger, and mindless rage eating food that will not fill it."

And he showed himself in his true form of

SMOKEY THE BEAR.

A handsome smokey-colored brown bear standing on his hind legs, showing that he is aroused and watchful.

Bearing in his right paw the Shovel that digs to the truth beneath appearances, cuts the roots of useless attachments, and flings damp sand on the fires of greed and war;

His left paw in the Mudra of Comradely Display—indicating that all creatures have the full right to live to their limits and that deer, rabbits, chipmunks, snakes, dandelions, and lizards all grow in the realm of the Dharma;

Wearing the blue work overalls symbolic of slaves and laborers, the countless people oppressed by a civilization that claims to save but only destroys;

Wearing the broad-brimmed hat of the West, symbolic of the forces that guard the Wilderness, which is the Natural State of the Dharma and the True Path of beings on earth—all true paths lead through mountains—

With a halo of smoke and flame behind, the forest fires of the kali yuga, fires caused by the stupidity of those who think things can be gained and lost whereas in truth all is contained vast and free in the Blue Sky and Green Earth of One Mind;

Round-bellied to show his kind nature and that the great Earth has food enough for everyone who loves her and trusts her;

Trampling underfoot wasteful freeways and needless suburbs; smashing the worms of capitalism and totalitarianism;

Indicating the Task: his followers, becoming free of cars, houses, canned food, universities, and shoes, master the Three Mysteries of their own Body, Speech, and Mind, and fearlessly chop down the rotten trees and prune out the sick limbs of this country America and then burn the left-over trash.

Wrathful but Calm, Austere but Comic, Smokey the Bear will illuminate those who would help him; but for those who would hinder or slander him,

HE WILL PUT THEM OUT.

Thus his great Mantra:

Namah samanta vajranam chanda maharoshana
Sphataya hum traka ham mam

"I DEDICATE MYSELF TO THE UNIVERSAL DIAMOND—
BE THIS RAGING FURY DESTROYED"

And he will protect those who love woods and rivers, Gods and animals, hoboes and madmen, prisoners and sick people, musicians, playful women, and hopeful children;

And if anyone is threatened by advertising, air pollution, or the police, they should chant SMOKEY THE BEAR'S WAR SPELL:

> DROWN THEIR BUTTS
> CRUSH THEIR BUTTS
> DROWN THEIR BUTTS
> CRUSH THEIR BUTTS

And SMOKEY THE BEAR will surely appear to put the enemy out with his vajra shovel.

> Now those who recite this Sutra and then try to put it
>   in practice will accumulate merit as countless as the
>   sands of Arizona and Nevada,
> Will help save the planet Earth from total oil slick,
> Will enter the age of harmony of humans and nature,
> Will win the tender love and caresses of men, women,
>   and beasts,
> Will always have ripe blackberries to eat and a sunny
>   spot under a pine tree to sit at,
>
> AND IN THE END WILL WIN HIGHEST PERFECT
> ENLIGHTENMENT.

> Thus have we heard.

(may be reproduced free forever)

Regarding "Smokey the Bear Sutra"

It's hard not to have a certain amount of devotional feeling for the Large Brown Ones, even if you don't know much about them. I met the Old Man in the Fur Coat a few times in the North Cascades—once in the central Sierra—and was suitably impressed. There are many stories told about humans marrying the Great Ones. I brought much of that lore together in my poem "this poem is for B__r," which is part of *Myths and Texts*. The Circumpolar B__r cult, we are told, is the surviving religious complex (stretching from Suomi to Utah via Siberia) of what may be the oldest religion on earth. Evidence in certain Austrian caves indicates that our Neanderthal ancestors were practicing a devotional ritual to the Big Fellow about seventy thousand years ago. In the light of meditation once it came to me that the Old One was no other than that Auspicious Being described in Buddhist texts as having taught in the unimaginably distant past, the one called "The Ancient Buddha."

So I came to realize that the U.S. Forest Service's "Smokey the B__r" publicity campaign was the inevitable resurfacing of our ancient benefactor as guide and teacher in the twentieth century, the agency not even knowing that it was serving as a vehicle for this magical reemergence.

During my years in Japan I had kept an eye out for traces of ancient B__r worship in folk religion and within Buddhism, and it came to me that Fudo Myo-ō, the patron of the Yamabushi (a Shinto-Buddhist society of mountain yogins), whose name means the "Immovable Wisdom King," was possibly one of those traces. I cannot provide an academic proof for this assertion; it's an intuition based on Fudo's usual habitat: deep mountains. Fudo statues and paintings portray a wickedly squinting fellow with one fang down and one fang up, a braid hanging down one side of the head, a funny gleam in his eye, wreathed in rags, holding a vajra sword and a lariat, standing on rough rock and surrounded by flames. The statues are found by waterfalls and deep in the wildest mountains of Japan. He also lurks in caves. Like the Ainu's Kamui Kimun, Lord of the Inner Mountains—clearly a B__r deity—Fudo has surpassing power, the capacity to quell all lesser violence. In the iconography he is seen as an aspect of Avalokiteãvara, the Bodhisattva of Compassion, or the consort of the beautiful Bodhisattva Tārā, She Who Saves.

It might take this sort of Buddha to quell the fires of greed and war and to help us head off the biological holocaust that the twenty-first century may well prove to be. I had such thoughts in mind when I returned to Turtle Island (North America) in December of 1968 from a long stay in Japan. A copy of the *San Francisco Chronicle* announced the Sierra Club Wilderness conference of February 1969; it was to be the following day. I saw my chance, sat down, and the sutra seemed to write itself. It follows the structure of a Mahayana Buddhist sutra fairly faithfully. The power mantra of the Great Brown One is indeed the mantra of Fudo the Immovable.

I got it printed overnight. The next morning I stood in the lobby of the conference hotel in my old campaign hat and handed out the broadsides, saying, "Smokey the B__r literature, sir." Bureau of Land Management and Forest Service officials politely took them. Forest beatniks and conservation fanatics read them with mad glints and giggles. The Underground News Service took it up, and it went to the *Berkeley Barb* and then all over the country. *The New Yorker* queried me about it, and when I told them it was both free and anonymous, they said they couldn't publish it. It soon had a life of its own, as intended.

{*This commentary was written to accompany the sutra's inclusion in the anthology* Working the Woods, Working the Sea, *edited by Finn Wilcox and Jeremiah Gorsline (Port Townsend, Wash.: Empty Bowl Press, 1986).*}

Four Changes, with a Postscript

I. Population

The Condition

POSITION: Human beings are but a part of the fabric of life—dependent on the whole fabric for their very existence. As the most highly developed tool-using animal, we must recognize that the unknown evolutionary destinies of other life forms are to be respected, and we must act as gentle steward of the earth's community of being.

SITUATION: There are now too many human beings, and the problem is growing rapidly worse. It is potentially disastrous not only for the human race but for most other life forms.

GOAL: The goal should be half of the present world population or less.

Action

SOCIAL / POLITICAL: First, a massive effort to convince the governments and leaders of the world that the problem is severe. And that all talk about raising food production—well intentioned as it is—simply puts off the only real solution: reduce population. Demand immediate participation by all countries in programs to legalize abortion, encourage vasectomy and sterilization (provided by free clinics); try to correct traditional cultural attitudes that tend to force women into childbearing; remove income-tax deductions for more than two children above a specified income level, and scale it so that lower-income families are forced to be careful, too, or pay families to limit their number. Take a vigorous stand against the policy of the right wing in the Catholic hierarchy and any other institutions that exercise an irresponsible social force in regard to this question; oppose and correct simpleminded boosterism that equates population growth with continuing prosperity. Work ceaselessly to have all political questions be seen in the light of this prime problem.

In many cases, the governments are the wrong agents to address. Their most likely use of a problem, or crisis, is as another excuse for extending their own powers. Abortion should be legal and voluntary. Great care should be taken that no one is ever tricked or forced into sterilization. The whole population issue is fraught with contradictions, but the fact stands that by standards of planetary biological welfare there are already too many human beings. The long-range answer is a steady low birthrate. Area by area of the globe, the measure of "optimum population" should be based on what is best for the total ecological health of the region, including its wildlife populations.

THE COMMUNITY: Explore other social structures and marriage forms, such as group marriage and polyandrous marriage, which provide family life but many less children. Share the pleasures of raising children widely, so that all need not directly reproduce in order to enter into this basic human experience. We must hope that no woman would give birth to more than one or two children during this period of crisis. Adopt children. Let reverence for life and reverence for the feminine mean also a reverence for other species and for future human lives, most of which are threatened.

OUR OWN HEADS: "I am a child of all life, and all living beings are my brothers and sisters, my children and grandchildren. And there is a child within me waiting to be born, the baby of a new and wiser self." Love, lovemaking, seen as the vehicle of mutual realization for a couple, where the creation of new selves and a new world of being is as important as reproducing our kind.

II. Pollution

The Condition

POSITION: Pollution is of two types. One sort results from an excess of some fairly ordinary substance—smoke, or solid waste—that cannot be absorbed or transmitted rapidly enough to offset its introduction into the environment, thus causing changes the great cycle is not prepared for. (All organisms have wastes and by-products, and these are indeed part of the total biosphere: energy is passed along the line and refracted in various ways. This is cycling, not pollution.) The other sort consists of powerful modern chemicals and poisons, products of recent technology that the biosphere is totally unprepared for. Such are DDT and similar chlorinated hydrocarbons; nuclear testing fallout and nuclear waste; poison gas, germ and virus storage and leakage by the military; and chemicals that are put into food, whose long-range effects on human beings have not been properly tested.

SITUATION: The human race in the last century has allowed its production and scattering of wastes, by-products, and various chemicals to become excessive. Pollution is directly harming life on the planet—which is to say, ruining the environment for humanity itself. We are fouling our air and water and living in noise and filth that no "animal" would tolerate, while advertising and politicians try to tell us we've never had it so good. The dependence of modern governments on this kind of untruth leads to shameful mind pollution, through the mass media and much school education.

GOAL: Clean air, clean clear-running rivers; the presence of pelican and osprey and gray whale in our lives; salmon and trout in our streams; unmuddied language and good dreams.

Action

SOCIAL/POLITICAL: Effective international legislation banning DDT and other poisons—with no fooling around. The collusion of certain scientists with the pesticide industry and agribusiness in trying to block this legislation must be brought out in the open. Strong penalties for water and air pollution by industries: Pollution is somebody's profit. Phase out the internal combustion engine and fossil fuel use in general; do more research into nonpolluting energy sources, such as solar energy, the tides. No more kidding the public about nuclear waste disposal: it's impossible to do it safely, so nuclear-generated electricity cannot be seriously planned for as it now stands. Stop all germ and chemical warfare research and experimentation; work toward a safe disposal of the present stupid and staggering stockpiles of H-bombs, cobalt gunk, germ and poison tanks and cans. Provide incentives against the wasteful use of paper and so on, which adds to the solid wastes of cities—develop methods of recycling solid urban wastes. Recycling should be the basic principle behind all waste-disposal thinking. Thus, all bottles should be reusable; old cans should make more cans; old newspapers should go back into newsprint again. Establish stronger controls and conduct more research on chemicals in foods. A shift toward a more varied and sensitive type of agriculture (more small-scale and subsistence farming) would eliminate much of the call for the blanket use of pesticides.

THE COMMUNITY: DDT and such: don't use them. Air pollution: use fewer cars. Cars pollute the air, and one or two people riding lonely in a huge car is an insult to intelligence and the earth. Share rides, legalize hitchhiking, and build hitchhiker waiting stations along the highways. Also—a step toward the new world—walk more; look for the best routes through beautiful countryside for long-distance walking trips: San Francisco to Los Angeles down the Coast Range, for example. Learn how to use your own manure as fertilizer if you're in the country, as people in the Far East have done for centuries. There's a way, and it's safe. Solid waste: boycott bulky wasteful Sunday papers, which use up trees. It's all just advertising anyway, which is artificially inducing more energy consumption. Refuse bags at the store and bring your own. Organize park and street cleanup festivals. Don't work in any way for or with an industry that pollutes, and don't be drafted into the military. Don't waste. (A monk and an old master were once walking in the mountains. They noticed a little hut upstream. The monk said, "A wise hermit must live there." The master said, "That's no wise hermit—you see that lettuce leaf floating down the stream? He's a Waster." Just then an old man came running down the hill with his beard flying and caught the floating lettuce leaf.) Carry your own jug to the winery and have it filled from the barrel.

OUR OWN HEADS: Part of the trouble with talking about something like DDT is that the use of it is not just a practical device, it's almost an establishment religion. There is something in Western culture that wants to wipe out creepy-crawlies totally and feels repugnance for toadstools and snakes. This is fear of one's own deepest inner-self wilderness areas, and the answer is to *relax*. Relax around bugs, snakes, and your own hairy dreams. Again, we all should share our crops with a certain percentage of bug life as a way of "paying our dues." Thoreau says, "How then can the harvest fail? Shall I not rejoice also at the abundance of the weeds whose seeds are the granary of the birds? It matters little comparatively whether the fields fill the farmer's barns. The true husbandman will cease from anxiety, as the squirrels manifest no concern whether the woods will bear chestnuts this year or not, and finish his labor with every day, relinquish all claim to the produce of his fields, and sacrificing in his mind not only his first but his last fruits also." In the realm of thought, inner experience, consciousness, as in the outward realm of interconnection, there is a difference between balanced cycle and the excess that cannot be handled. When the balance is right, the mind recycles from highest illuminations to the muddy blinding anger or grabbiness that sometimes seizes us all—the alchemical "transmutation."

III. Consumption

The Condition
POSITION: Everything that lives eats food and is food in turn. This complicated animal, the human being, rests on a vast and delicate pyramid of energy transformations. To grossly use more than you need, to destroy, is biologically unsound. Much of the production and consumption of mod-

ern societies is not necessary or conducive to spiritual and cultural growth, let alone survival, and is behind much greed and envy, age-old causes of social and international discord.

SITUATION: Humanity's careless use of "resources" and its total dependence on certain substances such as fossil fuels (which are being exhausted, slowly but certainly) are having harmful effects on all the other members of the life network. The complexity of modern technology renders whole populations vulnerable to the deadly consequences of the loss of any one key resource. Instead of independence we have over-dependence on life-giving substances such as water, which we squander. Many species of animals and birds have become extinct in the service of fashion fads, or fertilizer, or industrial oil. The soil is being used up; in fact, humanity has become a locustlike blight on the planet that will leave a bare cupboard for its own children—all the while living in a kind of addict's dream of affluence, comfort, eternal progress, using the great achievements of science to produce software and swill.

GOAL: Balance, harmony, humility, growth that is a mutual growth with redwood and quail; to be a good member of the great community of living creatures. True affluence is not needing anything.

Action

SOCIAL/POLITICAL: It must be demonstrated ceaselessly that a continually "growing economy" is no longer healthy, but a cancer. And that the criminal waste that is allowed in the name of competition—especially that ultimate in wasteful needless competition, hot wars and cold wars with "communism" (or "capitalism")—must be halted totally with ferocious energy and decision. Economics must be seen as a small subbranch of ecology, and production/distribution/consumption handled by companies or unions or cooperatives with the same elegance and spareness one sees in nature. Soil banks; open spaces; logging to be truly based on sustained yield (the U.S. Forest Service is—sadly—now the lackey of business). Protection for all scarce predators and varmints: "Support your right to arm bears." Damn the International Whaling Commission, which is selling out the last of our precious, wise whales; ban absolutely all further development of roads and concessions in national parks and wilderness areas; build auto campgrounds in the least desirable areas. Initiate consumer boycotts of dishonest and unnecessary products. Establish co-ops. Politically, blast both "communist" and "capitalist" myths of progress and all crude notions of conquering or controlling nature.

THE COMMUNITY: Sharing and creating. The inherent aptness of communal life, where large tools are owned jointly and used efficiently. The power of renunciation: if enough Americans refused to buy a new car for one given year, it would permanently alter the American economy. Recycling clothes and equipment. Support handicrafts, gardening, home skills, midwifery, herbs—all the things that can make us independent, beautiful, and whole. Learn to break the habit of acquiring unnecessary possessions—a monkey on everybody's back—but avoid a self-abnegating antijoyous self-righteousness. Simplicity is light, carefree, neat, and loving—not a self-punishing ascetic trip. (The great Chinese poet Tu Fu said, "The ideas of a poet should be noble and simple.") Don't shoot a deer if you don't know how to use all the meat and preserve what you can't eat, to tan the hide and use the leather—to use it all, with gratitude, right down to the sinew and hooves. Simplicity and mindfulness in diet are the starting point for many people.

OUR OWN HEADS: It is hard even to begin to gauge how much a complication of possessions, the notions of "my and mine," stand between us and a true, clear, liberated way of seeing the world. To live lightly on the earth, to be aware and alive, to be free of egotism, to be in contact with plants and animals, starts with simple concrete acts. The inner principle is the insight that we are interdependent energy fields of great potential wisdom and compassion, expressed in each person as a superb mind, a handsome and complex body, and the almost magical capacity of language. To these potentials and capacities, "owning things" can add nothing of authenticity. "Clad in the sky, with the earth for a pillow."

IV. Transformation

The Condition

POSITION: Everyone is the result of four forces: the conditions of this known universe (matter/energy forms and ceaseless change), the biology of one's species, individual genetic heritage, and the culture one is born into. Within this web of forces there are certain spaces and loops that allow to some persons the experience of inner freedom and illumination. The gradual exploration of some of these spaces constitutes "evolution" and, for human cultures, what "history" could increasingly be. We have it within our deepest powers not only to change our "selves" but to change our culture. If humans are to remain on earth, they must transform the five-millennia-long urbanizing civilization tradition into a new ecologically sensitive harmony-oriented wild-minded scientific-spiritual culture. "Wildness is the state of complete awareness. That's why we need it."

SITUATION: Civilization, which has made us so successful a species, has overshot itself and now threatens us with its inertia. There is also some evidence that civilized life isn't good for the human gene pool. To achieve the Changes, we must change the very foundations of our society and our minds.

GOAL: Nothing short of total transformation will do much good. What we envision is a planet on which the human population lives harmoniously and dynamically by employing various sophisticated and unobtrusive technologies in a world environment that is "left natural." Specific points in this vision:

- A healthy and spare population of all races, much less in number than today.
- Cultural and individual pluralism, unified by a type of world tribal council. Division by natural and cultural boundaries rather than arbitrary political boundaries.
- A technology of communication, education, and quiet transportation, land use being sensitive to the properties of each region. Allowing, thus, the bison to return to much of the High Plains. Careful but intensive agriculture in the great alluvial valleys; deserts left wild for those who would live there by skill. Computer technicians who run the plant part of the year and walk along with the elk in their migrations during the rest.
- A basic cultural outlook and social organization that inhibits power and property seeking while encouraging exploration and challenge in things like music, meditation, mathematics, mountaineering, magic, and all other ways of authentic being-in-the-world. Women totally free and equal. A new kind of family—responsible, but more festive and relaxed—is implicit.

Action

SOCIAL/POLITICAL: It seems evident that throughout the world there are certain social and religious forces that have worked through history toward an ecologically and culturally enlightened state of affairs. Let these be encouraged: Gnostics, hip Marxists, Teilhard de Chardin Catholics, Druids, taoists, Biologists, Witches, Yogins, Bhikkus, Quakers, Sufis, Tibetans, Zens, Shamans, Bushmen, American Indians, Polynesians, Anarchists, Alchemists—the list is long. Primitive cultures, communal and ashram movements, cooperative ventures. Since it doesn't seem practical or even desirable to think that direct bloody force will achieve much, it would be best to consider this change a continuing "revolution of consciousness," which will be won not by guns but by seizing the key images, myths, archetypes, eschatologies, and ecstasies so that life won't seem worth living unless one's on the side of the transforming energy. We must take over "science and technology" and release its real possibilities and powers in the service of this planet—which, after all, produced us and it.

(More concretely: no transformation without our feet on the ground.

Stewardship means, for most of us, find your place on the planet, dig in, and take responsibility from there—the tiresome but tangible work of school boards, county supervisors, local foresters, local politics, even while holding in mind the largest scale of potential change. Get a sense of workable territory, learn about it, and start acting point by point. On all levels, from national to local, the need to move toward steady state economy—equilibrium, dynamic balance, inner growth stressed—must be taught. Maturity/diversity/climax/creativity.)

THE COMMUNITY: New schools, new classes, walking in the woods and cleaning up the streets. Find psychological techniques for creating an awareness of "self" that includes the social and natural environment. Consideration of what specific language forms—symbolic systems—and social institutions constitute obstacles to ecological awareness. Without falling into a facile interpretation of McLuhan, we can hope to use the media. Let no one be ignorant of the facts of biology and related disciplines; bring up our children as part of the wildlife. Some communities can establish themselves in backwater rural areas and flourish, others can maintain themselves in urban centers, and the two types can work together—a two-way flow of experience, people, money, and homegrown vegetables. Ultimately cities may exist only as joyous tribal gatherings and fairs, to dissolve after a few weeks. Investigating new lifestyles is our work, as is the exploration of ways to explore our inner realms—with the known dangers of crashing that go with such. Master the archaic and the primitive as models of basic nature-related cultures—as well as the most imaginative extensions of science—and build a community where these two vectors cross.

OUR OWN HEADS: Are where it starts. Knowing that we are the first human beings in history to have so much of our past culture and previous experience available to our study, and being free enough of the weight of traditional cultures to seek out a larger identity; the first members of a civilized society since the Neolithic to wish to look clearly into the eyes of the wild and see our selfhood, our family, there. We have these advantages to set off the obvious disadvantages of being as screwed up as we are—which gives us a fair chance to penetrate some of the riddles of ourselves and the universe, and to go beyond the idea of "human survival" or "survival of the biosphere" and to draw our strength from the realization that at the heart of things is some kind of serene and ecstatic process that is beyond qualities and beyond birth and death. "No need to survive!" "In the fires that destroy the universe at the end of the kalpa, what survives?" "—The iron tree blooms in the void!"

Knowing that nothing need be done is the place from which we begin to move.

Postscript (1995)

Four Changes was written in 1969. Michael McClure, Richard Brautigan, Steve Beckwitt, Keith Lampe, Cliff Humphreys, Alan Watts, Allen Hoffman, Stewart Brand, and Diane di Prima were among those who read it during its formative period and offered suggestions and criticisms. It was widely distributed in several free editions. I added a few more lines and comments in 1974, when it was published together with the poems in *Turtle Island* (New York: New Directions, 1974). Now it's 1995, and a quarter century has elapsed. The apprehension we felt in 1969 has not abated. It would be a fine thing to be able to say, "We were wrong. The natural world is no longer as threatened as we said then." One can take no pleasure, in this case, in having been on the right track. Many of the larger mammals face extinction, and all manner of species are endangered. Natural habitat ("raw land") is fragmented and then destroyed ("developed"). The world's forests are being relentlessly logged by multinational corporations. Air, water, and soil are all in worse shape. Population continues to climb, and even if it were a world of perfect economic and social justice, I would argue that ecological justice calls for fewer people. The few remaining traditional people with place-based sustainable economies are driven into urban slums and cultural suicide. The quality of life for everyone everywhere has gone down, what with resurgent nationalism, racism, violence both random and organized, and increasing social and economic inequality. There are whole nations for whom daily life is an ongoing disaster. Naive and utopian as some of it sounds now, I still stand by the basics of "Four Changes." As I wrote in 1969,

> My Teacher once said to me,
> —become one with the knot itself,
> till it dissolves away.
> —sweep the garden.
> —any size.

"Energy Is Eternal Delight"

A young woman at Sir George Williams University in Montreal asked me, "What do you fear most?" I found myself answering "that the diversity and richness of the gene pool will be destroyed," and most people there understood what I meant.

The treasure of life is the richness of stored information in the diverse genes of all living beings. If the human race, following on some set of catastrophes, were to survive at the expense of many plant and animal species, it would be no victory. Diversity provides life with the capacity for a multitude of adaptations and responses to long-range changes on the planet. The possibility remains that at some future time another evolutionary line might carry the development of consciousness to clearer levels than our family of upright primates.

The United States, Europe, the Soviet Union, and Japan have a habit. They are addicted to heavy energy use, great gulps and injections of fossil fuel. As fossil fuel reserves go down, they will take dangerous gambles with the future health of the biosphere (through nuclear power) to keep up their habit.

For several centuries Western civilization has had a priapic drive for material accumulation, continual extensions of political and economic power, termed "progress." In the Judeo-Christian worldview humans are seen as working out their ultimate destinies (paradise? perdition?) with planet earth as the stage for the drama—trees and animals mere props, nature a vast supply depot. Fed by fossil fuel, this religio-economic view has become a cancer: uncontrollable growth. It may finally choke itself and drag much else down with it.

The longing for growth is not wrong. The nub of the problem now is how to flip over, as in jujitsu, the magnificent growth energy of modern civilization into a nonacquisitive search for deeper knowledge of self and nature. Self-nature. Mother Nature. If people come to realize that there are many nonmaterial, nondestructive paths of growth—of the highest and most fascinating order—it would help dampen the common fear that a steady state economy would mean deadly stagnation.

I spent a few years, some time back, in and around a training place. It was a school for monks of the Rinzai branch of Zen Buddhism, in Japan. The whole aim of the community was personal and universal liberation. In this quest for spiritual freedom every man marched strictly to the same drum in matters of hours of work and meditation. In the teacher's room one was pushed across sticky barriers into vast new spaces. The training was traditional and had been handed down for centuries—but the insights are forever fresh and new. The beauty, refinement, and truly civilized quality of that life has no match in modern America. It is supported by hand labor in small fields, gathering brushwood to heat the bath, drinking well water, and making barrels of homemade pickles.

The Buddhists teach respect for all life and for wild systems. A human being's life is totally dependent on an interpenetrating network of wild systems. Eugene Odum, in his useful paper "The Strategy of Ecosystem Development," points out how the United States has the characteristics of a young ecosystem. Some American Indian cultures have "mature" characteristics: protection as against production, stability as against growth, quality as against quantity. In Pueblo societies a kind of ultimate democracy is practiced. Plants and animals are also people and, through certain rituals and dances, are given a place and a voice in the political discussions of the humans. They are "represented." "Power to *all* the people" must be the slogan.

On Hopi and Navajo land, at Black Mesa, the industrial world is eating away at the earth in the form of strip-mining. This to provide electricity for Los Angeles. The defense of Black Mesa is being sustained by traditional Indians, young Indian militants, and longhairs. Black Mesa speaks to us through old stories. She is said to be sacred territory. To hear her voice is to give up the European word *America* and accept the new-old name for the continent, Turtle Island.

The return to marginal farmland on the part of some young people is not some nostalgic replay of the nineteenth century. Here is a generation of white people finally ready to learn from the Elders. How to live on the continent as though our children, and on down, for many ages, will still be here (not on the moon). Loving and protecting this soil, these trees, these wolves. Natives of Turtle Island.

A scaled-down, balanced technology is possible, if cut loose from the cancer of exploitation/heavy industry/perpetual growth. Those who have already sensed these necessities and have begun, whether in the country or the city, to "grow with less" are the only counterculture that counts. Electricity for Los Angeles is not exactly energy. As Blake said, "Energy is eternal delight."

{This was first published in the "Plain Talk" section of Turtle Island *(New York: New Directions, 1974).}*

Unnatural Writing

"Nature writing" has become a matter of increased literary interest in the last few years. The subject matter "nature," and the concern for it (and us humans in it), have come—it is gratifying to note—to engage artists and writers. This interest may be another strand of postmodernism, since the modernist avant-garde was strikingly urban-centered. Many would-be writers approach this territory in a mode of curiosity, respect, and concern, without necessarily seeking personal gain or literary reputation. They are doing it for love—and the eco-warrior's passion, not money. (There is still a wide range of views and notions about what nature writing ought to be. There is an older sort of nature writing that might be seen as largely essays and writing from a human perspective, middle-class, middlebrow Euro-American. It has a rhetoric of beauty, harmony, and sublimity. What makes us uncomfortable sometimes with John Muir's writing is an excess of this. He had contemporaries, now forgotten, who were far worse.)

Natural history writing is another branch. Semiscientific, objective, in the descriptive mode. Both these sorts are "naively realistic" in that they unquestioningly accept the front-mounted bifocal human eye, the poor human sense of smell, and other characteristics of our species, plus the assumption that the mind can, without much self-examination, directly and objectively "know" whatever it looks at. There has also always been a literature of heroic journals and adventure. And there is an old mix of science, nature appreciation, and conservation politics that has been a potent part of the evolution of the conservation movement in the United States. The best of this would be seen in the work of Rachel Carson and Aldo Leopold. All of these writings might be seen by some as mildly anthropocentric, but the work is worthy and good-hearted. We are in its debt.

Nature writing has been a class of literature held in less than full regard by the literary establishment, because it is focused on something other than the major subject matter of mainstream occidental writing, the moral quandaries, heroics, affairs of the heart, and soul searchings of highly gifted and often powerful people, usually male. Tales of the elites. In fact, up until a decade ago nature writing was relegated pretty much to a status like that of nineteenth-century women's writing—it was seen as a writing of sensibility and empathy and observation, but off to the side, not really serious, not important.

But if we look at the larger context of occidental history, educated elites, and literary culture, we see that the natural world is profoundly present in and an inescapable part of the great works of art. The human experience over the larger part of its history has been played out in intimate relationship to the natural world. This is too obvious even to say, yet it is often oddly forgotten. History, philosophy, and literature naturally foreground human affairs, social dynamics, dilemmas of faith, intellectual constructs. But a critical subtheme that runs through it all has to do with defining the human relationship to the rest of nature. In literature, nature not only provides the background, the scene, but also many of the characters. The "classical" world of myth is a world in which animal beings, supernatural figures, and humans are actors and interacters. Bears, bulls, and swans were not abstractions to the people of earlier times but real creatures in very real landscapes. The aurochs—the giant wild cow, *Bos primigenius,* who became Zeus to Europa—survived in pockets of the European forests until medieval times.

In *The Practice of the Wild,* I point out that through most of human history

> populations were relatively small and travel took place on foot, by horse, or by sail. Whether Greece, Germania, or Han China, there were always nearby areas of forest, and wild animals, migratory waterfowl, seas full of fish and whales, and these were part of the experience of every active person. Animals as characters in literature and as universal presences in the imagination and in the archetypes of religion are there because they were *there.* Ideas and images of wastelands, tempests, wildernesses, and mountains are born not of abstraction but of experience: cisalpine, hyperboreal, circumpolar, transpacific, or beyond the pale. [This is the world people lived in up until the late nineteenth century. Plentiful wildlife, open space, small human population, trails instead of roads—and human lives of individual responsibility and existential intensity. It is not "frontier" that we're considering, but the Holocene era, our *present* era, in all its glory of salmon, bear, elk, deer, and moose.] Where do the

sacred salmon of the Celts, the Bjorns and Brauns and Brun-(hilde)-s [bher = bear] of northern European literature, the dolphins of the Mediterranean, the Bear dances of Artemis, the Lion skin of Herakles come from but the wild systems the humans lived near?

> Those images that yet
> Fresh images beget
> That dolphin-torn, that gong-tormented sea.

Many figures in the literary field, the critical establishment, and the academy are not enthralled with the natural world, and indeed some positively doubt its worth when compared to human achievement. Take this quote from Howard Nemerov, a good poet and a decent man:

> Civilization, mirrored in language, is the garden where relations grow; outside the garden is the wild abyss.

The unexamined assumptions here are fascinating. They are, at worst, crystallizations of the erroneous views that enable the developed world to displace Third and Fourth World peoples and overexploit nature globally. Nemerov here proposes that language is somehow implicitly civilized or civilizing, that civilization is orderly, that intrahuman relations are the pinnacle of experience (as though all of us, and all life on the planet, were not interrelated), and that "wild" means "abyssal," disorderly, and chaotic.

First take language. Some theorists have latched onto "language" as that which somehow makes us different. They have the same enthusiasm for the "Logos" as the old Summer Institute of Linguistics had for Bible translation into unwritten languages. In fact, every recent writer who doesn't know what else to say about his or her work—when asked to give a sound bite—has declared, "Well, I'm just fascinated with language." The truth is language is part and parcel of consciousness, and we know virtually nothing about either one. Our study and respect should extend to them both.

On another tack, the European deconstructionists assume, because of their monotheistic background, that the Logos died along with God. Those who wish to decenter occidental metaphysics have begun to try to devalue both language and nature and declare them to be further tools of ruling-class mythology. In the past, the idea that the external world was our own invention came out of some variety of idealist thought. But *this* version leads to a weird philosophical position that, since the proponents are academic "meta-Marxists," might be called "materialist solipsism." But they are just talk.

There is some truly dangerous language in a term heard in some business and government circles: "sustainable development." Development is not compatible with sustainability and biodiversity. We must drop talking about development and concentrate on how to achieve a steady-state condition of real sustainability. Much of what passes for economic development is simply the further extension of the destabilizing, entropic, and disorderly functions of industrial civilization.

So I will argue that consciousness, mind, imagination, *and* language are fundamentally wild. "Wild" as in wild ecosystems—richly interconnected, interdependent, and incredibly complex. Diverse, ancient, and full of information. At root the real question is how we understand the concepts of order, freedom, and chaos. Is art an imposition of order on chaotic nature, or is art (also read "language") a matter of discovering the grain of things, of uncovering the measured chaos that structures the natural world? Observation, reflection, and practice show artistic process to be the latter.

Our school-in-the-mountains here at Squaw Valley is called "Art of the Wild." (I was wondering just what edible root might have been growing so profusely in this wet mountain bottomland to have caused it to be called "Squaw Valley." Any place with the word *squaw* in the name is usually where some early trappers saw numerous Native American women at work gathering wild food; here it might have been *Brodiaea* bulbs. This naming practice is as though some native women coming on a Euro-American farming community had called it White Boy Flats.)

The "art of the wild" is to see art in the context of the process of nature—nature *as* process rather than as product or commodity—because "wild" is a name for the way that phenomena continually actualize themselves. Seeing this also serves to acknowledge the autonomy and integrity of the nonhuman part of the world, an "Other" that we are barely beginning to be able to know. In disclosing, discovering, the wild world with our kind of writing, we may find ourselves breaking into unfamiliar territories that do not seem anything like what was called "nature writing" in the past. The work of the art of the wild can well be irreverent, inharmonious, ugly, frazzled, unpredictable, simple, and clear—or virtually inaccessible. Who will write of the odd barbed, hooked, bent, splayed, and crooked penises of nonhuman male creatures? Of sexism among spiders? Someone will yet come to write with the eye of an insect, write from the undersea world, and in other ways that step outside the human.

In *Practice* it says:

Life in the wild is not just eating berries in the sunlight. I like to imagine a "depth ecology" that would go to the dark side of nature— the ball of crunched bones in a scat, the feathers in the snow, the tales of insatiable appetite. Wild systems are in one elevated sense above criticism, but they can also be seen as irrational, moldy, cruel, parasitic. Jim Dodge told me how he had watched—with fascinated horror—orcas methodically batter a gray whale to death in the Chukchi Sea. Life is not just diurnal and a property of large interesting vertebrates, it is also nocturnal, anaerobic, cannibalistic, microscopic, digestive, fermentative: cooking away in the warm dark. Life is well maintained at a four mile ocean depth, is waiting and sustained on a frozen rock wall, and clinging and nourished in hundred-degree desert temperatures. And there is a world of nature on the decay side, a world of beings who do rot and decay in the shade. Human beings have made much of purity, and are repelled by blood, pollution, putrefaction. The other side of the "sacred" is the sight of your beloved in the underworld, dripping with maggots. Coyote, Orpheus, and Izanagi cannot help but look, and they lose her. Shame, grief, embarrassment, and fear are the anaerobic fuels of the dark imagination. The less familiar energies of the wild world, and their analogs in the imagination, have given us ecologies of the imagination. . . .

Narratives are one sort of trace that we leave in the world. All our literatures are leavings, of the same order as the myths of wilderness peoples who leave behind only stories and a few stone tools. Other orders of beings have their own literatures. Narrative in the deer world is a track of scents that is passed on from deer to deer, with an art of interpretation which is instinctive. A literature of bloodstains, a bit of piss, a whiff of estrus, a hit of rut, a scrape on a sapling, and long gone. And there might be a "narrative theory" among these other beings—they might ruminate on "intersexuality," or "decomposition criticism."

I propose this to turn us loose to think about "wild writing" without preconception or inhibition, but at the same time with craft. The craft could be seen as the swoop of a hawk, the intricate galleries of burrowing and tunneling under the bark done by western pine bark beetles, the lurking at the bottom by a big old trout—or the kamikaze sting of a yellow jacket, the insouciant waddle of a porcupine, the constant steadiness of a flow of water over a boulder, the chatter of a squirrel, hyenas moaning and excavating the bowels of a dead giraffe under a serene moon. Images of our art. Nature's writing has the potential of becoming the most vital, radical, fluid, transgressive, pansexual, subductive, and morally challenging kind of writing on the scene. In becoming so, it may serve to help halt one of the most terrible things of our time—the destruction of species and their habitats, the elimination of some living beings forever.

Finally, let us not get drawn too far into dichotomous views and arguments about civilization versus nature, the domesticated versus the wild, the garden versus the wild abyss. Creativity draws on wildness, and wildness confers freedom, which is (at bottom) the ability to live in the real physical daily world at each moment, totally and completely.

Some Points for a "New Nature Poetics"

- That it be literate—that is, nature literate. Know who's who and what's what in the ecosystem, even if this aspect is barely visible in the writing.
- That it be grounded in a place—thus, place literate: informed about local specifics on both ecological-biotic and sociopolitical levels. And informed about history (social history and environmental history), even if this is not obvious in the poem.
- That it use Coyote as a totem—the trickster, always open, shape shifting, providing the eye of other beings going in and out of death, laughing with the dark side.
- That it use Bear as a totem—omnivorous, fearless, without anxiety, steady, generous, contemplative, and relentlessly protective of the wild.
- That it find further totems—this is the world of nature, myth, archetype, and ecosystem that we must each investigate. "Depth ecology."
- That it fear not science. Go *beyond* nature literacy into the emergent new territories in science: landscape ecology, conservation biology, charming chaos, complicated systems theory.
- That it go further with science—into awareness of the problematic and contingent aspects of so-called objectivity.
- That it study mind and language—language as wild system, mind as wild habitat, world as a "making" (poem), poem as a creature of the wild mind.
- That it be crafty and get the work *done*.

{The original version of this essay was given as a talk the first year of the "Art of the Wild" nature-writing conference series, held at Squaw ("Brodiaea Harvesters") Valley in July 1992.}

The Porous World

Crawling

I was forging along the crest of a ridge, finding a way between stocky deep red mature manzanita trunks, picking the route and heading briskly on. Crawling.

Not hiking or sauntering or strolling, but *crawling,* steady and determined, through the woods. We usually visualize an excursion into the wild as an exercise of walking upright. We imagine ourselves striding through open alpine terrain—or across the sublime space of a sagebrush basin—or through the somber understory of an ancient sugar-pine grove.

But it's not so easy to walk upright through the late-twentieth-century midelevation Sierra forests. There are always many sectors regenerating from fire or logging, and the fire history of the Sierra would indicate that there have always been some areas of manzanita fields. So people tend to stay on the old logging roads or the trails, and this is their way of experiencing the forest. Manzanita and ceanothus fields, or the brushy ground cover and understory parts of the forest, are left in wild peace.

This crawl was in late December, and although the sky was clear and sunny, the temperature was around freezing. Patches of remnant snow were on the ground. A few of us were out chasing corners and boundary lines on the Bear Tree parcel (number 6) of the 'Inimim Community Forest with a retiring Bureau of Land Management forester, a man who had worked with that land many years before and still remembered the surveys. No way to travel off the trail but to dive in: down on your hands and knees on the crunchy manzanita leaf cover and crawl around between the trunks. Leather work gloves, a tight-fitting hat, long-sleeved denim work jacket, and old Filson tin pants make a proper crawler's outfit. Along the ridge a ways, and then down a steep slope through the brush, belly-sliding on snow and leaves like an otter—you get limber at it. And you see the old stumps from early logging surrounded by thick manzanita, still-tough pitchy limbs from old wolf trees, hardy cones, overgrown drag roads, four-foot butt logs left behind, webs of old limbs and twigs and the periodic prize of a bear scat. So, face right in the snow, I came on the first of many bear tracks.

Later, one of our party called us back a bit: "A bear tree!" And sure enough, there was a cavity in a large old pine that had opened up after a fire had scarred it. A definite black bear hangout, with scratches on the bark. To go where bears, deer, raccoons, foxes—all our other neighbors—go, you have to be willing to crawl.

So we have begun to overcome our hominid pride and learned to take pleasure in turning off the trail and going directly into the brush, to find the contours and creatures of the pathless part of the woods. Not really pathless, for there is the whole world of little animal trails that have their own logic. You go down, crawl swift along, spot an opening, stand and walk a few yards, and go down again. The trick is to have no attachment to standing; find your body at home on the ground, be a quadruped, or if necessary, a snake. You brush cool dew off a young fir with your face. The delicate aroma of leaf molds and mycelium rise from the tumbled humus under your hand, and a half-buried young boletus is disclosed. You can *smell* the fall mushrooms when crawling.

We began to fantasize on the broader possibilities of crawling. We could offer Workshops in Power Crawling! And in self-esteem—no joke! Carole said, "I've learned an important lesson. You can attain your goals, if you're willing to crawl!"

It's not always easy, and you can get lost. Last winter we took a long uphill cross-country transect on some of the land just above the Yuba Gorge; this soon turned into a serious crawl. We got into denser and denser old manzanita that had us doing commando-style lizard crawls to get under the very low limbs. It became an odd and unfamiliar ridge, and I had no idea where we might be. For hundreds of yards, it seemed, we were scuttling along, and then we came on a giant, totally fresh, worm-free *Boletus edulis,* the prize of all the boletes. That went into the little day pack. And a bit farther the manzanita opened and there we were! We were in a gap below an old cabin built half onto BLM land at the edge of the Hindu yoga camp, and soon we found the dirt road that led toward home. One more victorious expedition through the underbrush.

As wide open spaces shrink around us, maybe we need to discover the close-up charms of the brushlands, and their little spiders, snakes, ticks (yikes!), little brown birds, lizards, wood rats, mushrooms, and poison-oak vines. It's not for everyone, this world of little scats and tiny tracks. But for those who are bold, I'd say get some gloves and a jacket and a hat and go out and *explore California.*

Living in the Open

One can choose to live in a place as a sort of visitor, or try to become an inhabitant. My family and I decided from early on to try to be here, in the midelevation forests of the Sierra Nevada, as fully as we could. This brave attempt was backed by lack of resources and a lot of dumb bravado. We figured that simplicity would of itself be beautiful, and we had our own extravagant notions of ecological morality. But necessity was the teacher that finally showed us how to live as part of the natural community.

It comes down to how one thinks about screens, fences, or dogs. These are often used for keeping the wild at bay. ("Keeping the wild at bay" sounds like fending off hawks and bears, but it is more often a matter of holding back carpenter ants and deer mice.) We came to live a permeable, porous life in our house set among the stands of oak and pine. Our buildings are entirely opened up for the long Sierra summer. Mud daubers make their trips back and forth from inside the house to the edge of the pond like tireless little cement trucks, and pour their foundations on beams, in cracks, and (if you're not alert) in rifle-bore holes and backpack fire-pump nozzles. They dribble little spots of mud as they go. For mosquitoes, which are never much of a problem, the house is just another place to enjoy the shade. At night the bats dash around the rooms, in and out of the open skylights, swoop down past your cheek and go out an open sliding door. In the dark of the night the deer can be heard stretching for the lower leaves of the apple trees, and at dawn the wild turkeys are strolling a few yards from the bed.

The price we pay is the extra effort to put all the pantry food into jars or other mouse-proof containers. Winter bedding goes into mouse-proof chests. Then ground squirrels come right inside for fresh fruit on the table, and the deer step into the shade shelter to nibble a neglected salad. You are called to a hopeful steadiness of nerves as you lift a morsel of chicken to the mouth with four meat bees following it every inch of the way. You must sometimes (in late summer) cook and eat with the yellow jackets watching every move. This can make you peevish, but there is a kind of truce that is usually attained when one quits flailing and slapping at the wasps and bees.

It's true, living and cooking in the outdoor shade shelters someone occasionally gets stung. That's one price you might pay for living in the porous world, but it's about the worst that can happen. There's a faint risk of rattlesnake bite as we stride around the little trails, and the ever-present standoffishness of poison oak. But if you can get used to life in the semiopen, it's a great way to enjoy the forest.

It's also a form of conservation. As people increasingly come to inhabit the edges and inholdings of forest lands, they have to think carefully about how they will alter this new-old habitat. The number of people that can be wisely accommodated on the land cannot be determined simply by saying how many acres are required for a single household. This kind of planning is essential right now, and I'm all for it, but we have to remember that the cultural practices of households alone can make huge differences in impact.

Necessary roads should be thoughtfully routed and of modest width, with the occasional fire-truck turnout. Fire protections should be provided by having the roads well brushed along the edges, with plenty of thinning back into the woods, rather than building an excessively wide roadbed. If roads are a bit rough, it will slow cars down, and that's not all bad. If there are no or very few fences, if people are not pumping too heavily from their wells to irrigate pasture or orchards, if the number of dogs is kept modest, if the houses are well insulated and temperatures are held at the low sixties in the winter, if feral cats are not allowed, if an attitude of tolerance is cultivated toward the occasional mischief of critters, we will cause almost no impact on the larger forest ecosystem. But if there are too many people who hate insects and coyotes, who are perpetually annoyed by deer and who get hysterical about bears and cougars, there goes the neighborhood.

It's possible and desirable to take out firewood lightly, to cut some deliberately chosen sawlogs, to gather manzanita berries for the cider, to seek redbud for basketry supplies, and to pursue any of a number of other subtle economic uses of the forest. As we thin saplings, remove underbrush, and move tentatively toward the occasional prescribed burn, we are even helping the forest go its own direction. Maybe we will yet find ways to go past the dichotomy of the wild and the cultivated. Coyotes and screech owls make the night magic; log-truck airhorns are an early morning wakeup.

Permeability, porousness, works both ways. You are allowed to move through the woods with new eyes and ears when you let go of your little annoyances and anxieties. Maybe this is what the great Buddhist philosophy of interconnectedness means when it talks of "things moving about in the midst of each other without bumping."

{"Living in the Open" (1991) and "Crawling" (1992) appeared in numbers 2 and 3 of Tree Rings, *the newsletter of the Yuba Watershed Institute.}*

Coming into
the Watershed

I had been too long in the calm Sierra pine groves and wanted to hear surf and the cries of seabirds. My son Gen and I took off one February day to visit friends on the north coast. We drove out of the Yuba River canyon, and went north from Marysville—entering that soulful winter depth of pearly tule fog—running alongside the Feather River and then crossing the Sacramento River at Red Bluff. From Red Bluff north the fog began to shred, and by Redding we had left it behind. As we crossed the mountains westward from Redding on Highway 299, we paid special attention to the transformations of the landscape and trees, watching to see where the zones would change and the natural boundaries could be roughly determined. From the Great Valley with its tules, grasses, valley oak, and blue oak, we swiftly climbed into the steep and dissected Klamath range with its ponderosa pine, black oak, and manzanita fields. Somewhere past Burnt Ranch we were in the redwood and Douglas fir forests—soon it was the coastal range. Then we were descending past Blue Lake to come out at Arcata.

We drove on north. Just ten or fifteen miles from Arcata, around Trinidad Head, the feel of the landscape subtly changed again—much the same trees, but no open meadows, and a different light. At Crescent City we asked friends just what the change between Arcata and Crescent City was. They both said (to distill a long discussion), "You leave 'California.' Right around Trinidad Head you cross into the maritime Pacific Northwest." But the Oregon border (where we are expected to think "the Northwest" begins) is still many miles farther on.

So we had gone in that one afternoon's drive from the Mediterranean-type Sacramento Valley and its many plant alliances with the Mexican south, over the interior range with its dry pine-forest hills, into a uniquely Californian set of redwood forests, and on into the maritime Pacific Northwest: the edges of four major areas. These boundaries are not hard and clear, though. They are porous, permeable, arguable. They are boundaries of climates, plant communities, soil types, styles of life. They change over the millennia, moving a few hundred miles this way or that. A thin line drawn on a map would not do them justice. Yet these are the markers of the natural nations of our planet, and they establish real territories with real differences to which our economies and our clothing must adapt.

On the way back we stopped at Trinidad Head for a hike and a little birding. Although we knew they wouldn't be there until April, we walked out to take a look at the cliffs on the head, where tufted puffins nest. For tufted puffins, this is virtually the southernmost end of their range. Their more usual nesting ground is from southeastern Alaska through the Bering Sea and down to northern Japan. In winter they are far out in the open seas of the North Pacific. At this spot, Trinidad, we could not help but feel that we touched on the life realm of the whole North Pacific and Alaska. We spent that whole weekend enjoying "liminality," dancing on the brink of the continent.

I have taken to watching the subtle changes of plants and climates as I travel over the West. We can all tell stories, I know, of the drastic changes we have noticed as we raged over this or that freeway. This vast area called "California" is large enough to be beyond any one individual's ability (not to mention time) to travel over and to take it all into the imagination and hold it clearly enough in mind to see the whole picture. Michael Barbour, a botanist and lead author of *California's Changing Landscapes,* writes of the complexity of California: "Of the world's ten major soils, California has all ten. . . . As many as 375 distinctive natural communities have been recognized in the state. . . . California has more than five thousand kinds of native ferns, conifers, and flowering plants. Japan has far fewer species with a similar area. Even with four times California's area, Alaska does not match California's plant diversity, and neither does all of the central and northeastern United States and adjacent Canada combined. Moreover, about 30 percent of California's native plants are found nowhere else in the world."

But all this talk of the diversity of California is a trifle misleading. Of what place are we speaking? What is "California"? It is, after all, a recent human invention with hasty straight-line boundaries that were drawn with a ruler on a map and rushed off to an office in D.C. This is another illustration of Robert Frost's lines, "The land was ours before we were the land's." The political boundaries of the western states were established in haste and ignorance. Landscapes have their own shapes and structures, centers and edges, which must be respected. If a relationship to a place is like a marriage, then the Yankee establishment of a jurisdiction called California was like a shotgun wedding with six sisters taken as one wife.

California is made up of what I take to be about six regions. They are of respectable size and native beauty, each with its own makeup, its own mix of birdcalls and plant smells. Each of these proposes a slightly different lifestyle to the human beings who live there. Each led to different sorts of rural economies, for the regional differences translate into things like raisin grapes, wet rice, timber, cattle pasture, and so forth.

The central coast with its little river valleys, beach dunes and marshes, and oak-grass-pine mountains is one region. The great Central Valley is a second, once dominated by swamps and wide shallow lakes and sweeps of valley oaks following the streams. The long mountain ranges of the Sierra Nevada are a third. From a sort of Sonoran chaparral they rise to arctic tundra. In the middle elevations they have some of the finest mixed conifer forests in the world. The Modoc plateau and volcano country—with its sagebrush and juniper—makes a fourth. Some of the Sacramento waters rise here. The fifth is the northern coast with its deep interior mountains— the Klamath region—reaching (on the coast) as far north as Trinidad Head. The sixth (of these six sisters) consists of the coastal valleys and mountains south of the Tehachapis, with natural connections on into Baja. Although today this region supports a huge population with water drawn from the Colorado River, the Owens Valley, and the great Central Valley, it was originally almost a desert.

One might ask, What about the rest? Where are the White Mountains, the Mojave Desert, the Warner Range? They are splendid places, but they do not belong with California. Their watersheds and biological communities belong to the Great Basin or the lower Colorado drainage, and we should let them return to their own families. Almost all of core California has a summer-dry Mediterranean climate, with (usually) a fairly abundant winter rain. More than anything else, this rather special type of climate is what gives our place its fragrance of oily aromatic herbs, its olive-green drought-resistant shrubs, and its patterns of rolling grass and dark forest.

I am not arguing that we should instantly redraw the boundaries of the social construction called California, although that could happen some far day. But we are becoming aware of certain long-range realities, and this thinking leads toward the next step in the evolution of human citizenship on the North American continent. The usual focus of attention for most Americans is the human society itself with its problems and its successes, its icons and symbols. With the exception of most Native Americans and a few non-natives who have given their hearts to the place, the land we all live on is simply taken for granted—and proper relation to it is not considered a part of "citizenship." But after two centuries of national history, people are beginning to wake up and notice that the United States is located on a landscape with a severe, spectacular, spacy, wildly demanding, and ecstatic narrative to be learned. Its natural communities are each unique, and each of us, whether we like it or not—in the city or countryside—lives in one of them.

Those who work in resource management are accustomed to looking at many different maps of the landscape. Each addresses its own set of meanings. If we look at land ownership categories, we get (in addition to private land) the Bureau of Land Management, national forest, national park, state park, military reserves, and a host of other public holdings. This is the public domain, a practice coming down from the historic institution of the commons in Europe. These lands, particularly in the arid West, hold much of the water, forest, and wildlife that are left in America. Although they are in the care of all the people, they have too often been managed with a bent toward the mining or logging interests and toward short-term profits.

Conservationists have been working since the 1930s for sustainable forestry practices and the preservation of key blocks of public land as wilderness. They have had some splendid success in this effort, and we are all indebted to the single-minded dedication of the people who are behind every present-day wilderness area that we and our children walk into. Our growing understanding of how natural systems work brought us the realization that an exclusive emphasis on disparate parcels of land ignored the insouciant freeness of wild creatures. Although individual islands of wild land serving as biological refuges are invaluable, they cannot by themselves guarantee the maintenance of natural variety. As biologists, public land managers, and the involved public have all agreed, we need to know more about how the larger-scale natural systems work, and we need to find "on-the-ground" ways to connect wild zone to wild zone wherever possible. We have now developed the notion of biological corridors or connectors. The Greater Yellowstone Ecosystem concept came out of this sort of recognition. Our understanding of nature has been radically altered by systems theory as applied to ecology, and in particular to the very cogent subdisciplines called island biogeography theory and landscape ecology.

No single group or agency could keep track of grizzly bears, which do not care about park or ranch boundaries and have necessary, ancient territories of their own that range from late-summer alpine huckleberry fields to lower-elevation grasslands. Habitat flows across both private and public land. We must find a way to work with wild ecosystems that respects both the rights of landowners and the rights of bears. The idea of ecosystem management, all the talk now in land management circles, seems to go in the right direction. Successfully managing for the ecosystem will require as much finesse in dealing with miners, ranchers, and motel owners as it does with wild animals or bark beetles.

A "greater ecosystem" has its own functional and structural coherence. It often might contain or be within a watershed system. It would usually be larger than a county, but smaller than a western U.S. state. One of the names for such a space is "bioregion."

A group of California-based federal and state land managers who are trying to work together on biodiversity problems recently realized that their work could be better accomplished in a framework of natural regions. Their interagency "memorandum of understanding" calls for us to "move beyond existing efforts focused on the conservation of individual sites, species, and resources . . . to also protect and manage ecosystems, biological communities, and landscapes." The memorandum goes on to say that "public agencies and private groups must coordinate resource management and environmental protection activities, emphasizing regional solutions to regional issues and needs."

The group identified eleven or so such working regions within California, making the San Francisco Bay and delta into one, and dividing both the Sierra and the valley into northern and southern portions. (In landscapes as in taxonomy, there are lumpers and splitters.) Since almost 50 percent of California is public domain, it is logical that the chiefs of the BLM, the Forest Service, California Department of Fish and Game, California Department of Forestry, State Parks, the federal Fish and Wildlife Service, and such should take these issues on, but that they came together in so timely a manner and signed onto such a far-reaching plan is admirable.

Hearing of this agreement, some county government people, elected officials, and timber and business interests in the mountain counties went into a severe paranoid spasm, fearing—they said—new regulations and more centralized government. So later in the fall, an anonymous circular made its way around towns and campuses in northern California under the title "Biodiversity or New Paganism?" It says that "California Resource Secretary Doug Wheeler and his self-appointed bioregional soldiers are out to devalue human life by placing greater emphasis on rocks, trees, fish, plants, and wildlife." It quotes me as having written that "those of us who are now promoting a bioregional consciousness would, as an ultimate and long-range goal, like to see this continent more sensitively redefined, and the natural regions of North America—Turtle Island—gradually begin to shape the political entities within which we work. It would be a small step toward the deconstruction of America as a superpower into seven or eight natural nations—none of which have a budget big enough to support missiles." I'm pleased to say I did write that. I'd think it was clear that my statement is not promoting more centralized government, which seems to be a major fear, but these gents want both their small-town autonomy and the military-industrial state at the same time. Many a would-be westerner is a rugged individualist in rhetoric only, and will scream up a storm if taken too far from the government tit. As Marc Reisner makes clear in *The Cadillac Desert,* much of the agriculture and ranching of the West exists by virtue of a complicated and very expensive sort of government welfare: big dams and water plans. The real intent of the circular (it urges people to write the state governor) seems to be to resist policies that favor long-range sustainability and the support of biodiversity, and to hold out for maximum resource extraction right now.

As far as I can see, the intelligent but so far toothless California "bioregional proposal" is simply a basis for further thinking and some degree of cooperation among agencies. The most original part is the call for the formation of "bioregional councils" that would have some stake in decision making. Who would be on the bioregional councils is not spelled out. Even closer to the roots, the memorandum that started all this furor suggests that "watershed councils" would be formed, which, being based on stream-by-stream communities, would be truly local bodies that could help design agreements working for the preservation of natural variety. Like, let's say, helping to preserve the spawning grounds for the wild salmon that still come (amazingly) into the lower Yuba River gravel wastelands. This would be an effort that would have to involve a number of groups and agencies, and it would have to include the blessing of the usually development-minded Yuba County Water Agency.

The term *bioregion* was adopted by the signers to the Memorandum on Biological Diversity as a technical term from the field of biogeography. It's not likely that they would have known that there were already groups of people around the United States and Canada who were talking in terms of bioregionally oriented societies. I doubt they would have heard about the first North American Bioregional Congress held in Kansas in the late eighties. They had no idea that for twenty years communitarian ecology-minded dwellers-in-the-land have been living in places they call "Ish" (Puget Sound and lower British Columbia) or "Columbiana" (upper Columbia River) or "Mesechabe" (lower Mississippi), or "Shasta" (northern California), and all of them have produced newsletters, taken field trips, organized gatherings, and at the same time participated in local politics.

That "bioregion" was an idea already in circulation was the bad, or good, luck of the biodiversity agreement people, depending on how you look at it. As it happens, the bioregional people are also finding "watershed councils" to be the building blocks of a long-range strategy for social and environmental sustainability.

A watershed is a marvelous thing to consider: this process of rain fall-ing, streams flowing, and oceans evaporating causes every molecule of water on earth to make the complete trip once every two million years. The surface is carved into watersheds—a kind of familial branching, a chart of relationship, and a definition of place. The watershed is the first and last nation whose boundaries, though subtly shifting, are unarguable. Races of birds, subspecies of trees, and types of hats or rain gear often go by the watershed. For the watershed, cities and dams are ephemeral and of no more account than a boulder that falls in the river or a landslide that temporarily alters the channel. The water will always be there, and it will always find its way down. As constrained and polluted as the Los Angeles River is at the moment, it can also be said that in the larger picture that river is alive and well under the city streets, running in giant culverts. It may be amused by such diversions. But we who live in terms of centuries rather than millions of years must hold the watershed and its communi-ties together, so our children might enjoy the clear water and fresh life of this landscape we have chosen. From the tiniest rivulet at the crest of a ridge to the main trunk of a river approaching the lowlands, the river is all one place and all one land.

The water cycle includes our springs and wells, our Sierra snowpack, our irrigation canals, our car wash, and the spring salmon run. It's the spring peeper in the pond and the acorn woodpecker chattering in a snag. The watershed is beyond the dichotomies of orderly/disorderly, for its forms are free, but somehow inevitable. The life that comes to flourish within it constitutes the first kind of community.

The agenda of a watershed council starts in a modest way: like saying, "Let's try and rehabilitate our river to the point that wild salmon can suc-cessfully spawn here again." In pursuit of this local agenda, a community might find itself combating clear-cut timber sales upstream, water-sell-ing grabs downstream, Taiwanese drift-net practices out in the North Pacific, and a host of other national and international threats to the health of salmon.

If a wide range of people will join in on this effort—people from tim-ber and tourism, settled ranchers and farmers, fly-fishing retirees, the businesses and the forest-dwelling new settlers—something might come of it. But if this joint agreement were to be implemented as a top-down prescription, it would go nowhere. Only a grass-roots engagement with long-term land issues can provide the political and social stability it will take to keep the biological richness of California's regions intact.

All public land ownership is ultimately written in sand. The boundaries and the management categories were created by Congress, and Congress can take them away. The only "jurisdiction" that will last in the world of nature is the watershed, and even that changes slightly over time. If public lands come under greater and greater pressure to be opened for exploitation and use in the twenty-first century, it will be the local people, the watershed people, who will prove to be the last and possibly most effective line of defense. Let us hope it never comes to that.

The mandate of the public land managers and the Fish and Wildlife people inevitably directs them to resource concerns. They are proposing to do what could be called "ecological bioregionalism." The other movement, coming out of the local communities, could be called "cultural bioregionalism." I would like to turn my attention now to cultural bioregionalism and to what practical promise these ideas hold for fin-de-millennium America.

Living in a place—the notion has been around for decades and has usually been dismissed as provincial, backward, dull, and possibly reactionary. But new dynamics are at work. The mobility that has characterized American life is coming to a close. As Americans begin to stay put, it may give us the first opening in over a century to give participatory democracy another try.

Daniel Kemmis, the mayor of Missoula, Montana, has written a fine little book called *Community and the Politics of Place.* Mr. Kemmis points out that in the eighteenth century the word *republican* meant a politics of community engagement. Early republican thought was set against the federalist theories that would govern by balancing competing interests, devise sets of legalistic procedures, maintain checks and balances (leading to hearings held before putative experts) in place of direct discussion between adversarial parties.

Kemmis quotes Rousseau: "Keeping citizens apart has become the first maxim of modern politics." So what organizing principle will get citizens back together? There are many, and each in its way has its use. People have organized themselves by ethnic background, religion, race, class, employment, gender, language, and age. In a highly mobile society where few people stay put, thematic organizing is entirely understandable. But place, that oldest of organizing principles (next to kinship), is a novel development in the United States.

"What holds people together long enough to discover their power as citizens is their common inhabiting of a single place," Kemmis argues. Being so placed, people will volunteer for community projects, join school boards, and accept nominations and appointments. Good minds, which are often forced by company or agency policy to keep moving, will make notable contributions to the neighborhood if allowed to stay put. And since local elections deal with immediate issues, a lot more people will turn out to vote. There will be a return of civic life.

This will not be "nationalism" with all its danger, as long as sense of place is not entirely conflated with the idea of a nation. Bioregional concerns go beyond those of any ephemeral (and often brutal and dangerous) politically designated space. They give us the imagination of "citizenship" in a place called (for example) the great Central Valley, which has valley oaks and migratory waterfowl as well as humans among its members. A place (with a climate, with bugs), as Kemmis says, "develops practices, creates culture."

Another fruit of the enlarged sense of nature that systems ecology and bioregional thought have given us is the realization that cities and suburbs are all part of the system. Unlike the ecological bioregionalists, the cultural bioregionalists absolutely must include the cities in their thinking. The practice of urban bioregionalism ("green cities") has made a good start in San Francisco. One can learn and live deeply with regard to wild systems in any sort of neighborhood—from the urban to a big sugar-beet farm. The birds are migrating, the wild plants are looking for a way to slip in, the insects in any case live an untrammeled life, the raccoons are padding through the crosswalks at 2:00 A.M., and the nursery trees are trying to figure out who they are. These are exciting, convivial, and somewhat radical knowledges.

An economics of scale can be seen in the watershed/bioregion/city-state model. Imagine a Renaissance-style city-state facing out on the Pacific with its bioregional hinterland reaching to the headwaters of all the streams that flow through its bay. The San Francisco/valley rivers/Shasta headwaters bio-city-region! I take some ideas along these lines from Jane Jacobs's tantalizing book *Cities and the Wealth of Nations,* in which she argues that the city, not the nation-state, is the proper locus of an economy, and then that the city is always to be understood as being one with the hinterland.

Such a non-nationalistic idea of community, in which commitment to pure place is paramount, cannot be ethnic or racist. Here is perhaps the most delicious turn that comes out of thinking about politics from the standpoint of place: anyone of any race, language, religion, or origin is welcome, as long as they live well on the land. The great Central Valley region does not prefer English over Spanish or Japanese or Hmong. If it had any preferences at all, it might best like the languages it heard for thousands of years, such as Maidu or Miwok, simply because it's used to them. Mythically speaking, it will welcome whoever chooses to observe the etiquette, express the gratitude, grasp the tools, and learn the songs that it takes to live there.

This sort of future culture is available to whoever makes the choice, regardless of background. It need not require that a person drop his or her

Buddhist, Jewish, Christian, animist, atheist, or Muslim beliefs but simply add to that faith or philosophy a sincere nod in the direction of the deep value of the natural world and the subjecthood of nonhuman beings. A culture of place will be created that will include the "United States," and go beyond that to an affirmation of the continent, the land itself, Turtle Island. We could be showing Southeast Asian and South American newcomers the patterns of the rivers, the distant hills, saying, "It is not only that you are now living in the United States. You are living in this great landscape. Please get to know these rivers and mountains, and be welcome here." Euro-Americans, Asian Americans, African Americans can—if they wish—become "born-again" natives of Turtle Island. In doing so we also might even (eventually) win some respect from our Native American predecessors, who are still here and still trying to teach us where we are.

Watershed consciousness and bioregionalism is not just environmentalism, not just a means toward resolution of social and economic problems, but a move toward resolving both nature and society with the practice of a profound citizenship in both the natural and the social worlds. If the ground can be our common ground, we can begin to talk to each other (human and nonhuman) once again.

> California is gold-tan grasses, silver-gray tule fog,
> olive-green redwood, blue-gray chaparral,
> silver-hue serpentine hills.
> Blinding white granite,
> blue-black rock sea cliffs.
> —Blue summer sky, chestnut brown slough water,
> steep purple city streets—hot cream towns.
> Many colors of the land, many colors of the skin.

{This essay was first given as a talk for the California Studies Center at Sacramento State College, as part of their conference entitled "Dancing at the Edge," on February 6, 1992. It was published in the San Francisco Examiner *on March 1 and 2, 1992, and was soon reprinted in a number of other periodicals and anthologies in the United States and England.}*

Kitkitdizze:
A Node in the Net

Jets heading west on the Denver-to-Sacramento run start losing altitude east of Reno, and the engines cool as they cross the snowy Sierra crest. They glide low over the west-tending mountain slopes, passing above the canyon of the north fork of the American River. If you look north out the window you can see the Yuba River country, and if it's really clear you can see the old "diggings"—large areas of white gravel laid bare by nineteenth-century gold mining. On the edge of one of those is a little hill where my family and I live. It's on a forested stretch between the South Yuba canyon and the two thousand treeless acres of old mining gravel, all on a forty-mile ridge that runs from the High Sierra to the valley floor near Marysville, California. You're looking out over the northern quarter of the greater Sierra ecosystem: a vast summer-dry hardwood-conifer forest, with drought-resistant shrubs and bushes in the canyons, clear-cuts, and burns.

In ten minutes the jet is skimming over the levees of the Sacramento River and wheeling down the strip. It then takes two and a half hours to drive out of the valley and up to my place. The last three miles seem to take the longest—we like to joke that it's still the bumpiest road we've found, go where we will.

Back in the mid-sixties I was studying in Japan. Once, while I was on a visit to California, some friends suggested that I join them in buying mountain land. In those days land and gas were both still cheap. We drove into the ridge and canyon country, out to the end of a road. We pushed through manzanita thickets and strolled in open stretches of healthy ponderosa pine. Using a handheld compass, I found a couple of

277

brass caps that mark corners. It was a new part of the Sierra for me. But I knew the assembly of plants—ponderosa pine, black oak, and associates— well enough to know what the rainfall and climate would be, and I knew I liked their company. There was a wild meadow full of native bunch-grass. No regular creek, but a slope with sedges that promised subsurface water. I told my friends to count me in. I put down the money for a twenty-five-acre share of the hundred acres and returned to Japan.

In 1969, back for good in California, we drove out to the land and made a family decision to put our life there. At that time there were vir-tually no neighbors, and the roads were even worse than they are now. No power lines, no phones, and twenty-five miles—across a canyon—to town. But we had the will and some of the skills as well. I had grown up on a small farm in the Northwest and had spent time in the forests and moun-tains since childhood. I had worked at carpentry and been a Forest Service seasonal worker, so mountain life (at three thousand feet) seemed do-able. We weren't really "in the wilderness" but rather in a zone of ecological recovery. The Tahoe National Forest stretches for hundreds of square miles in the hills beyond us.

I had also been a logger on an Indian reservation in the ponderosa pine forests of eastern Oregon, where many trees were more than two hundred feet tall and five feet through. That land was drier and a bit higher, so the understory was different, but it grew the same adaptable cinnamon-col-ored pines. The trees down here topped out at about a hundred feet; they were getting toward being a mature stand, but a long way from old growth. I talked with a ninety-year-old neighbor who had been born in the area. He told me that when he was young he had run cattle over my way and had logged here and there, and that a big fire had gone through about 1920. I trimmed the stump on a black oak that had fallen and counted the rings: more than three hundred years. Lots of standing oaks that big around, so it was clear that the fires had not been total. Besides the pine stands (mixed with incense cedar, madrona, a few Douglas firs), our place was a mosaic of postfire manzanita fields with small pines com-ing through; stable climax manzanita; an eight-acre stand of pure black oak; and some areas of blue oak, gray pine, and grasses. Also lots of the low ground-cover bush called *kitkitdizze* in the language of the Wintun, a nearby valley people. It was clear from the very old and scattered stumps that this area had been selectively logged once. A neighbor with an incre-ment borer figured that some trees had been cut about 1940. The sur-rounding lands and the place I was making my home flowed together with unmarked boundaries; to the eye and to the creatures, it was all one.

We had our hands full the first ten years just getting up walls and roofs, bathhouse, small barn, woodshed. A lot of it was done the old way;

we dropped all the trees to be used in the frame of the house with a two-man falling saw, and peeled them with drawknives. Young women and men with long hair joined the work camp for comradeship, food, and spending money. (Two later became licensed architects; many of them stayed and are neighbors today.) Light was from kerosene lamps; we heated with wood and cooked with wood and propane. Wood-burning ranges, wood-burning sauna stoves, treadle-operated sewing machines, and propane-using Servel refrigerators from the fifties were the targets of highly selective shopping runs. Many other young settlers found their place in northern California in the early seventies, so eventually there was a whole reinhabitory culture living this way in what we like to call Shasta Nation.

I set up my library and wrote poems and essays by lantern light, then went out periodically, lecturing and teaching around the country. I thought of my home as a well-concealed base camp from which I raided university treasuries. We named our place Kitkitdizze after the aromatic little shrub.

The scattered neighbors and I started meeting once a month to talk about local affairs. We were all nature lovers, and everyone wanted to cause as little impact as possible. Those with well-watered sites with springs and meadows put in small gardens and planted fruit trees. I tried fruit trees, a chicken flock, a kitchen garden, and beehives. The bees went first. They were totally destroyed in one night by a black bear. The kitchen garden did fairly well until the run of dry winters that started in the eighties and may finally be over. And, of course, no matter how you fence a garden, deer find a way to get in. The chickens were constant targets of northern goshawks, red-tailed hawks, raccoons, feral dogs, and bobcats. A bobcat once killed twenty-five in one month. The fruit trees are still with us, especially the apples. They, of all the cultivars, have best made themselves at home. (The grosbeaks and finches always seem to beat us to the cherries.) But in my heart I was never into gardening. I couldn't see myself as a logger again either, and it wasn't the place to grow Christmas trees. Except for cutting fallen oak and pine for firewood, felling an occasional pole for framing, and frequent clearing of the low limbs and underbrush well back from the homestead to reduce fire hazard, I hadn't done much with the forest. I wanted to go lightly, to get a deep sense of it, and thought it was enough to leave it wild, letting it be the wildlife habitat it is.

Living in a place like this is absolutely delicious. Coyote-howl fugues, owl exchanges in the treetops, the almost daily sighting of deer (and the rattle of antlers at rutting season), the frisson of seeing a poky rattlesnake, tracking critters in the snowfall, seeing cougar twice, running across humongous bear scats, sharing all this with the children are more than worth the inconveniences.

My original land partners were increasingly busy elsewhere. It took a number of years, but we bought our old partners out and ended up with the whole hundred acres. That was sobering. Now Kitkitdizze was entirely in our hands. We were cash poor and land rich, and who needs more second-growth pine and manzanita? We needed to rethink our relation to this place with its busy—almost downtown—rush of plants and creatures. Do we leave it alone? Use it, but how? And what responsibility comes with it all?

Now it is two grown sons, two stepdaughters, three cars, two trucks, four buildings, one pond, two well pumps, close to a hundred chickens, seventeen fruit trees, two cats, about ninety cords of firewood, and three chainsaws later. I've learned a lot, but there still is plenty of dark and unknown territory. (There's one boundary to this land down in the chaparral—it borders the BLM—that I *still* haven't located.) Black bear leave pawprints on woodshed refrigerators, and bobcats, coyotes, and foxes are more in evidence than ever, sometimes strolling in broad daylight. Even the diggings, which were stripped of soil by giant nozzles washing out the scattered gold, are colonized by ever-hardy manzanita and bonsai-looking pine. The first major environmental conflict in California was between Sacramento Valley farmers and the hydraulic gold miners of the Yuba. Judge Lorenzo Sawyer's decision of 1884 banned absolutely all release of mining debris into the watershed. That was the end of hydraulic mining here. We now know that the amount of material that was washed out of the Sierra into the valley and onto good farmlands was eight times the amount of dirt removed for the Panama Canal.

The kerosene lights have been replaced by a photovoltaic array powering a mixed AC/DC system. The phone company put in an underground line to our whole area at its own expense. My wife Carole and I are now using computers, the writer's equivalent of a nice little chainsaw. (Chainsaws and computers increase both macho productivity and nerdy stress.) My part-time teaching job at the University of California, Davis, gives me an internet account. We have entered the late twentieth century and are tapping into political and environmental information with a vengeance.

The whole Sierra is a mosaic of ownership—various national forests, Bureau of Land Management, Sierra Pacific Industries, state parks, and private holdings—but to the eye of a hawk it is one great sweep of rocks and woodlands. We, along with most of our neighbors, were involved in the forestry controversies of the last decade, particularly in regard to the long-range plans for the Tahoe National Forest. The county boosters still seem to take more pleasure in the romance of the gold era than in the subsequent processes of restoration. The Sierra foothills are still described as "Gold Country," the highway is called "49," there are businesses called "Nugget" and "Bonanza." I have nothing against gold—I wear it in my teeth and in my ear—but the real wealth here is the great Sierran forest. My neighbors and I have sat in on many hearings and had long and complicated discussions with silviculturalists, district rangers, and other experts from the Forest Service. All these public and private designations seem to come with various "rights." With just "rights" and no land ethic, our summer-dry forests could be irreversibly degraded into chaparral over the coming centuries. We were part of a nationwide campaign to reform forest practices. The upshot was a real and positive upheaval on a national scale in the U.S. Forest Service and the promise of ecosystem management, which if actualized as described would be splendid.

We next turned our focus to the nearby public lands managed by the BLM. It wasn't hard to see that these public lands were a key middle-elevation part of a passageway for deer and other wildlife from the high country to the valleys below. Our own holdings are part of that corridor. Then we were catapulted into a whole new game: the BLM area manager for central California became aware of our interest, drove up and walked the woods with us, talked with us, consulted with the community, and then said, "Let's cooperate in the long-range planning for these lands. We can share information." We agreed to work with him and launched a biological inventory, first with older volunteers and then with our own wild teenagers jumping in. We studied close to three thousand forested acres. We bushwhacked up and down the canyons to find out just what was there, in what combinations, in what quantity, in what diversity.

Some of it was tallied and mapped (my son Kai learned Geographical Information Systems techniques and put the data into a borrowed Sun Sparc workstation), and the rest of our observations were written up and put into bundles of notes on each small section. We had found some very large trees, located a California spotted owl pair, noted a little wetland with carnivorous sticky sundew, described a unique barren dome with serpentine endemics (plants that grow only in this special chemistry), identified large stands of vivid growing forest, and were struck by the tremendous buildup of fuel. The well-intended but ecologically ignorant fire-exclusion policies of the government agencies over the last century have made the forests of California an incredible tinderbox.

The droughty forests of California have been shaped for millennia by fire. A fire used to sweep through any given area, forest historians are now saying, roughly every twenty-five years, and in doing so kept the undergrowth down and left the big trees standing. The native people also deliberately started fires, so that the California forests of two hundred years ago, we are told, were structured of huge trees in parks that were fire-safe. Of course, there were always some manzanita fields and recovering burns, but overall there was far less fuel. To "leave it be wild" in its present state would be risking a fire that might set the land back to first-phase brush again. The tens of thousands of homes and ranches mixed among the wooded foothills down the whole Sierra front could burn.

The biological inventory resulted in the formation of the Yuba Watershed Institute, a nonprofit organization made up of local people, sponsoring projects and research on forestry, biodiversity, and economic sustainability with an eye to the larger region. One of the conclusions of the joint-management plan, unsurprisingly, was to try to reduce fuel load by every available means. We saw that a certain amount of smart selective logging would not be out of place, could help reduce fuel load, and might pay some of the cost of thinning and prescriptive burning. We named our lands, with the BLM's blessing, the 'Inimim Forest, from the Nisenan word for *pine,* in recognition of the first people here.

The work with fire, wildlife, and people extends through public and (willing) private parcels alike. Realizing that our area plays a critical biological role, we are trying to learn the ground rules by which humans might live together with animals in an "inhabited wildlife corridor." A project for netting and banding migrant songbirds during nest season (providing information for a Western Hemisphere database) is located on some Kitkitdizze brushlands, rather than public land, simply because it's an excellent location. It is managed by my wife, Carole, who is deeply touched by the spirit of the vibrant little birds she bands. Our cooperative efforts here can be seen as part of the rapidly changing outlook on land management in the West, which is talking public-private partnership in a big way. Joint-management agreements between local communities and other local and committed interests, and their neighboring blocks of public lands, are a new and potent possibility in the project of responsibly "recovering the commons" region by region. The need for ecological literacy, the sense of home watershed, and a better understanding of our stake in public lands are beginning to permeate the consciousness of the larger society.

Lessons learned in the landscape apply to our own lands, too. So this is what my family and I are borrowing from the watershed work as our own Three-Hundred-Year Kitkitdizze Plan: We'll do much more understory thinning and then a series of prescribed burns. Some patches will be left untouched by fire, to provide a control. We'll plant a few sugar pines, and incense cedars where they fit (ponderosa pines will mostly take care of themselves), burn the ground under some of the oaks to see what it does for the acorn crop, burn some bunchgrass patches to see if they produce better basketry materials (an idea from the Native basket-weaving revival in California). We'll leave a percentage of dead oak in the forest rather than take it all for firewood. In the time of our seventh-generation granddaughter there will be a large area of fire-safe pine stands that will provide the possibility of the occasional sale of an incredibly valuable huge, clear, old-growth sawlog.

We assume something of the same will be true on surrounding land. The wildlife will still pass through. And visitors from the highly crowded lowlands will come to walk, study, and reflect. A few people will be resident on this land, getting some of their income from forestry work. The rest may come from the information economy of three centuries hence. There might even be a civilization with a culture of cultivating wildness.

You can say that this is outrageously optimistic. It truly is. But the possibility of saving, restoring, and wisely (yes!) using the bounty of wild nature is still with us in North America. My home base, Kitkitdizze, is but one tiny node in an evolving net of bioregional homesteads and camps.

Beyond all this studying and managing and calculating, there's another level to knowing nature. We can go about learning the names of things and doing inventories of trees, bushes, and flowers, but nature as it flits by is not usually seen in a clear light. Our actual experience of many birds and much wildlife is chancy and quick. Wildlife is often simply a call, a cough in the dark, a shadow in the shrubs. You can watch a cougar on a wildlife video for hours, but the real cougar shows herself but once or twice in a lifetime. One must be tuned to hints and nuances.

After twenty years of walking right past it on my way to chores in the meadow, I actually paid attention to a certain gnarly canyon live oak one day. Or maybe it was ready to show itself to me. I felt its oldness, suchness, inwardness, oakness, as if it were my own. Such intimacy makes you totally at home in life and in yourself. But the years spent working around that oak in that meadow and not really noticing it were not wasted. Knowing names and habits, cutting some brush here, getting firewood there, watching for when the fall mushrooms bulge out are skills that are of themselves delightful and essential. And they also prepare one for suddenly meeting the oak.

"The Great Clod" Project

"Wild" in China

Hsieh's Shoes

The people of mainstream China call themselves *"Han"* people, even today. The term is contrasted with any and all "ethnic" groupings—such as the people of the south known as the *Yüeh* (modern *Viet* of Vietnam), who "cut their hair short and tattooed themselves." (These days, cadres organizing and educating in Tibet who are too grossly contemptuous of local customs might be sent back labelled "Han chauvinists.")

Even in the fourth century A.D. we can assume that the forests and agriculturally marginal areas of greater China were inhabited, even if thinly, by either backwoods Han people or tribal people.

The post-Han "Six Dynasties" period witnessed a flourishing back-to-nature movement from within the ruling gentry class, a "nature" that extended from the fields and gardens of the suburbs to the really deep hills. Many people who might in less turbulent times have exercised their class prerogative of administrative employment turned instead toward an idea of purity and simplicity. Not all were wealthy or self-indulgent. The poet Tao Yuan-ming (Tao Ch'ien) 365–427) was a minor official whose early retirement to a small farm was his own choice. His poems are still the standard of a certain quietness, openness, emptiness, and also human frankness and frailty in the confusions of farm, family, and wine, that much later Chinese poetry aspires to. The Taoist idea of being nobody in the world, "behind instead of in front," gave strength to those who often must have missed the social life of their urban *literati* friends as they sat up late reading and drinking alone in their estates or homesteads out amongst the peasants.

Some of the Han dynasty poems portray the wild mountain world as horrible and scary. As Burton Watson points out, a gradual shift in the mode of *seeing* nature took place. In the songs of the *Classic of Songs,* which reflect so much of the life of the people, plants were named specifically; the scene was the ground and brush right before one—where one danced or harvested. By the Six Dynasties, the view moved back and became more panoramic. A case in point is the work of the poet Hsieh Ling-yün (385–433)—who has only a few rare poetic ancestors in earlier China. His aristocratic family had moved south, and he grew up in a biome that would have been considered exotic and barbarous by Confucius.

Hsieh was a lover of mountains. His fascination with the densely wooded, steep hills of South China (peaking between 4,000 and 6,000 feet) took him on long climbs and rambles, including one month-long trail-cutting exploration. He combined in himself would-be Taoist recluse and vigorous wilderness adventurer. An early follower of Buddhism (a new thing at that time, limited to upper-class circles), he wrote an essay expounding "instant enlightenment."

Hsieh's ambivalent pursuit of success in politics ended when he was banished to a minor position in a remote south coast town; he soon resigned totally from the administration and moved to a run-down family estate in the hills southeast of present-day Hangchhow. The place and life there is detailed in his long *fu* ("prose poem") called *Living in the Mountains.* The farther and nearer landscapes are described in detail. The fish, birds, plants, and mammals are listed. The whole is seen as an ideal place for pursuing Taoist and Buddhist meditations. Thus,

> I cast no lines for fish.
> I spread no nets for hare.
> I have no use for barbed shafts.
> Who would set out rabbit snares or fish traps?

And he says he "awoke to the complete propriety of loving what lives." Later in the poetical essay he describes his workers, "felling trees; they clear the thorns and cut bamboo," and sundry bark and reed and rush gathering activities; and charcoal-making. This faint contradiction, intensified later in history, can become a major problem: individual animals' lives are carefully spared, while the habitat that sustains them is heedlessly destroyed.

Hsieh is a puzzle. Arrogant and overbearing at court, he made enemies there. Intensely intellectual as a Buddhist, and careless of the needs or feelings of local people, he managed to get intrigued into a charge of rebellion, and was beheaded in the marketplace. Hsieh was probably already out of place in China—he should have joined the Rock Mountain Fur Company and gone out to be a trapper. He was "wild," and as an aristocrat that took some contradictory and nasty turns. But he opened up the landscape—"mountains and waters"—to the poetic consciousness for all time, and he was a fine poet.

Mountains were always foci of spirit power in China, beginning perhaps as habitat for the *hsien,* a shaman who gained "power" in the hills. Later they became a place of retreat for the taoist practitioner of "harmonizing with the Way" and again as sites for Buddhist monasteries. Hsieh Ling-yün plunged into the watercourses and thickets, camped in the heights alone, walked all night in the moonlight. These years and energies lie behind what we now take to be the Chinese sense of nature as reflected in art. Hsieh is also remembered as the inventor of a unique mountaineering shoe or clog—no one is quite sure how it looked.

Oxhead Mountain

Buddhism began and remains (at center) a set of ethical observances and meditation disciplines by means of which hardworking human beings can win through to self-realization and understanding of the way of existence. This effort is instructed by the content of Shakyamuni's enlightenment experience: a realization that all things are co-arising, mutually causing and being caused, "empty" and without "self."

In the time of the historical Buddha Gautama Shakyamuni, the community or *sangha* of Buddhists was an order of monks and nuns who had renounced the world. It was held that one could not really achieve enlightenment as a householder. Laypersons might build up a store of good merit by helping the Buddhist Order and living virtuous lives, but the deeper experiences were not for them.

The expansion of the concept of *sangha,* or community, is a key theme in the history of Buddhism. In the Mahayana, or "Great Vehicle" branch, laymen and women are also considered worthy aspirants and almost equal practicers with monks, or, at the very least, theoretically capable of achieving enlightenment while living the householder's life. The inherent capacity to achieve enlightenment is called "Buddha-nature." At one stage in Buddhist thought (around the second century A.D. in India), it was held that not quite all human beings had that capacity. Those excluded, called *icchantikas,* appear to have been aboriginal tribal people who lived by hunting.

Some early Chinese Buddhist thinkers were troubled by this. About a century later, other Indian Buddhist texts were brought to China that taught that salvation was accessible not only to all human beings but to all *sentient* beings, vindicating the Chinese thinkers. This was commonly understood to mean that animals and even plants are part of the Mahayana drama, working out their karma through countless existences, up to the point of being born into a human body. It was popularly assumed that a human body was a prerequisite to Buddhist practice.

The eighth century monk Chan-jan, of the T'ien T'ai sect, was one of the first to argue the final step. He concluded that nonsentient beings also have the Buddha-nature. "Therefore we may know that the single mind of a single particle of dust comprises the mind-nature of all sentient beings and Buddhas" and "The man who is of all-round perfection knows from beginning to end that truth is not dual and that no objects exist apart from mind. Who then, is 'animate' and who 'inanimate'? Within the Assembly of the Lotus, all are present without division."

The Chinese philosophical appreciation of the natural world as the visible manifestation of the Tao made a happy match with Indian Mahayana eschatology. Chinese Buddhists could say, "These beautiful rivers and mountains are Nirvana in the here and now." Buddhists located themselves on famous old numinous mountains, or opened up wilderness for new monasteries. In Ch'an (Zen) Buddhism, the masters were commonly known by the name of the mountain they lived and taught on. An early line of Ch'an (which died out in the eighth century) was called the "Oxhead Mountain" sect. These monks did more than just admire the scenery—they were on intimate terms with the local wildlife, including tigers. The Oxhead Master Tao Lin built a nest in a tree for his meditation. Sitting up in it, he once had a conversation with the poet Po Chü-i: "Isn't it dangerous up there?" Po asked, in his government official's robes. "Where you are is far more dangerous" was Tao-Lin's response. In this branch of Ch'an (and no other ever) when monks died, their bodies were left out in the forest for the animals to consume. It's also said, they had a great sense of humor.

The Chase in the Park

By Shang dynasty times hunting had already become an upper-class sport. The old hunters' gratitude for the food received, or concern for the spirits of the dead game, had evaporated. Hunting had become "the chase"—an expensive group activity requiring beaters who drove the game toward the waiting aristocrats who pursued and shot it with bows from chariots or horseback. Large-scale exercises of this sort were considered good training for warfare. They were followed by feasts with musicians, and slender dancers wearing diaphanous gowns. Warfare and hunting are popularly thought to be similar in spirit, and in post-civilized times this has often been the case. In hunting and gathering cultures the delicacy of preparation, and the care surrounding the act of taking life, puts hunting on a different level.

Chinese culture is strikingly free from food taboos, and the upper-class cuisine is the most adventurous in the world. Even so, from Shang times on, meat was a luxury that the common people could seldom afford. Furs and feathers of animals were vastly used in the costuming of officials. Idealized instructions can be found in the Li Chi or "Collected Rituals," which was put together in the Han dynasty.

> When a ruler wore the robe of white fox fur, he wore one of embroidered silk over it to display it. When the guards on the right of the ruler wore tigers' fur, those on the left wore wolves' fur. An ordinary officer did not wear the fur of the white fox. Great officers wore the fur of the blue fox, with sleeves of leopard fur, and over it a jacket of dark-colored silk to display it; with fawn's fur they used cuffs of the black wild dog, with a jacket of bluish yellow silk, to display it . . .

Han dynasty ritualism has an oddly alienated quality. The nature philosophy and the plant and mineral experimentation of the Taoists, or the direct knowledge of the natural world necessary to the life of working people, is far from the highly ordered ceremoniousness that surrounded government bureaus and the court. The Han upper class did admire those who were skilled and bold in gambling for power, but always against a background of strict propriety. Taking animal lives is easier for those accustomed to taking human life. Respect for nature comes with knowledge and contact, but attention to the observable order of nature is rarely practiced by those who think that wealth is purely a creation of human organization, labor, or ingenuity.

Still, all through history, the emperor continued to offer sacrifices to the Earth, to Heaven, and to the great mountains and rivers of the land. Calamitous floods, or prolonged drought, would bring the state up short, and the emperor himself would have to ask if he had somehow offended heaven. Whatever these offenses might be, it doesn't seem that destruction of wildlife habitat or waste of animal or human lives, or deforestation, was perceived as a possible offense against the unearthly power of T'ien (sky or heaven). The wealthy governors and emperors thus maintained large hunting parks. Edward Schafer's study of "Hunting Parks in China" (the source for all this information) suggests that they evolved from Bronze Age preserves established originally to continue supplying certain wild species for the periodic state sacrifices; species whose use had been established when their numbers were far greater. By the Chou dynasty such preserves were a place for sport and recreation that might contain exotic species as well as native animals, with artificial lakes and ponds, stables, hunting lodges, and pleasure pavilions. They were an ideal

[1]Beheading, or being boiled alive, was the fate of those who lost in the game of power.

place to lodge and entertain visiting heads of state. The park of the Han emperor Wu Ti, "The Supreme Forest," was about forty by twenty miles in size and contained thirty-six detached palaces and lodges. Within its varied terrain it contained both native and exotic species of fish, birds, amphibians, and mammals. Rivers were stocked with giant softshell turtle and alligator as well as sturgeon and other fish. Caribou, sambars, rhinoceroses, and elephants were symbolically (and perhaps practically) located in the "south" of the preserve, and wild horses and yaks in the "north." 'The ground of the Supreme Forest was prepared for the great winter hunt by the royal foresters. They burned clear a large open space and cut away brambles. Beaters, hunters, and athletes readied themselves for the onslaughts of wild beasts and forest demons with spells and periapts. When the royal party arrived, the birds and beasts were driven into the cleared areas, and the slaughter began:

> A wind of feathers, a rain of blood,
> Sprinkled the countryside, covered the sky.

Some advisors openly criticized parks as wasteful and politically inexpedient. In Ssu-ma Hsiang-ju's *fu* on "The Supreme Forest" the Emperor is urged to terminate the park and open it to the people for cultivation and firewood and fishing. It's interesting to note that no middle course is considered, such as keeping a wildlife preserve for its own natural, noumenal, or scientific interest. The virtuous alternative is to turn it over entirely to human use.

(No comparison could be made between Chinese hunting park wantonness and the destruction of animal, not to mention human, life that took place in the Roman Arena. There thousands of animals might be destroyed in a few days. The constant supplying of animals to the Arena made extinct numerous species throughout the Mediterranean basin.)

Hunting parks survived into T'ang times and later, but new ideas from Buddhism or old ideas revived from Taoism stressing compassion for all creatures enveloped them in a mist of moral doubt. T'ang was the high point of much poetry, and of Ch'an Buddhist creativity, but it must be remembered that it was not peopled by effete scholars in flowing robes who detested violence. It was a time of hardy Northern-derived gentry who were skilled horsepersons and archers and falconers, hard drinkers and fighters. Women were much freer then, and the custom of bound feet was yet to come. These aristocrats backed Buddhism, in part from a cosmopolitan interest in the cultural and trade exchanges possible with the little nations of Central Asia, but they kept their robust habits. An aristocratic maiden was once sought out by a suitor who was told by her parents she'd gone out hunting on horseback. That probably never happened again after T'ang.

China is wide. Travel was mostly on foot, maybe with a packhorse, sometimes also a riding horse. In the lowlands a network of canals provided channels for slow-moving passenger boats as well as freight barges. Travellers moved by boat on the big rivers, slowly and laboriously upstream, pulled by men on shore, and swiftly and boisterously back down. Boats sailed across the lakes and slow-moving lower river reaches. Horse and ox carts moved men and materials in the alluvial plains and rolling hills. In the mountains and deserts, long caravans of pack animals moved the goods of empire.

Government officials were accustomed to travelling weeks or even months to a new appointment, with their whole family. Buddhist monks and Taoist wanderers had a tradition of freely walking for months or years on end. In times of turmoil whole populations of provinces, and contending armies, might be tangled in frenzied travel on the paths and waterways. It was said, "If a man has his heart set on great things 10,000 *li* are his front yard." So the people of the watersheds of the Yang and Huang rivers came to know the shape of their territory.

The officials and monks (and most poets were one or the other) were an especially mobile group of literate people. Travellers' prose or rhymed-prose descriptions of landscapes were ingenious in evoking the complexity of gorges and mountains. Regional geographies with detailed accounts of local biomes were encouraged. Hsieh Ling-yun's *fu* on his mountain place is descriptive and didactic—but his poems in the *shih* (lyric) form already manifest the quiet intensity that becomes the definitive quality of Chinese *shih* poetry in its greatest creative T'ang and Sung dynasty phases.

The Chinese and Japanese traditions carry within them the most sensitive, mind-deepening poetry of the natural world ever written by civilized people. Because these poets were men and women who dealt with budgets, taxes, penal systems, and the overthrow of governments, they had a heart-wrenching grasp of the contradictions that confront those who love the natural world and are yet tied to the civilized. This must be one reason why Chinese poetry is so widely appreciated by contemporary Occidentals.

Yet it's hard to pin down what a "Chinese nature poem" might be, and why it is so effective. They are not really about landscapes or scenery. Space of distant hills becomes space in life; a condition the poet-critic Lu Chi called "calm transparency." Mountains and rivers were seen to be the visible expression of cosmic principles; the cosmic principles go back into silence, non-being, emptiness; a Nothing that can produce the ten thousand things, and the ten thousand things will have that marvelous emptiness still at the center. So the poems are also "silent." Much is left unsaid, and the reverberation or mirroring—a flight of birds across the mind of the sky—leaves an after-image to be savored, and finally leaves no trace. The Chinese poetic tradition is also where human emotions are revealed; where a still official can be vulnerable and frail. Lu Chi says poetry starts with a lament for fleeting life, and regard for the myriad growing things— taking thought of the great virtuous deeds of people past, and the necessity of making "maps" for the future. Chinese poetry steps out of narrow human-centered affairs into a big-spirited world of long time, long views, and natural processes; and comes back to a brief moment in a small house by a fence.

The strain of nostalgia for the self-contained hard-working but satisfying life of the farmer goes along somehow with delight in jumbled gorges. Nature is finally not a "wilderness" but a habitat, the best of habitats, a place where you not only practice meditation or strive for a vision, but grow vegetables, play games with the children, and drink wine with friends. In this there is a politics of a special order—the Chinese nature poet is harking back to the Neolithic village, never forgotten and constantly returned to mind by the Taoist classics—as a model for a better way of life. Sectarian Taoism and its secret societies fermented a number of armed peasant uprisings through history that unwittingly had "neolithic" on their standards. "Playing with your grandchildren"—"growing chrysanthemums"—"watching the white clouds"—are phrases from a dream of pre-feudal or post-revolutionary society.

Chinese poets of these centuries were not biologists or primitive hunters, though, and their poetics did not lead them to certain precisions. What they found were landscapes to match inner moods—and a deep sense of reverence for this mystery of a real world. In Burton Watson's analysis of nature imagery in T'ang poems he finds more references to non-living phenomena than living, and more than half of those looking upward to sky, weather, wind, clouds, and moon. Downward, rivers, waters, and mountains predominate. Among living things willow and pine are the most-mentioned trees, but the specific names of herbaceous plants and flowers are few—with "flowers" usually meaning the blossoms of trees like cherry or peach. Wild goose is the most common bird, associated with being separated from a friend; and monkey the most common mammal—because of its mournful cry. Cicada and moth are the most common insect. Many natural references, then, are used for their symbolic or customary human associations, and not for intrinsic natural qualities. No doubt the oral poetry of a pre-literate people will have more acquaintance with the actual living creatures as numinous intelligences in furry or scaly bodies. But this does not detract from what the Chinese poems are, highly disciplined and formal poems that open us to the dilemma of having "regard for the myriad growing things" while being literate monks or administrators or wives of officials in the world's first "great society." The reign of the Emperor Hsuan Tsung (712–756) is considered one of the high points of Chinese cultural history: the poets Wang Wei, Li Po, and Tu Fu were at the height of their powers during those years, and so were the brilliant and influential Ch'an Masters Shen-hui, Nan-yüeh, Ma-tsu, and Po-chang. The national population may have been as high as sixty million.

I first came onto Chinese poems in translation at nineteen, when my ideal of nature was a 45 degree ice slope on a volcano, or an absolutely virgin rain forest. They helped me to "see" fields, farms, tangles of brush, the azaleas in the back of an old brick apartment. They freed me from excessive attachment to wild mountains, with their way of suggesting that even the wildest hills are places where people, also, live.

> Empty mountains:
> > no one to be seen,
> Yet—hear—
> > human sounds and echoes.
> Returning sunlight
> > enters the dark woods;
> Again shining
> > on green moss, above.
> > > > *Wang Wei*

Walls Within Walls

City Walls

Dwelling within walls was normal for the Chinese people of the plains and valleys. In the early Han dynasty there were an estimated 37,844 walled settlements of various sizes, with perhaps 60 million people living behind them.[1] Walls are a striking part of the Chinese landscape even today, the gently slanted stone walls of a provincial capital, broken by occasional towers that project two or three stories higher yet, rising through the mist fronting a river or lake, or mirrored in half-flooded fields.

Early Neolithic settlements (called "Yang-shao") had no walls. Instead they were surrounded by ditches or moats about fifteen feet wide and deep. These were probably to keep out animals; deer are notorious nibblers on orchards and vegetable gardens. Digs of Yang-shao settlements have turned up few, if any, fighting weapons. Later Neolithic settlements (called "Lung-shan") have tamped-earth fortifications and weapons.[2]

Around the fifth century B.C., as the Eastern Chou dynasty slipped toward the era of "Warring States," the basic style of walled city began to take shape.

> The type consisted of at least three contrasting spatial units: a small enclosure which was the aristocratic and administrative centre, mixed (in early times) with dependent tradesmen and artisans; industrial and commercial quarters, with residences, in a large enclosure; farmlands immediately beyond the city walls. In the warring states period sometimes three successive ramparts were built, suggesting a need to extend protection to increasingly large areas of

[1]Yi-fu Tuan, *China* (Chicago: Aldine, 1970).
[2]Kwang-chih Chang, *The Archeology of Ancient China* (New Haven: Yale University Press, 1977), p. 152.

commercial activity. Another change lay in the strengthening of the outer walls at the expense of the walls of the inner citadel, which were allowed to go into decay.[3]

The city of Hsia-tu, in the state of Yen, is estimated to have been ten square miles within the walls.

There were also the "great walls" to keep out the northern nomad tribesmen, the walls originally built by the states of Ch'in, Yen, and Chao. When Ch'in became the first all-China empire, 221 B.C., it joined together previous sections to make a more continuous barrier.

The dominant element of the Han dynasty townscape was the wall. It separated a settlement from the outlying fields, and by creating an enclosure facilitated the regimentation of life within . . . it had the character of a succession of walled-in rectangles. There was the town wall with gates on the four sides. Within the wall the settlement was partitioned into a number of wards. Ch'ang-an itself had as many as 160 wards. Streets separated the wards, which were in turn surrounded by walls. Each ward had only one gate opening to the street during Han times, and contained up to one hundred households, each of which was again surrounded by a wall. The inhabitants, to get out of town, would thus have to pass through three sets of gates: that of their house, that of their ward, and that of their town. Moreover, all the gates were guarded and closed up at night.[4]

Lovers, criminals, and spies climbing over these walls after dark is a staple in Chinese storytelling.

T'ang dynasty cities had a little more nightlife than those of the Han, and larger, looser markets, with special quarters for the Persian, Turkish, and Arab traders. The plan of the capital city of Ch'ang-an followed in good part the old ritual ideal—"The Polar star and the celestial meridian writ small became the royal palace and the main north–south streets through the city."[5] The north–south streets were 450-feet wide. The upper classes were in the eastern sector and the working people in the west. Each wing had its own market area. There were also vacant lots with vegetable gardens and pasture within the walls. The great city was spacious and open.

Such city planning seemed to work, but no one could have foreseen the relentless (if fluctuating) rise of population, especially after the year 1100, when the number first exceeded one hundred million. Part of the later rise reflects an increase in the size of the Chinese territory and the inclu-

[3]Tuan, p. 67.
[4]Tuan, p. 104.
[5]Tuan, p. 106.

sion of people considered non-Chinese in earlier times. After 1100 there were five urban centers south of the Huai river with more than a million people each.

Flying Money

Between the ninth and the thirteenth centuries China became what it basically was to be into modern times. During the three centuries of the Sung dynasty not only people but wealth and high culture moved south and toward towns. In the early twelfth century only 6 percent of the population was urban, but by the fourteenth an estimated 33 percent were living in or around large cities.[6] In the second phase of the T'ang dynasty, after An Lu-shan's rebellion, the tax base was changed from per capita to a straight land tax. This meant that wealthy manors that had long been exempt began to pay taxes. It was the first of a series of shifts or tendencies with profound effects. Some of the changes were:

- a people's corvée army evolved into an army of mercenaries
- manor-owning country gentlemen often became absentee landlords
- cumbersome metal coin was replaced by paper money
- a rustic naïveté gave way to a street-wise hedonism
- interest in cultural diversity yielded to a China-centered cultural chauvinism
- regional agricultural self-sufficiency gave way to cash-crop specialization
- status determined by family connections declined, and a greater emphasis on status derived from high ranks in the government examinations developed
- hiking through the mountains was replaced by tending an artificially wild-looking backyard garden.

The society that began to emerge we can recognize at many points as analogous to what we now consider "modern"—but more convivial and peaceful. It was the best society one could hope to see in a world of high population and dwindling resources. It was a kind of human cultural climax, from which the contemporary world may still have much to learn. The sophistication of social devices was remarkable:

Local tax collectors developed the corollary function of wholesalers or brokers, gathering the local surplus of agricultural or manufactured goods for sale to transport to merchants. The latter ranged

[6]Mark Elvin, *The Pattern of the Chinese Past* (Stanford: Stanford University Press, 1973), p. 175.

from itinerant peddlers to large-scale, monopolistic operators. An extensive network of inns that developed to accommodate these traveling merchants became the inn system that was to continue with little change until recent times.[7]

Old and already effective farming skills were enhanced by new tools, seeds, plants, and a broad exchange of information through the exhaustive agricultural encyclopedias and treatises now made available by mass woodblock printing. The poet and administrator Su Shih wrote a prose piece on a unique new rice-transplanting device that looked like a wooden hobbyhorse. In rice seed alone a revolution took place: a drought-resistant seed from central Vietnam came to be used widely. It could be grown on poorer soil, and so expanded available rice acreage. "By Sung times almost all of the types in use before the middle of T'ang had disappeared . . . a southern Sung gazeteer for the county of Ch'ang-shu in the lower Yangtze delta lists twenty-one kinds of moderate gluten rice, eight of high gluten rice, four of low gluten rice and ten miscellaneous varieties as being cultivated there."[8] Mark Elvin says that by the thirteenth century China had the most sophisticated agriculture in the world, with India the only possible rival.[9]

Increased contact with the market made the Chinese peasantry into a class of adaptable, rational, profit-oriented, petty entrepreneurs. A wide range of new occupations opened up in the countryside. In the hills, timber was grown for the booming boatbuilding industry and for the construction of houses in the expanding cities. Vegetables and fruit were produced for urban consumption. All sorts of oils were pressed for cooking, lighting, waterproofing, and to go into haircreams and medicines. Sugar was refined, crystallized, used as a preservative. Fish were raised in ponds and reservoirs to the point where the rearing of newly-hatched young fish for stock became a major business.[10]

Trade and commerce weren't new to China, though. In the first century, B.C. Ssu-ma Ch'ien wrote:

from the age of Emperor Shun and the Hsia dynasty down to the present, ears and eyes have always longed for the ultimate in beautiful sounds and forms, mouths have desired to taste the best in

[7]Edwin O. Reischauer and John K. Fairbank, *East Asia: The Great Tradition* (New York: Houghton Mifflin, 1960), p. 213.
[8]Elvin, p. 121.
[9]Elvin, p. 129.
[10]Elvin, p. 167.

grass-fed and grain-fed animals, bodies have delighted in ease and comfort, and hearts have swelled with pride at the glories of powers and ability. So long have these habits been allowed to permeate the lives of the people that, though one were to go from door to door preaching the subtle arguments of the Taoists, he could never succeed in changing them.[11]

Ssu-ma did short biographies of famous commoners who made fortunes by buying low and selling high, gambling on surplus and dearth. The merchant Chi-jan of the fifth century B.C. said, "When an article has become extremely expensive, it will surely fall in price, and when it has become extremely cheap then the price will begin to rise. Dispose of expensive goods as though they were so much filth and dirt; buy up cheap goods as though they were pearls and jade. Wealth and currency should be allowed to flow as freely as water!"[12]

This trade was conducted with rolls of silk, bales of rice, salt, or copper cash as the media of exchange. Cash was often scarce, and by mid-T'ang it was noted that mining the copper and minting and transporting new coin cost twice as much as its face value as money. All sorts of "flying money"— promissory notes, letters of credit, and private-issue proto-money—were succeeded by government-issue paper money in the eleventh century. During the thirteenth century, and under the Mongols in the early fourteenth, the government even accepted paper money for the payment of taxes. Marco Polo was astonished to see paper used just as though it were metal. If the flow of currency began to falter, the government instantly offered silver or gold as payment for paper. "For seventeen or eighteen years the value of paper money did not fluctuate."[13]

The Southern Capital

In the coastal province of Chekiang, south of Shanghai, there are still some upland areas of Miao population. In the fifth century A.D., when Hsieh Ling-yun walked the hills and worked on his rural estate, the greater part of the province was considered barbarian. It is named for the Che River, which reaches into the southern slopes of the Huang mountains, and the 3000-foot hills on the Kiangsi-Anhwei border. The river is famous for the tidal bore that plays in its mouth at Hangchou bay. A decade after the fall of the Northern Sung capital K'ai-feng to the Juchen

[11]Ssu-ma Ch'ien, *Records of the Grand Historian,* Burton Watson, tr. (New York: Columbia University Press, 1961), vol. 2, pp. 476–77.
[12]Ssu-ma, p. 48.
[13]Elvin, p. 160.

(Chin), the town of Lin-an, at the river mouth, was declared the new capital. The émigré emperor, his court, and crowds of refugees of the northern ruling class settled in. The name was changed to Hang-chou.

In earlier times the Lin-an area had been a marsh. The main river was channelized and subsidiary streams dammed in the fifth century A.D. The original town grew then on land between the lake thus formed, "West Lake," and the main Che River. It has come to be considered one of the most scenic places in China. Great care has been taken to keep the shallow lake clean. It was a true public park, with laws against planting water-chestnut (which would rapidly spread) or dumping trash in the water. Public pavilions, docks, and shade areas were built. Zoning restrictions designated acceptable architectural styles. Buddhist temples were looked on with favor; one of the most famous structures overlooking the lake was the pagoda at Thunder Point. Built of blue glazed brick, it was 170 feet high.

Po Chu-I had served as prefect there in the ninth century, and Su Shih did major maintenance and improvement on the lake when he was briefly prefect in the late eleventh century. The causeway on the lake is named after him.[14]

In 1136 Hang-chou had a population of around two hundred thousand. In 1170 this had become half a million, and in 1275 it was well over a million and perhaps the largest single concentration of human beings in the world at that time.[15] It may also have been the richest. The capital fell to the Mongols in 1279, after a siege of several years. Marco Polo was in the city soon after it surrendered (he worked for Khubilai Khan for seventeen years) and has left eloquent description:

> On one side is a lake of fresh water, very clear. On the other is a huge river, which entering by many channels, diffused throughout the city, carries away all its filth and then flows into the lake, from which it flows out towards the Ocean. This makes the air very wholesome. And through every part of the city it is possible to travel either by land or by these streams. The streets and watercourses alike are very wide, so that carts and boats can readily pass along them to carry provisions for the inhabitants.
>
> There are ten principal marketplaces, not to speak of innumerable local ones. These are square, being a half a mile each way. In front of them lies a main thoroughfare, 40 paces wide, which runs straight from one end of the city to the other. It is crossed by many

[14]Jacques Gernet, *Daily Life in China on the Eve of the Mongol Invastion* (Stanford: Stanford University Press, 1962), pp. 51–52.
[15]Gernet, p. 28.

bridges . . . and every four miles, there is one of these squares. . . . And in each of these squares, three days in the week, there is a gathering of 40 to 50 thousand people, who come to market bringing everything that could be desired to sustain life. There is always abundance of victuals, both wild game, such as roebuck, stags, harts, hares, and rabbits, and of fowls, such as partridges, pheasants, francolins, quails, hens, capons, and as many ducks and geese as can be told. . . . Then there are the shambles, where they slaughter the bigger animals, such as calves, oxen, kid, and lambs, whose flesh is eaten by the rich and upper classes. The others, the lower orders, do not scruple to eat all sorts of unclean flesh.

All the ten squares are surrounded by high buildings, and below these are shops in which every sort of craft is practised and every sort of luxury is on sale, including spices, gems, and pearls. In some shops nothing is sold but spiced rice wine, which is being made all the time, fresh, and very cheap.[16]

Hang-chou was kept spotless. The authorities had the streets cleaned and refuse piled at key points where it was loaded into boats. The boats in turn converged and took it out to the country in convoys. Nightsoil (human waste) was collected by corporations each with their own gathering territory who sold it to the intensive truck gardens of the eastern suburbs.[17] (Contrary to common opinion in the West, the use of nightsoil does not pose a health problem if it is aged properly before applying—as it usually is. I poured and gardened with it myself as a Zen student in Japan.) Marco Polo's account of what he and the Mongols called *Kinsai* (from *Hsing-ts'ai,* "temporary residence of the emperor") describes 3000 public baths. "I assure you they are the finest baths and the best and biggest in the world—indeed they are big enough to accommodate a hundred men or women at once."[18]

The rich, bustling life of thirteenth-century southern China set the tone for seventeenth- and eighteenth-century Osaka and Tokyo. (In reading Jacques Gernet and Marco Polo on Hang-chou, I find myself reliving moments in the Kyoto of the 1950s and '60s. A coffee shop on Kawaramachi full of chic Western-dressed youth, called "Den-en" after T'ao Ch'ien's poetry of "fields and gardens." A public bath in the Gion proud of its tradition of extra-hot bathwater, to please the ladies of the quarter and the late-night drinkers and gamblers. A small modern-style bar called Tesu—when asked what the name meant, the modish lady who owned it

[16]Marco Polo, *The Travels,* R. E. Latham, tr. (New York: Penguin, 1958), p. 187.
[17]Gernet, p. 43.
[18]Marco Polo, p. 143.

said, "Why of course, from *Tess of the D'Urbervilles.*") Such cities, though crowded, are not dangerous. Our American image of a city as a faceless network of commercial canyons, bordered by suburbs where no one ever goes on foot, reflects little of the conditions of city life in pre-modern cultures. Like a huge village, Hang-chou had about fifteen major festivals a year. In one of these the emperor opened up part of the palace grounds for the street entertainers to put on a street-life show for the people of the court.

Marco Polo:

> The natives of Kinsia are men of peace . . . they have no skills in handling arms and do not keep any in their houses. There is prevalent among them a dislike and distaste for strife or any sort of disagreement. They pursue their trades and handicrafts with great diligence and honesty. They love one another so devotedly that a whole district might seem, from the friendly and neighborly spirit that rules among men and women, to be a single household.
>
> If they come across some poor man by day, who is unable to work on account of illness, they have him taken to one of the hospitals, of which there are great numbers throughout the city, built by the ancient kings and lavishly endowed. And when he is cured, he is compelled to practice some trade.[19]

Life in the city went on virtually without cease; the bars and brothels closed around two A.M. and the *abattoirs* started up at three. Till late at night, illuminated pleasure boats drifted on the lake with clan or guild or fraternity parties singing and drinking and eating. Boats of all sizes and styles were available for hire.

> They are roofed over with decks on which stand men with poles which they thrust into the bottom of the lake. . . . The deck is painted inside with various colours and designs and so is the whole barge, and all around it are windows that can be opened or shut so that the banqueters ranged along the sides can look this way and that and feast their eyes on the diversity and beauty of the scenes through which they are passing. . . . On one side it skirts the city, so that the barge commands a distant view of all its grandeur and loveliness, its temples, palaces, monasteries, and gardens with their towering trees, running down to the water's edge. On the lake itself is the endless procession of barges thronged with pleasure-seekers. For the people of this city think of nothing else, once they have done the work of their craft or their trade, but to spend a part of the day

[19]Marco Polo, pp. 191–92.

with their womenfolk or with hired women in enjoying themselves whether in these barges or in riding about the city in carriages.[20]

Produce and firewood came into the city by boat, the latter some distance from the hills of the interior. At the very least seventy tons of rice a day were consumed. Shoppers at the market discriminated between "new-milled rice, husked winter rice, first quality white rice, rice with lotus-pink grains, yellow-eared rice, rice on the stalk, ordinary rice, glutinous rice"[21] and many others. There were some great places to eat:

> Formerly the best known specialities were the sweet soya soup at the Mixed-wares Market, pig cooked in ashes in front of Longevity-and-Compassion Palace, the fish-soup of Mother Sung outside the Cash-reserve Gate, and rice served with mutton. Later, around the years 1241–1252, there were, among other things, the boiled pork from Wei-the-Big-Knife at the Cat Bridge, and the honey fritters from Chou-number-five in front of the Five-span Pavilion.[22]

By the tenth century, woodblock printing was in common use. Literacy and learning spread, so that the earlier, simpler division of society into an illiterate mass and a literate Confucian elite no longer applied. Merchants, wandering monks, peasant-entrepreneurs, daughters of substantial merchants—all read books. "Catalogs, encyclopedias, and treatises appeared which dealt with a wide variety of topics: monographs on curious rocks, on jades, on coins, on inks, on bamboos, on plum-trees . . . treatises on painting and calligraphy; geographical works. The first general and unofficial histories of China made their appearances."[23] The West Lake, already famous from its association with two of China's most highly regarded poets, gave its name to the "Poetry Society of the Western Lake," which counted both natives of the city and visiting literati among its members. It held picnics, banquets, and competitions, and the winning poems were circulated through the society. Hang-chou was a world of soft-handed scholars, dainty-stepping maidens raised behind closed doors, hustling town dandies, urban laborers, just-arrived country girls whose looks would determine if they'd work in a back kitchen or a teahouse.

> The best rhinoceros skins are to be found
>   at Ch'ien's, as you go down from the canal
>   to the little Ch'ing-hu lake.
> The finest turbans at K'ang-number-three's

[20]Marco Polo, p. 190.
[21]Gernet, p. 86.
[22]Gernet, p. 137.
[23]Gernet, pp. 229–30.

> in the street of the Worn Cash-coin;
> The best place for used books at the bookstalls
> under the big trees near the summer-house
>   of the Orange Tree Garden;
> Wicker cages in Ironwire Lane,
> Ivory combs at Fei's
> Folding fans at Coal Bridge.[24]

Most people rose early, finished work early, and left time in the afternoon for shopping and social calls. About three A.M. in the summer, and four in the winter, the bells of the Buddhist temples on the outskirts would begin to boom. At four or five in the morning, Buddhist and Taoist monks were walking down the lanes, beating a rhythm on the hand-held "wooden fish" and calling out the morning's weather—"a light snow just starting"—and announcing the day's events, whether preparations for a festival, a court reception, or a building-code hearing. "Imperial audiences were held at five or six o'clock in the morning. Seven o'clock was considered to be already late in the day."[25]

Hats and Buckles

At the time of the Mongol conquest poor people still had some meat to eat, a little pork or fish. In recent centuries meat has been a once or twice-a-year treat. The wealthy could also afford wild game. There were no sanctions, apparently, against market hunting, though shoppers were warned to beware of donkey or horsemeat being sold as venison.[26] The deforestation that had been predicted by Shen Kua two centuries earlier (he was almost exactly contemporary with Su Shih) was well underway. Sung economic expansion stimulated remarkable industrial development—"comparable to that which took place during the earlier phases of England's industrial revolution." The quantity of iron produced during the Northern Sung period was not matched again until the nineteenth century. Tuan Yi-fu summarizes:

> The rapid growth of ironworks exerted pressure on timber resources, which were already heavily pressed to meet the needs of large city populations and of shipbuilding. Many hundreds of thousands of tons of charcoal were swallowed up by the metal industries. In addition, there was the demand for charcoal in the manufacture of salt, alum, bricks, tiles and liquor. The Northern Sung period must be

[24]Gernet, p. 85.
[25]Gernet, p. 182.
[26]Gernet, p. 137.

seen as a time of rapid deforestation. North China suffered first. . . . Firewood and charcoal for the cities and the industries had to be transported from the South. There was an acute shortage which was partially met by the effective substitution of coal for charcoal in the eleventh century.[27]

Wetlands were drained. It seems the expansion of ricefields into "waste-lands" or marshes often went against the interests and desires of the local people, who relied on ponds and estuaries for fishing and gathering edible water plants. Large landowners or the government itself undertook these projects, looking for profits or taxes. (The chain of events that led to the execution of Hsieh Ling-yun started with his plan to drain the Hui-chung lake, near the modern town of Shao-hsing. This lake was on public land, but a landowner of Hsieh's stature could usually have expected to get away with it. The governor of the province however was an old rival, and his enmity combined with the reports of clashes between local peasants and Hsieh's armed retainers opened the way to a charge of rebellion.) In the late Sung the government encouraged small farmers, by granting tax exemptions, to go into marshy grounds on the Yangtze delta. The loss was not only wild food previously gathered by the poor, but habitat for waterfowl and other members of the marshy ecosystems.

Along with wetlands and forests, the people as a whole were losing accurate knowledge of nature. For the past few centuries it has been believed in China that tortoises were female to the male of snakes; a bronze statuette shows a tortoise and snake copulating. The correct infor-mation of sunburned naked boys or old fishermen who knew better became no account. The harmless gecko (wall lizard) and the toad came to be considered poisonous. The big-shouldered wild boar, *Sus scrofa,* which appears in Han hunting scenes, and is still the type of pig in T'ang art, is replaced in the art of later dynasties by the sway-backed droop-eared domestic pig type.[28]

From Shang to Ch'in times animals and insects appear in Chinese art in the conventionalized forms sometimes associated with the "Scythian" art of ancient central Asia. None of the designs are floral, and those which seem so are actually loops and spirals of insects and reptiles.[29] Realistic animals appear from the Han dynasty onward—deer being chased by hounds, a tiger with a collar. Later representation of animals tends more and more to cleave to symbolic and legendary significance. "Everything in their painting, carved panels, lacquered screens, pieces of tapestry or

[27]Tuan, pp. 130–31.
[28]Arthur de Carle Sowerby, *Nature in Chinese Art* (New York: John Day, 1940), pp. 65, 99.
[29]Sowerby, p. 129.

embroidery, stone bas-reliefs, or the decorations on furniture and buildings means something. It is this fact that helps to explain why certain animals appear with great frequency, while others equally well known occur but seldom, or are altogether absent."[30] Thus leopards were far more common in China than tigers, yet are rarely seen in art. Other animals that seldom appear are the hedgehog, shrews and moles, the common muskshrew of the southeast, the scaly anteater, the civets, and many rodents including the porcupine. Insects are often represented in many media. In Han times jade cicadas were placed in the mouth of the dead. Entirely lifelike hairy-clawed crabs were constructed in bronze. In Sowerby's study on "nature in Chinese art" we find included a glass snuff bottle with a butterfly in low relief on black glass; an unidentified fish in jade; a marble seal with a toad carved on the top; realistic scroll paintings of carp, minnows, knife-fish, mandarin fish, catfish, and bitterlings; a split bamboo with a wasp inside all carved in ivory; an unglazed statue of a Bactrian camel; a lifelike elephant with a harness from the Six Dynasties period; and a bronze buckle inlaid in silver, in the form of a rhinoceros.

The poor rhinoceros. A hat of some sort, and a girdle or belt with a buckle, were essential to male dress. Gernet says:

> These were the two things which distinguished the Chinese from the barbarian . . . the finest girdles had plaques or buckles in jade, in gold, or in rhinoceros horn. The horn was imported from India, and in particular Bengal, which was supposed to have the best horn. . . . "The Chinese" says an Arab account of the ninth century, "makes from this horn girdles which fetch a price of two or three thousand dinars or more. . . ." The astonishing prices fetched by these horns and the intense delight taken by Chinese in ornaments made from them can hardly be explained by their rarity value alone: superstition as well as artistic taste must lie at the root of this passion. And indeed we find that "sometimes the horn is in the image of a man, or a peacock, or a fish or some other thing.[31]

Distant Hills

For those men who passed the civil service examinations and accepted official posts, travel from place to place became a way of life. They were commonly transferred every three years. Su Shih was born in Szechwan near the foot of Mount Omei in 1037. Like many who rose to political

[30]Sowerby, p. 44.
[31]Gernet, pp. 131–32.

and literary eminence in the Sung, he came from relatively humble people, "connected with the local weaving industry." His grandfather had been illiterate. He and his younger brother were locally tutored by a Taoist priest. Together with their father they traveled the thousand-mile journey down the Yangtze and north to the capital of K'ai-feng, where both boys passed the examinations the first try, a striking feat. In his early poem "On the Yangtze Watching the Hills" (traveling by boat with his father and brother through the San-hsia Gorge) Su Shih opens some of that space for us:

> From the boat watching hills—swift horses:
> a hundred herds race by in a flash.
> Ragged peaks before us suddenly change shape,
> Ranges behind us start and rush away.
> I look up: a narrow trail angles back and forth,
> A man walking it, high in the distance.
> I wave from the deck, trying to call,
> But the sail takes us south like a soaring bird.[32]

All three were given employment. In 1066 the father died and the two sons returned to bury him in Szechwan. It was the last time Su Shih saw his native village. He was twenty-nine.

This mobility contributes to the impression we get from Su and his cohorts that they no longer cared about particular landscapes. Indeed, for many of them there was no place in China they called home enough to know the smells and the wild plants, but during their interminable journeys on river boats and canal barges the scenery slowly unrolled for them like a great scroll. At the same time there was a cheerful recognition and acceptance of the fact that "we live in society." The clear, dry funny poems of daily life with family and neighbors that came of this are marvelous. Taoist ideas of living in mountain isolation, or breaking conventions, came to be seen as romantic and irresponsible. Yoshikawa comments on the optimism of Sung poetry, and suggests that it echoes the optimism of the ancient *Classic of Songs (Shih Ching),* with its care for daily tasks and the busy space within the farmyard. The dominant emotion expressed in T'ang dynasty writing is sorrow and grief: humankind is all too impermanent, only mountains and rivers will remain.[33] Sung poets like Mei Yao-ch'en might write in rough plain language, or a low-key style, of things the elegantly intense T'ang poets would never touch. Such is Yang

[32]Su Tung-P'o, *Selections from a Sung Dynasty Poet,* Burton Watson, tr. (New York: Columbia University Press, 1965), p. 23.
[33]Kojiro Yoshikawa, *An Introduction to Sung Poetry,* Burton Watson, tr. (Cambridge: Harvard University Press, 1967), p. 25.

Wan-li's poem on a fly:

> Noted outside the window: a fly, the sun on
>   his back,
> rubbing his legs together, relishing the
>   morning brightness.
> Sun and shadow about to shift—already he
>   knows it,
> Suddenly flies off, to hum by a
>   different window.[34]

Su Shih, lying on his back in a boat, takes detachment a step further:

> I greet the breeze that happens along
> And lift a cup to offer to the vastness:
> How pleasant—that we have no thought of
>   each other![35]

Kojiro Yoshikawa's brief analysis of nature images in Sung poetry notes that "sunset" is a common reference in the T'ang with a strong overtone of sadness. Su Shih, writing on a sunset seen from a Buddhist temple:

> Faint wind: on the broad water,
>   wrinkles like creases in a shoe:
> Broken clouds: over half the sky,
>   a red the color of fish tails.[36]

Rain, Yoshikawa observes, is a frequent Sung reference—rain to listen to at night while talking with a bedmate, rain to burn incense and study by.

> Shall I tell you the way to become a god
>   in this humdrum world?
> Burn some incense and sit listening to the rain.
> *Lu Yu*[37]

In a society of such mobility, complexity, and size, it is to be expected that a "sense of place" would be hard to maintain. Humanistic concerns can be cultivated anywhere, but certain kinds of understanding and information about the natural world are only available to those who stay put

---

[34]Burton Watson, *Chinese Lyricism* (New York: Columbia University Press, 1971), p. 202.
[35]Yoshikawa, p. 23.
[36]Yoshikawa, p. 47.
[37]Yoshikawa, p. 48.

and keep looking. There is another kind of "staying put" that flourished in some circles during the Sung, namely the meditation practice of Ch'an Buddhism, zazen. What some Sung poets and thinkers might have lost in sense of natural place was balanced to some extent by a better understanding of natural self. A different sort of grounding occurred.

Much of the distinctive quality of Sung poetry can be attributed to the influence of the relentless and original Su Shih. Su was also an advanced Ch'an practicer, which is evident in his resolute, penetrating, sensitive body of work. The Ch'an influence is not at its best in the poems about monks or temples; we find it in plainer places. But when Su says of the sky, "How pleasant—that we have no thought of each other" it should not be taken as an expression of the heartlessness or remoteness of nature. Within the mutual mindlessness: of sky and self the Ch'an practicer enacts the vivid energy and form of each blade of grass, each pebble. The obsession that T'ang poets had with impermanence was a sentimental response to the commonly perceived stress of Mahayana Buddhism on transience and evanescence. Ch'an teachers never bothered with self-pity. They brought a playful and courageous style of give-and-take to the study of impermanent phenomena. I suspect that Sung poets were more dyed with the true spirit of Ch'an than those of the T'ang. From the standpoint of the natural environment, the T'ang view can almost be reversed—it seems the mountains and rivers, or at least their forests and creatures, soils and beds, are more fragile than we thought. Human beings grimly endure.

The Bore

The rulers and courtiers of Hang-chou never fully grasped the seriousness of the Mongol threat. Dallying in the parks, challenging each others' connoisseurship, they carried aestheticism to impressive levels. Mongka Khan, who ravaged Tibet, and his brother Kubilai left southern Sung on the back burner for a decade or so while they consolidated their northern and western borders.

In Hang-chou every September the people of the city thronged out to the banks of the Che River to witness a spectacle belonging to a scale even larger—their own unwitting point of contact with the dragons of the whole planetary water cycle. This was the annual high-point of the tidal bore which came in from the bay, up the river, and right by the town. Viewing platforms were erected for the emperor and his family. One year when the huge wall of water came rushing up, a surprise wind rose behind it, and the eagre went over the barriers and drowned hundreds of people.[38]

[38]Gernet, p. 195.

Sung dynasty China was a high-water mark of civilization. Joseph Needham and Mark Elvin believe thirteenth-century China was on the verge of
a Western-style technological revolution; at least many of the preconditions were there. (It would be foolish to assume that such an evolution is
necessarily desirable.) The Mongol conquest was a blow to the culture,
but even without it, China would probably have gone through the same
process—a stabilization, fading of innovation and experiment, and a long
slow retreat of both economy and creativity. Even after we grant this decline, it must be pointed out that no Occidental culture can approach the
time-scale of stability and relative prosperity this decline encompassed.
Reischauer's comment that "there are few historic parallels except among
primitive peoples"[39] strikes far.

Lively though it was, the Sung had severe problems. Half the people of
the Northern Sung were tenant farmers paying half their farm income as
rent to the landlords. Declining natural resources and growing population ended experimental ventures into labor-saving devices: materials
grew expensive as labor became cheap. Smaller farms, overworked soil,
and higher population brought tax revenue and personal income down.
The frontier territories of the south and southwest were saturated. In
spite of all the (almost self-congratulatory) social concern of the Neo-
Confucian philosophers, no analysis went deep enough. Thousands of people who worked in the salt marshes of the Huai River valleys were virtual
slaves.

Far north of the sinicized Juchen and their captured realm, across the
Ordos and the Gobi, lived the Mongol tribes. Some Mongol groups associated Mount Burkham Khaldun, near the head of the Onon River (a
tributary of the Amur) and south-southeast of Lake Baikal, with their
legendary ancestors the Blue Wolf and his wife the Fallow Deer. About
1185 an eighteen-year-old youth named Temujin fled for his life to the
slopes of this mountain, pursued by rival Mongol horsemen of the Merkit
tribe. For days they pursued him through the willow thickets and swamps
of the densely forested upland. They could follow his horse's tracks but
they could not catch up with him. Eventually the Merkit contented
themselves with taking some women from the camps below, and left. The
Secret History of the Mongols has Temujin saying, as he descends the mountain,

> Though it seemed that I'd be crushed like
> a louse, I escaped to Mount
> Burkham Khaldun.

[39]Reischauer, p. 241.

The mountain has saved my life and my horse.
Leading my horse down the elk-paths, making
     my tent from the willow branches, I
     went up Mount Burkhan.
Though I was frightened and ran like an insect,
     I was shielded by Mount Burkhan Khaldun.
Every morning I'll offer a sacrifice to
     Mount Burkhan.
Every day I'll pray to the mountains.
Then striking his breast with his hand,
     he knelt nine times to the sun.
Sprinkling offerings of mare's milk in the air,
And he prayed.[40]

This survivor, who had lived for years with his abandoned mother and brothers by trapping ground squirrels and marmots, snaring ducks, and fishing, went on to be chosen the supreme leader of all the Turko-Mongol tribes. At the gathering or *quriltai* of 1206 he was given the title "Jenghiz Khan." After that, he began his first campaign in northern China, attacking the cities of the Tungusic Chin. Many campaigns and victories later the Buddhist monk Li Chih-ch'ang visited him at his headquarters in Karakorum. Jenghiz Khan is reported as saying,

> Heaven is weary of the inordinate luxury of China. I remain in the wild region of the north, I return to simplicity and seek moderation once more. As for the garments that I wear and the meals that I eat, I have the same rags and the same food as cowherds and grooms, and I treat the soldiers as my brothers.[41]

Jenghiz Khan did not exactly live a simple life, but he was determined and tough. He was also a brilliant military strategist. Many grassland nomad warriors before him had won victories from the Chinese or Turko-Iranians, but none left behind an empire and the beginnings of an administration. This was partly because he paid close attention to the engineers and architects among his prisoners of war, and they taught him how to besiege a city and how to broach the walls.

[40]Yuan Ch'ai Pi Shih, *Secret History of the Mongols,* translated by Paul Kahn, tr. (Berkeley: North Point Press, 1984).
[41]René Grousset, *The Empire of the Steppes* (New Brunswick: Rutgers University Press, 1970), p. 249.

The Brush

The elites of premodern China's high civilization were urbane, bookish, secular, arty, and supremely confident. The Imperial Government rested in a ritualized relationship with Great Nature, and the seasonal exchanges between Heaven and Earth—sun, rains, and soils—were national sacraments conducted at elaborate Earth and Heaven shrines. (The most powerful of rituals were conducted in solitude by the Emperor himself.)

Nature and its landscapes were seen as realms of purity and selfless beauty and order, in vivid contrast to the corrupt and often brutal entanglements of politics that no active Chinese official could avoid. The price an intellectual paid for the prestige and affluence that came with being a member of the elite was the sure knowledge of the gap between humane Confucian theory and the actual practices of administering a county or a province—with multiple levels of graft, well-cooked books, and subtle techniques of coercion. And the higher one rose in the ranks, the more one's neck was exposed to the deadly intrigues of enemies.

The mountain horizons were a reminder of the vivid world of clear water, patient rocks, intensely focused trees, lively coiling clouds and mists—all the spontaneous processes that seemed to soar above human fickleness. The *fu* poet Sun Ch'o said of these processes, "When the Dao dissolves, it becomes rivers, when it coagulates it becomes mountains." Tsung Ping, an early fifth-century painter whose work does not survive, is described as having done mountain landscapes when ill and no longer able to ramble the hills he loved. He wrote the perfect program for a recluse:

> Thus by living leisurely, by controlling the vital breath, by wiping the goblet, by playing the *ch'in,* by contemplating pictures in silence, by meditating on the four quarters of space, by never resisting the influence of Heaven and by responding to the call of the

wilderness where the cliffs and peaks rise to dazzling heights and the cloudy forests are dense and vast, the wise and virtuous men of ancient times found innumerable pleasures which they assimilated by their souls and minds.[1]

He also stated a philosophy of landscape painting that stood for centuries to come: "Landscapes exist in the material world yet soar in the realms of the spirit . . . The Saint interprets the Way as Law through his spiritual insight, and so the wise man comes to an understanding of it. Landscape pays homage to the Way through Form, and so the virtuous man comes to delight in it."[2] Half a century later Hsieh Ho declared the first principle of landscape painting to be "spirit resonance and living moment"—meaning, a good painting is one in which the very rocks come alive, and one yearns to go walking in it. The basic aesthetics of the tradition had been articulated, but it was almost a thousand years before the implications of these statements were fully realized in painterly terms. The art of painting "mountains and waters" slowly unfolded through the centuries.

The concept of *ch'i*—a rich term that translates as indwelling energy, breath, and spirit—is a rich sophistication of archaic East Asian animism. Joseph Needham calls it "matter-energy" and treats it as a proto-scientific term. Contemporary people everywhere tend to see matter as lifeless. The notion of a rock participating in life and spirit—even as metaphor—is beneath adult consideration. Yet for those who work for long amid the forms of nature, the resonating presence of a river-system or prairie expanse or range of hills becomes faintly perceptible. It's odd but true that if too much human impact has hit the scene, this presence doesn't easily rise.

Archaic art worldwide is often abstract and geometrical. The spiral motif is widely found—from tattoos on the cheek to petroglyphs on a canyon wall. This representation of the *ch'i* of things becomes a design of volutes in early Chinese decorative art. Artists started tracing the lines of energy flow as observed in the clouds, running water, mist and rising smoke, plant growth—tendrils, rock formations, and various effects of light, in their patterns. They went on, according to Michael Sullivan, to draw images of fantastically formed animal/energy-bodied nature spirits, and this provided a main bridge from archetypal being to archetypal landform. The lines finally twisted themselves into ranges of mountains.[3]

[1]Quoted in Oswald Siren, *The Chinese on the Art of Painting* (New York: Schocken, 1963), p. 16.
[2]Quoted in J. L. Frodsham, *The Murmuring Stream* (Kuala Lumpur, U. of Malaya, 1976), Vol. I, p. 103.
[3]Michael Sullivan, "On the Origins of Landscape Representation in Chinese Art," *Archives of the Chinese Art Society of America* VII, 1953, pp. 61–62.

The word for civilization in Chinese is *wên-ming,* literally, "understanding writing." In the time of Confucius people wrote on slats of bamboo with a stylus. When paper and the soft-haired brush came into use, the fluidity of calligraphy became possible. In China calligraphy is considered the highest of the graphic arts. The painter uses the same equipment as a writer—the "four treasures" of brush, ink, inkstone, and paper. The brush usually has a bamboo handle with rabbit, badger, goat, deer, wolf, sable, fox, and other hairs for the tip. Even mouse-whiskers have been tried. Everything from a broken roof-tile to rare and unusual stones have been used for grinding the ink. Paper, which is said to have been invented in the first century A.D., is commonly made from paper mulberry, hemp, and bamboo. The paper preferred by Sung and Yüan dynasty painters was called "Pure Heart Hall" paper. It was smooth, white, and thin. Paintings were also done on silk, but paper lasts longer. Ink was made by burning dry pine logs in a kind of soot-collecting kiln. The soot was mixed with glue, one famous glue being made of donkey skin boiled in water from the Tung river. Fragrance was added, and the whole pressed into an inscribed stick.[4] Grinding the ink with a slow steady back-and-forth stroke, softening the brush, spreading the paper, amounts to a meditation on the qualities of rock, water, trees, air, and shrubs.

The earliest surviving landscape paintings (early T'ang, the seventh century) are more like perspective maps. Wang Wei's *Wang Chuan Villa* is a visual guide to a real place, with little labels on the notable locations. These first painted mountains are stark and centered, and the trees look stuck on. The painting might be a guidebook scene of a famous temple on a famous mountain. They are still half-tied to accounts of journeys, land-use records, or poems.

Then, with the Sung dynasty, in the eleventh century, paintings open out to great space. The rock formations, plants and trees, river and stream systems, flow through magically realistic spatial transitions. The painter-essayist Kuo Hsi reminded us that the mountains change their appearance at every step you take. Paintings distinguish the wider drier mountains of the north from the tighter, wetter, mistier valleys of the south. These vast scenes, with a few small fishing boats, little huts—cottages—travellers with pack stock—become visionary timeless lands of mountain-rocks and air-mist-breath and far calm vistas. People are small but are lovingly rendered, doing righteous tasks or reclining and enjoying their world.

Painters moved between extremes of wet ink-dripping brushes and drier sparser ink on the brush. From hard-boned fine-detailed meticulous workmanship leaf by leaf and pebble by pebble they moved to wet-flung

[4]Sze Mai Mai, *The Way of Chinese Landscape Painting* (New York: Vintage, 1959).

washes of lights and darks that capture a close hill, a distant range, a bank of trees with an effect that can be called impressionistic.

The Sung dynasty painters of large scale, including the horizontal handscrolls of a type sometimes called "Streams and Mountains without End," didn't always walk the hills they portrayed. With an established vocabulary of forms and the freedom of the brush they could summon up mountains that defied gravity and geomorphology, that seemed to float in mist. But these invented landscapes were somehow true to organic life and the energy cycles of the biosphere. The paintings show us the earth surface as part of a living being, on which water, cloud, rock, and plant growth all stream through each other—the rocks under water, waterfalls coming down from above clouds, trees flourishing in air. I overstate to make the point: the cycles of biosphere process to just this, stream vertically through each other. The swirls and spirals of micro- and macroclimate ("the tropical heat engine" for example) are all creations of living organisms; the whole atmosphere is a breath of plants, writhing over the planet in elegant feedback coils instructed by thermodynamics and whatever it is that guides complexity. "Nature by self-entanglement," said Otto Rössler, "produces beauty."

The mountains and rivers of the Sung dynasty paintings are remote. Yet they could be walked. Climbers take pleasure in gazing on ranges from a near distance and visualizing the ways to approach and ascend. Faces that seem perpendicular from afar are in fact not, and impossible-looking foreshortened spurridges or gullies have slopes, notches, ledges, that one can negotiate—a trained eye can see them. Studying Fan K'uan's "Travellers Among Streams and Mountains" (about A.D. 1000)—a hanging scroll seven feet tall—one can discern a possible climbing route up the chimneys to the left of the waterfall. The travellers and their packstock are safe below on the trail. They could be coming into the Yosemite Valley in the 1870s.[5] Southern Sung and Yüan dynasty landscape painting (especially with the horizontal handscroll format) tends to soften the hills. In the time of the evolution of the paintings, the mountains become easier, and finally can be easily rambled from one end to the other. As Sherman Lee says, the landscapes are no longer "mountain-and-water" but "rock-and-tree-and-water."[6]

The cities of the lower Yangtze became a haven for refugee artists and scholars during the Southern Sung dynasty, in the twelfth century, when

[5]Fan Kuan's painting can be seen in plate 11 in Wen Fong, *Summer Mountains* (New York: Metropolitan Museum of Art, 1975). Original is in the National Palace Museum, Taipei. Also in Lee and Fong, plate 8.
[6]Sherman E. Lee and Wen Fong, *Streams and Mountains Without End* (Ascona: Artibus Asiae, 1976), p. 19.

the northern half of the country fell to the Khitans, a forest-dwelling Mongol tribe from Manchuria. The long-established southern intelligentsia had always been closer to Daoism than the northerners. At that time Ch'an Buddhism and painting both were popularly divided into a northern and southern school. In both cases, the southern school was taken to be more immediate and intuitive. This large community of artists in the south launched new styles of painting. Lighter, more intimate, suggestive, swift, and also more realistic. Some of the painters—Hsia Kuei, Mu Ch'i, Liang K'ai, were much admired by the Japanese Zen monks and merchants, so many of their works were bought by the Japanese: traded for the exquisite Japanese swords that the Chinese needed to fight off the northern invaders. Many of the paintings ended up in the Zen Honzans ("Main Mountains"—headquarters temples) of Kyoto, where they are kept today.

The fact that some scrolls were landscapes of the imagination should not obscure the achievement of Chinese artists in rendering actual landscapes. The most fantastic-looking peaks of the scrolls have models in the karst limestone pinnacles of Kuangsi; misty cliffs and clinging pines are characteristic of the ranges of southern Anhwei province. The painting manual *Chieh-tzu Yuan Hua Chuan*, "Mustard-Seed Garden Guide to Painting" (about 1679), distinguishes numerous types of mountain formations, and provides a traditional menu of appropriate brush stroke-types for evoking them. Geological identifications of the forms indicated by different brush-strokes are described in Needham:

> Glaciated or maturely eroded slopes, sometimes steep, are shown by the technique called "spread-out hemp fibers," and mountain slopes furrowed by water into gullies are drawn in the *ho yeh ts'un* manner ("veins of a lotus-leaf hung up to dry"). "Unravelled rope" indicates igneous intrusions and granite peaks; "rolling clouds" suggest fantastically contorted eroded schists. The smooth roundness of exfoliated igneous rocks is seen in the "bullock hair" method, irregularly jointed and slightly weathered granite appears in "broken nets," and extreme erosion gives "devil face" or "skull" forms . . . cleavages across strata, with vertical jointed upright angular rocks, looking somewhat like crystals, are depicted in the "horse teeth" (*ma ya ts'un*) technique.[7]

The *Ta Ch'ing I T'ung Chih* is an eighteenth-century geographical encyclopedia with an illustrated chapter on "mountains and rivers." These woodblocks, based on the painting tradition, not only give a fair rendering of specific scenes, but do so with geological precision. Needham notes

---

[7]Joseph Needham, *Science and Civilization in China* III, p. 597.

how one can identify water-rounded boulder deposits, the Permian basalt cliffs of Omei-shan, the dipping strata of the Hsiang mountains near Po Chü-I's tomb, U-shaped valleys and rejuvenated valleys.[8]

Huang Kung-wang (born in 1269) was raised in the south. After a short spell with the civil service he became a Daoist teacher, poet, musician, and painter. He said to have recommended that one should "carry around a sketching brush in a leather bag" and to have called out to his students "look at the clouds—they have the appearance of mountain tops!"[9] His handscroll "Dwelling in the Fu-ch'un Mountains"[10] came to be one of the most famous paintings within China. He started it one summer afternoon in 1347, looking out from his house, and doing the whole basic composition on that one day. It took another three years to finish it. It's a clean, graceful painting that breathes a spirit of unmystified naturalness. The scene is not particularly wild or glamorous; it has the plain power of simply being its own quite recognizable place. This is in tune with the Ch'an demand for "nothing special" and its tenderness for every entity, however humble.

From around the Ming dynasty (1368 on) China had more and more people living in the cities. Painting helped keep a love of wild nature alive, but gradually many paintings were done by people who had never much walked the hills, for clients who would never get a chance to see such places. At the same time, there were painters like Wang Hui, who was a master of all historical styles, but also an acute observer of nature. His "Landscape in the Style of Chü-jan and Yen Wen-Kuei" (1713) carries the hills and slopes on out to sea as the painting fades away, by a portrayal of sea-fog twisting into scrolls and curls of water vapor / wind current / energy flow that faintly reminds us of the origins of Chinese paintings, and takes us back to the mineral and water cycle sources. Chinese painting never strays far from its grounding in energy, life, and process.

[8]*Ibid.*, pp. 593–7.
[9]James Cahill, *Hills Beyond a River* (New York: Weatherhill, 1976).
[10]*Ibid.* Plates 41–44; Color Plate 5. Original is in the National Palace Museum in Taipei.

The "Paris Review" Interview

The Art of Poetry

Gary Snyder is a rarity in the United States: an immensely popular poet whose work is taken seriously by other poets. He is America's primary poet-celebrant of the wilderness, poet-exponent of environmentalism and Zen Buddhism, and poet-citizen of the Pacific Rim—the first American poet to gaze almost exclusively west toward the East, rather than east toward Western civilization. A Snyder poem is instantly recognizable, and often imitated badly: an idiosyncratic combination of the plain speech of Williams, the free-floating, intensely visual images of Pound and the documentary information of both; the West Coast landscape first brought to poetry by Robinson Jeffers and Kenneth Rexroth; the precise and unallegorized observation of everyday life of the classical Chinese poets; and the orality of Snyder's fellow Beats.

He may well be the first American poet since Thoreau to devote a great deal of thought to the way one ought to live, and to make his own life one of the possible models. In person, he is full of humor and surprisingly undogmatic, with the charisma of one who seems to have already considered long and hard whatever one asks him. Snyder is an encyclopedia of things, both natural and artificial: what they are, how they were made, what they are used for, how they work. Then he quickly places that thing into a system that is ecological in its largest sense. Now in his mid-sixties, he would be a likely choice for a personal sage: sharp, wise, enthusiastic and an unexpectedly good listener.

Gary Snyder was born in San Francisco in 1930 and moved shortly after to the Pacific Northwest. Growing up in Washington state, he worked on his parents' farm and seasonally in the woods. He graduated in 1951 from Reed College with a degree in literature and anthropology. After a semester of linguistics study at Indiana University, he transferred to the University of California at Berkeley as a graduate student of Oriental languages, and became actively involved in the burgeoning West Coast poetry scene.

In the summer of 1955, Snyder worked on a trail crew in Yosemite National Park and began to write the first poems that he felt were truly his. That fall, he participated in the famous Six Gallery reading—featuring the first performance of Ginsberg's "Howl"—which launched the Beat movement. (Snyder appears as the character Japhy Ryder in Kerouac's The Dharma Bums.)

In 1956, he left the U.S. for what was to become a twelve-year residence abroad, largely in Japan. In Kyoto he pursued an intensive Zen Buddhist practice. During this period he also worked in the engine room of a tanker traveling along the Pacific Rim, and spent six months in India with Ginsberg and several others, where they had a notable discussion of hallucinogens with the Dalai Lama. In 1958, his translation of Han Shan's work, Cold Mountain Poems, *appeared. His first book of poetry,* Riprap, *was published in Japan in 1959. This was followed by* Myths & Texts *(1960) and the two pamphlets published by the Four Seasons Foundation in 1965 that gained him a wide readership;* Riprap and Cold Mountain Poems *and* Six Sections from Mountains and Rivers without End. *The first trade edition of his poetry,* The Back Country, *appeared in 1968.*

Snyder returned to the United States in 1969 to build a house in the foothills of the northern Sierra Nevada, where he still lives today in a family household that balances modern and archaic technologies. He continues to travel widely, reading poetry and lecturing on Buddhism, the environment and bioregional issues. He works with the local Yuba Watershed Institute, and since 1985 has been teaching at the University of California at Davis, where he helped to form a nature and culture discipline.

The interview took place before an audience at the Unterberg Poetry Center of the 92nd Street Y in New York City on October 26, 1992 and was later updated. The interviewer was Eliot Weinberger. What the transcript doesn't show is how often the conversation was punctuated by laughter. It began with some talk about the imminent presidential election and then turned to the question of poets and political power. Questions were then invited from the audience.

WEINBERGER: When Jerry Brown of California was running for president, people were kidding you that if he were elected, you would be named Secretary of the Interior. Now, the thing that interests me about this is that you are the only poet in America for whom there is any scenario, no matter how far-fetched, of actually entering into real political power. Is this something you think poets ought to do? Would you do it?

GARY SNYDER: I've never thought seriously about that question. Probably not, although I am foolish enough to think that if I did do it, I'd do it fairly well, because I'm pretty single-minded. But you don't want to be victimized by your lesser talents. One of my lesser talents is that I am a good administrator, so I really have to resist being drawn into straightening things out. The work I see for myself remains on the mythopoetic level of understanding the interface of society, ecology and language, and I think it is valuable to keep doing that.

WEINBERGER: But it is abnormal for poets not to be involved in the state. The United States remains an exception to most of the rest of the world, where poets commonly have served as diplomats or as bureauctats in some ministry.

SNYDER: Oh true. The whole history of Chinese poetry is full of great poets who played a role in their society. Indeed, I do too. I am on committees in my county. I have always taken on some roles that were there for me to take in local politics, and I believe deeply in civic life. But I don't think that as a writer I could move on to a state or national scale of politics and remain a writer. My choice is to remain a writer.

WEINBERGER: Let's get on to the writing and go back forty years or so. One of the amazing things about your work is that you seemed to burst on the scene fully formed with *Riprap* and *Cold Mountain Poems,* which were published in 1959 and 1958 but written earlier in the fifties when you were in your twenties. The poems in both books are unmistakably Snyder poems, and apparently, unlike the rest of us, you are not embarrassed by the work of your youth, for you picked eighteen of the twenty-three poems in *Riprap* for your *Selected Poems.*

SNYDER: Actually the poems in *Riprap* are not the poems of my youth. Those are the poems that I've kept because those were the ones I felt were the beginning of my life as a poet. I started writing poems when I was fifteen. I wrote ten years of poetry before *Riprap.* Phase one: romantic teenage poetry about girls and mountains.

WEINBERGER: You're still writing that!

SNYDER: I realized I shouldn't have said that as soon as the words were out of my mouth. I would like to think that they are not romantic poems but classical poems about girls and mountains. The first poet who touched me really deeply, as a poet, was D.H. Lawrence, when I was fifteen. I had read *Lady Chatterley's Lover* and I thought that was a nifty book, so I went to the library to see what else he had written, and there was something called *Birds, Beasts and Flowers.* I checked that out. I was disappointed to find out that it wasn't a sexy novel, but read the poems anyway, and it deeply shaped me for that moment in my life.

And then phase two, college. Poems that echoed Yeats, Eliot, Pound, Williams and Stevens. A whole five years of doing finger exercises in the modes of the various twentieth-century masters. All of that I scrapped, only a few traces of that even survive. I threw most of them in a burning barrel when I was about twenty-five.

So when I wrote the first poems in *Riprap* it was after I had given up poetry. I went to work in the mountains in the summer of 1955 for the U.S. Park Service as a trail crew laborer, and had already started classical Chinese study. I thought I had renounced poetry. Then I got out there and started writing these poems about the rocks and blue jays. I looked at them. They didn't look like any poems that I had ever written before. So I said, these must be my own poems. I date my work as a poet from the poems in *Riprap.*

WEINBERGER: What got you back to poetry at that moment? Was it primarily the landscape?

SNYDER: No, it just happened. What got me back to poetry was that I found myself writing poems that I hadn't even intended to write.

WEINBERGER: And what poets were important to you then? Who were the masters at this point?

SNYDER: When I was twenty-two or twenty-three, I began working with Chinese and found myself being shaped by what I was learning from Chinese poetry, both in translation and in the original. And I had been reading Native American texts and studying linguistics.

WEINBERGER: What were you finding in Chinese poetry at that time?

SNYDER: The secular quality, the engagement with history, the avoidance of theology or of elaborate symbolism or metaphor, the spirit of friendship, the openness to work and, of course, the sensibility for nature. For me it was a very useful balancing force to set beside Sidney, *The Faerie Queene,* Renaissance literature, Dante. The occidental tradition is symbolic, theological and mythological, and the Chinese is paradoxically more, shall we say, modern, in that it is secular in its focus on history or nature. That gave me a push.

WEINBERGER: Were you getting the ideogramic method from Pound or from the Chinese poetry directly?

SNYDER: From the Chinese poetry directly. I could never make sense of that essay by Pound. I already knew enough about Chinese characters to realize that in some ways he was off, and so I never paid much attention to it. What I found in Pound were three or four dozen lines in the *Cantos* that are stunning—unlike anything else in English poetry—which touched me deeply and to which I am still indebted.

WEINBERGER: Pound as a landscape poet?

SNYDER: No, as an ear. As a way of moving the line.

WEINBERGER: Since we are talking about Chinese poetry I wanted to ask you about the Han Shan translations, *Cold Mountain Poems.* It is curious because Chinese poetry is so canonical, and Han Shan is not in the canon. I think at the time there were people who thought that you made him up. I wondered how you discovered him?

SNYDER: Well, he is only noncanonical for Europeans and Americans. The Chinese and the Japanese are very fond of Han Shan, and he is widely known in the Far East as an eccentric and as possibly the only Buddhist poet that serious Far Eastern *littérateurs* would take seriously. They don't like the rest of Buddhist poetry—and for good reason, for the most part.

To give you an example: in 1983 I was in China with a party of American writers—Toni Morrison, Allen Ginsberg, Harrison Salisbury, William Gass, Francine du Plessix Grey and others—and we were introduced to some members of the Politburo upstairs in some huge building. The woman who was our simultaneous interpreter introduced me to these bureau members—I am embarrassed to say I don't remember who these impressive Chinese persons were—by saying, "He is the one who translated Han Shan." They instantly started loosening up, smiling and quoting lines from Han Shan in Chinese to me. He is well known. So whose canon are we talking about?

WEINBERGER: You haven't continued to translate much. Was this just something you felt you should do at the moment but that later there was too much other work to do?

SNYDER: There is a line somewhere—is it Williams who says it?—"You do the translations. I can sing." Rightly or wrongly, I took that somehow, when I ran into it, as a kind of an instruction to myself, not to be drawn too much into doing translation. I love doing Chinese translations, and I have done more that I haven't published, including the longest *shih* in Chinese, the *Ch'ang-hen ko,* "The Long Bitter Song" of Po Chü-i. So I am not just translating these tiny things. I am working right now on finishing up the *P'i-p'a hsing,* the other long Po Chü-i poem about the woman who plays the lute. And I've done a few T'ang poems. Maybe someday I'll get to doing more Chinese translations.

WEINBERGER: Getting back to the early poems: it's interesting that the American West is essentially invented in literary American poetry by two of your immediate predecessors, Robinson Jeffers and Kenneth Rexroth. Did you feel that they opened it up for you somehow, made it acceptable to write about?

SNYDER: Definitely. Jeffers and Rexroth both, as you say, were the only two poets of any strength who had written about the landscapes of the American West, and it certainly helped give me the courage to start doing the same myself.

WEINBERGER: What about the community of poets at the time? Philip Whalen, Lew Welch, Allen Ginsberg, Michael McClure, Robert Duncan, among others. One gets the sense that this was the only community of poets in which you were an active participant, that since that time you've been involved in other things. How important is a community of poets to you or to any poet? And what has happened since?

SNYDER: I think that rather than the term *community* it would be more accurate to speak of a *network* of poets. *Community* is more properly applied to diverse people who live in the same place and who are tied together by their inevitable association with each other, and their willingness to engage in that over a long period of time. But that is just a quibble.

When you are in your twenties, in particular, and you are a working, dissenting intellectual and artist, you need nourishment. Up in Portland, where I went to college, there were only a couple of other people you could talk to about poetry—Philip Whalen and Lew Welch and William Dickey. We started hearing little echoes of things in California and ended up there, all of us—for the comradeship, for the exchange of ideas. That was before the Beat generation broke onto the scene. I met Jack Spicer, Robin Blaser, Robert Duncan, Madeline Gleason, Tom Parkinson, Josephine Miles, William Everson, Kenneth Rexroth—that whole wonderful circle of San Francisco Renaissance people, such brilliant minds, such dedication to the art and such unashamed radical politics. Most of them were conscientious objectors in World War II, had rejected Stalinism early on, and with Kenneth Rexroth had formulated an antistatist, neo-anarchist political philosophy, anarcho-pacifism, which at that time in American history made great sense. I was proud to be part of that circle at that time.

That group was enlarged when Allen Ginsberg and Jack Kerouac came onto the scene and the phenomenon that we are more commonly aware of as the San Francisco Beat generation poetry emerged. But it came out of that group of Duncan, Spicer, Rexroth and Blaser that was already eight or ten years old—it wasn't just created by Allen and his friends. Through Allen I began to meet people from the East Coast. I met Kenneth Koch, Ed Sanders, Anne Waldman, Jerome Rothenberg, Don Hall, James Laughlin, Robert Creeley, Ed Dorn and many others. I still keep in touch with many of them. A wonderful circle.

WEINBERGER: Has the Beat thing been a burden for the rest of your life? Are you tired of hearing about the Beats?

SNYDER: I was for a while, but nobody has been beating me on the head with it lately.

WEINBERGER: I am surprised that very young people now are so fascinated by the Beats, compared to the hippie movement. As an old hippie I think we're much more interesting. What do you think they see in the Beats?

SNYDER: Gee, I don't know if I should say this to you. When I look at the differences, one that emerges is that the political stance of the West Coast Beats was clear. They were openly political and, in terms of the Cold War, it was a kind of a pox-on-both-your-houses position. Clearly our politics were set against the totalitarianism of the Soviet Union and China, and at the same time would have no truck with corporate capitalism. Today you might say, "Okay what else is new? Do you have any solutions to suggest?" I understand that, of course, but at that time the quality of our dissent alone was enough to push things in a slightly new direction. What it led to in the poetry was a populist spirit, a willingness to reach out for an audience and an engagement with the public of the United States. This swell of poetry readings, going to all of the college towns and the big cities, which started around 1956, transformed American poetry. It was a return to orality and the building of something closer to a mass audience.

I do feel that there was a visionary political and intellectual component in the hippie phenomenon, but it is harder to track out what it is. It wasn't so clearly spoken and it was outrageously utopian, whereas the Beat generation's political stance was in retrospect more pragmatic, more hardheaded, easier to communicate, and it didn't rely on so much spiritual rhetoric. So that might be one reason, just as the punks rejected hippie spiritual rhetoric and went for a harder-edged politics, well, the Beat generation had a harder-edged politics.

WEINBERGER: As long as we're talking about hippies, what about drugs? Obviously in the fifties and sixties you experimented with hallucinogens. Did it help or hurt the writing? Tear down obstacles or erect new ones? Or was it ultimately irrelevant?

SNYDER: That's a whole topic in itself, that deserves its own time. I'll just say that I am grateful that I came to meet with peyote, psilocybin, LSD and other hallucinogens in a respectful and modest frame of mind. I was suitably impressed by their powers, I was scared a few times, I learned a whole lot and I quit when I was ahead.

WEINBERGER: Going back—you basically left the scene in 1956 to go to Japan.

SNYDER: In May of 1956 I sailed away in an old ship, headed across the Pacific for Japan.

WEINBERGER: Why did you go? It seems like it was an exciting moment in America when you left.

SNYDER: Well, exciting as the scene was looking in 1956, I was totally ready to go to Japan. I had laid plans to go to the Far East, oh, three years prior to that, and had had several setbacks. The State Department denied me a passport for some of my early political connections.

WEINBERGER: Would you have gone to China if the political situation had been different at the time?

SNYDER: I certainly would have.

WEINBERGER: It would have completely changed the course of the rest of your life.

SNYDER: I'm sure it would have changed my life, although I don't know just how much, because my focus in going to the Far East was the study of Buddhism, not to find out if socialism would work, and the only Buddhists I would have found in China would have been in hiding at that time and probably covered with bruises. So it wouldn't have been a good move.

WEINBERGER: I get the sense that you are much more attracted to Chinese poetry than Japanese poetry.

SNYDER: To some extent that's true. It is a karmic empathy that is inexplicable. I love Japanese literature and Japanese poetry too, but I feel a deep resonance with Chinese poetry.

WEINBERGER: You stayed in Japan for ten years?

SNYDER: I was resident in Japan for about ten years, and I maintained residence there for twelve. I was away part of the time working on oil tankers and teaching at the University of California-Berkeley for a year.

WEINBERGER: And how many years were you in the monastery there?

SNYDER: I was in and out of the monastery. That was where my teacher lived, and I was resident in it for sesshin—for meditation weeks—and then out, then in again. I had a little house that I rented just five minutes walk from the Daitoku-ji monastery.

WEINBERGER: Are you still a practicing Buddhist? Do you sit every day?

SNYDER: Almost every day. Zazen becomes a part of your life, a very useful and beautiful part of your life—a wonderful way to start the day by sitting for at least twenty, twenty-five minutes every morning with a little bit of devotional spirit. My wife and I are raising a thirteen-year-old adopted daughter. When you have children you become a better Buddhist too, because you have to show them how to put the incense on the altar and how to make bows and how to bow to their food and so forth. That is all part of our culture, so we keep a Buddhist culture going. My grown sons say, when they are asked what they are, because they were raised that way, "Well, we are ethnic Buddhists. We don't know if we really believe it or not, but that is our culture."

WEINBERGER: What does zazen do for the poetry? Do you feel that there is a relation there that helps somehow in the writing?

SNYDER: I was very hesitant to even think about that for many years, out of a kind of gambler's superstition not to want to talk too much or think too much about the things that might work for you or might give you luck. I'm not so superstitious anymore, and to demystify zazen, Buddhist meditation, it can be said that it is a perfectly simple, ordinary activity to be silent, to pay attention to your own consciousness and your breath, and to temporarily stop listening or looking at things that are coming in from the outside. To let them just pass through you as they happen. There's no question that spending time with your own consciousness is instructive. You learn a lot. You can just watch what goes on in your own mind, and some of the beneficial effects are you get bored with some of your own tapes and quit playing them back to yourself. You also realize—I think anyone who does this comes to realize—that we have a very powerful visual imagination and that it is very easy to go totally into visual realms where you are walking around in a landscape or where any number of things can be happening with great vividness. This taught me something about the nature of thought and it led me to the conclusion—in spite of some linguists and literary theorists of the French ilk—that language is not where we start thinking. We think before language, and thought-images come into language at a certain point. We have fundamental thought processes that are prelinguistic. Some of my poetry reaches back to that.

WEINBERGER: You've written that language is wild, and it's interesting that, in your essays and in some of the poems, you track down words as though you're hunting or gathering. But do you believe that language is more a part of nature than a part of culture?

SNYDER: Well, to put it quite simply, I think language is, to a great extent, biological. And this is not a radical point of view. In fact, it is in many ways an angle of thought that has come back into serious consideration in the world of scientific linguistics right now. So, if it's biological, if it's part of our biological nature to be able to learn language, to master complex syntax effortlessly by the age of four, then it's part of nature, just as our digestion is part of nature, our limbs are part of nature. So, yes, in that sense it is. Now of course, language takes an enormous amount of cultural shaping, too, at some point. But the structures of it have the quality of wild systems. Wild systems are highly complex, cannot be intellectually mastered—that is to say they're too complex to master simply in intellectual or mathematical terms—and they are self-managing and self-organizing. Language is a self-organizing phenomenon. Descriptive linguistics come after the fact, an effort to describe what has already happened. So if you define the wild as self-managing, self-organizing, and self-propagating, all natural human languages are wild systems. The imagination, we can say, for similar reasons, is wild. But I would also make the argument that there is a prelinguistic level of thought. Not always, but a lot of the time. And for some people more than other people. I think there are people who think more linguistically, and some who think more visually, or perhaps kinesthetically, in some cases.

WEINBERGER: Getting back to Buddhism for a second. For many poets, poetry is the religion of the twentieth century. And I'm curious what you get, in that sense, from Buddhism that you don't get from poetry?

SNYDER: I had a funny conversation with Clayton Eshleman, the editor and poet, many years ago while he was still in Kyoto. Clayton was talking, at length and with passion, about poetry. And I said to him, "But Clayton, I already have a religion. I'm a Buddhist." It's like the Pope telling Clare Boothe Luce, "I already am a Catholic." I don't think art makes a religion. I don't think it helps you teach your children how to say thank you to the food, how to view questions of truth and falsehood, or how not to cause pain or harm to others. Art can certainly help you explore your own consciousness and your own mind and your own motives, but it does not have a program to do that, and I don't think it should have a program to do that. I think that art is very close to Buddhism and can be part of Buddhist practice, but there are territories that Buddhist psychology and Buddhist philosophy must explore, and that art would be foolish to try to do.

WEINBERGER: So you mainly draw that line on ethical grounds?

SNYDER: Well, there's ethics, there is philosophy, there is the spirit of devotion, and there is simply its capacity to become a cultural soil, a territory within which you transmit a way of being, which religion has a very strong role in. And then there is the other end of religious practice and Buddhist practice, which is to leave art behind. Which is to be able to move into the territory of the completeness and beauty of *all* phenomena. You really enter the world, you don't need art because everything is remarkable, fresh and amazing.

WEINBERGER: So how do you keep writing?

SNYDER: Because you don't want to live in that realm very much of the time. We live in the realm of forms, we should act in the realm of forms. Jim Dodge and I once went to a Morris Graves exhibit in Oakland, where he was arguing with me about this Buddhist position in regard to art. I was saying, "You don't need art in a certain sense, Jim." So he went to the Morris Graves exhibit looking at the Morris Graves paintings, and I went through it looking at the spaces between the paintings with as much attention, and pointing out wonderful little hairline cracks in the plaster, the texture of the light and so forth. There is a point you can make that anything looked at with love and attention becomes very interesting.

WEINBERGER: So you think people should read the margins of your books?

SNYDER: This is an oral art. They should listen to the unsaid words that resonate around the edge of the poem.

WEINBERGER: Just as Chinese poetry is full of empty words, deliberately empty words for the *ch'i,* the sort of breath, to circulate through. In 1970 you moved back to the Sierra Nevadas, and you've been there ever since. I think from that moment on, when you finally settle down, you're talking much more about a poetry rooted in place.

SNYDER: Certainly a number of the poems written since 1970 reflect the position of being in a place, a spot in the world to which I always return. A lot of poems, however, do come out of my hunting and gathering trips to other territories. The idea of being a person of place never excludes the possibility of travel. To the contrary, it reminds people of place—everybody else in the world except Canadians, Australians, and Americans—that they know where they come from. They have a place to go back to. They have no difficulty answering the question, "Where are you from?" But Americans often can't answer that question. They say, "Well, do you mean where I was born or where I went to high school, or where my parents live now, or where I went to college, or where my job is, or where I'm going to move next year?" That's an American dilemma. So having a place means that you know what a place means. And if somebody asks you, "What folk songs do you sing where you come from?" you have a song you can sing to them. Like in Japan, say, where you're always being asked to sing a song from your native place.

WEINBERGER: Yes. Ours is "I Love New York in June." Do you think that sense of place is primary for the poetry?

SNYDER: Not in any simple or literal way. More properly I would say it's a sense of what *grounding* means. But place has an infinite scale of expansion or contraction. In fact, if somebody asks me now, "What do you consider to be your place?" my larger scale answer is, "My place on earth is where I know most of the birds and the trees and where I know what the climate will be right now, roughly, what should be going on there on that spot on earth right now, and where I have spent enough time to know it intimately and personally." So that place for me goes from around Big Sur on the California coast all the way up the Pacific coast through British Columbia, through southeast Alaska, out through southwest Alaska, out onto the Aleutian chain, and then comes down into Hokkaido and the Japanese islands, and goes down through Taiwan. Now that's the territory I have moved and lived in and that I sort of know. So that's my place.

WEINBERGER: Since we're talking about your map of the world, people have wondered about the general absence of European civilization—or at least Europe after the Paleolithic—in your work. To me it's no more shocking than the absence of Asia—not to mention Africa—from everyone else's work. But still the question comes up. Is this a deliberate criticism of Eurocentrism or merely just the track your interest followed?

SNYDER: It's true that I haven't visited Europe much, but it isn't totally absent from my poetry, and there are some key points in my work that connect with occidental cultural insights that are classical, if not Paleolithic. The scholar Robert Torrance even wrote a little paper on the occidental aspect of my work. Much of the value I find in the West is in the pre-Christian, the pagan and the matrifocal aspects, however. And I track things like connections I fancy that I can see from Greek poetics to the Arabic poetry of Spain, in turn to Lorca, in turn to Jack Spicer. And the Bogomils, Waldenses, Albigenses, shepherds of Montaillou, Anabaptists, Quakers, Luddites, Amish and Wobblies have my gratitude, of course.

And now that I'm getting old enough to enjoy hotels as well as camping I think I'll start visiting Europe. I loved Spain—I went there recently.

WEINBERGER: I want to change gears and talk about the word *work,* which is central to all of your writing. You've written, to take one of many examples, "Changing the filter, wiping noses, going to meetings, picking up around the house, washing dishes, checking the dip stick, don't let yourself think these are distracting you from your more serious pursuits." What does this mean for a writer who would feel that her or his "real work" is the writing, and that all these other things are overwhelming?

SNYDER: If one's real work is the writing and if one is a fiction writer, I guess one's work as a writer really holds one to the literally physical act of writing and visualizing and imagining and researching and following out the threads of one's project. However, if one is a nonfiction prose writer or a poet, one is apt to be much more closely engaged with daily life as part of one's real work, and one's real work actually becomes life. And life comes down to daily life. This is also a very powerful Buddhist point: that what we learn and even hopefully become enlightened by is a thorough acceptance of exactly who we are and exactly what it is we must do, with no evasion, no hiding from any of it, physically or psychologically. And so finding the ceremonial, the almost sacramental quality of the moves of daily life is taught in Buddhism. That's what the Japanese tea ceremony is all about. The Japanese tea ceremony is a model of sacramental tea drinking. Tea drinking is taken as a metaphor for the kitchen and for the dining room. You learn how to drink tea, and if you learn how to drink tea well, you know how to take care of the kitchen and dining room every day. If you learn how to take care of the kitchen and the dining room, you've learned about the household. If you know about the household, you know about the watershed. *Ecology* means house, *oikos,* you know, from the Greek. *Oikos* also gives us economics. *Oikos nomos* means "managing the household." So that's one way of looking at it. I understand that there are other lines and other directions that poets take and I honor them. I certainly don't believe there's only one kind of poetry.

WEINBERGER: I have a line from Auden here that "the goal of everyone is to live without working." And basically what he's saying in the rest of the passage is that work is something that other people impose on us.

SNYDER: I would agree with Auden. The goal of living is not to consider work work, but to consider it your life and your play. That's another way of looking at it.

WEINBERGER: But how is that different from Calvinism, in the sense of extolling the virtues of work?

SNYDER: Well, work per se does not bring about salvation, nor is it automatically virtuous. It has more the quality of acknowledgment and recognition and making necessity charming. And it's not always charming, and nothing I've said should lead us to think that an oppressed worker should swallow and accept the conditions of his life without fighting back. It's none of that really. Your question catches me a little bit by surprise because I am so far removed from being a puritan in any way, and so is Buddhism, incidentally. There is a very funny quality in Buddhism, which is enjoying and acknowledging badness. So you can be bad and still be a good Buddhist. So everything I say has its reverse. "I hate work," you know, let it all go. Or as W. C. Fields once said, "If a thing is worth doing at all, it's worth doing poorly."

WEINBERGER: Speaking of the doing of things, let me ask you about your mechanics of writing. I gather you have some complicated system of file cards, even for the poems. Can you describe that?

SNYDER: Most writers I know, and certainly prose writers, have a well-organized shop. There are moves in longer poetic projects that are very like the work of researchers. I tell young would-be poets not to fear organization, that it won't stultify their scope. I use some systems I learned from anthropologists and linguists. Now I use a computer too. A friend who's a professional hydrologist gives a good caution, "Write up your field notes at the end of each day!" And then get them into your hard disk fairly soon and always back that up. The main thing though is to give full range to the mind and learn to walk around in memory and imagination smelling and hearing things.

WEINBERGER: Your poems are notable both for their extreme condensation and their musicality. Do the lines come out in such compact form? Are the poems initially much longer and then chipped away? Do you consciously count syllables or stresses, or do you mainly write by ear?

SNYDER: There is one sort of poem I write that is highly compressed and has a lot of ear in it. As a poem comes to me, in the process of saying and writing it, the lines themselves establish a basic measure, even a sort of musical or rhythmic phrase for the whole poem. I let it settle down for quite a while and do a lot of fine-tuning as part of the revision. Doing new poems at readings brings out subtle flaws in the movement or music to be immediately noted. I don't count syllables or stresses, but I discover after the fact what form the poem has given itself, and then I further that. Of course I write other sorts of poems as well—longer, less lyrical, formal, borrowings or parodies, and so forth. I am experimenting with switching back and forth between a prose voice and a lyric voice in some of the work I'm doing now.

WEINBERGER: I gather that, unlike many writers, you publish very slowly—allowing things to sit for years before they're brought out in the world. Why is that? And what works are currently hanging up to dry?

SNYDER: Well, I have found that if you let a poem sit around long enough, you come to see and hear it better. Not that a poem in progress doesn't reach a point of being pretty much finished. So I don't rush it—it's a matter of allowing intuition and taste to come into play; you choose to hold onto a piece, waiting for some little turn of insight. This is true of prose writing, too. But letting it wait might be a kind of luxury sometimes because there are often urgent reasons to get things into the world, especially essays dealing with current issues. I recently finished a project I called *Mountains and Rivers Without End*—a series of longish poems that I have been working at for decades. And I'm glad I let it wait that long, it is more tasty.

WEINBERGER: Why do you think it took so long?

SNYDER: Well of course when I launched myself into this in 1956, having just finished the book-length poem *Myths and Texts*—which only took three years—I thought it would be wrapped up in five or six years. I started studying the *Lotus Sutra* and some geomorphology and ecology texts as a bit of beginning research, and also I set sail for Japan. It all got more complicated than I had predicted, and the poems were evasive. So I relaxed, and thought, However long it takes. I kept my eye on it, walking, reflecting and researching, but didn't make any big demands on the mountain-goddess muse. So it worked out to about one section a year for forty years.

WEINBERGER: How does it feel, having completed a forty-year-long project like *Mountains and Rivers Without End?*

SNYDER: How does it feel to finish it? I'm truly grateful. Now I have further work with it though—I'm learning how to read it aloud, and I'm still learning more about its workings.

WEINBERGER: As with Pound and the *Cantos,* did you find it impossible to tear yourself away from *Mountains and Rivers* to work on other things?

SNYDER: As I say, I was pretty relaxed about results for a long time. But I did keep a really sharp focus going, never neglected it. Through those years I also wrote and published fifteen or sixteen books. Then, between 1992 and 1996, seeing the shape of the whole forming up, I put *Mountains and Rivers* ahead of everything else—stopped all other sorts of writing, neglected the garden, let the pine needles pile up on the road, quit giving poetry readings, didn't answer mail, quit going to parties, my old truck quit running—till it was done.

WEINBERGER: Working on a book for forty years, do you carry the germ of your next project? What *are* you going to do next?

SNYDER: What I want to do next is restart the garden and the truck, go out with the young people to some deserts and rivers and maybe cities, and reengage with a bunch of old friends. And then back to prose and the thorny problems of our time.

WEINBERGER: You're one of the few poets whose work is accessible to a non-poetry-reading public. Yet somewhere you say—you're talking about Robert Duncan—that it's the poetry you never fully comprehend that most engages you. I was wondering whether you consciously strike out obscurities, thinking of the general reader, to make the poetry accessible?

SNYDER: Semiconsciously. I've written a number of different sorts of poems and there's a percentage of my poetry—maybe twenty-five percent, maybe forty—that is accessible. I think partly that has been a function of my regard for the audience, my desire to have some poems that I knew that I could share with people I lived and worked with. Certainly a number of the work poems, and poems of travel and poems of place, are works that I could and did share with neighbors or with fellow workers on the job. I've always enjoyed that enormously. At the same time there are territories of mind and challenges that are not easily accessible. I've written a number of rather difficult poems. I just don't read them at poetry readings as a rule.

WEINBERGER: Let me quickly ask you about your book of selected poems. *No Nature,* as a title, obviously takes many aback. It seems apocalyptic until you realize that it's a kind of Buddhist joke: the true nature is no nature, the nature of one's self is no nature. Is that correct?

SNYDER: Yes, and it's also a critical-theory joke.

WEINBERGER: In what sense?

SNYDER: In that some folks hold that everything is a social construction, and I add that society is a natural construction, including the industrial and the toxic.

WEINBERGER: It's interesting that, for someone involved as much as you are in the environmental movement, your work is surprisingly without disasters. There's very little bad news in the poetry—no Bhopals, no Chernobyls. Are you setting positive examples? Or are you just cheerful?

SNYDER: There are several poems that have some very bad news in them. Going all the way back to a poem written in 1956 called "This Tokyo." And the poem that I wrote as an op-ed piece for the *New York Times* in 1972 called "Mother Earth: Her Whales." However, I feel that the condition of our social and ecological life is so serious that we'd better have a sense of humor. That it's too serious just to be angry and despairing. Also, frankly, the environmental movement in the last twenty years has never done well when it threw out excessive doom scenarios. Doom scenarios, even though they might be true, are not politically or psychologically effective. The first step, I think, and that's why it's in my poetry, is to make us love the world rather than to make us fear for the end of the world. Make us love the world, which means the nonhuman as well as the human, and then begin to take better care of it.

WEINBERGER: Many are surprised to discover that you're not a vegetarian and not a Luddite, but rather a carnivore with a Macintosh. This sets you apart from, on the one hand, many Buddhists, and, on the other, from a certain branch of the environmental movement. Any comments?

SNYDER: Come, come, I'm not a carnivore, I'm an omnivore. Carnivores have ridiculously short intestines! I am a very low-key omnivore at that, as are most of the Third World people who eat very little fish or meat, but who certainly wouldn't spurn it. I did a whole discussion of this question—for Buddhists—in a recent issue of *Ten Directions,* from the Zen Center of Los Angeles. The key is still the first precept: "Cause least harm." We have to consider the baleful effects of agribusiness on the global environment, as well as have concern for the poor domestic critters. Ethical behavior is not a matter of following a rule, but examining how a precept might guide one, case by case.

Now, as for environmentalists, my Earth First! and Wild Earth friends are pretty diverse, but one thing they all share is that they are not prigs or puritans. They do ecological politics as a kind of contact sport. I'm all for that.

As for computers: the word processor is not the agent of transformation, it's language that is the agent. The word processor is just a facilitating device. Keep your eye on the ball!

AUDIENCE MEMBER: I was on the phone this afternoon with my teacher, who is a Lakota. I mentioned that I was going to see Gary Snyder. And she said, "Oh, Gary Snyder. He's an Indian. Ask him if he knows it." Do you know that you are an Indian? A Native American.

SNYDER: That was very kind of her to say that. I don't know if I know I'm an Indian or not. However, I do know that I'm a Native American. Here again is a Turtle Island bioregional point. Anyone is, metaphorically speaking, a Native American who is "born again on Turtle Island." Anyone is a Native American who chooses, consciously and deliberately, to live on this continent, this North American continent, with a full spirit for the future, and for how to live on it right, with the consciousness that says, "Yeah, my great-great-grandchildren and all will be here for thousands of years to come. We're not going on to some new frontier, we're here now." In that spirit, African-Americans, Euro-Americans, Asian-Americans, come together as Native Americans. And then you know that those continents that your ancestors came from are great places to visit, but they're not home. Home is here.

WEINBERGER: But do you think that the myths that come out of here belong to everyone?

SNYDER: They belong to the place, and they will come to belong to those who make themselves members of this place. It's not that easy, however. It takes real practice.

WEINBERGER: I'm just playing devil's advocate for a moment. I know in the seventies there were Native Americans who were criticizing you— I don't think rightly—essentially saying, "Hey, white boy, keep your hands off our coyote."

SNYDER: You know, coyote—the trickster image—is found all over the globe. In myth and world folklore, it blankets the planet from forty thousand years ago on. It is totally cosmopolitan, and we know this. So, in that sense, mythology and folklore are archaic international world heritages. The question is to understand what to do with them and how to respond to them. The stories about Coyote Old Man are in fact genuinely something that came out of Native American experience, broke through the civilization-history time barrier and are now fully rooted in twentieth-century literature. That's something that has come across. It's quite amazing. And I'm sure that other things will prove in time to have come across like that. You can't be against it. It makes both worlds, the old and new, richer, and it testifies to the openness of the imagination.

AUDIENCE MEMBER: There are a lot of things that are splitting the country apart nowadays. Does this scare you?

SNYDER: Well, along with everyone else, I have very troubled moments about the future of the United States and our society. And it would be foolish to say that I've got any easy answers. For those who can do it, one of the things to do is not to move. To stay put. Now staying put doesn't mean don't travel. But it means have a place and get involved in what can be done in that place. Because without that we're not going to have a representative democracy that works in America. We're in an oligarchy right now, not a democracy. Part of the reason that it slid into oligarchy is that nobody stays anywhere long enough to take responsibility for a local community and for a place.

AUDIENCE MEMBER: In a radio interview several years ago, you were asked about your politics and you responded that you were an anarchist. Can you explain that, and how that really works?

SNYDER: You know I really regretted saying that on the radio. That was on "Fresh Air." I try not to say that on the radio. In fact, I try not to even use the word *anarchist* because it immediately raises the question that you just raised which is, "Can you explain that?" The term shouldn't be used, it has too many confusing associations. Anarchism should refer to the creation of nonstatist, natural societies as contrasted with legalistically organized societies, as alternative models for human organization. Not to be taken totally literally, but to be taken poetically as a direction toward the formation of better and more viable communities. Anarchism, in political history, does not mean chaos, it means self-government. So a truly anarchist society is a self-governing society. We all need to learn better how to govern ourselves. And we can do that by practice, and practice means you have to go to meetings, and going to meetings means you'll be bored, and so you better learn how to meditate.

WEINBERGER: The dao of bureaucracy.

SNYDER: That's right. The dao of bureaucracy. Anybody who meditates knows how to handle boredom so then you can go to meetings. That's how I got into politics.

AUDIENCE MEMBER: You've had to submit to a very rigorous discipline in your religious practice, learning of languages and study of poetry. Do you find your students now willing to submit to that kind of discipline?

SNYDER: You know, I never felt like I was submitting to discipline. Since I was about sixteen or seventeen, I've never done anything I didn't want to do. It was always my own choice. When I was studying Chinese, it was what I wanted to do. I could have left at any time, nobody was paying me to do it, and I didn't have any parents insisting that I do it. So, I don't know how to answer that. I've always operated from my own free choice. However, I certainly would say that a highly motivated person, willing to engage intensely with something, is not easy to find among the students I've run into. But there are always a few that have some sort of fire under them.

AUDIENCE MEMBER: What would you tell sixteen-year-olds with the world before them, what should they do?

SNYDER: This is one of the occupational hazards of being a poet. You're asked questions that you really don't know an answer for. I'd say the same thing that I say to my eighteen-year-old stepdaughter: you're going to have to get a lot of formal education. And don't think that a four-year education is the end of it. Nowadays you have to go on a little bit farther or it isn't going to mean a whole lot. But even while doing education, don't think it makes you superior to uneducated people or illiterate people, because there's a tremendous amount of cultural wisdom and skill out in the Third World, out in the preliterate world that is intrinsically every bit as viable as anything that Euro-American society has created. And then the fundamental ethical precept: whatever you do, try not to cause too much harm.

Selections
from Journals

Japan, "Of All the Wild Sakura"

Some notes from Kyoto Journals taken between March and June, 1959

10. III. 1959

Tuesday Coming in to Yokohama

Dreamed I was climbing a steep railway embankment with an old hobo; he talked funny, dipthongizing certain vowels—/hwa: yeyus/"why yes"/— I realized that was how Ed McCullough talked at Warm Springs Logging Camp A; I said to myself, Now I know what hobo-dialect is.

A ship passes us, outward bound; a light gray drizzle & a warmish south wind. Six hours from Yokohama.

And now, again, Japan—

Passing the two lights and the breakwater of Yokohama, I can see where the *Sappa Creek* was anchored a year and a half back. The "roads" of Tokyo Bay. Fuji's white dome above smoggy haze. Later: a clear day: waiting in Yokohama Eki for the Kyoto train. Another walk up the stairs to Immigration. The scene is people: warm, noise of it all; I feel quite at home.

And down the Tōkaidō. That big mountain east of Biwa-ko: I recall the time I came back from skiing here with Shimizu; and the arrogant young sumo apprentices on the train.

Red plum blossoms out now—one in the dark shade of farm gully.

Rinko-in {Rinzai temple in Shokoku-ji}

Back at Rinko-in—"Tada ima"—Later to see Philip Yampolsky, and Will Petersen; Ami-ko looks like an Indian. —beautiful skull and black black hair.

Will P. now worrying about painting, "oil painting and Buddhism don't go together" he says—his paintings are rich, and I don't see what he worries about.

Last night it snowed a little. & this morning, 5 A.M., riding with Walter Nowick to Daishû-in, it snowed more, thick and wet.

Goto Rōshi {Walter's teacher and the teacher of Oda Sessô Rōshi} dark-faced & funny.

White hills around the edge of town.

(The time T. & I went to the summit of Grizzly Peak to make love: full moon, a brush fire north, and surprising another couple in the warm grass—September 1955.)

(—thinking back on Crater Mt. Lookout: I was the last one to ever sit in Crater Mountain—built in the thirties—abandoned after my year, '52.

A photo of a woman hung on the window; [Lisa Fonssagrives] her nipple just poking Mt. Challenger, Mt. Sourdough by her thigh. Shave-headed, bearded, reading, melting last winter's snow to make my tea.) Boys, he said, "don't mourn for me, meditate."

sit down & fly.

—Last night dinner at Pete's with the recently-arrived-from-Europe Cid Corman. Stories of poverty in Southern Italy.

leavingtaking (copied from ship board notebook—
It's not real until the
gap between the ship and the dock
gets too wide to jump—Pier 9 Saturday
afternoon at 5 o'clock, the twenty-first
of February 19 hundred fifty-nine.
All of Berkeley hills curved out behind
the Bay—the strange suburban view—
lot homes—that flash back, a brutal
orange sum—glare at the eye
Clarity of spring: Mt. Diablo can be seen
(I never went there) Regrets that quicken
as the ship backs off Potrero Hill
—ah, San Francisco is my home.

Monday Rinko-in
Preparing to leave Shokoku-ji and move to the Kitano river valley. The last few days cleaning the little house I'll rent at Yasek, "Eight Sandbars." Yesterday Petersen and I were out there taking up all the tatami, peering under the floor, shoring up busted boards. Dust everywhere from the road. Yesterday it rained; smoking and sitting on the porch-edge; the white puffs of cloud on the hillsides almost too oriental. Dust and cobwebs, old sake bottles. Today I finished the job, beating the tatami in spots of sun between showers, reading at old *Mainichi* as I laid them out with bug powder.

Mrs. Ishiguro brought bancha for lunch. No dreams since I got here. The big old Rinko-in tom disappeared. & now a brindled male kitten roams about looking for food and warm spots. The temple family rises at 5:30, dust the shoji, cough and piss and talk—barefooted on chill floors, splashing cold water on the face. Camellia blooms / cherry begins / tombi sails over the hinoki tops slowly, twisting and angling his wide flat tail feathers.

24. III.
Cid Corman tearing into much of *Myths and Texts* [just-then published book of poems by GS], it isn't "real" he says of "Io" and other borrowings from Occidental sources. The Native-American-derived stuff he thinks makes it. Digs the concrete and directly experienced portions—finds the language not compressed or sharp enough often. He's a very scrupulous critic but not always right.

Kerosene stoves, gasoline stoves, propane.

28. III.
Saturday Yase
—living at Yase. Sunlight from over Hiei; rice cooking in the kamado and *kai* on the konro. The house feels too big and the road is terrible dusty; perhaps I won't be able to make it here. But will see. Yesterday Pete brought Glen Grosjean out—looking young, chapped, red-faced, & more relaxed. He is moving to a new job up at Sendai—says he couldn't do decent sanzen with his roshi because he didn't respect him. Only stayed til 11 A.M. Afternoon Corman came—we climbed the hill in back, talking poetry as we crashed through the underbrush.

29. III.
& last night dinner with Mrs. [Ruth Fuller Everett] Sasaki: She seems much less inclin'd to arrogance.

& I much less inclined to be annoyed with her simply because she has money and is of the middle class. Today—chilly dusty—I come to recognize the tombi (kite) that works up and down the river—the sense of the place is growing.

What one has to do to fix up a house to live in the country:

I had to order 2 wooden well-buckets (*oke*), buy a rope, two short chains, a coil of copper wire, hook it all up over the sheave and seize the eyes with wire—to get water out of the courtyard well.

Had to buy a dustpan, a broom for tatami, & a broom for the daidokoro [*niwaboke*].

The gardners came & trim'd the poor pine trees.

The electricity man—upon request—came and put up a meter. There seem to be no fuses. Then bought: friction tape, coat-hangers, scouring powder, laundry soap, a mirror, a wire to broil fish on, a basket for sumi, a chopping block, a kitchen knife, a *nata* (axe), a sugar can and 2 kilo brown sugar; kitchen scrub brushes, a pair of zoris, a knife sharpen stone, & *hibashi,* fire tongs.

Walter gave me a *shichirin* (charcoal brazier) to cook on. Complete. & a huge stack of Rinko-in plates, bowls, etc.

Had to order a *shikibuton* (bottom futon) made at cost of Y.3000 in a fine dark *unsui* (Zen monk) blue.

Ordered a personal *han* (seal). & bought a basketload of sumi, charcoal, & six bundles of firewood, from a little old local woman with horny hands.

Bought US mountain white gas stove at the surplus store.

Took all the mats out, beat them, & swept the under-flooring with Pete. Wiped off everything. Hired a 3-wheel truck to bring me & all my goods out—stopping on-route at Pete's to get desk & all that cost Y.600.

Now there remains much cleaning yet to be done.

The complicated and numerous objects one requires even for simple life.

30. III.

Workman came into Sakyo-ku *yakusho* (city office); seat stoutly patched & sewn in square spirals of classic design.

Literary Languages:

Far East: Chinese / Japanese . . . Tibetan, Mongol, Korean

India: Sanskrit into: Bengali / Hindi / etc. Also Tamil, off on its own.

Islamic: Arabic / Persian / Urdu etc.

Classical: Greek / Latin

Romance: French / Italian / Spanish

Ancient: Coptic, Zend, Hebrew etc.

others are—Germanic, Slavic, Celtic. The three root traditions are Graeco-Roman, Sanskrit India, & China.

Last night Yampolsky and I ate out and wandered a bit the bars. I feel weird. As though the Sappa Creek and San Francisco knocked all the shit out of my head.
It starts all over again.
am I young?
this time clear.
ears, nose, eye, skin,
mind, mouth.

The taste of iron and vinegar. Those fools.
irony [L.G. dissimulation, pretence.
clinch [beat back the end. cf. / clench /
buxom [AS bu-an, "bow"] flexible, yielding, gentle] blithe, comely,
as per girls] vigorous, good-tempered] plump.
dint—a blow or stroke. cf. dent. By dint of; by force of.
re/ my dusty road, [kanji]
quoth Petersen.
Modern psychology is just beginning to recognize the existence of creatures and images of the mind that Buddhism learned to exorcise as illusion long ago.

Sunday
Today at Kawamura Nōgakudō, with Ami and Will Petersen, Corman. Program was Tadanori, Uneme, Sumidagawa, Kantan. *Sumidagawa* gets absolutely hair-raising when the Kokata (this time actually a little girl of four) quavers out "Namu amida butsu" from the tomb. The whole of *Kantan* is superb. And riding home at night in April rain. Soaking wet.

A *butsudan* needs:
    1 sentatte (incense holder)
    2 rosokutatte (candle holders)
    2 kabin (vases)
    3 buppan or bukki (to hold rice)
    1 chatōki (for tea)
    —Yoshida the Butsuguya-san. Ordering a few items for Marin-an

Zendo below Mt. Tamalpais in California. & riding my new Honda Dream 250 motorcycle everywhere. Joanne Kyger says she will come to Japan.

Wa! Spring! By the river.
frogs all creaking
bugs begin to fly in at night to
bang on the light-bulb.
seeking the light! pow! like me.

Poverty and appreciation of the mind, in the far east.

& though it may take years to make a man wise, he cannot put off the necessity *right now* for dealing with the problems of himself and people. The woes of the world. & it is at that point we judge.

30. IV. Yase

/ *Jinchû-an* / *Hermitage in the Dust*
"Well, do you think you'll ever amount to anything?"—1st Engineer USNS Sappa Creed sd to me.

And start regular sanzen interviews with Oda Sessō Rōshi {Monastic rōshi and Kanchō of Daitoku-ji}. Rain at 3 A.M. teisho at 9. Koan received: Hear the sound of a single hand. "Sekishu no onjo wo kiite koyō."—Hakuin.

(The question I must pose, to myself or someone: can Zen Buddhism bless a marriage, or merely consider it a second-rate expedient. If not, then not really a religion; but a psychological discipline, sect, or cult.

A religion must, as one of its functions, serve to relate and define the individual in relation to his wife, his family, and society, as well as the metaphysical absolute. Existenz.)

8. V.

29 years old this morn—and this morning after sanzen, took a ride up Northwest of the city and into the hills—what green jumbled and twisty mountain views. Gunning the cycle around steep gravelly curves and bouncing on the ruts & boulders. Frogs & birds. Turned back at a road-head in an unexpected high hamlet. But electricity everywhere. This place, the quad tells me later, was Himuro, "Ice House."

10. V.

Installation of the new Abbot of Shokoku-ji

Shokoku-ji ceremony installing—*jōza*—"climbing into the chair" for Otsu Rōshi as new Kanchō. Jan the Dutchman [Janwillem Van de Wetering], Paul Wienpahl [Philosopher from Santa Barbara, Spinoza-specialist], & me.

Hatto./ Dharma Hall

Otsu Rōshi sits in a chair on the floor before the high platform. Monks start beating the two drums on each side of the hatto. 2 blows each, alternating ⸱ / ⸱ / ⸱ —gradually speeding up. The shokoku priests file in from North door. Rhythm gradually speeds up, then breaks and starts slow again. Builds up.

Audience is older men and women. The women talk a lot. The men are in suits, a few in swallow-tail coats and morning pants. Old Kyoto women—with a certain sneaky humility.

Drumbeats shift to alternate single beats on center of drum. Great reverberation. Hitting the drum with both mallets at the same time. Builds up again to a low roar on both drums, then starts slow again.

The walls open, sunshine outside, a huge system of hanging pennants over the platform limply moving.

Oda Rōshi comes in. Other priests keep coming in. Four tall candles in 6 foot high holders on the floor before the platform. A green pine-top on the west side of it, on top.

The high hall, wood pillars, dragon, and thunder-drum.

Drums stop. Otsu Rō climbs the stairs to the top of the platform and the jōza in big Chinese slippers. With lots of young monks' help, gets in the chair and carefully adjusts his robes. His kesa is magnificent stiff gold brocade. All the priests, row by row, come and bow before him. He acknowledges each with a gassho. Then monk hands him his hossu, he swishes it about.

He sits up and starts to yell in a weird voice—Chinese *goroku* chanting voice I think. Incomprehensible to everyone. But a spectacle. Outside some little kid with a voice like a magpie shouts.

Now he takes his staff, with what looks like a frog gig on the bottom, thumps it, and chants out again in the Chinese Voice.

Vowels drawn out, strange rises and drops, breaks, falling to a growl and other times rather high and clear.

Then from Chinese Voice to sutra chant.

He gets down from his chair, comes back to the floor, walks out, all the other priests following him.

28. V.

The fourth good day in a row, and I burned the rest of the leaves and limbs from when the trees were trimmed; cleared weeds and turned over the soil—Jan the Dutchman and Walter N. came at 9:00 with seeds and plants, and we put in cucumbers, eggplant, 3 kinds of beans, spinach, radishes, and dill.

Then had tea and strawberries, and Jan and Walter returned. Napped in the sun, and afternoon made a jar of strawberry jam; a shelf in the shoebox, and Spanish rice. How nice the sun. I sit here below Mt Hiei, along-side the Kitano river, Kyoto city just downstream, working on a koan, recalling friends, and gazing across the steep mountain slopes. I should write friend Valery about Japanese gardens.

(The woman planet. Naked Greek Athletes. How.)

—of all the wild sakura,
one small tree alone on the far hill,
surrounded by dark straight sugi
is best.

Australia

September–October, 1982, with John Stokes and Nanao Sakaki

Gossip Around Ayers' Rock

Clive the guitarist speaks of the mysterious creation of a brand-new dingo dreaming myth—coming out of the events of last year when a dingo supposedly stole an infant girl out of a tent over at the public campground, dragged it off, and the baby (whose name was Azaria) was never seen again. An aboriginal tracker was brought in, tried to track the dingo but after a while refused to continue, saying that it was not a dingo he was tracking but an evil spirit.

Other elder aboriginal people said a dingo could not and would not steal a baby. A cloud of innuendo began to surround the case when police investigated the parents, and a suspicion arose (in all the newspapers of Australia) that perhaps the parents themselves did the baby in. So there is still a great search going on to try and find some of the child's remains. And Clive says another level of the myth is that the devil dingo, which appeared once long ago in the dreamtime, appeared to take Baby Azaria away and raise her, and that in the year 2000 she will return as the Mother Goddess, or something like that—spiritual White Kids latching onto the old indigenous stories. The new dingo dreamtime story being made right now.

Stokes then reports what Robert Bly said at a talk in Adelaide. Bly was commenting on the thirteen young women who all mysteriously disappeared from a picnic at Hanging Rock in the 1890s. No one found out what happened to any of them. Bly says, "You want to know what happened to the girls at Hanging Rock? Because you Australians won't give the aborigines their land back, your women are going to disappear. What happens then? They turn into black swans and the black swans turn into B52s. How do I know? Because that's what happened in America." Very useful commentary, Mr. Bly.

Singing at the School at the Ranch

Schoolchildren in the class. Maybe five of the little girls and one of the boys absolutely stark naked. The others only partly dressed. They are all between four and six. We sit together on a big mat. The youngsters on one side, Nanao and John and me on the other. We drum for them, sing for them, sit crosslegged with them, show them full lotus. One little black naked four year old looking intently at me as I play the jaw harp for maybe a full five minutes. Eyes meeting across what gulf.

Shiva shiva shiva. Black skin, dusty sheen, matted tangled locks. White ash on the body. Hot sun burning down red rock, red soil. Barefoot beings. All these are the mark of Shiva. Shiva really is the lord of the Old Ways. The lord of wild people. Wild hair. So it was right to chant the Shiva mantra in the kindergarten and first-grade classes today.

I can see why they are right and how they are right. Even down to destroying an old house. Right—like, right to be naked. Correct to be sitting on the sand. Correct to be keeping the women on one side and the men on the other. Right to put white ash on the skin. Precisely right, to sit in the shade of a bush all afternoon. Not correct for the outside world, but so precisely correct for themselves and for their place.

And the ranch is where the two worlds meet. In the late afternoon, go with Ronnie a mile or so beyond the settlement to where a horse muster is taking place, a paddock with mares and colts rounded up in it. Six or eight black stockmen. Some of those cowboys barefoot. Some starting a little brush fire and heating water for tea. One lad at top speed on a black horse galloping through the scrub. A wild horse coming from outside the paddock and standing up to the fence, communicating with the horses inside. One black cowboy comes over from the fire to our truck and passes out chunks of cold wild cooked rabbit for an afternoon snack. That loose arm-swinging relaxed easygoing powerful gait. Chief stockman's name is Murray. Says the brand here is 72W.

And later yet, Bruce Sweet takes me out the fenceline to the north to see an old Comet windmill pump installed out there with his new-style cement and brick watering trough. He says that they've got a range here for their cattle that extends 90 miles to the west. And that from there, the last fence, there is not another fence or human settlement through the deserts of western Australia for 1200 miles.

Dreaming at Papunya

We will get away from Alice Springs when our three aboriginal elders are found. Nose-peg, and the one with a green headband is here, but the third is nowhere to be seen. In Billy Marshall's truck, and Neal Murray in his station wagon, we cruise Alice Springs for an hour looking for the third old man. Stop at the fringe camps, where groups of three or four people are sitting in straggly eucalyptus shade (ghost gum trees), some sleeping, others distant, ambling leisurely along the dry creekbed—broad, dry sandy arroyo. Sitting on the ground. Little circles of people in any bit of shade on the outskirts of Alice Springs, the white man's town. And the fringe camps, half open buildings—toilets and showers—places for out-skirts aborigines to live part time. The old man is nowhere here, but finally we get the rumor that he went ahead in somebody else's car. So we head out of town, west, for the settlement of Pupunya.

Old men's white hair pulled back by headbands, tied down with ban-danas, bristly white beards. The dark heavy brows and broad nose, deeply set, fierce twinkly eyes. Skinny legs. About halfway to Pupunya we pull off the dirt road to a little *molga* shade littered with tin cans and bottles— the midway rest point. Everybody out of the car. Another car pulls in too. It's the teacher from Yuenduma—Rex Granite, spiffy educated school-teacher—but we all sit on the ground and have a beer and a toke. Much kangaroo droppings here. We ask old Nose-peg what's the aboriginal name for the spot. He says "Kangaroo Droppings." He says this in Wal-biri. We don't know if he is kidding or serious.

Farther down the long straight road leaving the red dust trail—scrag-gly occasional cattle—red clay ant hills, openings of vast dry grass—tus-sock grass—pastures, closed in again by acacia scrub, vegetation always changing—see in sunset far mountains silhouetted with steep pinnacles. They would be right on the tropic of Capricorn, Billy says. "One of the least seen ranges in all Australia."

The long straight roads from just north of Alice Springs coming west-ward across 200 miles of desert to Papunya. Warm desert air tonight, and in Pupunya the dogs bark and rock-and-roll comes across the flats from the scattered cement settlement houses.

Just before sunset we have dinner outside in the dark cooking over an open fire. No place to sit but the dirt with the dogs. Then we went to the next house, Neal's, to sleep. Neal Murray, the youthful poet who works as an outstation teacher here, is a single man who lives in a full-size regula-tion government house, and there is nothing in his house to indicate any-one ever lives there, except some musical instruments. The rest is empty and dirty. So strangely so that Nanao, John, and I don't want to sleep in it—also such bright lights—so we spread our bedrolls outside.

All night outside, the bright light of the moon, the light of the street-lights, the roar of the distant settlement generator, and the periodic uproar of dogs. A few hundred yards away a small outdoor sitting, sleeping out group of black people, making speeches most of the night. Swarms of tiny ants clinging to the bedroll—they don't bite.

Clive and Jeannie, Billy Marshall—this whole generation of whites teaching and working with outback people are able to relax, laugh, enjoy the company and the problems of living here with some humor. Clive tells the story of how his favorite western boots were stolen from his house, so he went to the village council leader, mentioned it to him, that man saying that—sure, it must have been stolen by petrol sniffers—and that then a few days later he saw the village council leader wearing his boots around the settlement. So Clive says with a big laugh, "I said to him, 'hey, what about giving me my boots back'—and the man said, also laughing, 'Oh I was just keeping them for you till I saw you to return them.'"

These are the ways to be: sleep a lot in the daytime. Do your walks at night and take the whole family traveling at night when it's cool. Stop again in the day and everybody sleep under the shade of a tree. Sleep in the daytime a lot anyway, and on moonlit nights hunt. On moonlit nights go food gathering. Have your parties late at night. Dance. Paint your bodies. Make music till dawn. Catch up on sleep in the shade of a tree in the daytime. Never bother to make the children go to sleep at any time. Let them sleep whenever they will. Have strict rules about who can have sex with whom, punishment of death, and then at certain parties and ceremonies— break all the rules.

A chasm crosses through the mountains to the desert south of us. Billy Marshall says, "Going through those hills. Inside of that is an owl dreaming place". Owl dreaming place—place of owl essence. Place ideal to owls. Sphere of being of owls. Optimal owl habitat, curious superior owl occasion, this is how it becomes an aboriginal way of seeing essence-of-owlness. Like northern California Sierra as one wide ponderosa pine dreaming-ground. And its Spotted owl dreamers.

Australia: a poor biomass, arid landscape, no real rivers, so people take it easy. No way to change the world. No way to hurt the world. No world to lose. No world to save.

Ladakh

In Ladakh, on the western Tibetan Plateau, in the state of Jammu-Kashmir India, drainage of the Indus river, September 1992, with Gen Snyder.

The Tara-puja at the Spitok Temple / Gompa

Spitok Gompa is a complex of rusty-red–painted stone-and-adobe buildings up on an isolated rocky little hill on the valley floor. We explore through several rooms and halls, and then come on the main Buddha-hall. Four monks are sitting around a table along the left side of the hall, making a sand-painting mandala. On the left wall of the hall, behind glass doors, visible in tied bundles, is a set of volumes of the Kanjur, on the right side of hall is a set of the Tanjur. At the back is a huge Shakyamuni. On his left a Tara, and on the right a Tsong-kha-pa. The sand-painting monks, seated up on a platform, bending forward, crosslegged over their sand painting, working with these colored minerals, making this complex painting out of the rock of the world. They said they went for special studies in south India—where the experts in this Tibetan art are gathered and teaching. And they said that the tradition of sand-painting mandalas comes, originally from India, forgotten now there, remembered in Tibet.

Some notes on the female Bodhisattva, Tara. There is a whole room here, a whole chamber aside, that is full of additional small Tara figures on shelves. Tara, her face and body, her aspect, is full and lovely, but not erotic or maternal, somewhere between; a complex figure with a savvy and sympathetic gaze. Although she is described as a figure of compassion, she has more of calm aloofness and gentle but unmistakable intelligence. There is one figure in the Tara hall, only 9 or 10 inches tall, a standing figure, that was described to us by the lama as a "wrathful Tara." There are very striking wrathful female images in India culminating in Kali—so he said, "This is our Kali-Tara." But when we look at her face closely it has none of the bloodthirsty mind-splitting rage of the Kali face. The features not contorted, the teeth bared but not open—a kind of understated, elegant but fierce annoyance. These figures combine dignity, intelligence, half-naked beauty, and ease—never overly stiff or formal, yet thoroughly dignified.

We're standing out on the highest of the flat roofs of Spitok Gompa and looking eastward up the Indus Valley—the bottoms are a broad green irrigated territory almost a mile wide. The barley crop is now being cut and stacked and taken in and dried. A steep bank along the far shore of the river and a long dry *bajada* that rises behind it—then beyond that is a range of mountains with snow. The upstream Indus makes a bend to the south beyond the ridges. White clouds, blue sky.

The conches begin to blow from another rooftop. The Tara puja is about to begin. We are invited into the Tara-hall, and sit against the back wall—in zazen, crowded. Many Ladakhis and Indian tourists and soldiers also push in. The leader is a boy, probably a tulku, reincarnated lama, who takes the center seat facing the Tara-image, and bows, stands, prostrates, does the gestures, sometimes with a faint grin, and a certain insouciant flair. The monks chanting and playing instruments along each side are equally relaxed.

We are all served a bit from the puja, receiving dabs of tea, barley flour, an apple, and plain bread by younger monks who circulate through the crowd. Each gets a sip of *chang,* the homemade barley wine. An old lama in a sleeveless red sweater, with his robe top off, has the big callous on his ankle of a man who sits in meditation a lot. What a gang, I think. In this multi-storied mud-brick tower of rooms and icons, libraries and bells and gongs—funny serious men all ages celebrating the generosity of the Great Bodhisattva Goddess Tara, in a landscape of almost zero fertility.

The Large Women's Gathering

In the afternoon: at the low end of town, we all attend a gathering of women from the villages around Leh, women's meeting. All of these are farm women. Yellow tent, banner set up, something for all of us—some reason that this was all put together. So the first part was a very large circle dance of traditional women. Most of our group was led to seats under the tent. Rows of narrow sitting carpets, with the colorful little low tables. Many women sat in rows under the tent without dancing, as well. Hundreds, three hundred?—and we're constantly served salted Tibetan tea, little tiny apples and then *tsampa* cakes. I sat next to a lama on the one side and Aman Sinkh from the ashram in Rajasthan on the other side.

And then, the second part of this, which Helena Norberg-Hodge put together, is the presentation of a play, partly in English and partly in Ladakhi; the actors being Ladakhi kids and some of the foreign tourist youth, all drafted into working on this together—satirizing Western culture and making the point that the attractions of occidental materialism are not so great—so they've got the characters of an old man with Parkinson's Disease—a drunken father—a bag lady wandering around and through the audience. I can't see much of it, the crowd is so dense, and can't hear well because their voices aren't loud enough, but people are laughing and what a goofy idea to try this anyway. Three army people, one with an automatic rifle over his shoulder, are standing around watching it, looking at the play, seeming very relaxed, handsome, cool.

This is said to be the largest gathering of traditional people in the Leh area for eighty or ninety years. Women here a powerful presence, all in their traditional clothes, under the canvas, tight-packed, sitting on the rugs, serving each other and talking, chatting, all with a kind of relaxed dignity and yet at no point while we were there, any official talks or speeches given. Almost continuously some women are moving in the stately circle dances. The dance: a slow, graceful, short step with a kind of occasional skip.

The left hand holding the sash down, the right-hand sash over the shoulder holding it out. Intricacies in these little skip steps that are very subtle. The circle will be going one way and then at a point it turns and goes the other way a short distance. Segments of the circle will turn and go one way and another segment, the other. And then they'll rejoin and be again a full circle. At another time, the dance changes, and the difference is seen in the way the dancers are holding their right hand, which would be, as I saw, one sequence.

Gen said it's Noh drama. Later men also joined the dance, and younger women. I got the sense that anyone who wished to could dance. Very much indeed in the flavor of Noh dance.

Ladakhi women also served us guests cup after cup of Tibetan tea and some occasional chang. And when I got up and went out in the field around the lights and the canvas, I came onto the kitchen, the cooking area, seven four-foot-wide flat-bottomed tureens sitting across rock rings, with firewood and dung burning underneath each one—seven in a row and then an eighth one backed up against a boulder. All of it lit by one light bulb hanging from a tree limb. A group of women squatting nearby laying out *chapatis* and yet another group squatting pounding spices. Little stacks of food and supplies on plastic sheets and burlap. It's mostly men putting together this big meal for the hundreds of traditional women and their guests.

The Fields and Mountains Around Rumbak Village

Rumbak is a settlement that can only be reached by a seven-hour walk from the Indus River valley up a rocky creekbed trail. Coming into the high valley of Rumbak, we stretched out on a little grassy place and napped half an hour. And then the sun went behind the mountain and the cold shadow overtook us, woke us, and we went the next mile up to Rumbak village. Angdu's parents were still out in the fields so we stepped into a half-built house up the hill and were served both salt tea and black tea. It had a small Tara shrine and a little old table and a rug. Across from that on a square torn out of an old tarp on the floor something drying on it— tasting it, it was caraway seed. And Angdu says, not cultivated but it grows wild here. I chanted the Tara mantra in a soft voice for the Tara shrine and Angdu picked up on it and finished the mantra with me. Then down to the house and through the yard, part of which was full of penned-up goats, another part two cows and another stone corral, the two horses. Picked our packs up from the stone step and went into the unlit interior of the first floor. Ploughs and tools along the side and then up very steep stairs, second floor, also dark, up to the third floor, toilet to the left, and then step out onto the roof. And a room off the roof full of folded mattresses and rugs, a sewing machine, a table, a few other odds and ends. A Tibetan calendar is given to us, we spread out two beds, put rugs on them, put our sleeping bags down and simply rest—so tired.

Angdu's oldest brother lives here, runs the farm. His sister is married, living in Sabu. And one brother in the army, another brother will soon join the army. Another brother works for the government in Leh, and a final brother is a ponyman. Angdu learned English in Leh. He occasionally guides people over the pass.

This place puts me in mind of Neolithic semi-pastoralists living in mud-brick houses showing countless collapse and rebuilding and renovating over the centuries. Old abandoned buildings being reincorporated, the sheep and cows in tight stone pens against the house. Right now off the roof in the twilight I look down on a woman milking a cow.

An ancient lady here on the roof—in another rooftop room—cooking her own dinner with a single candle for light. Then she sits in the entrance: thick glasses, dark wrinkled skin and wispy white hair, and a white sheepskin over her back for warmth. The family eats on the floor below. Up through the square smoke-hole come beams of gas-mantle lamplight. Then comes again more tea and at eight a dinner of rice and potato with a little curry sauce. Gen and I blow out the candle and go to sleep at 8:30.

Next day we take a walk up a westerly branch canyon toward Gandha

Pass. On the rocks above us wild sheep. Up here the final highest household, called Urutay, just one building. Two choughs, black birds slightly smaller than a crow with a kind of piping cry, come down the canyon together and then settle on an outcropping. Across the canyon a herd of goats being driven over the dry talus toward higher ground. Yaks and Dzos wandering the narrow barleyfield edges. (The bird is a yellow-billed chough—looked it up—found all through the Himalayas at higher elevations.)

More wild blue sheep up a side canyon resting on ledges. Past the village some fields of caraway. We pull the seeds off the heads and just eat them—delicious. A golden eagle flying in the sky. Up a side canyon now looking across to Stok pass which is steep looking indeed and to the right going up toward some snowy peaks, snowy hills, I guess that's the Rumbak Glacier.

A big flat rock by the side of the trail painted in English, " Save Wildlife" which I gassho to almost unconsciously say, om mani padme hum ... "Om Save Wildlife Hum"—that would be a great mantra.

On the return over to Rumbak—at the bench of barleyfields, workers are singing. We sit at the edge of a field and a woman, her children, her baby stop by. We get a shot of warm thermos butter-tea, *guguti.*

Truly, songs in the fields. Sitting on a grassy strip between one harvested and one yet unharvested barleyfield, Angdu making tea in a little pot, which is perched on a rough stone tripod fired with dung and twigs. A young mother carrying a baby came over with three other children and they sat in a cluster near us, six feet away, three elegant, really raggedy, dirty-faced, grinning kids, each attending to and playing with the youngest, who could not be satisfied by nursing, and so keeps crying. And then Angdu put powdered milk and sugar in the tea and made a passable chai. We sat in the setting sun drinking with the people finishing up their work for the day, driving stock and beginning to walk back toward the village.

The confluence of countless villages can be refined to a high culture expressed in this essence: A harvest song.

We continue ascending the side-drainage back to the village. Up on the roof dusk comes as two yaks are unloaded below. Yongden finally goes down to the prayer-wheel chapel beside the trail and is in there a long time, the bell ringing as he spins the wheel. A multitude of prayers for the world.

We eat dinner sitting on the floor of our rooftop room on a rug, by candle, bowls of *dhal-bat,* which is "lentil stew and rice" and nothing else. I study the Flemings' *Birds of Nepal* by candlelight. Tomorrow we cross Stok Pass.

Next morning mindful of walking; haul of the lungs, articulation of the ankle, heels, and toes, and the knee bending back, and the weight carried forward on the hip joints. Heartbeat rhythm, somehow tangled with breath, and eyes not straying from the trail, staying on the beat.

(Islamic and Christian fundamentalism can be seen as the desperately sincere but somewhat witless effort to establish a bulwark against the world, which is to say, against the institutionalized forces of greed and commercialism in the larger society. The Buddhist answer would be non-attachment: at its best an attitude giving full recognition to the intrinsic worth of things, including even crummy consumer items, but with a clear grasp of where real values lie.)

Now up here only a few minutes from the Pass are Blue Gentians, in bloom. In bloom at the end of September—what a cycle. Approaching the crest, I go tenderly, slow down a little, don't breathe too fast, be gentle, and approach the crest, gently to the top.

At the pass, elevation 16,072 feet, three hours exactly from the village to here, snow falling lightly but through those flurries views both ways.

Tan, reddish, yellowish, bare bands of intense vertical strata, blades running parallel. Uninhabitable mountains and a far view down to the Indus Valley, a back look to Rumbak. Clouds and mist and mountains coming through and the gold and orange of the plants—we are in the midst of them now. And then down toward the outflow from the Stok glacier; soft, slidey, steep slopes switchbacking, chough calls from above us. And around, back and forth across this cirque.

I just got it—going downhill from Stok Pass—these mountains are so steep, vertical, eroded, pointed, without meadow or lake—because they're so new—they're the newest mountains on the planet. "Say hello to the Baby Himalayas." The sheep love the Himalayas, the Himalayas love sheep. Each blue sheep thinks the Himalaya is hers alone. Mountains always folding and in-folding, like dough, like bread dough.

More stone walls even way high here. This is post-agriculture toil. I don't believe the hunters & gatherers ever worked this hard.

And who is the Ancient One in these mountains? It's the wild sheep whose horns are on the top of the roof, pre-Buddhist, earliest people who came here, came hunting blue sheep. Little shamanist touch from before.

Stok River coming out of Stok Glacier joining with our creek is a sizable body of water now with some big tough bushy 20 foot tall willows filling in the bottoms. High above us on a most unlikely set of pinnacles are the stone remnants of what Angdu says are some old fort or palace—way up there, way out of the way.

Remember that in our earlier world in which everyone walked or rode a horse everywhere, places like this were not so remote—they're more equal—climbing mountains isn't that much harder than walking anywhere else and our perception of the isolation of a region like this is skewed by the age of railroads and cars. Descending down and down, switchbacks and slides, to gentler ground, the gravel alluvium and skirting along the edges of the irrigation canals and half-ruined pathways between the water, the alluvium, the fields and the walls, and now entering into the actual lanes of the upper end of the village of Stok.

Back to Leh that night. At eve, gentle biologist Nurbu comes by to retrieve his *Birds of Nepal*—it's a rare book now.

Botswana
and Zimbabwe

Travels with Gen Snyder and Kai Snyder,
who worked there in April of 1994.

Baboon Camp in the Okavango Delta

The slightly higher, forested ground called is "islands"—the grass fields "Molapo." Out walking this morning with baboon scientist Ryne Palombit, on his morning observation tour. Little baboons riding on the backs of their moms, or males, not even necessarily the father.

Ryne's method:
1) a regular tracking of individuals/while noting group behavior
2) call playback to establish an objective basis for describing social status/rank and interaction/carefully done/specific set-up

7:20 A.M. east of Camp about 1.5 mile, driving along the rough track, come on the band—Savanna baboon—in a strip of trees with the grass fields, *molapos*, on each side. Five or six tree species. Sandy soil—with a three-canopy plant cover. Baboons right now eating a type of wild fig.

Females' peritoneal tissue externalized and gets very pink—a whole exposed labia-minor?

Tracks everywhere; cover the ground—roadbed shows it. The constant little calls are a keeping-in-touch.

Impalas fight, skirmish, kick up dust. Impala bucks in groups dancing away down the glade. Truly some sort of "peaceable kingdom" if you don't mind the predators bringing down their meals.

Females assume rank under mothers, sisters, without much big aggression. Eating the beans of the pods of the camelthorn tree

(Yogin or yogini, nun or monk's deliberate choice of nonreproductive "low status" celibate role could be seen as a truly *revolutionary* move in the over-all history of biological evolution where so much hinges on reproductive success.)

Baboons eat various acacia species—succulent fruit, jackal berry, figs, grass seeds, water lily roots, insects, termites. While moving, the band as a whole will spread over as much as eight hundred yards. They drift through the trees, walking, climbing, leaping down—plucking and eating. Baboon as a broad-spectrum user of a wide range of resources. They don't crowd or herd up—move through the tall grass now drying out. Leisurely, spaciously, nibbling & tasting as they pass. The females live out their lives in a home range. The young males must move out, and join a new group.

Ryne: "I get the feeling that the males follow the females along. The females have kids or they're pregnant & need lots of food—so *they* follow the food, and the males follow *them*."

Calls: vervets and baboons slap kids for making fake alarm calls. They have different calls that will identify different predators. A young one learns not to mistake a vulture for a turkey. The basic call vocabulary is for food items, and to point out predators. Says Ryne.

—Baboons up in the "Sycamore Fig" *muchabe,* as I study washtub-size elephant droppings in the 4-wheel drive dirt road.

A Walk in the Delta Forests & Wetlands

From Baboon Camp. The green tent on its welded steel pipe frame is like a small cabin—shaded porch projecting—a blue-green plastic floor, sur-rounded by a clean-raked sand clearing right up to where suddenly the jungly vegetation starts. This is to protect us from snakes. And looking out on the green field stretch of waterway, beyond that, grasses, and then reeds; beyond that walls of papyrus stems and a few tree clumps, and beyond that a line of large trees. Behind that rank after rank of white and steely gray clouds against a steely blue sky. Some white-headed fish eagle aizles over the reed beds, the grass beds and rushes, something in his sights.

Out for the day with two local men who work as *mokoro,* dugout polers. The younger, barefoot, speaks no English, wears shorts, big smile. And the older, the leader, says his name is Jameson. He is wearing polyester glen plaid permanent-crease trousers and dark brown polyester short sleeve shirt, here as part of the Goodwill movement of used clothes to the third world.

These two old silvery dugouts, slightly asymmetrical, with a little bundle of rushes on the bottom, which provides a seat that stays dry. Kai and Gen in one, me in the other, one man each poling each with a long, clean, limber pole—sends us scooting along the waterway and out to the main channel. They pole us upstream against the current, dodging from bank to bank, skillfully finding the slack waters and the easy poling as they go.

A Reed-buck that gives a sharp-cry and then dashes off from the boat. We turn off the main channel into a shallower one and scoot around inland toward a ridge of big trees. Finally beach up and step out, pick up the food and we are in a vast grassy plain with occasional clumps of trees. We begin to walk. The grass is shoulder or waist high, swishing against our bare legs and shorts—wearing teva sandals—I wonder if it's smart to be so lightly dressed. Off on the left, thirty or forty wildebeests look at us this way and that way and then break into a run and dash, leaving dust. Right behind them three warthogs do the same—with little stubby tails erected like flags as they go. We press on through field after field, molapo after molapo, walking steadily on, another clump of warthogs. We see more warthogs dashing off, several more wildebeests, come up on a little rise of shady trees and there's a jackal dashing off. It's a "black-backed jackal." Sit in the shade and rest.

We're not far from the river channel now and so we turn downstream walking parallel with it and see the flight of saddle-beaked storks and wattled cranes, rising, sailing, dropping behind the trees. Crossing some low marshy ground and around another rise there's a moist depression stretching away, in which the cranes and storks are now standing, and as I step into another marshy place to wade, hear a loud splashing sound and see something half swimming half running away, I think it's a young crocodile, but no, it is a six-foot-long monitor lizard on a dash. We come to a rise and a grove, and decide to stop for lunch—go into a deeply shaded space under arching trees, clearly an animal sheltering place, with lots of dung—cape buffalo—but it's old and dry so Jameson says they aren't here now. We've hardly started to settle in and we hear a little noise just beyond the bushes. We look more closely and first there's the head of one, and then a total of four big Cape Buffaloes fifty or sixty feet away. Standing and looking at us.

This is supposed to be scary, and so we all joke and pick out a tree to climb if they charge, but they don't, they turn in a moment and amble off, going off across the grass opening, so we sit here and share our lunch with our polers, relax a while sitting on the dry leaves among lots of buffalo droppings in the shade.

Lunch over, we head east across another grassy plain. This time the grass species is very sharp and bladelike for a spell—rasping on the skin but it doesn't draw blood. We go past little tree islands, up seven or eight feet above us, built on maybe old termite nests. Across the stretches the gray-white termite lingams, raised up by these pale underground creatures in celebration of six-legged Shiva. Sometimes they are plastered right into and among the many trunks of a tree, intertwining the termite nest with the tree trunk. Farther eastward we come on a two-acre or so torn-up slight depression, with shallow pits each scooped or dug out areas seven feet across. A lot of warthogs have been rooting here. Next we see a group of zebras and another little group of warthogs.

And saddle-bill storks and a family of warthogs getting alarmed and running off at the same moment. (Saw earlier reed bucks fleeing as storks sailed off over them, birds and reed bucks flying away together. High in the sky, a fish-eagle soars and turns, looking so much like an American bald eagle.) In making this big circuit, we are really turned around. I could not hope to find my way easily back to the little boat. But there we are—suddenly on the mokoro, and poling back downstream. At first only eighteen inches deep, filled with grass and streamers of water plants. And then back again into deeper channels and then suddenly a big splash and waving of the grasses ahead of us. So something has gone into the water. Jameson says it's a crocodile. He says, more crocodiles in here than people think. Gliding along, then, between banks of reed and papyrus. In this slow quiet way, I think of the Tigris/Euphrates world where people lived in the wetlands and glided along in little boats, in the world of hippopotamus, fish, and waterfowl as they built up their reed and mud villages to turn them eventually into urban agrarian civilizations.

We reach the main channel—a steady current. The main channel's about twenty-five to thirty feet wide with a seven-foot depth in the center—the running (and rising) water rustling the leaves and grasses along the banks. We scare up a lechwe—the little antelope with broad footpads for living in the wetlands—we could barely see through the reeds and papyrus, but we could hear them, splash, splash, splashing in large numbers as they ran from the approach of our dugout. Silent as our dugouts are, they take alarm. Lions and hyenas cannot pursue them into the swamps so they have an advantage here. We go back down river swiftly, and turn into a little side channel that brings us to Baboon Camp.

The landscape mosaic is made up of these elements: starting from the wet center the permanent marsh has permanent river channels and arms. Above that, there are seasonally inundated grasslands in degrees of depressions so that some are wetter and under water slightly longer than others. This is registered in changes of vegetation and color, just as it is visible now in some areas of the molapos; some being greener and others more golden-tan; depressions and greener swales and then slightly higher and drier grass species, stretches of broad fields and plains of mixed grass species, mixed grasses, and herbs. There is the periodic, solitary island of three or four trees that is a little higher; the trees are perhaps built around old termite nest towers. Then there are the sandy rises, some long and skinny and some more round—they remain as islands when everything else is flooded. These are riparian forests of large mixed glossy-leafed, broad-leaved hardwoods—ebonys, figs, acacia, and others.

This combination of elements is constantly repeated in various arrangements. There must be five or six species of larger trees that make up the islands with characteristic leaf and bough forms distinctive from each other so that they make an elegant set of shapes on the horizon. And grasslands, too, are not always pure grass, but there is sage and many other little bushes—and annual and perennial grasses and tiny herbs.

Along the water channels an edging of papyrus—dense and tall, or kinds of bulrushes and reeds, each in their own pattern. I keep thinking, is this Sumeria? Something like ancient Egypt?

The Northern Botswana Elephant Range

Mid-morning, about ready to drive on. This morning so cool that we put on long pants. Elevation here about 3900 feet—most of Africa is up around 3000 feet, though you wouldn't know it. With the sun out, it's soon warm.

Driving over from the Savute marshes we were pushing through miles of tall grass. Cleaning the mats of grass seeds out of the radiator, front of the car, so that the cooling will work—using a switch of a green leafy limb with leaves to reach down in and sweep. Today is Kai's twenty-sixth birthday. Little would I have thought a quarter century back, in Kyoto, that he and his yet unborn brother and I might be bouncing around in Africa one day. What do we ever know?

Tracks/Traces:

— A beetle dragging down the sand path, leaving its neat repetitive
   record—
— Lion paws in the road ahead over old car-trace
— Our own walking leaves our shoe-style for a while.
— The Buddha, the Tathagata, "thus come"; NO trace.

Some of these elephants like to scoop out holes about four feet across and two feet deep at one end, tapering up on a gradual angle at the other end. Sometimes they do it right in the middle of the dirt road so that we have to watch for these holes where you could drop a wheel and maybe break an axle.

Mixed dry sparse grassy cover, with a largely shrubby tree forest and scattered tall trees, same species. The whole landscape crossed by well-worn animal trails of various gauges though none of these trails are anywhere near as clear as the well-beaten elephant roads.

Eastward, a band of baboons sifts through the woods. A freshly broken treetop being munched by elephants. A six-foot jaw bone in the road. Pile after pile of elephant dung. Huge piles. Holy shit, one finally thinks.

The melodic moans of hyenas. The relentless absurdness of baboon calls. Back in woodland again now. Butterfly split leaves of the mopane tree, and termite nests again showing that there's water in the subsoil here.

Stopped to look at very clear elephant footprints in this fine sand, so fine that the impression is perfect and complete: what you get is a whole network of delicate lines etched on the inch or two width reticulate bumps—the whole elephant foot a big fingerprint made up of a number of well-lined bumps. Along with that is some semicircular dragging or scooping marks in the sand, which we're thinking might be the trunk as it goes along. Huge tooth in another old jaw bone down the track—honor the ancestors!

Miles of sand, as fine as that on any beach. Soft, reddish-tan or faintly pink. Out of what ancient system of lakes or oceans? I'm watching from my lookout in the hatch of the truck. Quite suddenly soil type changes. Kai says this is like the soils in Zambia.

Yesterday afternoon's period of steady climb: from the map can see we might be around 4100 feet now. I realize that what we're driving through is the vast range of the greatest wild elephant herd in Africa, the northern Botswana elephant range. This is it, with all of this dung and all of these broken trees. Somewhere, someone must be singing "The song of following the elephant."

We get to the ruins of the Ngezumba Dam. Whatever dam was here has crumbled out and washed away. There are just a series of shattered cement walls and buttresses. It's about 150 feet across the little canyon, only 30 feet deep—and not a trace of water down there.

Parking the wagon on the berm of the dam in the grass and scanning around with binoculars, Kai said, wow and hey, and it turns out he accidentally put his glasses on a python hanging on the wall on the opposite side of the canyon, draped over some tree roots. We walked across to look at it. Very slowly, pulled its way into a hiding place of leaves and roots. About eight feet long if all stretched out.

The hornbills—birds with beaks that don't quite close, wattled red naked neck, and a kind of a red ring of bare skin around the eye.

In this network of dirt roads east of Ngezumba Dam, various road forks marked with stone pylons but the signs are mostly missing. . . . Finally we come into the old campsite of Nogatsaa. We turn in the roadway and coast to a stop under some trees at the edge of a broad dry ex-marsh plain. This official campground looks like a Mexican movie village that has recently been sacked by bandits. A number of chalets and rondavels, but not a soul in sight, broken windows, roofs fallen in, walls caved in on most buildings. The whole thing is in shambles. As the guy said at Sabuti, elephants. Some of the little tourist cabins are still usable, though dusty inside with beer cans, candle wax, and old flashlight batteries. The game lookout perch with round stone walls is half collapsed. A sign, "FREE REPUBLIC OF NOGATSAA," written in English and German, above the door of one of these semicollapsed cabins.

Kai walks back from one of those dirt lanes and says, you want to see what happened? So I follow him, we go through a brushy wall with logs and suddenly I'm standing in front of a dug-out moat of dirt, and then I see there is a toppled water tank, the whole thing down, that was surrounded by a moat, and then surrounded by a barrier wall of logs. And the elephants breached the log wall and the moat, got onto the little island in the center where the water tower stood and pushed over the whole water tower, tank and all. The Elephant Board of Governors decided against a tourist establishment at Nogatsaa, and ordered the destruction of the water system. Then they had their young bulls and females with attitude go trash the rest. Only hornbills and a few squirrels left, remembering the days of busy campers.

Mid-afternoon, a refreshing breeze—I'm still in the shade of the parked truck, my back against a tire. Gen naps on the big tan mattress—Kai has just gotten up from a nap and is in the circular observation post of stone—no roof but chickenwire. Hornbills clucking in synch over and over—(It seems that many trees serve as elephant-rubbing trees.) A wide grass prairie—seasonal swamp—stretching south.

Dinner of cheese, smoked salmon paste, gooseberry jam, pilot bread, and apples. Not bad. Water from the containers has an old flavor. We have a little more than ½ tank of gas. A dust-devil passes near, throwing up a whirl of dry grasses. Late sun lowering—long-cast shade, wind rustles grasses. The many sounds of Africa—doves coo & twang—a faint far lion roar—the mournful rise-and-fall of a hyena.

It grows dark. We Sing "Happy Birthday" to Kai with a Pemmican bar served on a tin plate—makes a cake—and he blows out the single utility candle flame.

At Victoria Falls

I am drawn back to the Falls for a second visit. I leave Kai and Gen and walk back the half-mile path and set out to do another stroll along the cliff-edge.

As the river approaches this edge of old basalt from an ancient volcanic flow, it widens its channel out until it's a mile wide. Then it drops hugely and suddenly over the mile-wide system of ledges to fall anywhere from 300 to 360 feet down, along that face. The water all spills into a narrow channel that runs at right angles to the direction of the flow of the river, so that rather than heading on down a stream through a gorge, it hits a trough and runs sharply north in a great flurry. It then makes a sharp and narrow U-bend and turns south again, makes another sharp U-bend north, and after a few milder meanders finally becomes a normal river channel heading east. One walks from the south side out along the tongue of table land just opposite the falls. You can look right across at the whitewater streaming, it seems like only a few hundred feet away. I feel the cool wet air rising up against my face, misting through the increasingly bushier canopy and undergrowth. Then stepping out at an open place for a view and a blast of cloud and spray, a hovering perpetual rainbow. The first great cataract is dead ahead heaving over the stone lip. On north a little, a kind of island juts out with some falls dropping off beyond that, and this cliff "island" has a little forest with cliffs, and water going off both sides. I keep walking north toward the point. Found myself opposite another broad stretch of falls with first, a great flow, then a thinner flow over a rocky jumble, then an increased flow again, then another small point of dry land, and then another very long arc of breaking water going directly over and down. I make my way, outlook by outlook, to the final far end, taking my shirt off and putting it in my pack— getting drenched now, and the few other tourists walking this far, black and white alike, all getting soaked. A couple of white girls in high-thigh bathing suits looking totally un-African in their bareness and sexiness—they'll put on clothes again as soon as they get back toward the entrance. Finally I'm at the end of the peninsula, all rocky and wet grasses now, where the rising water of the falls is constantly falling back in a steady heavy drenching. The path is awash with a constant flow of inch-deep water flooding back, going over to all the edges of rocks and trails to the big cliff. It's a marsh now and the outcroppings are covered with moss. The downpour comes in pulses, as do waves of rising mist.

I stand in a cloud of spray and chant the Fudo mantra, old Yamabushi waterfall ascetic practice style, standing straight in the cold downpour, eyes closed, meditating in the midst of the stream—the meeting of ceaseless flow and obdurate uprightness—the synthesis of the vertical of asce- tic energy and horizontal unconditional compassion. I do my weird sort of Yamamba, old mountain woman, dance. I think of the energy-package this represents: volcanism, tectonics, subduction, the planetary "heat engine" that makes the cycles of weather and water. Looking over the edge from the very far point I find a handhold on the wet rocks, then lean way out and gaze straight down into the whirling, frothing channels. Reticulated foam rolls over in a quick shaft of sunlight between the mist—huge rain- drops falling, while between and through them, fine mist is rising, all at the same time.

This is surely one of the most beautiful places, events, cases of what is, on our broad blue planet.

And walk slowly back beyond the reach of the heavy rains. Just a few hundred yards up the path it's drier and much warmer—getting African hot and dry again. Take off my canvas shorts and wring them out and then continue ambling back, harking to the roar, verging from time to time on the mist where the trail draws near the edge.

I've seen a mother and daughter, eleven-year-old sort of girl in a swim suit, ecstatically jumping up and down, waving her arms, all wet— thoroughly taken by the scene. At the juncture of the trails our paths rejoin, there's this light in the girl's face. She's still doing jumping jacks and waving her arms and rubbing the water on her face and on her arm. I say to the mother, "This is a place you can't stay dry in, isn't it? I was here yesterday and I couldn't help but come back again." And she laughs, and speaks with an American accent, "Well we were here this morning and did all of this one time already, and my daughter insisted we come back again."

Walking back toward the gate note the gradual change in vegetation away from the almost cloud-forest that has formed along the lip where the spray rises from the falls into the more common arid crackly dry leaves on the ground, trees and bushes. Trees: red-leaf fig and *Acacia galpinii,* with big vines on it. By the time I get to the gate my chest has already dried off, my hair is half dry, I put my t-shirt back on. In dampish shorts and dry t-shirt, a little day-pack, I walk back via the Victoria Falls Hotel path, spattered with elephant droppings, through the backside of the famous, wealthy, old colonial Victoria Falls Hotel with its broad clipped lawn, its starched waiters, its patio laid out for tea or dinner, and pass right through the lobby and reception room in a decor of white and light green, and on down the steps to the limousine stop and down the gated driveway of the Hotel to the broad half-dirt main street that runs between Victoria Falls town proper and the waterfalls. Heading for our tent at the public camp- ground. A continuous stream, both sides of the road, of wildly variously dressed African people, walking, walking, everywhere.

Uncollected
Essays

Walking the Great Ridge Ōmine on the Womb-Diamond Trail

I started climbing snowpeaks in the Pacific Northwest when I was fifteen. My first ascent was on Mt. St. Helens, a mountain I honestly thought would last forever. After I turned eighteen I worked on ships, trail crews, fire lookouts, or in logging camps for a number of seasons. I got into the habit of hiking up a local hill when I first arrived in a new place, to scan the scene. For the Bay Area, that meant a walk up Mt. Tamalpais.

I first arrived in Kyoto in May, 1956. Because the map showed Mt. Atago to be the highest mountain on the edge of the Kitano River watershed, I set out to climb it within two or three days of my arrival. I aimed for the highest point on the western horizon, a dark forested ridge. It took several trains and buses to get me to a complex of *ryokan* in a gorge right by a rushing little river. The map had a shrine icon on the summit, so I knew there had to be a trail going up there, and I found it. Dense *sugi* groves, and only one other person the whole way, who was live-trapping small songbirds. Up the last slope, wide stone steps, and a bark-roofed shrine on top. Through an opening in the sugi trees, a long view north over hills and villages, the Tamba country. A few weeks later I described this hike to a Buddhist priest-scholar at Daitokuji, who was amused ("I've never been up there") and mischievous enough to set me up with a friend who had Yamabushi connections. I was eventually invited to join a ritual climb of the northern summit of Ōmine, the "Great Ridge." As it turned out I was inducted as a novice Yamabushi (*sentachi*) and introduced to the deity of the range, Zaō Gogen, and to Fudō Myō-ō.

After that experience on Mt. Ōmine I took up informal mountain walking meditations as a complement to my Zen practice at Daitoku-ji. I spent what little free time I had walking up, across, and down Hieizan or out the ridge to Yokkawa, or on other trails in the hills north of Kyoto. I did several backpacking trips in the Northern Japan Alps. I investigated Kyoto on foot or by bike and found an occasional Fudō Myō-ō—with his gathered intensity—in temples both tiny and huge, both old and new. (Fierce as he looks, he's somehow comforting. There is clearly a deep affection for this fellow from a wide range of Japanese people.) I studied what I could on the Yamabushi tradition. What follows, by way of prelude to a description of a pilgrimage down the length of the Great Ridge, barely touches the complexity and richness of this rich and deeply indigenous teaching. My own knowledge of it is, needless to say, rudimentary.

It must have started as prehistoric mountain-spirit folk religion. The Yamabushi ("those who stay in the mountains") are back country Shaman-Buddhists with strong Shinto connections, who make walking and climbing in deep mountain ranges a large part of their practice. The tradition was founded in the 7th or 8th centuries A.D. by En-no-Gyōja, "En the ascetic," who was the son of a Shinto priest from Shikoku. The tradition is also known as Shugendō, "the way of hard practice." The Yamabushi do not constitute a sect, but rather a society with special initiations and rites whose members may be lay or priesthood, of any Buddhist sect, or also of Shinto affiliation. The main Buddhist affinity is with the Shingon sect, which is the Sino-Japanese version of Vajrayana, esoteric Buddhism, the Buddhism we often call "Tibetan." My mountain friends told me that the Yamabushi have for centuries "borrowed" certain temples from the Shingon sect to use as temporary headquarters. In theory they own nothing and feel that the whole universe is their temple, the mountain ranges their worship halls and zendos, the mountain valleys their guest-rooms, and the great mountain peaks are each seen as boddhisattvas, allies, and teachers.

The original Yamabushi were of folk origin, uneducated but highly spiritually motivated people. Shugendō is one of the few [quasi] Buddhist groups other than Zen that make praxis primary. Zen, with its virtual requirement of literacy and its upper class patrons, has had little crossover with the Yamabushi. The wandering Zen monk and the travelling Yamabushi are two common and essential figures in Nō dramas, appearing as bearers of plot and resolvers of karma. Both types have become Japanese folk figures, with the Yamabushi the more fearful for they have a reputation as sorcerers. Except that the Zen people have always had a fondness for Fudō, and like to draw mountains even if they don't climb them.

Yamabushi outfits make even Japanese people stop and stare. They wear a medieval combination of straw *waraji* sandals, a kind of knicker, the deer or *kamoshika* (a serow or "goat-antelope" that is now endangered) pelt hanging down in back over the seat, an underkimono, a hemp cloth over-robe, and a conch shell in a net bag across the shoulder. They carry the *shakujo* staff with its loose jangling bronze rings on top, a type of sistrum. A small black lacquered cap is tied onto the head. (I have a hemp over-robe with the complete text of the Hannya Shingyo brush-written on it, as well as black block-printed images of Fudō Myō-ō, En-no-Gyōja, some little imps, and other characters. The large faint red seals randomly impressed on it are proof of pilgrimages completed. The robe was a gift from an elder Yamabushi who had done these trips over his lifetime. He had received it from someone else and thought it might be at least a century old.) Yamabushi will sometimes be seen flitting through downtown Kyoto begging and chanting sutras, or standing in inward-facing circles jangling their sistrum-staffs in rhythm at the train station while staging for a climb. They prefer the cheap, raw Golden Bat cigarettes. Yamabushi have a number of mountain centers, especially in the Dewa Sanzan region of Tohoku. Then there's Mt. Ontake, where many women climb, and shamanesses work in association with Yamabushi priests who help them call down gods and spirits of the dead. At one time the men and women practitioners of mountain religion in its semi-Buddhist form provided the major religious leadership for the rural communities, with hundreds of mountain centers.

The "Yamabushi" aspect of mountain religion apparently started at Ōmine, in eastern Wakayama Prefecture, the seat of En-no-Gyōja's life-long practice. The whole forty-mile-long ridge with its forests and streams was En's original zendo. Two main routes lead the seven or eight miles up, with wayside shrines all along the route. Although the whole ascent can be done by trail, for those intent on practice the direct route is taken—cliffs scaled while chanting the Hannya Shingyo. Near the top there is an impressive face over which the novices are dangled upside down. There are two temples on the main summit in the shade of big conifers. When you step in it is cooler, and heady with that incense redolence that only really old temples have.

> A jangling of shakujo staffs and the blowing of
> conches in the courtyard between buildings.
> A fire-circle for the *goma* or fire ceremony—mudras
> hid under the sleeves—and the vajra-handled sword
> brought forth. Oil lanterns and a hard-packed
> earthen floor, the *uguisu* echoing in the dark
> woods. A Fudō statue in the shadows,

> focussed and steadfast on his rock,
>> backed by carved flames,
>>> holding the vajra-sword and a noose.

He is a great Spell-holder and protector of the Yamabushi brotherhood. His name means "Immovable Wisdom-king." Fudō is also widely known and seen in the larger Buddhist world, especially around Tendai and Shingon temples. Some of the greatest treasures of Japanese Buddhist art are Fudō paintings and statues. His faintly humorous glaring look (and blind or cast eye) touches something in the psyche. There are also crude little Fudō images on mountains and beside waterfalls throughout central Japan. They were often placed there by early Yamabushi explorers.

A great part of the Shingon teaching is encoded onto two large mandala-paintings. One is the "Vajra-realm" (Kongō-kai) and the other the "Garbha-realm" (Taizō-kai). They are each marvelously detailed. In Sanskrit "Vajra" means diamond (as drill tip, or cutter), and "Garbha" means womb. These terms are descriptive of two complementary but not exactly dichotomous ways of seeing the world, and representative of such pairs as: mind / environment, evolutionary drama / ecological stage, mountains / waters, compassion / wisdom, the Buddha as enlightened being / the world as enlightened habitat, etc.

For the Yamabushi these meanings are projected onto the Ōmine landscape. The peak Sanjo-ga-dake at the north is the Vajra Realm center. The Kumano Hongu shrine at the south end is at the center of the Garbha Realm. There was a time when—after holding ceremonies in the Buddha-halls at the summit, the Yamabushi ceremonists would then walk the many miles along the ridge—with symbolic and ritual stations the whole way—and down to the Kumano River for another service at the shrine. Pilgrims from all over Japan, by the tens of thousands, were led by Yamabushi teachers through this strict and elaborate symbolic journey culminating in a kind of rebirth. A large number of pilgrims now make a one-day hike up from the north end, a few do a one-day hike up at the south end, but it's rare to walk the whole Great Ridge.

In early June of 1968 three friends and I decided to see what we could find of the route. My companions were Yamao Sansei, artist and fellow worker from Suwa-no-se Island; Saka, also an island communard and spear fisherman; and Royall Tyler, who was a graduate student at that time. He is now an authority on Japanese religion.

My Notes: First Day

Early morning out of town. From Sanjo *eki* in Kyoto take the train to Uji. Then hitchhike along thru Asuka, by a green mounded *kofun* ancient emperor's tomb shaped like a keyhole, as big as a high school. Standing by quiet two-lane paved roads through the lush fields, picked up by a red tradesman's van, a schoolteacher's sedan—reflecting on long-gone emperors of the days when they hunted pheasants in the reedy plains. All ricefields now.

As we get into the old Yamato area it's more lush—deeper green and more broad-leaf trees. Arrive in Yoshino about noon—meet up with Royall & Saka (we split up into two groups for quicker hitching—they beat us) at the Zaō Dō, an enormous temple roofed old-style with *sugi* bark. A ridge rises directly behind the village slanting up and back to the massive mountains, partly in light cloud. Yoshino village of sakura-blooming hills, cherries planted by En-no-Gyōja ("ascetic" but it would work to translate it "mountaineer") as offerings to Zaō the Mountain King. In a sense the whole of Yoshino town stands as a *butsudan* / altar. So the thousands of cherry trees make a perennial vase of flowers—(and the electric lights of the village the candle?)—offerings to the mountain looming above. Here in the Zaō Dō is the large dark image, the mountain spirit presented in a human form, Zaō Gongen—"King of the Womb Realm." ("Manifestation (*gongen*) of the King (ō) of the Womb (*za*).")

I think he was seen in a flash of lightning, in a burst of mountain thunder, glimpsed in an instant by En the Mountaineer as he walked or was sitting. Gleaming black, Zaō dances, one leg lifted, fierce-faced, hair on end. We four bow to this wild dancing energy, silently ask to be welcome, before entering the forest. Down at the end of the vast hall two new Yamabushi are being initiated in a lonely noon ceremony by the chief priest.

Zaō is not found in India or China, nor is he part of an older Shinto mythology. He is no place else because this mountain range is the place. This mountain deity is always here, a shapeshifter who could appear in any form. En the Mountaineer happened to see but one of his possible incarnations. Where Fudō is an archetype, a single form which can be found in many places, Zaō is always one place, holding thousands of shapes.

We adjust our packs and start up the road. Pass a small shrine and the Sakuramoto-bo—a hall to En the Mountaineer. Walk past another little hall to Kanki-ten, the seldom-seen deity of sexual pleasure. Climb onward past hillsides of cherry trees, now past bloom. (Saigyō, the monk-poet, by writing about them so much, gave these Yoshino cherry blossoms to the whole world.) The narrow road turns to trail, and we walk uphill til dusk. It steepens and follows a ridge-edge, fringe of conifers, to a run-down old *koya*—mountain hut—full of hiker trash. With our uptight Euro-American conservationist ethic we can't keep ourselves from cleaning it up and so we work an hour and then camp in the yard. No place else level enough to lay a bag down.

I think of the old farmers who followed the mountain path, and their sacraments of Shamanist / Buddhist / Shinto style—gods and Buddha-figures of the entranceway, little god of the kitchen fire, of the outhouse, gods of the bath house, the woodshed, the well. A procession of stations, of work-dharma-life. A sacramental world of homes and farms, protected and nourished by the high, remote, rainy, transcendent symbolic mountains.

Second Day

Early morning, as the water is bubbling on the mountain stove, a robust Yamabushi in full gear appeared before the hut. He had been up since before dawn and already walked up from Yoshino, on his way to the temples at the top. He is the priest of Sakuramoto-bo, the little temple to En the Mountaineer. Says he's doing a 200-day climbing and descending practice. And he is grateful that we cleaned up the mess. The racket of a *kakesu:* Japanese Jay.

The Ōmine range as headwaters sets the ancient boundaries between the countries of Kii, Yamato, and Ise. These mountains get intense rainfall, in from the warm Pacific. It is a warm temperate rainforest, with streams and waterfalls cascading out of it. Its lower elevations once supported dense beech and oak forests, and the ridges are still thick with fir, pine, hemlock, and fields of wild azalea and camellia. The slopes are logged right up to the ridge edge here & there, even though this is in the supposed Yoshino-Kumano "National Park." (National Park does not mean protected land wholly owned by the public, as in the U.S. In Japan and many other countries the term is more like a zoning designation. Private or village-owned land may be all through the area, but it is subject to management plans and conservation restrictions.)

On the summit, center of the Diamond Realm, we visit the two temple halls, one to En the founder, and the other to Zaō. He makes me think of underground twists and dips of strata, the deep earth thrust brought to light and seen as a slightly crazed dance. And like Fudō, he is an incarnation of deep and playful forces. In Buddhist iconography, sexual ecstasy is seen as an almost ferocious energy, an ecstatic grimace that might be taken for pain.

We blow our conch, ring our shakujo, chant our sutras and dharanis, while standing at the edge of the five-hundred-foot cliff over which I was once suspended by three ascetics who then menacingly interrogated me on personal and Dharma points. In the old days, some stories say, they would just let a candidate drop if he lied or boasted. From the seventh century on no women have been allowed on this mountain. [Several college women who loved hiking changed that in 1969]. Elevation 5675 feet.

We descend from the summit plateau and are onto the branch trail that follows the ridge south. It is rocky, brushy, and narrow—no wide pilgrim paths now. We go clambering up the narrow winding trail, steps made by tree-roots, muddy in parts, past outcroppings and tiny stone shrines buried in *kumazasa,* the mountain "bear bamboo-grass" with its springy thriving erect bunches and sharp-edged leaves. We arrive at the Adirondack-type (open on one side) shelter called "Little *Sasa*" hut and make our second camp.

Third Day

Rhododendron blossoms, mossy rocks, fine-thread grasses—
running ridges—wind and mist—it had rained in the night.
A full live blooming little tree of white bell flowers its
limbs embracing a dead tree standing—
moss & a tuft of grass on the trunk.
The dead tree twisting—wood grain rising laid bare white—
sheen in the misty brightness. When a tree dies
its life goes on, the house of moss and countless bugs.
Birds echoing up from both steep slopes of the ridge.

And now we are in the old world, the old life. The Japan of gridlock cities, cheerful little bars, uniformed schoolkids standing in lines at castles, and rapid rattling trains, has retreated into dreamlike ephemerality. This is the perennial reality of vines and flowers, great trees, flitting birds. The mist and light rain blowing in gusts uphill into your wet face, the glimmer of mountains and clouds at play. Each step picked over mossy rock, wet slab, muddy pockets between vines. Long views into blue-sky openings, streaks of sunlight, arcs of hawks.

A place called Gyôja-gaeri—"Where the ascetics turn back." For a rice-ball-lunch stop. These trails so densely overgrown they're almost gone.

Now at Mi-san peak, the highest point along the Great Ridge, 6283 feet. Another place to stop and sit in zazen for a while, and to chant another round of sutras and dharanis. A little mountain hut a bit below the summit. White fir and spruce-mist blowing afternoon. Yellow-and-black eye of a snake. A fine polish and center line on each scale.

Here for the night. Tending the fire in the hut kitchen—open firepit on the dirt floor—weeping smoky eyes sometimes but blinking and cooking—sitting pretty warm, the wind outside is chilly. Lost somehow our can of *sencha,* good green tea. We have run onto our first hikers, the universal college student backpackers with white towels around their necks and Himalayan-style heavy boots. They had come up a lateral trail, and were shivering in the higher altitude cool. Hovering over the cook-fire, stirring, I mused on my family at home, and my two-month-old baby son. Another sort of moment for mountain travellers.

Fourth Day

Oyama renge—a very rare flowering tree, *Magnolia sieboldii,* found here.

A *darshan,* the gift of a clear view of, a Japanese Shika Deer's white rump. Deep water—deep woods—wide. Green leaves—jagged and curved ones, a line-energy to play in. White-flowering low trees with red-rimmed glossy leaves.

We angle up an open flowery ridge and leafy forest to Shaka-dake, Shakyamuni Peak, and have lunch. Chant here the Sanskrit mantra of Shakyamuni learned in Nepal—"Muni muni mahamuni Shakyamuni ye svaha"—"Sage, sage, great sage, sage of the Shakyas, ye svaha." Shakya means "oak." Gautama's people were known as the "Oak Nation."

All this trip we have stayed over 5000 feet. Then stroll down a slope to the west into a high basin of massive broad-leafed trees, without a hint of any path, open and park-like. An old forest. A light wind rustling leaves, and a dappled golden light. Thick soft fine grass—Tibetan cat's eye green—between patches of exposed rock. A rest, sitting on the leaves: sighing with the trees. Then a sudden chatter shocks us—a rhesus monkey utters little complaints and gives us the eye.

(Old men and women who live alone in the woods.
in a house with no trail or sign—characters of folktale or drama—)

To hear the monkey or the deer
leave the path.

And I realize that this is the stillest place I had ever been—or would ever be—in Japan. This forgotten little corner of a range, headwaters of what drainage? Totsugawa River? Is it striking because it is seems so pristine and pure? Or that it is anciently wise, a storehouse of experience, hip? A place that is full, serene, needing nothing, accomplished, and—in the most creative sense—half rotten. Finished, so on the verge of giving and changing.

Maybe this is what the *Za* of Zaō's name suggests—za (or *zō*—Chinese *tsang*) means a storehouse, an abundance, a gathering, or in esoteric Buddhism, "womb." Sanskrit *alaya,* as in "storehouse of consciousness" (*alaya-vijñana*) or Storehouse of Snow: Himalaya. The three divisions of Buddhist literature are called zō. *Pitaka* in Sanskrit, "basket." Baskets full of the wealth of teachings. Could it be analogous to the idea of climax in natural systems? (Translating "Zaō" as "King of the Womb Realm" is the Imperial Chinese reading of his name. "Chief of Storage Baskets" would be the Neolithic translation. "Master of the Wilds" is the Paleolithic version.)

We walk back up to our packs. Down the east ridge, loggers are visible and audible high on the slope. Load up and push through sasa on down the trail. A view of a large hawk: some white by the head. Likely a *hayabusa*—falcon—to judge by its flight and dive.

(I find myself thinking we in America must do a Ghost Dance: for *all* the spirits, humans, animals, that were thrown aside.)

—And come on a small Buddha-hall below Shaka-peak. We slip into it, for halls and temples are never locked. It is clean swept, decked out, completely equipped, for a simple *goma* service, with a central fire pit, an altar tray with vajra-tools, all fenced off with a five-colored cord, and a mediation seat before the fire spot. We know thus that there are villages below from which ascetics climb to meditate here. We are nearing the south end of the Great Ridge.

Another hour or so later, the trail that was following the top of the ridge has totally disappeared into the *kumazasa* and brush. It has started raining again. We stop, unload, study the maps, confer, and finally decide to leave the ridge at this point. We take the lateral trail east, swiftly steep and endlessly descending, stepping and sliding ever downward. Go past a seven-layer dragon-like waterfall in the steady rain. Sloshing on down the overgrown trail, find leeches, *hiru* on our ankles, deduced from the visible threads of blood. They come right off—no big deal. And still descending, until dark, we arrive at a place called Zenki, "Front Devil." (Zenki is one of Fudō's two boy imp helpers. Somewhere there's a place called "Back Devil.") We camp in another damp wooden hut along the trail. Someone has kindly left dry wood, so we cook by smoky firelight, and I reflect on the whole Ōmine route as we cook.

We are not far now from the Kitayama River, and the grade from here will be gentle. The Kitayama flows to the Kumano, and goes on out to the seacoast, ancient site of fishing villages and Paleolithic salmon runs. It would seem likely that from very early times, Neolithic or before, anyone wishing to travel between the pleasant reed plains of Yamato and this southern coast would have followed the Great Ridge. No other route so direct, for the surrounding hills are complex beyond measure, and the Great Ridge leads above it all, headwaters of everything, and sinuous though it be, clear to follow. The mountain religion is not a religion of recluses and hermits (as it would look to contemporary people, for whom the mountains are not the direct path) but a faith of those who move simultaneously between different human cultures, forest ecosystems, and various spiritual realms. The mountains are the way to go! And Yamabushi were preceded, by a mix of vision-questing mountain healers and sturdy folk who were trading dried fish for grains. In a world where everyone walks, the "roadless areas" are perfectly accessible.

The humans were preceded by wildlife, who doubtless made the first trails. The great ridge a shortcut for bears between seacoast fish and inland berries? All these centuries Ōmine has also been a wildlife corridor and a natural refuge, a core zone, protecting and sustaining beings. A Womb of Genetic Diversity.

Fifth Day

Next morning find the start of a dirt road going on down to the river. A pilgrims / hikers register on a post there, where we write "Sansei, Saka, Royall, Gary—followed the old Yamabushi route down the Ōmine ridge 5000 above the valleys walking 4 days from Yoshino and off the ridge at Zenki. June 11 to 16, 1968."

By bus and hitchhiking we make it to the coast and camp a night by the Pacific. Hitching again, parting with Saka who must head back to Kyoto, we make our way to the Kumano "new shrine," Shingu. Dark red fancy shrine boat in the museum and an old painting of whaling. A coffeeshop has a little slogan on the wall, "chiisa no, heibon na shiawase de ii—" "A small, ordinary happiness is enough."

Travelling on, riding the back of a truck. Up the Kumano river valley running parallel to cascades of cool sheets of jade riverwater strained through the boulders. Houses on the far side tucked among wet sugi and hinoki, we are let off directly in front of Kumano Hongu at dusk. Found a nook to make a camp in, cook in, sleep the night. Riverbed smoothwashed granite stones now serve as the floor of the god's part of the shrine. Grown with moss, now that no floods wash over.

Then dreamed that night of a "Fudō Mountain" that was a new second peak to Mt. Tamalpais in Northern California. A Buddhist Picnic was being held there. I walked between the two peaks—past the "Fudō Basketball Court"—and some *kami* shrines (God's House is like the house the Ainu kept their Bear in?) and got over to the familiar parking-lot summit of Mt. Tamalpais. I was wondering how come the Americans on the regular peak of Tam didn't seem to know or care about Fudō Mountain, which was so close. Then I went into a room where a woman was seated crosslegged, told she was a "Vajra-woman"—*Vajrakanha*—a tanned Asian woman on a mat, smiling, who showed me her earrings—like the rings of a shakujo. Smiled & smiled.

6:30 A.M. the next morning we enter the center of the Garbhadhātu at Kumano Hongu, "The Main Shrine at Bear-fields." On a wood post is carved: "The most sacred spot in Japan, the main holy ground of the Womb Realm."

And it goes on to say that on April 15 every year a major fire ceremony is conducted here. Shinto, way of the spirits, outer; Buddha, way of the sentient beings, inner. It's always like this when you walk in to the shrine and up to the god's house. It is empty; or way back within, in the heart of the shrine, is a mirror: *you* are the outside world.

> They say—Kannon is water—Fudō is uplift—Dainichi is
> 　　　　　　　　　　　　　　　　　　　energy.
> Mountain and Water practice. Outer pilgrimages & inner
> 　　　　　　　　　　　　　　　　　　　meditations.
> They are all interwoven: headwaters and drainages,
>
> The whole range threatens & dances,
> The subsiding
> Mountain of the past
> The high hill of the present
> The rising peak that will come.
>
> Bear　　　Field.

And poking around there, in back, we come on a carpentry shed, mats on the ground, and workers planing hinoki beams. With that great smell. We have run onto a *miya daiku,* a shrine builder, Yokota Shin'ichi. We chat at length on carpentry tools, and forestry, and the ancient routes of supply for perfect sugi and hinoki logs to be used in the repair of temples, and the making of sacred halls and their maintenance. I ask him how would one build a sacred hall in America? He says, "know your trees. Have the tools. Everyone should be pure when you start. Have a party when you end." And he says "go walking on the mountain." He gives us fresh fish, he was just given so much.

> deep in the
> older hills
> one side rice plains
> 　　　　　Yamato
> one side black pebble
> whale-spearing beach.
> who built such shrine?
> such god my face?
> planing the beam
> shaping the eave

blue sky
Keeps its shape.

Thinking,
"symbols" do not stand for things,
but for the states of mind that engage those things.
/ Tree / = tree intensity of mind.

We hitchhike up on the Totsugawa gorge, cross the pass, and in some hours are out in the Nara prairies and ricefields. With *ayu* ("sweetfish") and *funa* (a silver carp, a gibel; *Lyrinus auratus*) given us by Shin'ichi-san—tucked into a cookpot along with shredded ice to keep it cool, arrive in Kyoto by train and bus by 9 P.M. We hello and hug and all cook up the fish—and brown rice for our meal. And I hold the baby, crosslegged on the tatami, back from the Great Ridge, linking the home hearth and the deep wilds.

That was 1968. It is doubtless drastically changed by now. The Yamabushi have much given way to hikers and tourists. Roads, logging, and commercial tourist enterprises spread throughout the Japanese countryside. Japan has extended its baleful forest-product extraction habits to the world. We in North America have nothing to be proud of, however. In the twenty-some years since I returned to Turtle Island we have worked steadily to reform the US Forest Service and private logging practices. We are finally beginning to see a few changes. Nonetheless, in these years since 1968 Northern California, Oregon, Washington, British Columbia, and Southeast Alaska have been subjected to some of the heaviest logging and destruction of habitat in the twentieth century. As Nanao Sakaki ruefully suggests, "Perhaps we shall have to change Tu Fu's line to read 'The State remains, but the mountains and rivers are destroyed.'"

Walking
Downtown Naha

My friend Yamazoto gave me a sketchy idea of how to walk into the old shopping alleys of downtown Naha. I followed the flow of cars and trucks on a main road to a green-painted iron pedestrian overcross and dropped down to a narrower set of streets. The world of buildings seen from the overpass was almost entirely a post–World War II regrowth. The city was flattened during the World War II invasion of Okinawa, particularly by the air raid of October 10, 1944, which is referred to as *tetsu no bofu*—the "typhoon of iron." The earlier city was composed of compact one-story wooden houses with red tile hip roofs. It was rebuilt into a rolling and staggered colony of reinforced concrete cubes. The designs though hasty were creative. Countless tiny cement buildings were poured, each somewhat unique. The warm climate allows exterior staircases winding up the wall with balconies projecting out, gridwork rail designs, stairstepped floors with tiny observation rooms or final bedrooms on the roof. The most elaborate are ziggurat-like, with green plantings on the ledges and spreading up the walls. They are painted all colors, but mostly cream or tan, or they are left natural concrete. The last take on free-form gray mold and stain patterns in time that give them the mottled earthy look of Bizen pottery. Laundry flaps from balconies and rooftops. They are mini build ings, with rarely more than three short stories. They follow the street layout of the old city, not a right-angled grid, so they are jumbled, skewed, winding, tangential, and they rise and break with the rolling terrain.

Okinawa is mild in winter and hot and breezy in summer so the balcony and roof spaces are well-used. In time the buildings will become covered with vines and creepers, trees will grow taller and thicker alongside, and the narrow streets with their tiny delivery vans and motorscooters will be over-arched with a glowing canopy.

I had picked out an alley from the overpass that ran a northeast course toward my rough destination, though against the grain of the many lanes that entered it. It was raining and I unfurled a small folding umbrella. The upper stories are homes or apartments but the street level is almost all small shops and services. Hair-do parlors and Tabako shops ("Tabako" the Carib Indian word that has entered most of the world's languages)— strong coffee shops—on a relatively quiet lane where you must hug the wall when a car passes. Ads and signs everywhere: my eyes couldn't leave the writing alone. Some part of my mind effortlessly soaked up long-forgotten Chinese characters and syllabary-written loan-words and sallied out to reassemble its old fluency. A few more bends and the lane was heading due east. Too far this way would be off. There were path-wide breaks paved in between structures, some might be passages. A student in a blue dress came up one so I took it and was carried through (descending steps and being funneled between old stone walls) to a wider street totally packed with cars and trucks, lined with storefronts and signs, a basin of rumbling and honking. An intersection brought in a street I had been seeking, *Kokusai dori,* "International Street," which should take me to the shopping bazaars of long ago. The stores were more various here. Some were for the Japanese tourists, selling jewelry of shell and coral, traditional Ryukyuan fabrics, and a large conch shell such as I dived for and brought up when I lived on Suwa-no-se island a few hundred miles to the north. In the sixties.

The street went over a canal. Looked down, and there was a two-foot-diameter drain line entering the ten-foot-wide stream with a gush of brown water. The stream surface was a solid with five-inch fish crowded up to the incoming water. The smell was too rank and rich. I hoped those fish were built to handle that stuff. There was a space beyond the canal where a few buildings had been torn down, and it looked like a mini-freeway right-of-way was being taken. Through the break in the wall of buildings I could see into some elder structures: dark gray wood with the old-style roof. More south Chinese than Japanese in look, solid and subtropical with those tiles each mortared down against the typhoon winds. These houses in their little cluster near the canal were survivors from the typhoon of iron. A tiny island of relict architecture, a bit of highly endangered diversity.

Okinawa was once the Ryukyu Kingdom, the "Great Loo Choo," an independent island nation that had separate relations with the Chinese court. China declared that this nation of less than a million people was the most skilled in courtly manners of all the tributary realms. The Shimada Clan Lord of southern Kyushu invaded the unarmed Ryukyu capital of Shuri in the seventeenth century, made the king into a puppet, and gradually transformed the islands into a fellaheen colony growing cash-crop sugar cane. Many Okinawans hoped they would regain their freedom after World War II and felt betrayed when the US handed them back to the control of the Japanese.

The forests of Okinawa, mostly gone, once supplied wood for housing. The shortage of wood pushed postwar builders into the ingenious forms of poured concrete. New habitat, new energy, new style. Though the thought of a greenly overgrown garden city of boulders and cliffs is charming, I doubt that these small buildings are the final phase. They are already being shaded out, here and there, by new high-rise hotels and office buildings that are owned and financed from Japan—a flow of investment southward following *naichi* ("mainland" Japanese) tourism. Eventually all these tangled boxy and crenellated multicolored houses will fade before a monoculture of tall buildings, to look like the new Hong Kong. (The high-rise buildings, like the little ones, are all built of aggregate: river or beach-washed gravels and sands, borrowed a while from the earth and made to stand on end.) The tall buildings will be a sort of climax for this town, at least until the cash-and-energy-flow osmosis that lifts such things skyward fades away.

It was past noon and I stepped into a noodle shop. It served Okinawan soba and with a few deft touches (indigo-blue fake *kasuri* cloth, goza mats on the benches, folksy pottery) echoed ethnicity and the rural. The waitress was not up to trying her English so she absolutely did not see me until I spoke out in Japanese—"Elder sister, some Okinawa soba please." Smiles of instant rapport. The noodles came in a ten-inch bowl with large chunks of pork, and a cup of chilled country-style tea.

I walked on up the intensely active street. I began to feel the landscape with my skin, a somatic sensation of mirroring or echoing that comes with re-cognitions that are below the conscious threshold. Then I saw my conscious goal: the short slope down into a roofed shopping lane, a gate to a cave, with the words above it, *Heiwa dori,* "Peace Lane." I stopped before the cave-mouth full of memories of a different Naha City, 1957, when I had explored the town on foot as a seaman ashore off a tanker. It had all been so much poorer and plainer then, and only Heiwa-dori had the glitter and bustle that seems to cover the whole town now. I had been taking a break to earn money between Kyoto Zen Buddhist study sessions, and the Naha tanker stop was enroute to the Persian Gulf. So the bazaar was a place to buy a 3×6 goza mat, a small teapot and a teacup, some green tea, and a carpenter's saw. (The saw I saved till much later, but the mat, pot, and cup served me well on shipboard. In the Indian Ocean I spread the mat on the boat-deck, slipped off my zori, sat down crosslegged, faced the sunset, and poured *ocha.* Sometimes a shipmate would join me. They amiably said, "Snyder, you've gone totally Asian.") I catch myself standing there watching the self of thirty-two years earlier walk up the same lane — "You can dive into the past and emerge in the future," the Hua-yen commentaries say.

So I walked it again. An arching canvas roof covered the length of it, beginning to drum in the increasing rain. Herbs, snacks, boutiques, a shopful of Mainland China products, but no loose green tea or carpentry tools today. Halfway back down the lane I noticed a side path with ragged cobble paving. I checked it out. At first it looked like a dead end, going around a shabby shed to a stone wall. Looking above, a rare sight: the tops of large leafy trees. Something is *there.* The stone path didn't end, it took a turn and went through a break in the wall up steps to a wooded hillock park surrounded by the town. Birds were calling and flying from tree to tree — evergreen glossy broad-leafed trees like camphor and *Tabu.* Several stairflights higher, at the top, I stood in the shelter of an overarching banyan tree as the rain pelted down.

Wind and rain from the sea. The birds flitting back and forth, and a young cat stalking. Stone benches, old cut stone edges to the dirt platform, and below, one tiny "ancient house" from the prewar city. Standing there watched and washed by this world of sky and rain — and the trades and jobs and families of my fellow humans in this wide warm newgrowth city, for a moment I was completely at home. At home in the rain with the cat, the banyan, the alleys and the apartments, in a world I barely knew, a stranger in Okinawa, and yet as at home — for this moment, here — as I would be anywhere. And maybe back home as much a stranger there as here, only not seeing it. Memories and our old pathways are woven like ghost nets invisibly filling the landscape of our days. I stood for a moment with the image of ancient forests, clearcuts, and the fresh green new growth of my native West Coast mountains shining through these thoughts of the rise and fall of cities and families, all one in the net of nature.

Down the other side of the hill was another maze of little houses and shops, and in great good cheer I plunged on down to find a way back to camp, in this case simply my hotel.

Is Nature Real?

I'm getting grumpy about the slippery arguments being put forth by high-paid intellectuals trying to knock nature and knock the people who value nature and still come out smelling smart and progressive.

The idea of nature as a "social construction"—a shared cultural projection seen and shaped in the light of social values and priorities—if carried out to the full bright light of philosophy, would look like a subset of the world view best developed in Mahayana Buddhism or Advaita Vedanta, which declares (as just one part of its strategy) the universe to be *maya,* or illusion. In doing so the Asian philosophers are not saying that the universe is ontologically without some kind of reality. They are arguing that, across the board, our seeing of the world is biological (based on the particular qualities of our species' body-mind), psychological (reflecting subjective projections), and cultural construction. And they go on to suggest how to examine one's own seeing, so as to see the one who sees and thus make seeing more true.

The current use of the "social construction" terminology, however, cannot go deeper, because it is based on the logic of European science and the "enlightenment." This thought-pod, in pursuing some new kind of meta-narrative, has failed to cop to its own story—which is the same old occidental view of nature as a realm of resources that has been handed over to humanity for its own use. As a spiritually (politically) fallen realm, this socially constructed nature finally has no reality other than the quantification provided by economists and resource managers. This is indeed the ultimate commodification of nature, done by supposedly advanced theorists, who prove to be simply the high end of the "wise use" movement. Deconstruction, done with a compassionate heart and the intention of gaining wisdom, becomes the Mahayana Buddhist logical and philosophical exercise that plumbs to the bottom of deconstructing and comes back with compassion for all beings. Deconstruction without compassion is self-aggrandizement.

So we understand the point about wilderness being in one sense a cultural construct, for what isn't? What's more to the point, and what I fail to find in the writings of the anti-nature crowd, is the awareness that wilderness is the locus of big rich ecosystems, and is thus (among other things) a living place for beings who can survive in no other sort of habitat. Recreation, spirituality, aesthetics—good for people—also make wilderness valuable, but these are secondary to the importance of biodiversity. The protection of natural variety is essential to planetary health for all.

Some of these critical scholars set up, then attack, the notion of "pristine wilderness" and this again is beating a dead horse. It is well known that humans and proto-humans have lived virtually everywhere for hundreds of millenia. "Pristine" is only a relative term, but humanly used as the landscape may have been, up until ninety years ago the planet still had huge territories of wild terrain that are now woefully shrunken. Much of the wild land was also the territory of indigenous cultures that fit well into what were inhabited wildernesses.

The attacks on nature and wilderness from the ivory towers come at just the right time to bolster global developers, the resurgent timber companies (here in California the Charles Hurvitz Suits at Pacific Lumber) and those who would trash the Endangered Species Act. It looks like an unholy alliance of Capitalist Materialist and Marxist Idealists in an attack on the rural world that Marx reputedly found idiotic and boring.

Heraclitus, the Stoics, the Buddhists, scientists, and you average alert older person all know that everything in this world is ephemeral and unpredictable. Even the earlier ecologists who worked with Clemenstain succession theory know that! Yet now a generation of resource biologists, inspired by the thin milk of Daniel Botkin's theorizing, are promoting what they think is a new paradigm that relegates the concept of climax to the dustheap of ideas. Surely none of the earlier scientific ecologists ever doubted that disturbances come and go. It looks like this particular bit of bullying also comes just in time to support the corporate clear-cutters and land-developers. (Despite blow-downs, bugs, fires, drouth, and landslides, vast plant communities lasted in essence for multimillions of years prior to human times.)

It's a real pity that many in the humanities and social sciences are finding it so difficult to handle the rise of "nature" as an intellectually serious territory. For all the talk of "the other" in everybody's theory these days, when confronted with a genuine Other, the nonhuman realm, the response of the come-lately anti-nature intellectuals is to circle the wagons and declare that nature is really part of culture. Which maybe is just a strategy to keep the budget within their specialties.

A lot of this rhetoric, if translated into human politics, would be like saying "African-American people are the social construction of whites." And then they might as well declare that South Central Los Angeles is a problematic realm that has been exaggerated by some white liberals, a realm whose apparent moral issues are also illusory, and that the real exercise in regard to African Americans is a better understanding of how white writers and readers made them up. But liberal critical theorists don't talk this way when it comes to fellow human beings because they know what kind of heat they'd get. In the case of nature, because they are still under the illusion that it isn't seriously *there,* they indulge themselves in this moral and political shallowness.

Conservationists and environmentalists have brought some of this on themselves. We still have not communicated the importance of biodiversity. Many if not most citizens are genuinely confused over why such importance appears to be placed on hitherto unheard-of owls or fish. Scientists have to be heard from, but the writers and philosophers among us (myself included) should speak our deep feelings for the value of the nonhuman with greater clarity. We need to stay fresh, write clean prose, reject obscurity, and not intentionally exaggerate. And we need to comprehend the pain and distress of working people everywhere.

A *Wilderness* is always a specific place, because it is there for the local critters that live in it. In some cases a few humans will be living in it too. Such places are scarce and must be rigorously defended. *Wild* is the process that surrounds us all, self-organizing nature: creating plant-zones, humans and their societies, all ultimately resilient beyond our wildest imagination. Human societies create a variety of dreams, notions, and images about the nature of nature. But it is not impossible to get a pretty accurate picture of nature with a little first-hand application—no big deal, I'd take these doubting professors out for a walk, show them a bit of the passing ecosystem show, and maybe get them to help clean up a creek.

{*An earlier version of this essay was published in* Wild Earth, Winter 1996/1997, *under the title "Nature as Seen from Kitkitdizze Is No 'Social Construction.'"*}

Entering the
Fiftieth Millennium

Let's say we're about to enter not the twenty-first century but the fiftieth millennium. Since the various cultural calendars (Hindu, Jewish, Islamic, Christian, Japanese) are each within terms of their own stories, we can ask what calendar would be suggested to us by the implicit narrative of Euro-American science—since that provides so much of our contemporary educated worldview. We might come up with a "Homo sapiens calendar" that starts at about 40,000 years before the present, BP, in the Gravettian/Aurignacian era when the human tool kit (already long sophisticated) began to be decorated with graphs and emblems and when figurines were produced not for practical use but apparently for magic or beauty.

Rethinking our calendar in this way is made possible by the research and discoveries of the last century in physical anthropology, paleontology, archaeology, and cultural anthropology. The scholars of hominid history are uncovering a constantly larger past in which the earlier members of our species continually appear to be smarter, more accomplished, more adept, and more complex than we had previously believed. We humans are constantly revising the story we tell ourself about ourselves. The main challenge is to keep this unfolding story modestly reliable.

One of my neopagan friends, an ethnobotanist and prehistorian, complains about how the Christians have callously appropriated his sacred solstice ceremonies. "Our fir tree of lights and gifts," he says, "has been swept into an orgy of consumerism, no longer remembered as a sign of the return of the sun," and, "People have totally forgotten that the gifts brought from the north by Santa Claus are spiritual, not material; and his red clothes, white trim, round body, and northern habitat show that he represents the psychoactive mushroom *Amanita muscaria*."

My friend is one of several poet-scholars I know who study deep history (a term he prefers to "prehistory")—in this case that of Europe—for clues and guides to understanding the creature that we are and how we got here, the better to steer our way into the future. Such studies are especially useful for artists.

I went to France last summer to pursue my interest in the Upper Paleolithic. Southwest Europe has large areas of karst plateau, which allows for caves by the thousands, some of them enormous. Quite a few were decorated by Upper Paleolithic people. With the help of the poet and paleo-art historian Clayton Eshleman, my wife and I visited many sites and saw a major sampling of the cave art of southwest Europe, in the Dordogne and the Pyrenees. Places like Pêche-merle, Cougnac, Niaux, El Portel, Lascaux, and Trois Frères. The cave art, with its finger tracings, engravings, hand stencils, outline drawings, and polychrome paintings, flourished from 10,000 to 35,000 years ago. The Paleolithic cave and portable art of Europe thus constitute a 25,000-year continuous artistic and cultural tradition. The people who did this were fully Homo sapiens and, it must be clearly stated, not just ancestors of the people of Europe but (in a gene pool that old) to some degree ancestors to everyone everywhere. The art they left us is a heritage for people of the whole world.

This tradition is full of puzzles. The artwork is often placed far back in the caves, in almost inaccessible places. The quality fluctuates wildly. Animals can be painted with exquisite attention, but there are relatively few human figures, and the ones that are there are strangely crude. Almost no plants are represented. Birds and fish are scarce compared to mammals (one cave provides an exception). Some animal paintings, as at Niaux, appear unfinished, with the feet left off.

The theories and explanations from the twentieth-century cave-art specialists—the great Abbé Breuil and the redoubtable André Leroi-Gourhan—don't quite work. The hunting-magic theory, which holds that the paintings of animals were to increase the take in the hunt, is contradicted by the fact that the majority of animal representations are of wild horses, which were not a big food item, and that the animals most commonly consumed, red deer and reindeer, are depicted in small number. The horse was not yet domesticated, so why this fascination for horses? (My wife, Carole, suggests that maybe the artists were a guild of teenage girls.) The bison is a close second, however, and was a food source.

The other most commonly represented animals, the huge Pleistocene bison and the aurochs, a huge *bos* (which was living in the forests of northern Europe up until the sixteenth century), were apparently too large and dangerous to be major hunting prey. Ibex, chamois, and panther occasionally show up, but they were not major food items. (There are also pictures of animals long extinct now—wooly rhinoceros, mammoth, cave bear, giant elk.)

In the art of early civilized times, there was a fascination with large predators—in particular, the charismatic Anatolian lions and the brown bears from which the word *arctic* derives. Big predators were abundant in the Paleolithic, but sketches or paintings of them are scarce in all caves but one. It was the bears who first used the caves and entirely covered the walls of some, like Rouffignac, with long scratches. Seeing this may have given the first impetus to humans to do their own graffiti.

The theory that these works were part of a shamanistic and ceremonial cultural practice, though likely enough, is still just speculation. There have been attempts to read some narratives out of certain graphic combinations, but that too cannot be tested.

After several decades of research and comparison, it came to seem to the archeologists and art historians that cave art began with hand stencils and crude engravings starting around 32,000 years BP and progressively evolved through time to an artistic climax at the Lascaux cave. This is the most famous of caves, discovered during World War II. It is generally felt to contain the most remarkable and lovely of all the world's cave art. The polychrome paintings are dated at around 17000 BP. Last summer I had the rare good fortune to be admitted to *le vrai grotte* of Lascaux (as well as the replica, which is in itself excellent and what all but a handful of people now see). I can testify to its magic. There's an eighteen-foot-long painting of an auroch arcing across a ceiling twelve feet above the floor. A sort of Lascaux style is then perceived as coming down in other, later caves, excellent work, up to the Salon Noir in the Niaux cave in the Ariège, dated about 11500 BP. After that, cave art stops being made, and many caves closed up from landslides or cave-ins and were forgotten.

Until quite recently everyone was pretty comfortable with this theoretical evolutionary chronology, which fits our contemporary wish to believe that things get better through time. But in 1994 some enthusiastic speleologists found a new cave, on the Ardèche, a tributary of the Rhone. Squeezing through narrow cracks and not expecting much, they almost tumbled into a fifty-foot-high hall and a quarter mile of passageways of linked chambers full of magnificent depictions that were the equal of anything at Lascaux. There are a few animals shown here that are totally new to cave art. Images of woolly rhinoceros and the Pleistocene maneless lion, which are rare in other caves, are the most numerous. This site is now known, after one of the lead discoverers, as the Chauvet cave.

The French scientists did their initial carbon dating, were puzzled, looked again, and had to conclude that these marvelous paintings were around 32,000 years old: 15,000 years older than those at Lascaux—almost as distant in time from Lascaux as Lascaux is from us. The idea of a progressive history to cave art is seriously in question. A new, and again larger, sense of the Homo sapiens story has opened up for us, and the beginnings of art are pushed even further back in time.

I wrote in my notebook:

Out of the turning and twisting calcined cave walls, a sea of fissures, calcite concretions, stalactites, old claw-scratchings of cave bears, floors of bear wallows & slides; the human finger-tracings in clay, early scribblings, scratched-in lines and sketchy little engravings of half-done creatures or just abstract signs, lines crossed over lines, images over images; out of this ancient swirl of graffiti rise up the exquisite figures of animals: swimming deer with antler cocked up, a pride of lions with noble profiles, fat wild horses, great bodied bison, huge-horned wild bulls, antlered elk; painted and powerfully outlined creatures alive with the life that art gives: on the long-lost mineraled walls below ground. Crisp, economical, swift, sometimes hasty; fitting into the space, fitting over other paintings, spread across . . . outlined in calligraphic confident curving lines. Not photo-realistic, but true.

To have done this took a mind that can clearly observe and hold within it a wealth of sounds, smells, and images and then carry them underground and re-create them. The effort took organization and planning to bring off: we have found the stone lamps and evidence of lighting supplies and traces of ground pigments sometimes obtained from far away. The people must have gathered supplies of food, dried grass for bedding, and poles for scaffolding. Someone was doing arts administration.

One important reminder here is, as T. S. Eliot said when writing of Magdalenian art, that "art never improves." There is no progress in art. It is either good or it isn't. Art that moves us today can be from anywhere, from any time.

The cave paintings had their own roles to play back in the late Pleistocene. Having been protected by the steady temperatures of the underground, they return to human eyes again today, and across the millennia can move us. No master realist painter of the past five hundred years could better those painted critters of the past: they totally do what they do, without room for improvement.

This is quite true, in certain ways, for the literary arts as well.

And there may be no "progress" in religion, in practice, or in the Dharma, either. There was an Ancient Buddha. There were archaic Bodhisattvas. All that we have to study, of them, is their shards and paintings.

What *was* the future? One answer might be, "The future was to have been further progress, an improvement over our present condition." This is more in question now. The deep past confounds the future by suggesting how little we are agreed on what is good.

If our ancient rock artists skipped out on painting humans, it just may be that they knew more than enough about themselves and could turn their attention wholeheartedly to the nonhuman other. The range of their art embraces both abstract and unreadable signs and graphs and a richly portrayed world of what today we call "faunal biodiversity." They gave us a picture of their animal environment with as much pride and art as if they were giving us their very selves.

Maybe in some way they speak from a spirit that is in line with Dōgen's comment "We study the self to forget the self. When you forget the self, you can become one with all the other phenomena."

We have no way of knowing what the religious practices, the rituals, or the verbal arts of 35,000 years ago might have been. It is most likely that the languages of that time were in no way inferior in complexity, sophistication, or richness to the languages spoken today. I get this opinion in a recent personal communication from the eminent linguist William Bright. It's not far-fetched to think that if the paintings were so good, the poems and songs must have been of equal quality.

One can imagine myths and tales of people, places, and animals. In poetry or song, I fancy wild horse chants, "salutes" (as are sung in some parts of Africa) to each creature, little lyrics that intensify some element in a narrative, a kind of deep song—*cante jondo*—to go together with deep history; or on the other side, quick "bison haiku."

It was all in the realm of orality, which as we well know can support a rich and intense "literary" culture that is often interacting with dance, song, and story. Such are our prime high arts today: opera and ballet.

Today, then: the Franco-Germanic-Anglian creole known as English has become the world's second language and as such is a major bearer of diverse literary cultures. English is and will be all the more a future host to a truly multicultural "rainbow" realm of writings. The rich history of the English-language tradition is like a kiva full of lore, to be studied and treasured by writers and scholars wherever they may find themselves on the planet. It will also continue to diversify and to embrace words and pronunciations that will move it farther and farther from London Town. Even as I deliberately take my membership to be North American and feel distant from much of European culture, I count myself fortunate to have been born a native speaker of English. Such flexibility, such variety of vocabulary! Such a fine sound system! We can look forward to its future changes. Performance and poetry, storytelling and fiction are still alive and well. Orality and song stay with poetry as long as we are here.

We might wonder through what images *our* voices, our practices, will carry to the people of 10,000 years hence. Through the swirls of still-standing freeway off-ramps and on-ramps? Through the ruins of dams? For those future people will surely be there, listening for some faint call from us, when they are entering the sixtieth millennium.

Poetry

Riprap

Mid-August at
Sourdough Mountain Lookout

Down valley a smoke haze
Three days heat, after five days rain
Pitch glows on the fir-cones
Across rocks and meadows
Swarms of new flies.

I cannot remember things I once read
A few friends, but they are in cities.
Drinking cold snow-water from a tin cup
Looking down for miles
Through high still air.

Piute Creek

One granite ridge
A tree, would be enough
Or even a rock, a small creek,
A bark shred in a pool.
Hill beyond hill, folded and twisted
Tough trees crammed
In thin stone fractures
A huge moon on it all, is too much.
The mind wanders. A million
Summers, night air still and the rocks
Warm.   Sky over endless mountains.
All the junk that goes with being human
Drops away, hard rock wavers
Even the heavy present seems to fail
This bubble of a heart.
Words and books
Like a small creek off a high ledge
Gone in the dry air.

A clear, attentive mind
Has no meaning but that
Which sees is truly seen.
No one loves rock, yet we are here.
Night chills. A flick
In the moonlight
Slips into Juniper shadow:
Back there unseen
Cold proud eyes
Of Cougar or Coyote
Watch me rise and go.

Milton by Firelight

Piute Creek, August 1955

"O hell, what do mine eyes
            with grief behold?"
Working with an old
Singlejack miner, who can sense
The vein and cleavage
In the very guts of rock, can
Blast granite, build
Switchbacks that last for years
Under the beat of snow, thaw, mule-hooves.
What use, Milton, a silly story
Of our lost general parents,
            eaters of fruit?

The Indian, the chainsaw boy,
And a string of six mules
Came riding down to camp
Hungry for tomatoes and green apples.
Sleeping in saddle-blankets
Under a bright night-sky
Han River slantwise by morning.
Jays squall
Coffee boils

In ten thousand years the Sierras
Will be dry and dead, home of the scorpion.
Ice-scratched slabs and bent trees.
No paradise, no fall,
Only the weathering land
The wheeling sky,
Man, with his Satan
Scouring the chaos of the mind.
Oh Hell!

Fire down
Too dark to read, miles from a road
The bell-mare clangs in the meadow
That packed dirt for a fill-in
Scrambling through loose rocks
On an old trail
All of a summer's day.

Above Pate Valley

We finished clearing the last
Section of trail by noon,
High on the ridge-side
Two thousand feet above the creek
Reached the pass, went on
Beyond the white pine groves,
Granite shoulders, to a small
Green meadow watered by the snow,
Edged with Aspen—sun
Straight high and blazing
But the air was cool.
Ate a cold fried trout in the
Trembling shadows. I spied
A glitter, and found a flake
Black volcanic glass—obsidian—
By a flower. Hands and knees
Pushing the Bear grass, thousands
Of arrowhead leavings over a
Hundred yards. Not one good
Head, just razor flakes
On a hill snowed all but summer,
A land of fat summer deer,
They came to camp. On their
Own trails. I followed my own
Trail here. Picked up the cold-drill,
Pick, singlejack, and sack
Of dynamite.
Ten thousand years.

Hay for the Horses

He had driven half the night
From far down San Joaquin
Through Mariposa, up the
Dangerous mountain roads,
And pulled in at eight a.m.
With his big truckload of hay
            behind the barn.
With winch and ropes and hooks
We stacked the bales up clean
To splintery redwood rafters
High in the dark, flecks of alfalfa
Whirling through shingle-cracks of light,
Itch of haydust in the
            sweaty shirt and shoes.
At lunchtime under Black oak
Out in the hot corral,
—The old mare nosing lunchpails,
Grasshoppers crackling in the weeds—
"I'm sixty-eight" he said,
"I first bucked hay when I was seventeen.
I thought, that day I started,
I sure would hate to do this all my life.
And dammit, that's just what
I've gone and done."

Riprap

Lay down these words
Before your mind like rocks.
            placed solid, by hands
In choice of place, set
Before the body of the mind
            in space and time:
Solidity of bark, leaf, or wall
            riprap of things:
Cobble of milky way,
            straying planets,
These poems, people,
            lost ponies with
Dragging saddles
            and rocky sure-foot trails.
The worlds like an endless
            four-dimensional
Game of *Go*.
            ants and pebbles
In the thin loam, each rock a word
            a creek-washed stone
Granite: ingrained
            with torment of fire and weight
Crystal and sediment linked hot
            all change, in thoughts,
As well as things.

Myths and Texts

1

The morning star is not a star
Two seedling fir, one died
                    Io, Io,
Girdled in wistaria
Wound with ivy
                    "The May Queen
Is the survival of
A pre-human
Rutting season"

The year spins
Pleiades sing to their rest
                    at San Francisco
                    dream
                    dream
Green comes out of the ground
Birds squabble
Young girls run mad with the pine bough,
                                        Io

2

But ye shall destroy their altars,
    break their images, and cut down their groves.
                                Exodus 34:13

The ancient forests of China logged
    and the hills slipped into the Yellow Sea.
Squared beams, log dogs,
    on a tamped-earth sill.
San Francisco 2x4s
    were the woods around Seattle:
Someone killed and someone built, a house,
    a forest, wrecked or raised
All America hung on a hook
    & burned by men, in their own praise.

Snow on fresh stumps and brush-piles.
The generator starts and rumbles
                    in the frosty dawn

I wake from bitter dreams,
Rise and build a fire,
Pull on and lace the stiff cold boots
Eat huge flapjacks by a gloomy Swede
In splintery cookhouse light
                            grab my tin pisspot hat
Ride off to the show in a crummy-truck
And start the Cat.

"Pines grasp the clouds with iron claws
like dragons rising from sleep"
250, 000 board-feet a day
If both Cats keep working
& nobody gets hurt

3

"Lodgepole Pine: the wonderful reproductive
power of this species on areas over which its
stand has been killed by fire is dependent upon
the ability of the closed cones to endure a fire
which kills the tree without injuring its seed.
After fire, the cones open and shed their seeds
on the bared ground and a new growth springs up."

Stood straight
                holding the choker high
As the Cat swung back the arch
                piss-firs falling,
Limbs snapping on the tin hat
                bright D caught on
Swinging butt-hooks
                ringing against cold steel.

Hsü Fang lived on leeks and pumpkins.
Goosefoot,
            wild herbs,
                        fields lying fallow!

But it's hard to farm
Between the stumps:
The cows get thin, the milk tastes funny,

The kids grow up and go to college
They don't come back.
            the little fir-trees do

            Rocks the same blue as sky
Only icefields, a mile up,
                      are the mountain
Hovering over ten thousand acres
Of young fir.

8

Each dawn is clear
Cold air bites the throat.
Thick frost on the pine bough
Leaps from the tree
      snapped by the diesel

Drifts and glitters in the
        horizontal sun.
In the frozen grass
        smoking boulders
        ground by steel tracks.
In the frozen grass
        wild horses stand
        beyond a row of pines.
The D8 tears through piss-fir,
Scrapes the seed-pine
            chipmunks flee,
A black ant carries an egg
Aimlessly from the battered ground.
Yellowjackets swarm and circle
Above the crushed dead log, their home.
Pitch oozes from barked
        trees still standing,
Mashed bushes make strange smells.
Lodgepole pines are brittle.
Camprobbers flutter to watch.

A few stumps, drying piles of brush;
Under the thin duff, a toe-scrape down

Black lava of a late flow.
Leaves stripped from thornapple
Taurus by nightfall.

14

The groves are down
                cut down
Groves of Ahab, of Cybele
Pine trees, knobbed twigs
     thick cone and seed
     Cybele's tree this, sacred in groves
Pine of Seami, cedar of Haida
Cut down by the prophets of Israel
     the fairies of Athens
     the thugs of Rome
             both ancient and modern;
Cut down to make room for the suburbs
Bulldozed by Luther and Weyerhaeuser
Crosscut and chainsaw
     squareheads and finns
     high-lead and cat-skidding
Trees down
Creeks choked, trout killed, roads.

Sawmill temples of Jehovah.
Squat black burners 100 feet high
Sending the smoke of our burnt
Live sap and leaf
To his eager nose.

15

Lodgepole
          cone/seed waits for fire
And then thin forests of silver-gray.
     in the void
     a pine cone falls
Pursued by squirrels
What mad pursuit! What struggle to escape!

Her body a seedpod
Open to the wind
"A seed pod void of seed
We had no meeting together"
        so you and I must wait
Until the next blaze
Of the world, the universe,
Millions of worlds, burning
        —oh let it lie.

Shiva at the end of the kalpa:
Rock-fat, hill-flesh, gone in a whiff.
Men who hire men to cut groves
Kill snakes, build cities, pave fields,
Believe in god, but can't
Believe their own senses
Let alone Gautama. Let them lie.

Pine sleeps, cedar splits straight
Flowers crack the pavement.
        Pa-ta Shan-jen
(A painter who watched Ming fall)
        lived in a tree:
"The brush
May paint the mountains and streams
Though the territory is lost."

1

first shaman song

In the village of the dead,
Kicked loose bones
        ate pitch of a drift log
        (whale fat)
Nettles and cottonwood. Grass smokes
        in the sun
Logs turn in the river
        sand scorches the feet.

Two days without food, trucks roll past
        in dust and light, rivers

are rising.
Thaw in the high meadows. Move west in July.

Soft oysters rot now, between tides
    the flats stink.

I sit without thoughts by the log-road
Hatching a new myth
watching the waterdogs
    the last truck gone.

6

this poem is for bear

"As for me I am a child of the god of the mountains."

A bear down under the cliff.
She is eating huckleberries.
They are ripe now
Soon it will snow, and she
Or maybe he, will crawl into a hole
And sleep. You can see
Huckleberries in bearshit if you
Look, this time of year
If I sneak up on the bear
It will grunt and run

The others had all gone down
From the blackberry brambles, but one girl
Spilled her basket, and was picking up her
Berries in the dark.
A tall man stood in the shadow, took her arm,
Led her to his home. He was a bear.
In a house under the mountain
She gave birth to slick dark children
With sharp teeth, and lived in the hollow
Mountain many years.
    snare a bear: call him out:
honey-eater
forest apple
light-foot
Old man in the fur coat, Bear! come out!

Die of your own choice!
Grandfather black-food!
              this girl married a bear
Who rules in the mountains, Bear!
              you have eaten many berries
              you have caught many fish
              you have frightened many people

Twelve species north of Mexico
Sucking their paws in the long winter
Tearing the high-strung caches down
Whining, crying, jacking off
(Odysseus was a bear)

Bear-cubs gnawing the soft tits
Teeth gritted, eyes screwed tight
              but she let them.
Til her brothers found the place
Chased her husband up the gorge
Cornered him in the rocks.
Song of the snared bear:
      "Give me my belt.
      "I am near death.
      "I came from the mountain caves
      "At the headwaters,
      "The small streams there
      "Are all dried up.

—I think I'll go hunt bears.
              "hunt bears?
Why shit Snyder,
You couldn't hit a bear in the ass
              with a handful of rice!"

8

this poem is for deer

"I dance on all the mountains
 On five mountains, I have a dancing place
 When they shoot at me I run
 To my five mountains"

Missed a last shot
At the Buck, in twilight
So we came back sliding
On dry needles through cold pines.
Scared out a cottontail
Whipped up the winchester
Shot off its head.
The white body rolls and twitches
In the dark ravine
As we run down the hill to the car.
                              deer foot down scree
Picasso's fawn, Issa's fawn,
Deer on the autumn mountain
Howling like a wise man
Stiff springy jumps down the snowfields
Head held back, forefeet out,
Balls tight in a tough hair sack
Keeping the human soul from care
                         on the autumn mountain
Standing in late sun, ear-flick
Tail-flick, gold mist of flies
Whirling from nostril to eyes.

                    ℰ

Home by night
                  drunken eye
Still picks out Taurus
Low, and growing high:
            four-point buck
Dancing in the headlights
            on the lonely road
A mile past the mill-pond,
With the car stopped, shot
That wild silly blinded creature down.

Pull out the hot guts
            with hard bare hands
While night-frost chills the tongue
            and eye
The cold horn-bones.
The hunter's belt

                    just below the sky
Warm blood in the car trunk.
Deer-smell,
                the limp tongue.

                        ❧

Deer don't want to die for me.
            I'll drink sea-water
Sleep on beach pebbles in the rain
Until the deer come down to die
                in pity for my pain.

                    # 9

Sealion, salmon, offshore—
Salt-fuck desire driving flap fins
North, south, five thousand miles
Coast, and up creek, big seeds
Groping for inland womb.

Geese, ducks, swallows,
                        paths in the air
I am a frozen addled egg on the tundra

My petrel, snow-tongued
            kiss her a brook her mouth
of smooth pebbles her tongue a bed
            icewater flowing in that
Cavern dark, tongue drifts in the creek
                —blind fish

On the rainy boulders
On the bloody sandbar
I ate the spawned-out salmon
I went crazy
Covered with ashes
Gnawing the girls breasts
Marrying women to whales
Or dogs, I'm a priest too
I raped your wife
I'll eat your corpse

10

Flung from demonic wombs
        off to some new birth
A million shapes—just look in any
        biology book.
And the hells below mind
        where ghosts roam, the heavens
Above brain, where gods & angels play
        an age or two
& they'll trade with you,
Who wants heaven?
        rest homes like that
Scattered all through the galaxy.

     "I kill everything
     I fear nothing but wolves
     From the mouth of the Cowlitz
           to its source,
     Only the wolves scare me,
     I have a chief's tail"
—Skunk.
       "We carry deer-fawns in our mouths
       We carry deer-fawns in our mouths
       We have our faces blackened"
—Wolf-song.
"If I were a baby seal
           every time I came up
I'd head toward shore—"

16

How rare to be born a human being!
Wash him off with cedar-bark and milkweed
        send the damned doctors home.
Baby, baby, noble baby
Noble-hearted baby

One hand up, one hand down
"I alone am the honored one"
   Birth of the Buddha.

And the whole world-system trembled.
"If that baby really said that,
I'd cut him up and throw him to the dogs!"
said Chao-chou the Zen Master. But
Chipmunks, gray squirrels, and
Golden-mantled ground squirrels
                    brought him each a nut.
Truth being the sweetest of flavors.

Girls would have in their arms
A wild gazelle or wild wolf-cubs
And give them their white milk,
                    those who had new-born infants home
Breasts still full.
Wearing a spotted fawnskin
                    sleeping under trees
                    bacchantes, drunk
On wine or truth, what you will,
Meaning: compassion.
Agents: man and beast, beasts
Got the buddha-nature
All but
Coyote.

3
Maudgalyâyana saw hell

Under the shuddering eyelid
Dreams gnawing the nerve-strings,
The mind grabs and the shut eye sees:
Down dimensions floating below sunlight,
Worlds of the dead, Bardo, mind-worlds
& horror of sunless cave-ritual
Meeting conscious monk bums
Blown on winds of karma from hell
To endless changing hell,
Life and death whipped
On this froth of reality (wind & rain
Realms human and full of desire) over the cold
Hanging enormous unknown, below
Art and History and all mankind living thoughts,

Occult & witchcraft evils each all true.
The thin edge of nature rising fragile
And helpless with its love and sentient stone
And flesh, above dark drug-death dreams.

Clouds I cannot lose, we cannot leave.
We learn to love, horror accepted.
Beyond, within, all normal beauties
Of the science-conscious sex and love-receiving
Day-to-day got vision of this sick
Sparkling person at the inturned dreaming
Blooming human mind
Dropping it all, and opening the eyes.

8

John Muir on Mt. Ritter:

After scanning its face again and again,
I began to scale it, picking my holds
With intense caution. About half-way
To the top, I was suddenly brought to
A dead stop, with arms outspread
Clinging close to the face of the rock
Unable to move hand or foot
Either up or down. My doom
Appeared fixed. I MUST fall.
There would be a moment of
Bewilderment, and then,
A lifeless rumble down the cliff
To the glacier below.
My mind seemed to fill with a
Stifling smoke. This terrible eclipse
Lasted only a moment, when life blazed
Forth again with preternatural clearness.
I seemed suddenly to become possessed
Of a new sense. My trembling muscles
Became firm again, every rift and flaw in
The rock was seen as through a microscope,
My limbs moved with a positiveness and precision
With which I seemed to have
Nothing at all to do.

10
Amitabha's vow

"If, after obtaining Buddhahood, anyone in my land
    gets tossed in jail on a vagrancy rap, may I
    not attain highest perfect enlightenment.

    wild geese in the orchard
    frost on the new grass

"If, after obtaining Buddhahood, anyone in my land
    loses a finger coupling boxcars, may I
    not attain highest perfect enlightenment.

    mare's eye flutters
    jerked by the lead-rope
    stone-bright shoes flick back
    ankles trembling: down steep rock

"If, after obtaining Buddhahood, anyone in my land
    can't get a ride hitch-hiking all directions, may I
    not attain highest perfect enlightenment.
    wet rocks buzzing
    rain and thunder southwest
    hair, beard, tingle
    wind whips bare legs
    we should go back
    we don't

13

Spikes of new smell driven up nostrils
Expanding & deepening, ear-muscles
Straining and grasping the sounds
Mouth filled with bright fluid coldness
Tongue crushed by the weight of its flavors
        —the Nootka sold out for lemon drops
(What's this talk about not understanding!
        you're just a person who refuses to see.)

Poetry a riprap on the slick rock of metaphysics
"Put a Spanish halter on that whore of a mare
& I'll lead the bitch up any trail"

(how gentle! He should have whipped her first)

   the wind turns.
   a cold rain blows over the shale
   we sleep in the belly of a cloud.
(you think sex art and travel are enough?
      you're a skinful of cowdung)

South of the Yellow River the Emperor Wu
Set the army horses free in the mountain pastures,
Set the Buffalo free on the Plain of the Peach Grove.
Chariots and armor were smeared with blood
   and put away. They locked up
   the Arrows bag.
Smell of crushed spruce and burned snag-wood.
   remains of men,
Bone-chopped foul remains, thick stew
Food for crows—
   (blind, deaf, and dumb!
   shall we give him another chance?)
At Nyahaim-kuvara
Night has gone
Traveling to my land
   —that's a Mohave night
Our night too, you think brotherhood
Humanity & good intentions will stop it?
As long as you hesitate, no place to go.

Bluejay, out at the world's end
   perched, looked, & dashed
Through the crashing: his head is squashed.
   symplegades, the *mumonkwan,*
It's all vagina dentata
   (Jump!)
"Leap through an Eagle's snapping beak"

Actaeon saw Dhyana in the Spring.

it was nothing special,
misty rain on Mt. Baker,
Neah Bay at low tide.

15

Stone-flake and salmon.
The pure, sweet, straight-splitting
                        with a ping
Red cedar of the thick coast valleys
Shake-blanks on the mashed ferns
                        the charred logs
Fireweed and bees
An old burn, by new alder
Creek on smooth stones,
Back there a Tarheel logger farm.
(High country fir still hunched in snow)

From Siwash strawberry-pickers in the Skagit
Down to the boys at Sac,
Living by the river
            riding flatcars to Fresno,
Across the whole country
Steep towns, flat towns, even New York,
And oceans and Europe & libraries & galleries
And the factories they make rubbers in
This whole spinning show
            (among others)
Watched by the Mt. Sumeru L.O.

From the middle of the universe
& them with no radio.
"What is imperfect is best"
            silver scum on the trout's belly
            rubs off on your hand.
It's all falling or burning—
            rattle of boulders
            steady dribbling of rocks down cliffs
            bark chips in creeks
Porcupine chawed here—
                        Smoke

From Tillamook a thousand miles
Soot and hot ashes. Forest fires.
Upper Skagit burned I think 1919
Smoke covered all northern Washington
        lightning strikes, flares,
Blossoms a fire on the hill.
Smoke like clouds. Blotting the sun
Stinging the eyes.
The hot seeds steam underground
        still alive.

16

"Wash me on home, mama"
                —song of the Kelp.
  A chief's wife
  Sat with her back to the sun
  On the sandy beach, shredding cedar-bark.
  Her fingers were slender
  She didn't eat much.

"Get foggy
  We're going out to dig
  Buttercup roots"

  Dream, Dream,
  Earth! those beings living on your surface
  none of them disappearing, will all be transformed.
  When I have spoken to them
  when they have spoken to me, from that moment on,
  their words and their bodies which they
  usually use to move about with, will all change.
  I will not have heard them. Signed,
                ( )
                Coyote

The Back Country

A Berry Feast

For Joyce and Homer Matson

I

Fur the color of mud, the smooth loper
Crapulous old man, a drifter,
Praises! of Coyote the Nasty, the fat
Puppy that abused himself, the ugly gambler,
Bringer of goodies.

    In bearshit find it in August,
    Neat pile on the fragrant trail, in late
    August, perhaps by a Larch tree
    Bear has been eating the berries.
            high meadow, late summer, snow gone
    Blackbear
            eating berries, married
    To a woman whose breasts bleed
    From nursing the half-human cubs.

        Somewhere of course there are people
        collecting and junking, gibbering all day,

"Where I shoot my arrows
"There is the sunflower's shade
        —song of the rattlesnake
        coiled in the boulder's groin
"K'ak, k'ak, k'ak!
        sang Coyote. Mating with
        humankind—
        The Chainsaw falls for boards of pine,
        Suburban bedrooms, block on block
        Will waver with this grain and knot,
        The maddening shapes will start and fade
        Each morning when commuters wake—
        Joined boards hung on frames,
                a box to catch the biped in.

            and shadow swings around the tree
    Shifting on the berrybush
        from leaf to leaf across each day
    The shadow swings around the tree.

2

Three, down, through windows
Dawn leaping cats, all barred brown, grey
Whiskers aflame
                    bits of mouse on the tongue

Washing the coffeepot in the river
                    the baby yelling for breakfast,
Her breasts, black-nippled, blue-veined, heavy,
Hung through the loose shirt
                    squeezed, with the free hand
                              white jet in three cups.
Cats at dawn
                    derry derry down

Creeks wash clean where trout hide
We chew the black plug
Sleep on needles through long afternoons
                    "you shall be owl
                    "you shall be sparrow
                    "you will grow thick and green, people
                    "will eat you, you berries!
Coyote: shot from the car, two ears,
A tail, bring bounty.
      Clanks of tread
                    oxen of Shang
                    moving the measured road

Bronze bells at the throat
Bronze balls on the horns, the bright Oxen
Chanting through sunlight and dust
                    wheeling logs down hills
                    into heaps,
                              the yellow
                    Fat-snout Caterpillar, tread toppling forward
                    Leaf on leaf, roots in gold volcanic dirt.

When
      Snow melts back
                    from the trees
      Bare branches   knobbed pine twigs
            hot sun on wet flowers

Green shoots of huckleberry
Breaking through snow.

3

Belly stretched taut in a bulge
Breasts swelling as you guzzle beer, who wants
                         Nirvana?
Here is water, wine, beer
Enough books for a week
A mess of afterbirth,
A smell of hot earth, a warm mist
Steams from the crotch

"You can't be killers all your life
"The people are coming—
                —and when Magpie
Revived him, limp rag of fur in the river
Drowned and drifting, fish-food in the shallows,
"Fuck you!" sang Coyote
                and ran.
Delicate blue-black, sweeter from meadows
Small and tart in the valleys, with light blue dust
Huckleberries scatter through pine woods
Crowd along gullies, climb dusty cliffs,
Spread through the air by birds;
Find them in droppings of bear.

"Stopped in the night
"Ate hot pancakes in a bright room
"Drank coffee, read the paper
"In a strange town, drove on,
        singing, as the drunkard swerved the car
"Wake from your dreams, bright ladies!
"Tighten your legs, squeeze demons from
        the crotch with rigid thighs
"Young red-eyed men will come
"With limp erections, snuffling cries
"To dry your stiffening bodies in the sun!

Woke at the beach. Grey dawn,
Drenched with rain. One naked man
Frying his horsemeat on a stone.

4

Coyote yaps, a knife!
Sunrise on yellow rocks.
People gone, death no disaster,
Clear sun in the scrubbed sky
              empty and bright
Lizards scurry from darkness
We lizards sun on yellow rocks.
    See, from the foothills
    Shred of river glinting, trailing,
    To flatlands, the city:
           glare of haze in the valley horizon
    Sun caught on glass gleams and goes.
    From cool springs under cedar
    On his haunches, white grin,
           long tongue panting, he watches:

Dead city in dry summer,
Where berries grow.

The Spring

Beating asphalt into highway potholes
            pickup truck we'd loaded
road repair stock shed & yard
a day so hot the asphalt went in soft.
            pipe and steel plate tamper
took turns at by hand
then drive the truck rear wheel
a few times back and forth across the fill—
finish it off with bitchmo round the edge.

the foreman said let's get a drink
& drove through woods and flower fields
            shovels clattering in back
into a black grove by a cliff
            a rocked in pool
            feeding a fern ravine
                        tin can to drink
numbing the hand and cramping in the gut
surging through the fingers from below
            & dark here—
let's get back to the truck
get back on the job.

A Walk

Sunday the only day we don't work:
Mules farting around the meadow,
                    Murphy fishing,
The tent flaps in the warm
Early sun: I've eaten breakfast and I'll
                    take a walk
To Benson Lake. Packed a lunch,
Goodbye. Hopping on creekbed boulders
Up the rock throat three miles
                    Piute Creek—
In steep gorge glacier-slick rattlesnake country
Jump, land by a pool, trout skitter,
The clear sky. Deer tracks.
Bad place by a falls, boulders big as houses,
Lunch tied to belt,
I stemmed up a crack and almost fell
But rolled out safe on a ledge
                    and ambled on.
Quail chicks freeze underfoot, color of stone
Then run cheep! away, hen quail fussing.
Craggy west end of Benson Lake—after edging
Past dark creek pools on a long white slope—
Lookt down in the ice-black lake
                    lined with cliff
From far above: deep shimmering trout.
A lone duck in a gunsightpass
                    steep side hill
Through slide-aspen and talus, to the east end,
Down to grass, wading a wide smooth stream
Into camp. At last.
                    By the rusty three-year-
Ago left-behind cookstove
Of the old trail crew,
Stoppt and swam and ate my lunch.

Burning the Small Dead

Burning the small dead
       branches
broke from beneath
   thick spreading
        whitebark pine.

        a hundred summers
snowmelt   rock   and   air

hiss in a twisted bough.

   sierra granite;
        mt. Ritter—
        black rock twice as old.

Deneb, Altair

windy fire

Foxtail Pine

bark smells like pineapple: Jeffries
cones prick your hand: Ponderosa

nobody knows what they are, saying
"needles three to a bunch."

      turpentine tin can hangers
      high lead riggers

"the true fir cone stands straight,
the doug fir cone hangs down."

—wild pigs eat acorns in those hills
cascara cutters
tanbark oak bark gatherers
myrtlewood burl bowl-makers
little cedar dolls,
      baby girl born from the split crotch
          of a plum
        daughter of the moon—

foxtail pine with a
clipped curve-back cluster of tight
    five-needle bunches
  the rough red bark scale
and jigsaw pieces sloughed off
        scattered on the ground.
—what am I doing saying "foxtail pine"?
these conifers whose home was ice
age tundra, taiga, they of the
    naked sperm
to whitebark pine and white pine seem the same?

    a sort of tree
    its leaves are needles
    like a fox's brush
(I call him fox because he looks that way)
    and call this other thing, a
      foxtail pine.

Oil

soft rainsqualls on the swells
south of the Bonins, late at night. Light
from the empty mess-hall
throws back bulky shadows
of winch and fairlead
over the slanting fantail where I stand.

but for men on watch in the engine room,
the man at the wheel, the lookout in the bow,
the crew sleeps. in cots on deck
or narrow iron bunks down drumming
passageways below.

the ship burns with a furnace heart
steam veins and copper nerves
quivers and slightly twists and always goes—
easy roll of the hull and deep
vibration of the turbine underfoot.

bearing what all these
crazed, hooked nations need:
steel plates and
long injections of pure oil.

After Work

The shack and a few trees
float in the blowing fog

I pull out your blouse,
warm my cold hands
      on your breasts.
you laugh and shudder
peeling garlic by the
      hot iron stove.
bring in the axe, the rake,
the wood

we'll lean on the wall
against each other
stew simmering on the fire
as it grows dark
      drinking wine.

Four Poems for Robin

Siwashing it out once in Siuslaw Forest

I slept under   rhododendron
All night   blossoms fell
Shivering on   a sheet of cardboard
Feet stuck   in my pack
Hands deep   in my pockets
Barely   able   to   sleep.
I remembered   when we were in school
Sleeping together   in a big warm bed
We were   the youngest lovers
When we broke up   we were still nineteen.
Now our   friends are married
You teach   school back east
I dont mind   living this way
Green hills   the long blue beach
But sometimes   sleeping in the open
I think back   when I had you.

A spring night in Shokoku-ji

Eight years ago this May
We walked under cherry blossoms
At night in an orchard in Oregon.
All that I wanted then
Is forgotten now, but you.
Here in the night
In a garden of the old capital
I feel the trembling ghost of Yugao
I remember your cool body
Naked under a summer cotton dress.

An autumn morning in Shokoku-ji

Last night watching the Pleiades,
Breath smoking in the moonlight,
Bitter memory like vomit
Choked my throat.

I unrolled a sleeping bag
On mats on the porch
Under thick autumn stars.
In dream you appeared
(Three times in nine years)
Wild, cold, and accusing.
I woke shamed and angry:
The pointless wars of the heart.
Almost dawn. Venus and Jupiter.
The first time I have
Ever seen them close.

December at Yase

You said, that October,
In the tall dry grass by the orchard
When you chose to be free,
"Again someday, maybe ten years."

After college I saw you
One time. You were strange.
And I was obsessed with a plan.

Now ten years and more have
Gone by: I've always known
          where you were—
I might have gone to you
Hoping to win your love back.
You still are single.

I didn't.
I thought I must make it alone. I
Have done that.

Only in dream, like this dawn,
Does the grave, awed intensity
Of our young love
Return to my mind, to my flesh.

We had what the others
All crave and seek for;
We left it behind at nineteen.

I feel ancient, as though I had
Lived many lives.

And may never now know
If I am a fool
Or have done what my
        karma demands.

Work to Do Toward Town

Venus glows in the east,
        mars hangs in the twins.
Frost on the logs and bare ground
        free of house or tree.
Kites come down from the mountains
And glide quavering over the rooftops;
        frost melts in the sun.
A low haze hangs on the houses
        —firewood smoke and mist—
Slanting far to the Kamo river
        and the distant Uji hills.
Farmwomen lead down carts
        loaded with long white radish;
I pack my bike with books—
        all roads descend toward town.

The Manichaeans

for Joanne

Our portion of fire
     at this end of the milky way
(the Tun-huang fragments say, Eternal Light)
Two million years from M 31
     the galaxy in Andromeda—
My eyes sting with these relics.
Fingers mark time.
     semen is everywhere
Two million seeds in a spurt.

Bringing hand close to your belly
     a shade off touching,
Until it feels the radiating warmth.

Your far off laughter
Is an earthquake in your thigh.
Coild like Ourabouros
     we are the Naga King
This bed is Eternal Chaos
     —and wake in a stream of light.

Cable-car cables
Whip over their greast rollers
Two feet underground.
     hemmed in by mysteries
     all moving in order.
A moment at this wide intersection,
Stoplights change, they are
     catastrophes among stars,
A red whorl of minotaurs
          gone out.
The trumpet of doom
     from a steamship at Pier 41.
Your room is cold,
     in the shade-drawn dusk inside
Light the oven, leave it open
Semi transparent jet flames rise
          fire,

Together we make eight pounds of
Pure white mineral ash.

Your body is fossil
As you rest with your chin back
   —your arms are still flippers
                your lidded eyes lift from a swamp
Let us touch—for if two lie together
Then they have warmth.

We shall sink in this heat
          of our arms
Blankets like rock-strata fold
           dreaming as
              Shiva and Shakti
And keep back the cold.

Artemis

Artemis,
Artemis,
so I saw you naked—
well GO and get your goddam'd
      virginity back
me, me,
I've got to feed my hounds.

Mother of the Buddhas, Queen of Heaven, Mother of the Sun; Marici, Goddess of the Dawn

for Bhikku Ghosananda

old sow in the mud
bristles caked black
down her powerful neck

tiny hooves churn
squat body slithering
deep in food dirt

her warm filth,
deep-plowing snout,
dragging teats

those who keep her
or eat her
are cast out

she turns her small eye
from earth to
look up at me.

Nalanda, Bihar

Nature   Green Shit

The brittle hollow stalks of sunflower
    heads broke over full of dusty seed
    peeld, it tastes good, small

Why should dirt be dirty when you clean up.
    stop to like the dead or dying plants,
    twisted witherd grass

Picking the last peppers
Soft and wrinkld; bright green, cool

    what a lump of red flesh *I* am!

Violet dawn sky—no more Arcturus—
    beside the sugi nursery where we
    pulld down vines
    house lights constellations
    still   on the hill.

Heavy frosted cabbage.
    (all night porch bulb—)
    paper boy squealing bike brakes

    hey that's my cat!
Coming home.

Twelve Hours Out of New York After Twenty-Five Days at Sea

The sun always setting behind us.
I did not mean to come this far.
   —baseball games on the radio
      commercials that turn your hair—
The last time I saild this coast
Was nineteen forty eight
Washing galley dishes
     reading Gide in French.
In the rucksack I've got three *nata*
Handaxes from central Japan;
The square blade found in China
    all the way back to Stone—
A novel by Kafu NAGAI
About geisha in nineteen-ten
With a long thing about gardens
And how they change through the year;
Azalea ought to be blooming
    in the yard in Kyoto now.
Now we are north of Cape Hatteras
Tomorrow docking at eight.
     mop the deck round the steering gear,
Pack your stuff and get paid.

19.IV.1964

Hop, Skip, and Jump

for Jim and Annie Hatch

      the curvd lines toe-drawn, round cornerd squares
bulge out doubles from its single pillar line, like,
Venus of the Stone Age.
she takes stone,
with a white quartz band for her lagger.
                            she
     takes a brown-staind salt-sticky cigarette
                   butt.
he takes a mussel shell. he takes a clamshell. she takes
a stick.
he is tiny, with a flying run & leap—
shaggy blond—misses all the laggers,
          tumbles from one foot.
          they are dousing
a girl in a bikini down the beach
          first with cold seawater
            then with wine.
double-leg   single-leg   stork stalk turn
on the end-square—   hop, fork, hop, scoop the lagger,
     we have all trippt and fallen.
     surf rough and full of kelp,
   all the ages—
draw a line on another stretch of sand—
                  and—
                 everybody try
to do the hop, skip, and jump.

                   4.X.1964 Muir Beach

Through the Smoke Hole

for Don Allen

I

There is another world above this one; or outside of this one; the way to it
is thru the smoke of this one, & the hole that smoke goes through. The
ladder is the way through the smoke hole; the ladder holds up, some say,
the world above; it might have been a tree or pole; I think it is merely
a way.

Fire is at the foot of the ladder. The fire is in the center. The walls are round.
There is also another world below or inside this one. The way there is
down thru smoke. It is not necessary to think of a series.

Raven and Magpie do not need the ladder. They fly thru the smoke holes
shrieking and stealing. Coyote falls thru; we recognize him only as a
clumsy relative, a father in old clothes we don't wish to see with our
friends.

It is possible to cultivate the fields of our own world without much thought
for the others. When men emerge from below we see them as the
masked dancers of our magic dreams. When men disappear down, we
see them as plain men going somewhere else. When men disappear up
we see them as great heroes shining through the smoke. When men
come back from above they fall thru and tumble; we don't really know
them; Coyote, as mentioned before.

II

Out of the kiva come
masked dancers or
plain men.
        plain men go into the ground.

out there out side all the chores
        wood and water, dirt,
wind, the view across the flat,

                    here, in the round
                                no corners
            head is full of magic figures—
            woman your secrets aren't my secrets
            what I cant say I wont
            walk round
            put my hand flat down.
            you in the round too.
            gourd vine blossom.
            walls and houses drawn up
            from the same soft soil.

            thirty million years gone
                        drifting sand.
                cool rooms pink stone
            worn down fort floor, slat sighting
                heat shine on jumna river

            dry wash, truck tracks in the riverbed
            coild sand pinyon.

                        seabottom
                        riverbank
                        sand dunes
            the floor of a sea once again.
                        human fertilizer
                        underground water tunnels
                        skinny dirt gods
                        grandmother berries
                                        out
            through the smoke hole.
                (for childhood and youth *are* vanity

            a Permian reef of algae,

            out through the smoke hole
            swallowd sand
                        salt mud
            swum bodies,   flap
            to the limestone blanket—

            lizzard tongue,   lizzard tongue

wha, wha, wha   flying
in and *out* thru the smoke hole

plain men
come out of the ground.

Nanao Knows

for Nanao Sakaki

Mountains, cities, all so
            light, so loose.   blankets
Buckets—throw away—
Work left to do.
            it doesn't last.

Each girl is real
            her nipples harden, each has damp,
            her smell, her hair—
—What am I to be saying.
There they all go
Over the edge, dissolving.

Rivetters bind up
Steel rod bundles
For wet concrete.
In and out of forests, cities, families
            like a fish.

Regarding Wave

Wave

Grooving clam shell,
        streakt through marble,
sweeping down ponderosa pine bark-scale
      rip-cut tree grain
            sand-dunes, lava
           flow

Wave   wife.
      woman—wyfman—
"veiled; vibrating; vague"
  sawtooth ranges pulsing;
           veins on the back of the hand.

Forkt out: birdsfoot-alluvium
        wash

     great dunes rolling
Each inch rippld, every grain a wave.

Leaning against sand cornices til they blow away

   —wind, shake
   stiff thorns of cholla, ocotillo
   sometimes I get stuck in thickets—

Ah, trembling spreading radiating wyf
         racing zebra
  catch me and fling me wide
To the dancing grain of things
          of my mind!

In the House of the Rising Sun

Skinny kids in shorts get cups
    full of rice-gruel—steaming
    breakfast—sling
    their rifles, walk
    hot thickets.
    eyes peeled for U S planes.

Kyoto   a bar girl in pink
    with her catch for the night
    —but it's already morning—half-
    dazed, neat suit,
    laugh toward bed,

A guy I worked at logging with in Oregon
    fiddles his new lead-belcher cannons
        in South Yüeh.
    tuned better than chainsaws,
        at dawn,
    he liked mush.   with raisins.

Sleeping out   all night
  in warm rain.
Viet Nam uplands burned-off jungles
  wipe out a few rare birds
Fish in the rice paddy ditches
  stream a dry foul taste thru their gills
New Asian strains of clap
  whip penic   ill in.

Making toast, heating coffee,
    blue as Shiva—
    did I drink some filthy poison
    will I ever learn to love?

Did I really have to kill my sick, sick cat.

Song of the Taste

Eating the living germs of grasses
Eating the ova of large birds

    the fleshy sweetness packed
    around the sperm of swaying trees

The muscles of the flanks and thighs of
            soft-voiced cows
    the bounce in the lamb's leap
    the swish in the ox's tail

Eating roots grown swoll
        inside the soil

Drawing on life of living
   clustered points of light spun
        out of space
hidden in the grape.

Eating each other's seed
        eating
  ah, each other.

Kissing the lover in the mouth of bread:
      lip to lip.

Kyoto Born in Spring Song

Beautiful little children
    found in melons,
   in bamboo,
  in a "strangely glowing warbler egg"
   a perfect baby girl—

baby, baby,
   tiny precious
    mice and worms:

   Great majesty of Dharma turning
   Great dance of Vajra power

lizard baby by the fern
centipede baby scrambling toward the wall
cat baby left to mew for milk alone
mouse baby too afraid to run

    O sing   born in spring
  the weavers swallows babies in Nishijin
    nests below the eaves

    glinting mothers wings
    swoop to the sound of looms

    and three fat babies
  with three human mothers
every morning doing laundry
        "good
morning how's your baby?"
Tomoharu, Itsuko, and Kenji—

    Mouse, begin again.
Bushmen are laughing
  at the coyote-tricking
    that made us think machines

   wild babies
in the ferns and plums and weeds.

Everybody Lying on Their Stomachs, Head Toward the Candle, Reading, Sleeping, Drawing

The corrugated roof
Booms and fades night-long to

million-darted rain
squalls   and

outside

lightning

Photographs in the brain
Wind-bent bamboo.
through

the plank shutter
set

Half-open   on eternity

Shark Meat

In the night fouled the nets—
Sonoyama's flying-fish fishing
Speared by the giant trident
     that hung in the net shed
      we never thought used

Cut up for meat on the beach.
At seven in the morning
Maeda's grandson
       the shy one
      —a slight harelip
Brought a crescent of pale red flesh
     two feet long, looped on his arm
Up the bamboo lanes to our place.

The island eats shark meat at noon.

Sweet miso sauce on a big boiled cube
     as I lift a flake

        to my lips,

Miles of water, Black current,
Thousands of days
     re-crossing his own paths
     to tangle our net
       to be part of
       this loom.

The Bed in the Sky

Motorcycle strums   the empty streets
Heading home at one a. m.
     ice slicks shine in the moon
          I weave a safe path through

Naked shivering light flows down
Fills the basin over Kyoto
     and the plain
          a ghost glacier dream

From here a hundred miles are clear
The cemetery behind
     Namu   Amida   Butsu
          chiselled   ten thousand times

Tires crackle the mud-puddles
The northern hills gleam white
     I ought to stay outside   alone
          and watch the moon all night

But the bed is full and spread and dark
I hug you and sink in the warm
     my stomach against your big belly

          feels our baby turn

Regarding Wave

The voice of the Dharma
    the voice
      now

A shimmering bell
    through all.

      ॐ

Every hill,   still.
Every tree alive. Every leaf.
All the slopes   flow.
      old woods, new seedlings,
      tall grasses plumes.

Dark hollows;   peaks of light.
   wind stirs   the cool side
Each leaf living.
     All the hills.

      ॐ

    The Voice
    is a wife
      to

    him still.

   ōṃ   ah   hūṃ

Revolution in the Revolution
in the Revolution

The country surrounds the city
The back country surrounds the country

"From the masses to the masses" the most
Revolutionary consciousness is to be found
Among the most ruthlessly exploited classes:
Animals, trees, water, air, grasses

We must pass through the stage of the
"Dictatorship of the Unconscious" before we can
Hope for the withering-away of the states
And finally arrive at true Communionism.

ॐ

If the capitalists and imperialists
      are the exploiters, the masses are the workers.
          and the party
          is the communist.

If civilization
      is the exploiter, the masses is nature.
          and the party
          is the poets.

If the abstract rational intellect
      is the exploiter, the masses is the unconscious.
          and the party
          is the yogins.

& POWER
comes out of the seed-syllables of mantras.

Sours of the Hills

barbed seeds   in double ranks
sprung for sending off;

half-moon hairy seeds in the hair of the wrist

majestic fluff
sails. . . . rayed and spined . . . up hill at eye level
    hardly a breeze;

amber fruit with veins
on a bending stem,
size of an infant pea.

plumes wave,
seeds spill.

blueblack berry on a bush turned leaf-purple

deep sour, dark tart, sharp
    in the back of the mouth.

in the hair and from head to foot
stuck with seeds—burrs—
    next summer's mountain weeds—

a strolling through vines and grasses:

into the wild sour.

To Fire

(Goma / Homa)

        I have raised pure flames
        With mystic fists and muttered charms!

All the poems I wrote before nineteen
Heaps of arty cards from Christmas
Straw shoes
Worn clogs
The English Daily—Johnson's, Wilson's Ho Chi Minh
    —face crumpling inward licked by yellow locks

The contracting writhing plastics
And orange skins that shrink and squeak
             peace! peace! grace!

        Using sanctified vajra-tongs of blue
        I turn the mass and let in air

        Those letters forwarded now to Shiva
        the knots of snot in kleenex,
             my offering—my body!

And here the drafts of articles and songs
Words of this and that

Bullshit—renounce
           the leather briefcase no one wants
           the holey socks.

As sun moves up and up;
And motorcycles warm the street;
And people at the bus stop steam
      GREAT BRILLIANT KING
        Unshakeable!
    —halo of flame—

these   sweets   of   our   house   and   day:

Let me unflinching burn
Such dross within
With joy
I pray!

Love

Women who were turned inside-out
Ten times over by childbirth

On the wind-washed lonely islands
Lead the circle of *obon* dancers
Through a full moon night in August

The youngest girl last;

Women who were up since last night
Scaling and cleaning the flying fish

Sing about love.

Over and over,
Sing about love.

Suwa-no-se Island

Meeting the Mountains

He crawls to the edge of the foaming creek
He backs up the slab ledge
He puts a finger in the water
He turns to a trapped pool
Puts both hands in the water
Puts one foot in the pool
Drops pebbles in the pool
He slaps the water surface with both hands
He cries out, rises up and stands
Facing toward the torrent and the mountain
Raises up both hands and shouts three times!

Kai at Sawmill Lake VI.69

Long Hair

Hunting season:

Once every year, the Deer catch human beings. They
do various things which irresistibly draw men near them;
each one selects a certain man. The Deer shoots the man,
who is then compelled to skin it and carry its meat home
and eat it. Then the Deer is inside the man. He waits
and hides in there, but the man doesn't know it. When
enough Deer have occupied enough men, they will strike
all at once. The men who don't have Deer in them will
also be taken by surprise, and everything will change
some. This is called "takeover from inside."

Deer trails:

Deer trails run on the side hills
       cross county access roads
       dirt ruts to bone-white
       board house ranches,
       tumbled down.

Waist high through manzanita,
Through sticky, prickly, crackling
       gold dry summer grass.

Deer trails lead to water,
Lead sidewise all ways
Narrowing down to one best path—
And split—
And fade away to nowhere.
Deer trails slide under freeways
       slip into cities
       swing back and forth in crops and orchards
       run up the sides of schools!

Deer spoor and crisscross dusty tracks
Are in the house: and coming out the walls:

And deer bound through my hair.

Turtle Island

Without

the silence
of nature
within.

the power within.
the power

without.

the path is whatever passes—no
end in itself.

the end is,
grace—ease—

healing,
not saving.

singing
the proof

the proof of the power within.

I Went Into the Maverick Bar

I went into the Maverick Bar
In Farmington, New Mexico.
And drank double shots of bourbon
                    backed with beer.
My long hair was tucked up under a cap
I'd left the earring in the car.

Two cowboys did horseplay
                    by the pool tables,
A waitress asked us
                    where are you from?
a country-and-western band began to play
"We don't smoke Marijuana in Muskokie"
And with the next song,
                    a couple began to dance.

They held each other like in High School dances
                    in the fifties;
I recalled when I worked in the woods
                    and the bars of Madras, Oregon.
That short-haired joy and roughness—
                    America—your stupidity.
I could almost love you again.

We left—onto the freeway shoulders—
                    under the tough old stars—
In the shadow of bluffs
                    I came back to myself,
To the real work, to
                    "What is to be done."

No Matter, Never Mind

The Father is the Void
The Wife   Waves

Their child is Matter.

Matter makes it with his mother
And their child is Life,
                    a daughter.

The Daughter is the Great Mother
Who, with her father/brother Matter
                    as her lover,

Gives birth to the Mind.

The Bath

Washing Kai in the sauna,
The kerosene lantern set on a box
    outside the ground-level window,
Lights up the edge of the iron stove and the
    washtub down on the slab
Steaming air and crackle of waterdrops
    brushed by on the pile of rocks on top
He stands in warm water
Soap all over the smooth of his thigh and stomach
    "Gary don't soap my hair!"
    —his eye-sting fear—
    the soapy hand feeling
    through and around the globes and curves of his body
    up in the crotch,
And washing-tickling out the scrotum, little anus,
    his penis curving up and getting hard
    as I pull back skin and try to wash it
Laughing and jumping, flinging arms around,
    I squat all naked too,
                is this our body?

Sweating and panting in the stove-steam hot-stone
    cedar-planking wooden bucket water-splashing
    kerosene lantern-flicker wind-in-the-pines-out
    sierra forest ridges night—
Masa comes in, letting fresh cool air
    sweep down from the door
    a deep sweet breath
And she tips him over gripping neatly, one knee down
    her hair falling hiding one whole side of
    shoulder, breast, and belly,
Washes deftly Kai's head-hair
    as he gets mad and yells—
The body of my lady, the winding valley spine,
    the space between the thighs I reach through,
    cup her curving vulva arch and hold it from behind,
    a soapy tickle   a hand of grail
The gates of Awe
That open back a turning double-mirror world of

wombs in wombs, in rings,
  that start in music,
                    is this our body?

The hidden place of seed
The veins net flow across the ribs, that gathers
    milk and peaks up in a nipple—fits
    our mouth—
The sucking milk from this our body sends through
    jolts of light; the son, the father,
    sharing mother's joy
That brings a softness to the flower of the awesome
    open curling lotus gate I cup and kiss
As Kai laughs at his mother's breast he now is weaned
    from, we
    wash each other,
                    this our body

Kai's little scrotum up close to his groin,
    the seed still tucked away, that moved from us to him
In flows that lifted with the same joys forces
    as his nursing Masa later,
    playing with her breast,
Or me within her,
Or him emerging,
                    this is our body:

Clean, and rinsed, and sweating more, we stretch
    out on the redwood benches hearts all beating
Quiet to the simmer of the stove,
    the scent of cedar
And then turn over,
    murmuring gossip of the grasses,
    talking firewood,
Wondering how Gen's napping, how to bring him in
    soon wash him too—
These boys who love their mother
    who loves men, who passes on
    her sons to other women;

The cloud across the sky. The windy pines.
    the trickle gurgle in the swampy meadow

this is our body.

Fire inside and boiling water on the stove
We sigh and slide ourselves down from the benches
    wrap the babies, step outside,

black night & all the stars.

Pour cold water on the back and thighs
Go in the house—stand steaming by the center fire
Kai scampers on the sheepskin
Gen standing hanging on and shouting,

"Bao! bao! bao! bao! bao!"

This is our body. Drawn up crosslegged by the flames
    drinking icy water
      hugging babies, kissing bellies,

Laughing on the Great Earth

Come out from the bath.

Control Burn

What the Indians
here
used to do, was,
to burn out the brush every year.
in the woods, up the gorges,
keeping the oak and the pine stands
tall and clear
with grasses
and kitkitdizze under them,
never enough fuel there
that a fire could crown.

Now, manzanita,
(a fine bush in its right)
crowds up under the new trees
mixed up with logging slash
and a fire can wipe out all.

Fire is an old story.
I would like,
with a sense of helpful order,
with respect for laws
of nature,
to help my land
with a burn. a hot clean
burn.
      (manzanita seeds will only open
      after a fire passes over
      or once passed through a bear)

And then
it would be more
like,
when it belonged to the Indians

Before.

Prayer for the Great Family

Gratitude to Mother Earth, sailing through night and day—
    and to her soil: rich, rare, and sweet
        in our minds so be it.

Gratitude to Plants, the sun-facing light-changing leaf
    and fine root-hairs; standing still through wind
    and rain; their dance is in the flowing spiral grain
        in our minds so be it.

Gratitude to Air, bearing the soaring Swift and the silent
    Owl at dawn. Breath of our song
    clear spirit breeze
        in our minds so be it.

Gratitude to Wild Beings, our brothers, teaching secrets,
    freedoms, and ways; who share with us their milk;
    self-complete, brave, and aware
        in our minds so be it.

Gratitude to Water: clouds, lakes, rivers, glaciers;
    holding or releasing; streaming through all
    our bodies salty seas
        in our minds so be it.

Gratitude to the Sun: blinding pulsing light through
    trunks of trees, through mists, warming caves where
    bears and snakes sleep—he who wakes us—
        in our minds so be it.

Gratitude to the Great Sky
    who holds billions of stars—and goes yet beyond that—
    beyond all powers, and thoughts
    and yet is within us—
    Grandfather Space.
    The Mind is his Wife.

      so be it.

                after a Mohawk prayer

Source

To be in
to the land
where croppt-out rock
can hardly see
the swiftly passing trees

Manzanita clans
cluster up and fan out on their soils
in streaks and sweeps
with birds and woodrats underneath

And clay swale keeps wet,
free of trees, the bunch-grass
like no Spaniard ever came

I hear no news

Cloud finger dragons dance and
tremble down the ridge
and spit and spiral snow then pull in
quivering, on the sawtooth
spine

Clears up, and all the stars.
the tree leaves catch
some extra tiny source
all the wide night

Up here
out back
drink deep
that black light.

For Nothing

Earth a flower
A phlox on the steep
slopes of light
hanging over the vast
solid spaces
small rotten crystals;
salts.

Earth a flower
by a gulf where a raven
flaps by once
a glimmer, a color
forgotten as all
falls away.

A flower
for nothing;
an offer;
no taker;

Snow-trickle, feldspar, dirt.

The Egg

"A snake-like beauty in the living changes of syntax"
Robert Duncan

Kai twists
rubs "bellybutton"
rubs skin, front and back
two legs kicking
anus a sensitive center
    the pull-together
    between there and the scrotum,
the center line,
with the out-flyers changing
—fins, legs, wings,
feathers or fur,
they swing and swim
but the snake center
fire pushes through:
    mouth to ass,
    root to
    burning, steady,
    single eye.

breeze in the brown grasses
high clouds deep
blue.   white.
blue.   moving
changing

my Mother's old
soft arm. walking
helping up the
path.

Kai's hand
in my fist
the neck bones,
a little thread,
a garland,
of consonants and vowels
from the third eye

---

through the body's flowers
a string of peaks,
a whirlpool
sucking to the root.

It all gathers,
humming,
in the egg.

Pine Tree Tops

in the blue night
frost haze, the sky glows
with the moon
pine tree tops
bend snow-blue, fade
into sky, frost, starlight.
the creak of boots.
rabbit tracks, deer tracks,
what do we know.

By Frazier Creek Falls

Standing up on lifted, folded rock
looking out and down—

The creek falls to a far valley.
hills beyond that
facing, half-forested, dry
—clear sky
strong wind in the
stiff glittering needle clusters
of the pine—their brown
round trunk bodies
straight, still;
rustling trembling limbs and twigs

listen.

This living flowing land
is all there is, forever

We *are* it
it sings through us—

We could live on this Earth
without clothes or tools!

Mother Earth: Her Whales

An owl winks in the shadows
A lizard lifts on tiptoe, breathing hard
Young male sparrow stretches up his neck,
      big head, watching—

The grasses are working in the sun. Turn it green.
Turn it sweet. That we may eat.
Grow our meat.

Brazil says "sovereign use of Natural Resources"
Thirty thousand kinds of unknown plants.
The living actual people of the jungle
      sold and tortured—
And a robot in a suit who peddles a delusion called "Brazil"
      can speak for *them?*

      The whales turn and glisten, plunge
         and sound and rise again,
      Hanging over subtly darkening deeps
      Flowing like breathing planets
         in the sparkling whorls of
            living light—

And Japan quibbles for words on
      what kinds of whales they can kill?
A once-great Buddhist nation
      dribbles methyl mercury
      like gonorrhea
         in the sea.

Père David's Deer, the Elaphure,
Lived in the tule marshes of the Yellow River
Two thousand years ago—and lost its home to rice—
The forests of Lo-yang were logged and all the silt &
Sand flowed down, and gone, by 1200 AD—
Wild Geese hatched out in Siberia
      head south over basins of the Yang, the Huang,
      what we call "China"
On flyways they have used a million years.

Ah China, where are the tigers, the wild boars,
               the monkeys,
                       like the snows of yesteryear
Gone in a mist, a flash, and the dry hard ground
Is parking space for fifty thousand trucks.
IS man most precious of all things?
—then let us love him, and his brothers, all those
Fading living beings—

North America, Turtle Island, taken by invaders
               who wage war around the world.
May ants, may abalone, otters, wolves and elk
Rise! and pull away their giving
               from the robot nations.

Solidarity. The People.
Standing Tree People!
Flying Bird People!
Swimming Sea People!
Four-legged, two-legged, people!

How can the head-heavy power-hungry politic scientist
Government   two-world   Capitalist-Imperialist
Third-world   Communist   paper-shuffling male
          non-farmer   jet-set   bureaucrats
Speak for the green of the leaf? Speak for the soil?

(Ah Margaret Mead . . . do you sometimes dream of Samoa?)

The robots argue how to parcel out our Mother Earth
To last a little longer
               like vultures flapping
Belching, gurgling,
               near a dying Doe.
"In yonder field a slain knight lies—
We'll fly to him and eat his eyes
               with a down
          derry derry derry down down."

          An Owl winks in the shadow
          A lizard lifts on tiptoe

breathing hard
The whales turn and glisten
plunge and
Sound, and rise again
Flowing like breathing planets

In the sparkling whorls

Of living light.

Stockholm: Summer Solstice 40072

Why Log Truck Drivers Rise Earlier Than Students of Zen

In the high seat, before-dawn dark,
Polished hubs gleam
And the shiny diesel stack
Warms and flutters
Up the Tyler Road grade
To the logging on Poorman creek.
Thirty miles of dust.

There is no other life.

"One Should Not Talk to a Skilled Hunter About What Is Forbidden by the Buddha"

Hsiang-yen

A gray fox, female, nine pounds three ounces.
39 5/8" long with tail.
Peeling skin back (Kai
reminded us to chant the *Shingyo* first)
cold pelt. crinkle; and musky smell
mixed with dead-body odor starting.

Stomach content: a whole ground squirrel well chewed
plus one lizard foot
and somewhere from inside the ground squirrel
a bit of aluminum foil.

The secret.
and the secret hidden deep in that.

Magpie's Song

Six A.M.,
Sat down on excavation gravel
by juniper and desert S.P. tracks
interstate 80 not far off
    between trucks
Coyotes—maybe three
        howling and yapping from a rise.

Magpie on a bough
Tipped his head and said,

> *"Here in the mind, brother*
> *Turquoise blue.*
> *I wouldn't fool you.*
> *Smell the breeze*
> *It came through all the trees*
> *No need to fear*
> *What's ahead*
> *Snow up on the hills west*
> *Will be there every year*
> *be at rest.*
> *A feather on the ground—*
> *The wind sound—*

Here in the Mind, Brother,
Turquoise Blue"

O Waters

O waters
wash us, me,
under the wrinkled granite
straight-up slab,

and sitting by camp in the pine shade
Nanao sleeping,
mountains humming and crumbling
snowfields melting
soil
building on tiny ledges
for wild onions and the flowers
Blue
Polemonium

great
earth
sangha

For the Children

The rising hills, the slopes,
of statistics
lie before us.
the steep climb
of everything, going up,
up, as we all
go down.

In the next century
or the one beyond that,
they say,
are valleys, pastures,
we can meet there in peace
if we make it.

To climb these coming crests
one word to you, to
you and your children:

stay together
learn the flowers
go light

As for Poets

As for poets
The Earth Poets
Who write small poems,
Need help from no man.

Ꙇ

The Air Poets
Play out the swiftest gales
And sometimes loll in the eddies.
Poem after poem,
Curling back on the same thrust.

Ꙇ

At fifty below
Fuel oil won't flow
And propane stays in the tank.
Fire Poets
Burn at absolute zero
Fossil love pumped back up.

Ꙇ

The first
Water Poet
Stayed down six years.
He was covered with seaweed.
The life in his poem
Left millions of tiny
Different tracks
Criss-crossing through the mud.

Ꙇ

With the Sun and Moon
In his belly,
The Space Poet
Sleeps.

No end to the sky—
But his poems,
Like wild geese,
Fly off the edge.

A Mind Poet
Stays in the house.
The house is empty
And it has no walls.
The poem
Is seen from all sides,
Everywhere,
At once.

FROM

Axe Handles

Axe Handles

One afternoon the last week in April
Showing Kai how to throw a hatchet
One-half turn and it sticks in a stump.
He recalls the hatchet-head
Without a handle, in the shop
And go gets it, and wants it for his own.
A broken-off axe handle behind the door
Is long enough for a hatchet,
We cut it to length and take it
With the hatchet head
And working hatchet, to the wood block.
There I begin to shape the old handle
With the hatchet, and the phrase
First learned from Ezra Pound
Rings in my ears!
"When making an axe handle
            the pattern is not far off."
And I say this to Kai
"Look: We'll shape the handle
By checking the handle
Of the axe we cut with—"
And he sees. And I hear it again:
It's in Lu Ji's *Wê Fu,* fourth century
A.D. "Essay on Literature"—in the
Preface: "In making the handle
Of an axe
By cutting wood with an axe
The model is indeed near at hand."
My teacher Shih-hsiang Chen
Translated that and taught it years ago
And I see: Pound was an axe,
Chen was an axe, I am an axe
And my son a handle, soon
To be shaping again, model
And tool, craft of culture,
How we go on.

River in the Valley

We cross the Sacramento River at Colusa
follow the road on the levee south and east
find thousands of swallows nesting
on the underside of a concrete overhead
roadway? causeway? abandoned. Near
                        Butte Creek.

    Gen runs in little circles looking up
    at swoops of swallows—laughing—
           they keep
    flowing under the bridge and out,

    Kai leans silent against a concrete pier
    tries to hold with his eyes the course
    of a single darting bird,

    I pick grass seeds from my socks.

The coast range. Parched yellow front hills,
blue-gray thornbrush higher hills behind,
and here is the Great Central Valley,
drained, then planted and watered,
    thousand-foot deep soils
    thousand-acre orchards

    Sunday morning,
only one place serving breakfast
in Colusa, old river and tractor men
sipping milky coffee.

From north of Sutter Buttes
we see snow on Mt. Lassen
and the clear arc of the Sierra
south to the Desolation peaks.
One boy asks, "where do rivers start?"

in threads in hills, and gather down to here—
but the river
is all of it everywhere,
all flowing at once,
all one place.

Changing Diapers

How intelligent he looks!
    on his back
    both feet caught in my one hand
    his glance set sideways,
    on a giant poster of Geronimo
    with a Sharp's repeating rifle by his knee.

I open, wipe, he doesn't even notice
    nor do I.
Baby legs and knees
    toes like little peas
    little wrinkles, good-to-eat,
    eyes bright, shiny ears,
    chest swelling drawing air,

No trouble, friend,
    you and me and Geronimo
    are men.

Walking Through Myoshin-ji

Straight stone walks
    up lanes between mud walls

. . . the sailors who handled the ships
    from Korea and China,
the carpenters, chisels like razors,

    young monks working on *mu,*

and the pine trees
    that surrounded this city.
    the Ancient Ones, each one
anonymous.
    green needles,
      lumber,
        ash.

VII, 81, Kyoto

Working on the '58 Willys Pickup

For Lu Yu

The year this truck was made
I sat in early morning darkness
Chanting sūtra in Kyoto,
And spent the days studying Chinese.
Chinese, Japanese, Sanskrit, French—
Joys of Dharma-scholarship
And the splendid old temples—
But learned nothing of trucks.

Now to bring sawdust
Rotten and rich
From a sawmill abandoned when I was just born
Lost in the young fir and cedar
At Bloody Run Creek
So that clay in the garden
Can be broken and tempered
And growing plants mulched to save water—
And to also haul gravel
From the old placer diggings,
To screen it and mix in the sand with the clay
Putting pebbles aside to strew on the paths
So muddy in winter—

I lie in the dusty and broken bush
Under the pickup
Already thought to be old—
Admiring its solidness, square lines,
Thinking a truck like this
would please Chairman Mao.

The rear end rebuilt and put back
With new spider gears,
Brake cylinders cleaned, the brake drums
New-turned and new brake shoes,
Taught how to do this
By friends who themselves spent
Youth with the Classics—

The garden gets better, I
Laugh in the evening
To pick up Chinese
And read about farming,
I fix truck and lock eyebrows
With tough-handed men of the past.

For / From Lew

Lew Welch just turned up one day,
 live as you and me. "Damn, Lew" I said,
"you didn't shoot yourself after all."
"Yes I did" he said,
 and even then I felt the tingling down my back.
"Yes you did, too" I said—"I can feel it now."
"Yeah" he said,
"There's a basic fear between your world and
 mine. I don't know why.
What I came to say was,
 teach the children about the cycles.
The life cycles. All the other cycles.
That's what it's all about, and it's all forgot."

Getting in the Wood

The sour smell,
    blue stain,
        water squirts out round the wedge,

Lifting quarters of rounds
    covered with ants,
    "a living glove of ants upon my hand"
the poll of the sledge a bit peened over
so the wedge springs off and tumbles
    ringing like high-pitched bells
        into the complex duff of twigs
        poison oak, bark, sawdust,
        shards of logs,

And the sweat drips down.
    Smell of crushed ants.
The lean and heave on the peavey
that breaks free the last of a bucked
    three-foot round,
        it lies flat on smashed oaklings—

Wedge and sledge, peavey and maul,
    little axe, canteen, piggyback can
    of saw-mix gas and oil for the chain,
knapsack of files and goggles and rags,

All to gather the dead and the down.
    the young men throw splits on the piles
    bodies hardening, learning the pace
and the smell of tools from this delve
    in the winter
        death-topple of elderly oak.
Four cords.

True Night

Sheath of sleep in the black of the bed:
From outside this dream womb
Comes a clatter
Comes a clatter
And finally the mind rises up to a fact
Like a fish to a hook
A raccoon at the kitchen!
A falling of metal bowls,
 the clashing of jars,
 the avalanche of plates!
I snap alive to this ritual
Rise unsteady, find my feet,
Grab the stick, dash in the dark—
I'm a huge pounding demon
That roars at raccoons—
They whip round the corner,
A scratching sound tells me
 they've gone up a tree.

I stand at the base
Two young ones that perch on
Two dead stub limbs and
Peer down from both sides of the trunk:
 Roar, roar, I roar
 you awful raccoons, you wake me
 up nights, you ravage
 our kitchen

As I stay there then silent
The chill of the air on my nakedness
Starts off the skin
I am all alive to the night.
Bare foot shaping on gravel
Stick in the hand, forever.

Long streak of cloud giving way
To a milky thin light
Back of black pine bough,
The moon is still full,

Hillsides of Pine trees all
Whispering; crickets still cricketting
Faint in cold coves in the dark

I turn and walk slow
Back the path to the beds
With goosebumps and loose waving hair
In the night of milk-moonlit thin cloud glow
And black rustling pines
I feel like a dandelion head
Gone to seed
About to be blown all away
Or a sea anemone open and waving in
cool pearly water.
Fifty years old.
I still spend my time
Screwing nuts down on bolts.

At the shadow pool,
Children are sleeping,
And a lover I've lived with for years,
True night.
One cannot stay too long awake
In this dark

Dusty feet, hair tangling,
I stoop and slip back to the
Sheath, for the sleep I still need,
For the waking that comes
Every day

With the dawn.

24:JV:40075, 3:30 PM, n. of Coaldale, Nevada, A Glimpse Through a Break in the Storm of the Summit of the White Mountains

O Mother Gaia

sky   cloud   gate   milk   snow

wind-void-word

I bow in roadside gravel

Dillingham, Alaska,
the Willow Tree Bar

Drills chatter full of mud and compressed air
all across the globe,
    low-ceilinged bars, we hear the same new songs

All the new songs.
In the working bars of the world.
After you done drive Cat. After the truck
       went home.
       Caribou slip,
       front legs folded first
       under the warm oil pipeline
       set four feet off the ground—

On the wood floor, glass in hand,
       laugh and cuss with
       somebody else's wife.
       Texans, Hawaiians, Eskimos,
       Filipinos, Workers, always
       on the edge of a brawl—
       In the bars of the world.
       Hearing those same new songs
               in Abadan,
       Naples, Galveston, Darwin, Fairbanks,
       White or brown,
Drinking it down,

the pain
of the work
of wrecking the world.

Breasts

That which makes milk can't
                    help but concentrate
Out of the food of the world,
Right up to the point
                    where we suck it,
Poison, too

But the breast is a filter—
The poison stays there, in the flesh.
Heavy metals in traces
                    deadly molecules hooked up in strings
                    that men dreamed of;
Never found in the world til today.
                    (in your bosom
                    petrochemical complex
                    astray)

So we celebrate breasts
We all love to kiss them
                    —they're like philosophers!
Who hold back the bitter in mind
To let the more tasty
Wisdom slip through
                    for the little ones.
                    who can't take the poison so young.

The work that comes later
After child-raising
For the real self to be,
Is to then burn the poison away.
Flat breasts, tired bodies,
That will snap like old leather,
                    tough enough
                    for a few more good days,

And the glittering eyes,
Old mother,
Old father,
                    are gay.

Old Woman Nature

Old Woman Nature
naturally has a bag of bones
            tucked away somewhere.
            a whole room full of bones!

A scattering of hair and cartilage
      bits in the woods.

A fox scat with hair and a tooth in it.
      a shellmound
            a bone flake in a streambank.

A purring cat, crunching
      the mouse head first,
            eating on down toward the tail—

The sweet old woman
      calmly gathering firewood in the
                  moon . . .

Don't be shocked,
She's heating you some soup.

                    VII. '81, Seeing Ichikawa Ennosuke
                    in "Kurozuka" — "Demoness" —
                    at the Kabuki-za in Tokyo

The Canyon Wren

for James and Carol Katz

I look up at the cliffs
But we're swept on by   downriver
                the rafts
Wobble and slide over roils of water
        boulders shimmer
        under the arching stream
Rock walls straight up on both sides.
A hawk cuts across that narrow sky
              hit by sun,

We paddle forward, backstroke, turn,
Spinning through eddies and waves
Stairsteps of churning whitewater.
        above the roar
        hear the song of a Canyon Wren.

A smooth stretch, drifting and resting.
Hear it again, delicate downward song

      ti ti   ti ti tee tee tee

Descending through ancient beds.
A single female mallard flies upstream —

Shooting the Hundred-Pace Rapids
Su Shih saw, for a moment,
        it all stand still
"I stare at the water:
        it moves with unspeakable slowness"

Dōgen, writing at midnight,

      "mountains flow

      "water is the palace of the dragon
      "it does not flow away.

We beach up at China Camp
Between piles of stone

Stacked there by black-haired miners,
        cook in the dark
        sleep all night long by the stream.

These songs that are here and gone,
Here and gone,
To purify our ears.

The Stanislaus River runs through Central Miwok country and down to the San Joaquin valley. The twists and turns of the river, the layering, swirling stone cliffs of the gorges are cut in nine-million-year-old latites. For many seasons lovers of rocks and water have danced in rafts and kayaks down this dragon-arm of the high Sierra. Not long ago Jim Katz and friends, river runners all, asked me to shoot the river with them, to see its face once more before it goes under the rising waters of the New Mellones Dam. The song of the Canyon Wren stayed with us the whole voyage; at China Camp, in the dark, I wrote this poem.

April, 40081, Stanislaus River,
Camp 9 to Parrott's Ferry

For All

Ah to be alive
            on a mid-September morn
            fording a stream
            barefoot, pants rolled up,
            holding boots, pack on,
            sunshine, ice in the shallows,
            northern rockies.

Rustle and shimmer of icy creek waters
stones turn underfoot, small and hard as toes
            cold nose dripping
            singing inside
            creek music, heart music,
            smell of sun on gravel.

            I pledge allegiance

I pledge allegiance to the soil
            of Turtle Island,
and to the beings who thereon dwell
            one ecosystem
            in diversity
            under the sun
With joyful interpenetration for all.

Left Out
in the Rain

Poem Left in
Sourdough Mountain Lookout

I the poet Gary Snyder
Stayed six weeks in fifty-three
On this ridge and on this rock
& saw what every Lookout sees,
Saw these mountains shift about
& end up on the ocean floor
Saw the wind and waters break
The branchéd deer, the Eagle's eye,
& when pray tell, shall Lookouts die?

(A later lookout told me this poem was still pinned up in the cabin in 1968.)

Seeing the Ox

Brown ox
Nose snubbed up
Locking his big head high
    against telephone pole
    right by Daitoku temple—
Slobbering, watching kids play
    with rolling eye,

Fresh dung pile under his
    own hind hooves.

Kyoto

Longitude 170° West, Latitude 35° North

For Ruth Sasaki

This realm half sky half water,
    night black with white foam
    streaks of glowing fish
    the high half black too lit with
    dots of stars,
The thrum of the diesel engine twirling
    sixty-foot drive shafts of twin screws,
Shape of a boat, and floating
    over a mile of living seawater, underway,
    always westward, dropping
    land behind us to the east,
Brought only these brown Booby birds that trail
    a taste of landfall feathers in the craw
    hatchrock barrens—old migrations—
    flicking from off stern into thoughts,
Sailing jellyfish by day, phosphorescent
    light at night,
    shift of current on the ocean floor
    food chains climbing to the whale.

Ship hanging on this membrane infinitely
    tiny in the "heights" the "deep"
    air-bound beings in the realm of wind
    or water, holding hand to wing or fin
Swimming westward to the farther shore,
    this is what I wanted? so much
    water in the world and so much crossing,
    oceans of truth and seas of doctrine
Salty real seas of our westering world,
    Dharma-spray of lonely slick on deck
Sleepy, between two lands, always a-
    floating world,
               I go below.

M. S. Arita Maru

For Example

There was an old Dutch lady
Lived in a room in the house
In front of my small shack
Who sat all day in the garden
By my door and read.
She said she knew the East
And once had seen a book
On Buddhist monks. "And you
Gott no business going to
Japan. The thing to be
Is life, is young and travel
Much and love. I know
The way you are, you study hard
But you have friends that
Come and stay, and bike, and
There's the little tree you
Planted by the wall" As I
Filled my water bucket from
A hose. The sun lit up
Her thin white hair a bird
Squawked from the Avocado at the air
& Bodhisattvas teach us everywhere.

English Lessons at
the Boiler Company

The western hills curve down from Mt. Atago
Toward Osaka plains and the inland sea.
Sun, snow, clouds, flurry and glitter,

From long high sheds comes the rivetting,
Shriek of steam pressure tests,
They make boilers—

File into the small, heated, carpetted,
Office room: start teaching language,
Strange feeling sounds, odd puffs and buzzes,
Bend tongues, re-wrap the brain,

Over the plains,   snow-whirling clouds.

Farewell to Burning Island

A white bird lands on the ship
—The smoking island from afar
Feet scorch on the white deck
—Sailing east across the ocean
Once more.

Suwa-no-se Island, East China Sea

No Shoes No Shirt No Service

Padding down the street, the
Bushmen, the Paiute, the Cintas Largas
    are refused.
The queens of Crete,
The waiting-ladies of the King of Bundelkhand.
Tārā is kept out,
Bare-breasted on her lotus throne.

    (officially, no one goes through
    unofficially, horses go through,
    carriages go through—)

The barefoot shepherds, the bare-chested warriors

    (what is this gate,
    wide as a highway
    that only mice can enter?)

The cow passed through the window nicely—
Only the tail got stuck,

And the soils of this region will be fertile again
After another round of volcanoes
Nutrient ash—
    Shiva's dancing feet
    (No shoes)

Poetry Is the Eagle of Experience

All the little mice of writing letters,
Sorting papers,
And the rabbits of getting in the wood,
The big Buck of a lecture in town.

Then, walk back into the brush
To keep clearing a trail.
High over even that,
A whistle of wings!
Breath of a song.

Calcium

The doe munches on rotten cow-skull
bone, she is pregnant.
Back of the woodshed
hooves rustling dry poison oak.

Cement hardens up at the footings
poured for the barn.

Molecule by molecule
drawn in and saved by
single swimming cells,
a few sparks of Calcium
like Blue Whales
far apart, and streaming through the sea.

At White River Roadhouse in the Yukon

For Gary Holthaus

At White River Roadhouse   in the Yukon
A bell rings   in the late night:
A lone car   on the Alaska highway
Hoping to buy gas   at the shut roadhouse.

For a traveller sleeping   in a little room
The bell ring   is a temple in Japan,
In dream I put on   robes and sandals
Chant sūtras   in the chilly Buddha-hall.

Ten thousand miles   of White Spruce taiga.
The roadhouse master   wakes to the night bell
Enters the dark   of ice and stars,
To sell the car some gas.

The Persimmons

In a cove reaching back between ridges
the persimmon groves:
leaves rust-red in October
ochre and bronze
scattering down from the
hard slender limbs of this
slow-growing hardwood
that takes so much nitrogen
and seven years to bear,
and plenty of water all summer
to be bearing so much and so well
as these groves are this autumn.
Gathered in yard-wide baskets
of loose open weave
with mounds of persimmons just picked
still piled on the ground.
On tricycle trucks
pedaled so easy and slow down the lanes,
"Deep tawnie cullour" of sunset
each orb some light left from summer
glowing on brown fall ground,
the persimmons are flowing
on streams of more bike-trucks
til they riffle and back up
alongside a car road
and are spread on the gravel by sellers.
The kind with a crease round the middle,
Tamopan, sweet when soft,
ripening down from the top to the base.
Persimmons and farmers
a long busy line on the roadside,
in season, a bargain, a harvest
of years, the peace of
this autumn again, familiar,
when found by surprise at
the tombs of the dead Ming emperors.
Acres of persimmon orchards
surrounding the tumuli
of kings who saw to it they kept on consuming

even when empty and gone.
The persimmons outlive them,
but up on the hills
where the Great Wall wanders
the oaks had been cut for lumber or charcoal
by Genghis Khan's time.
People and persimmon orchards prevail.
I walked the Great Wall today,
and went deep in the dark of a tomb.
And then found a persimmon
ripe to the bottom
one of a group on a rough plaited tray
that might have been drawn by Mu Ch'i.
Tapping its infant-soft skin
to be sure that it's ready,
the old man laughing,
he sees that I like my persimmons.
I trade him some coin
for this wealth of fall fruit
lined up on the roadside to sell to the tourists
who have come to see tombs,
and are offered as well
the people and trees that prevail.

Beijing, Peoples Republic

For Berkeley

City of buds and flowers

Where are your fruits?

Where are your roots.

"There are those
who love to get dirty"

There are those who love to get dirty
    and fix things.
They drink coffee at dawn,
    beer after work,

And those who stay clean,
    just appreciate things,
At breakfast they have milk
    and juice at night.

There are those who do both,
    they drink tea.

Sestina of the End of the Kalpa

You joyous Gods, who gave mankind his Culture,
And you, brave nymphs, who taught him love of Nature,
You sturdy Mountains, Prairies, in your Pattern
Breeding from Uncouth Ape the various Races,
Give ear to what I sing, of place and Structure,
Troubling the simple air with blushing Language.

Because, astride his horse, a Siouan's Language
As well as painted steed, is part of Culture,
We soon find Substance melted into Structure.
And pitying poor Mankind's silly Nature—
An equal meagre blandness in all Races:
We look beyond mere Man to find a Pattern.

Each blotch and wiggle has distinctive Pattern,
And order lurks within each mumbling Language.
Hermes the sneaky watcher of the Races,
If caught might tell the sins of every Culture.
Each bungles life according to its Nature,
Which is to say, each has a faulty Structure.

But Man is taught necessity of Structure,
And Birth and Death whirl in a single Pattern;
The bleating Dewey says, "But this is Nature"—
And Law and Order, if you know the Language.
To have a God (The Possum sez) is Culture,
And God is Order, for most Human Races.

Apollo: let us wander through the Races,
Sifting each hiss and glottal for its Structure,
And come to make conclusion of all Culture.
Poor Kwakiutl! Tangled in their Pattern;
Stern Indo-Aryans; slaves to Language.
And somehow through this, Science fingers Nature.

A use is found for every law of Nature,
The future planned (humanely) for all Races,
Wisdom wallows in decay of Language.
Fierce *Siva!* These Greeks defend their "Structure,"
The God of Christians, in the same old Pattern
Perpetuates the form and force of Culture,

Destroyer: with fire inform the Races
That Chaos is the Pattern under Structure.
Language and Culture burn! and death to Nature.

Berkeley

How Zen Masters Are Like Mature Herring

So few become full grown
And how necessary all the others;
    gifts to the food chain,
    feeding another universe.

These big ones feed sharks.

Cold Mountain Poems

[TRANSLATIONS]

Preface to the Poems of Han-shan by Lu Ch'iu-yin, Governor of T'ai Prefecture

Kanzan, or Han-shan, "Cold Mountain" takes his name from where he lived. He is a mountain madman in an old Chinese line of ragged hermits. When he talks about Cold Mountain he means himself, his home, his state of mind. He lived in the T'ang dynasty—traditionally A. D. 627–650, although Hu Shih dates him 700–780. This makes him roughly contemporary with Tu Fu, Li Po, Wang Wei, and Po Chü-i. His poems, of which three hundred survive, are written in T'ang colloquial: rough and fresh. The ideas are Taoist, Buddhist, Zen. He and his sidekick Shih-te (Jittoku in Japanese) became great favorites with Zen painters of later days—the scroll, the broom, the wild hair and laughter. They became Immortals and you sometimes run onto them today in the skidrows, orchards, hobo jungles, and logging camps of America.

No one knows just what sort of man Han-shan was. There are old people who knew him: they say he was a poor man, a crazy character. He lived alone seventy li west of the T'ang-hsing district of T'ien-t'ai at a place called Cold Mountain. He often went down to the Kuo-ch'ing Temple. At the temple lived Shih-te, who ran the dining hall. He sometimes saved leftovers for Han-shan, hiding them in a bamboo tube. Han-shan would come and carry it away; walking the long veranda, calling and shouting happily, talking and laughing to himself. Once the monks followed him, caught him, and made fun of him. He stopped, clapped his hands, and laughed greatly—Ha Ha!—for a spell, then left.

He looked like a tramp. His body and face were old and beat. Yet in every word he breathed was a meaning in line with the subtle principles of things, if only you thought of it deeply. Everything he said had a feeling of the Tao in it, profound and arcane secrets. His hat was made of birch bark, his clothes were ragged and worn out, and his shoes were wood. Thus men who have made it hide their tracks: unifying categories and interpenetrating things. On that long veranda calling and singing, in his words of reply Ha Ha!—the three worlds revolve. Sometimes at the villages and farms he laughed and sang with cowherds. Sometimes intractable, sometimes agreeable, his nature was happy of itself. But how could a person without wisdom recognize him?

I once received a position as a petty official at Tan-ch'iu. The day I was to depart, I had a bad headache. I called a doctor, but he couldn't cure me and it turned worse. Then I met a Buddhist Master named Feng-kan, who said he came from the Kuo-ch'ing Temple of T'ien-t'ai especially to visit me. I asked him to rescue me from my illness. He smiled and said, "The four realms are within the body; sickness comes from illusion. If you want to do away with it, you need pure water." Someone brought water to the Master, who spat it on me. In a moment the disease was rooted out. He then said, "There are miasmas in T'ai prefecture, when you get there take care of ourself." I asked him, "Are there any wise men in your area I could look on as Master?" He replied, "When you see him you don't recognize him, when you recognize him you don't see him. If you want to see him, you can't rely on appearances. Then you can see him. Han-shan is a Man-jusri hiding at Kuo-ch'ing. Shih-te is a Samantabhadra. They look like poor fellows and act like madmen. Sometimes they go and sometimes they come. They work in the kitchen of the Kuo-ch'ing dining hall, tending the fire." When he was done talking he left.

I proceeded on my journey to my job at T'ai-chou, not forgetting this affair. I arrived three days later, immediately went to a temple, and questioned an old monk. It seemed the Master had been truthful, so I gave orders to see if T'ang-hsing really contained a Han-shan and Shih-te. The District Magistrate reported to me: "In this district, seventy li west, is a mountain. People used to see a poor man heading from the cliffs to stay awhile at Kuo-ch'ing. At the temple dining hall is a similar man named Shih-te." I made a bow, and went to Kuo-ch'ing. I asked some people around the temple, "There used to be a Master named Feng-kan here. Where is his place? And where can Han-shan and Shih-te be seen?" A monk named Tao-ch'iao spoke up: "Feng-kan the Master lived in back of the library. Nowadays nobody lives there; a tiger often comes and roars. Han-shan and Shih-te are in the kitchen." The monk led me to Feng-kan's yard. Then he opened the gate: all we saw was tiger tracks. I asked the monks Tao-ch'iao and Pao-te, "When Feng-kan was here, what was his job?" The monks said, "He pounded and hulled rice. At night he sang songs to amuse himself." Then we went to the kitchen, before the stoves. Two men were facing the fire, laughing loudly. I made a bow. The two shouted HO! at me. They struck their hands together—Ha Ha!—great laughter. They shouted. Then they said, "Feng-kan—loose-tongued, loose-tongued. You don't recognize Amitabha, why be courteous to us?" The monks gathered round, surprise going through them. "Why has a big official bowed to a pair of clowns?" The two men grabbed hands and ran out of the temple. I cried, "Catch them"—but they quickly ran away. Han-shan returned to Cold Mountain. I asked the monks, "Would those two men be willing to settle down at this temple?" I ordered them to find a house, and to ask Han-shan and Shih-te to return and live at the temple.

I returned to my district and had two sets of clean clothes made, got some incense and such, and sent it to the temple—but the two men didn't return. So I had it carried up to Cold Mountain. The packer saw Han-shan, who called in a loud voice, "Thief! Thief!" and retreated into a mountain cave. He shouted, "I tell you man, strive hard!"—entered the cave and was gone. The cave closed of itself and they weren't able to follow. Shih-te's tracks disappeared completely.

I ordered Tao-ch'iao and the other monks to find out how they had lived, to hunt up the poems written on bamboo, wood, stones, and cliffs—and also to collect those written on the walls of people's houses. There were more than three hundred. On the wall of the Earth-shrine Shih-te had written some *gatha*. It was all brought together and made into a book.

I hold to the principle of the Buddha-mind. It is fortunate to meet with men of Tao, So I have made this euology.

The path to Han-shan's place is laughable,
A path, but no sign of cart or horse.
Converging gorges—hard to trace their twists
Jumbled cliffs—unbelievably rugged.
A thousand grasses bend with dew,
A hill of pines hums in the wind.
And now I've lost the shortcut home,
Body asking shadow, how do you keep up?

In a tangle of cliffs I chose a place—
Bird-paths, but no trails for men.
What's beyond the yard?
White clouds clinging to vague rocks.
Now I've lived here—how many years—
Again and again, spring and winter pass.
Go tell families with silverware and cars
"What's the use of all that noise and money?"

Men ask the way to Cold Mountain
Cold Mountain: there's no through trail.
In summer, ice doesn't melt
The rising sun blurs in swirling fog.
How did I make it?
My heart's not the same as yours.
If your heart was like mine
You'd get it and be right here.

I settled at Cold Mountain long ago,
Already it seems like years and years.
Freely drifting, I prowl the woods and streams
And linger watching things themselves.
Men don't get this far into the mountains,
White clouds gather and billow.
Thin grass does for a mattress,
The blue sky makes a good quilt.
Happy with a stone underhead
Let heaven and earth go about their changes.

I have lived at Cold Mountain
These thirty long years.
Yesterday I called on friends and family:
More than half had gone to the Yellow Springs.
Slowly consumed, like fire down a candle;
Forever flowing, like a passing river.
Now, morning, I face my lone shadow:
Suddenly my eyes are bleared with tears.

In my first thirty years of life
I roamed hundreds and thousands of miles.
Walked by rivers through deep green grass
Entered cities of boiling red dust.
Tried drugs, but couldn't make Immortal;
Read books and wrote poems on history.
Today I'm back at Cold Mountain:
I'll sleep by the creek and purify my ears.

There's a naked bug at Cold Mountain
With a white body and a black head.
His hand holds two book-scrolls,
One the Way and one its Power.
His shack's got no pots or oven,
He goes for a walk with his shirt and pants askew.
But he always carries the sword of wisdom:
He means to cut down senseless craving.

Cold Mountain is a house
Without beams or walls.
The six doors left and right are open
The hall is blue sky.
The rooms all vacant and vague
The east wall beats on the west wall
At the center nothing.

Borrowers don't bother me
In the cold I build a little fire
When I'm hungry I boil up some greens.
I've got no use for the kulak
With his big barn and pasture—
He just sets up a prison for himself.
Once in he can't get out.
Think it over—
You know it might happen to you.

❧

Some critic tried to put me down—
"Your poems lack the Basic Truth of Tao"
And I recall the old-timers
Who were poor and didn't care.
I have to laugh at him,
He misses the point entirely,
Men like that
Ought to stick to making money.

❧

When men see Han-shan
They all say he's crazy
And not much to look at
Dressed in rags and hides.
They don't get what I say
& I don't talk their language.
All I can say to those I meet:
"Try and make it to Cold Mountain."

FROM

Miyazawa Kenji

[TRANSLATIONS]

Miyazawa Kenji (1896–1933)

. . . was born and lived most his life in Iwate prefecture in northern Japan. This area, sometimes called the Tibet of Japan, is known for poverty, cold, and heavy winter snows. His poems are all from there.

He was born and lived his life among the farmers: a school teacher (Chemistry, Natural Sciences, Agriculture) and a Buddhist. His poems have many Buddhist allusions, as well as scientific vocabulary.

The bulk of his work is colloquial and metrically free. His complete work, published after his death, contains seven hundred free-verse poems, nine hundred *tanka* poems, and ninety children's stories.

Spring and the Ashura

From the ash-colored steel of images:
akebia tendrils coil round clouds,
wildrose thicket, swampy leafmold—
everywhere a pattern of flattery
    (amber splinters flooding down
      thicker than woodwinds at noon)
the bitter taste of anger, the blueness.
at the depths in the brilliance of this april air
spitting, gnashing, pacing back and forth
I am an Ashura!
    (the scene gets blurred by tears)
smashed bits of cloud cross my vision,
    a holy crystal wind sweeps
      the translucent sea of the sky.
        Zypressen—one line of spring
      blackly draws in ether,
        —through those dark footsteps
          the edge of the mountain of heaven shines.
        (the shimmering mist, white polarization)
    the true words are lost.
    turn, clouds flying
  ah, in the radiant depths of april
 gnashing, BURNING, wander
I am one of the Ashuras:
  (chalcedony clouds flowing
    where is that singing, that spring bird?)
  Sun Wheel shimmering blue
    ashura echoing in the forest
      heaven's bowl giddily tilting over
        clusters of giant coal-fern stretch up toward it.
      pitifully dense—those branches
  this whole double scene.
  flash of a crow flapping
            up from a treetop
    —spiritless woods—
    —the atmosphere clearer and clearer
      cypress trees standing to heaven
         in a dead hush—
a thing in the golden meadow:
just a person.
farmer wearing a straw cape looking at me

can he really see me
at the bottom of this shining sea of air?
      blue over blue, deepening my sadness.
zypressen silently quivering
      bird again cuts the blue
            (my real feelings are not here
            ashura tears on the ground)

breathing anew   in the sky
lungs faintly contracting
      (this body totally dispersed
         mixed with the atoms of space)

twigs of a gingko still reflecting
cypress blacker and blacker
sparks of cloud pour down.

NOTE

Ashura is a Sanskrit Buddhist term for beings inhabiting one of the six realms of existence. They are malevolent giants in constant strife, often represented in art as human
warriors, samurai, killing each other. The ashura realm is the warring, contentious, hostile
area of the mind. The other five realms are hell-dwellers, hungry ghosts, animals, mankind, and devas.

Floating World Picture: Spring in the Kitagami Mountains

I

Nobody at the edge of the firepit
snowboots and jute leggings.
white birch flaming
jetting out sour hot sap
—a child sings the kite song
skinning badgers.
housepillars gleaming with soot
   —like shaped with stone axes—
the sheer ceiling
full of the blue smoke of breakfast
—vault of a temple—
one shaft of sunlight shooting down and
         all is at the bottom in that
                  sensual beam of light.

Spring—at the chilly horsebarn
glimmer of dry hay and snow
yearning for sunny hills
the horses stamp their hooves.

2

The willow puts out honey flowers
birds flow over hill after hill
horses hurry:
      hot-breatht Arab
      glistening light-bodies thoroughbred
invisible cuneiform wind
in the stiff gloomy limbs of the walnut—
a dog rustles in bamboo grass.

      heavy work horse
      flashing his tufty tail
      like a monstrous lizard

                              navigating in the sun
horses one by one coming,
chewing at the edge of the marl,
climbing along the misty run of snowmelt
under a malachite sky
—bright noisy market—
being led to the
stud inspection center.

Cloud Semaphore

Ah, it's great! clear—clean—
wind blowing
farm tools twinkling
vague mountains
    —lava-plug   magma
all in a dream where there's no time

        when cloud semaphores
        were already hung
        in the stark blue east

the vague mountains . . .
        wild geese will come
            down to the four
                cedars tonight!

The Politicians

Running around here & there
stirring up trouble and bothering people
a bunch of lushes—
       fern leaves and cloud:
the world was so chilly and dark—

Before long that sort
will up and rot all by themselves
and be washed away by the rain
and afterwards, only green fern.

And when humanity is laid out like coal
somewhere some earnest geologist
will note them in his notebook.

Thief

About when the stars of the Skeleton
       were paling in the dawn:
Striding the crackly glitter
       —frozen mud—
The thief who had just stolen a celadon vase
       from the front of a store
Suddenly stopped those long black legs
Covered his ears with his hands
And listened to the humming of his mind.

Sixteen T'ang Poems

[TRANSLATIONS]

Note for Sixteen T'ang Poems

In the early fifties I managed to get myself accepted into the Department of Oriental Languages at UC Berkeley as a graduate student. I took seminars in the reading of T'ang and Sung poems with Professor Ch'en Shih-hsiang, a remarkable scholar, calligrapher, poet, and critic who had a profound appreciation for good poetry of any provenance. Ch'en hsien-sheng introduced me to the Han-shan poems, and I published those translations back in the sixties. The poems translated here also got their start in those seminars, but I never considered them quite finished. From Berkeley I went to Japan and for the subsequent decade was working almost exclusively with Ch'an texts. Another twenty years went into developing a farmstead in the Sierra Nevada and working for the ecological movement. In the last few years I have had a chance to return to my readings in Chinese poetry and bring a few of the poems I started back then to completion. This little collection is dedicated to the memory of Ch'en Shih-hsiang.

14.I.93

Two Poems by Meng Hao-jan

Spring Dawn

Spring sleep, not yet awake to dawn,
I am full of birdsongs.
Throughout the night the sounds of wind and rain
Who knows   what flowers fell.

Mooring on Chien-te River

The boat rocks at anchor by the misty island
Sunset, my loneliness comes again.
In these vast wilds the sky arches down to the trees,
In the clear river water, the moon draws near.

Five Poems by Wang Wei

Deer Camp

Empty mountains:
   no one to be seen.
Yet—hear—
   human sounds and echoes.
   Returning sunlight
   enters the dark woods;
Again shining
   on green moss, above.

Bamboo Lane House

Sitting alone, hid in bamboo
Plucking the lute and gravely whistling.
People wouldn't know that deep woods
Can be this bright   in the moon.

Saying Farewell

Me in the mountains   and now you've left.
Sunset,   I close the peelpole door.
Next spring   when grass is green,
Will you   return once more?

Thinking of Us

Red beans grow in the south
In spring they put out shoots.
Gather a lapful for me—
And doing it, think of us.

Poem

You who come from my village
Ought to know its affairs
The day you passed the silk window
Had the chill plum bloomed?

Three Poems for Women in the Service of the Palace

Autumn Evening
    Tu Mu

A silver candle in the autumn gloom
        by a lone painted screen
Her small light gauze fan
        shivers the fireflies
On the stairs of heaven, night's color
        cool as water;
She sits watching the Herd-boy,
        the weaving-girl, stars.

The Herd-boy is Altair, in Aquila.
The Weaving-girl Vega, in Lyra.

The Summer Palace
    Yuan Chen

Silence settles on the old Summer Palace
Palace flowers   still   quiet   red.
White-haired concubines
Idly sit and gossip   of the days of Hsüan Tsung.

Palace Song
    Po Chü-i

Tears soak her thin shawl
    dreams won't come.
In the dark night, from the front palace,
    girls rehearsing songs.
Still fresh and young,
    already put down,
She leans across the brazier
    to wait the coming dawn.

Spring View
   Tu Fu

The nation is ruined,   but mountains and rivers remain.
This spring the city   is deep in weeds and brush.
Touched by the times   even flowers weep tears,
Fearing leaving   the birds tangled hearts.
Watch-tower fires   have been burning for three months
To get a note from home   would cost ten thousand gold.
Scratching my   white hair thinner
Seething hopes   all in a trembling hairpin.

Events of the An Lushan rebellion.

Parting from Ling Ch'e
   Liu Ch'ang-ch'ing

Green, green
            bamboo-grove temple
Dark, dark,
            the bell-sounding evening.
His rainhat catches
            the slanting sunlight,
Alone returning
            from the distant blue peaks.

Climbing Crane Tower
   Wang Chih-huan

The white sun has gone over the mountains
The yellow river is flowing to the sea.
If you wish to see a thousand *li*
Climb one story higher in the tower.

River Snow
      Lo Tsung-yuan

These thousand peaks cut off the flight of birds
On all the trails, human tracks are gone.
A single boat—coat—hat—an old man!
Alone fishing chill river snow.

Parting with Hsin Chien at Hibiscus Tavern
      Wang Ch'ang-ling

Cold rain on the river
    we enter Wu by night
At dawn I leave
    for Ch'u-shan, alone.
If friends in Lo-yang
    ask after me, I've
"A heart like ice
    in a jade vase."

Two Poems Written at Maple Bridge Near Su-chou

Maple Bridge Night Mooring
  Chang Chi

Moon set, a crow caws,
              frost fills the sky
River, maple, fishing-fires
              cross my troubled sleep.
Beyond the walls of Su-chou
              from Cold Mountain temple
The midnight bell sounds
              reach my boat.

                              (circa 765 AD)

At Maple Bridge
  Gary Snyder

Men are mixing gravel and cement
At Maple bridge,
Down an alley by a tea-stall
From Cold Mountain temple;
Where Chang Chi heard the bell.
The stone step moorage
Empty, lapping water,
And the bell sound has travelled
Far across the sea.

                      1984 AD

Long Bitter Song

[TRANSLATIONS]

Bai Juyi's "Long Bitter Song"

translated by Gary Snyder

The "Long Bitter Song" (Chang hen ge) of Bai Juyi (Po Chü-I) is probably the best known and most widely popular poem in the whole Chinese cultural-sphere. Bai and his friend Wang Shifu (Wang Shih-fu) were visiting the Xienfu Chan Buddhist training center in 806, and were talking one night of the events of the reign of Emperor Xuanzong (Hsüan Tsung) and the An Lushan rebellion, sixty years earlier. Xuanzong was one of China's better rulers and presided over what has since been considered the golden age of both Chan Buddhist creativity and Chinese poetry. He took power in 712 and led a strong and innovative administration up to about 745. At that time he became totally infatuated with Yang Gui Fei (Yang Kuei-fei), the wife of one of his many sons. She became his concubine, the Sogdian-Turkish general An Lushan became an intimate of the couple and perhaps also a lover of Yang, the restive Northeast revolted under An, he led his troops into the capital, Xuanzong, Yang Gui Fei and the palace guard fled the city, and outside town at Horse Cliff the troops stopped, refused to go on, and insisted on putting Yang Gui Fei to death. That was in 755. The rebellion was quelled by 762, about the same time Xuanzong died. This rebellion marked a watershed in the fortunes of the Tang dynasty, beginning a period of somewhat more decentralized power, a rise of Chinese cultural chauvinism and contempt for the "third world" border peoples, and a greater weakness in relation to the borders.

The story of the Emperor and his lovely concubine had become legend. After that evening's reminiscences. Bai was inspired to write the story as a long poem. Within his own lifetime he then heard it sung on the canals and in the pleasure quarters by singing-girls and minstrels. Bai lived from A.D. 772 to 846. He was born in a poor family, passed the examinations partly on the strength of his literary brilliance, and became a lifelong political functionary of great integrity and compassion who wrote many stirring poems on behalf of the common people. He was a Chan Buddhist, and studied under the master Wei Kuan, who was a disciple of the outstanding Chan teacher Mazu (Ma-tsu).

This poem is in the seven character line, which gives it (in Chinese) this sort of rhythm:

tum tum / tum tum: tum tum tum

I have tried to keep to this beat as far as possible in my translation. I did the first version of it with the aid of Ch'en Shih-hsiang who was my teacher in graduate seminars at U.C. Berkeley in Tang poetics, in the early fifties.

I must take full responsibility, however, for idiosyncratic aspects of the translation—cases of both stripped-down literalism, and occasional free flights. My debt to his gracious, learned, unquenchable delight in all forms of poetry is deep indeed, and I am pleased to honor his memory with this publication of a poem that we took much pleasure in reading together.

Gary Snyder 28.X.86

Long Bitter Song

Han's Emperor wanted a Beauty
         one to be a "Destroyer of Kingdoms"
Scouring the country, many years,
         sought, but didn't find.
The Yang family had a girl
         just come grown;
Reared deep in the inner-apartments,
         men didn't know of her.
Such Heaven-given elegance
         could not be concealed
One morning she was taken to
         the Emperor's household.
A turn of the head, one smile,
         —a hundred lusts were flamed
The Six Palaces rouge-and-eyebrow
         without one beautiful face.
In the Spring cold she was given a bath
         at the Flower-pure Pool
Warm pool, smooth water,
         on her cold, glowing skin
Servant girls helping her rise,
         languorous, effortless beauty—
This was the beginning of her new role:
         glistening with Imperial favour.
Hair like a floating cloud, flower-face,
         ripple of gold when she walked.
—In the warm Hibiscus curtains
         they spent the Spring night.
Spring night is bitterly short
         it was noon when they rose;
From this time on the Emperor
         held no early court.
Holding feasts and revels
         without a moment's rest
Spring passed, Spring dalliance,
         all in a whirl of nights.
Beautiful girls in the outer palace:
         three thousand women:

Love enough for three thousand
                    centered in one body.
In Gold House, perfectly attired
                    her beauty served the night;
In the Jade Tower the parties ended
                    with drunk, peaceful Spring.
Her sisters and brothers
                    all given land,
Splendor and brilliance
                    surprised her humble family.
Following this, on all the earth,
                    fathers & mothers hearts
No longer valued bearing males
                    but hoped to have girls.
The high-soaring Li palace
                    pierces blue clouds
Delights of Immortals, whirled on wind
                    were heard of everywhere.
Slow song, flowing dance,
                    music like frost-crystal
                    sifting from the lute-strings—
The Emperor could exhaust a day
                    watching—and still not full

II

Then Yuyang war drums,
                    approached, shaking the earth;
Alarming, scattering, the "Rainbow Skirt"
                    the "Feathered Robe" dances.
From the nine great City-Towers,
                    smoke, dust, rose.
Thousands of chariots, ten thousand horsemen
                    scattered Southwest—
Kingfisher banner fluttering, rippling,
                    going and then stopping;
West out the city walls
                    over a hundred li
And the six armies won't go on:
                    nothing can be done—
Writhing, twisting, Moth-eyebrows
                    dies in front of the horses.

Her flower comb falls to the ground
                    not a man will pick it up—
Kingfisher feathers, "little golden birds",
                    jade hair-pin;
The Emperor hides his face
                    no way to help
Turns, looks, blood, tears,
                    flow, quietly mingle.
Yellow dust eddies and scatters.
                    Desolate winds blow.
Cloud Trail winds and twists
                    climbing to Sword-point Peak
Under Omei Shan
                    the last few came.
Flags, banners, without brightness,
                    A meagre-coloured sun.
Shu river waters blue
                    Shu mountains green
And the Emperor, days, days,
                    nights, nights, brooding.
From the temporary palace, watching the moon
                    colour tore his heart
The night-rain bell-tinkle
                    —bowel-twisting music.

III

Heaven turns, earth revolves,
                    The Dragon-Chariot returned.
But he was irresolute,
                    didn't want to go;
And at the foot of Horse Cliff,
                    in the sticky mud,
Couldn't find the Jade Face
                    at her death-place.
Court officials watching him
                    soaked their clothes with tears.
Looking east to the Capital walls,
                    they returned on horses
Came back to Pond Park
                    —all was as before.
Taiye Hibiscus,
                    Weiyang Willow.

But Hibiscus flowers were like her face,
   the Willows like her brow:
Seeing this, how could he
   keep tears from falling.
Spring wind, peach, plum,
   flowers open in the sun;
Autumn rain, Wutong trees,
   leaf-fall time.
Western palace, the inner court,
   many autumn grasses.
Falling leaves fill the stairs
   red: and no one sweeps.
The Pear-garden players
   white-haired young.
Pepper-court eunuchs
   watched beautiful girls age.
Evening, palace, glow-worm flight,
   —his thoughts were soundless
He picked his single candle-wick down,
   couldn't reach sleep.
Slow, slow, the night bell
   begins the long night,
Glimmering, fading, the Milky Way,
   and day about to dawn.
Silent tile roof-ducks
   are heavy with frost-flowers
The Kingfisher quilt is cold—
   who will share his bed?
Far, far, the living and the dead
   and the light years—cut apart.
Her spirit already dissolving,
   not even entering dreams.

IV

A Linqiong Daoist priest
   of the Hongdu school
Was able to deeply concentrate
   and thus call up the spirits.
Hearing this, the Emperor
   —troubled, twisting thoughts.
Ordered the Daoist priest
   to make a thorough search.

Pushing the sky, riding air,
                    swift as a thunderbolt,
Harrowing the heavens, piercing Earth,
                    he sought everywhere
Above exhausting the blue void,
                    below, the Yellow Springs.
The ends of earth—vast, vast,
                    and nowhere did he find her.
Then he heard—that out on the ocean—
                    was a mountain of Immortals
A mountain at—nowhere—
                    a cloudy, unreal place.
Palace towers, tinkling gems,
                    where Five Clouds rise.
Within—lovely, wanton, chaste,
                    many faery people.
There was there one faery
                    called Taizhen;
Snow skin, flower appearance,
                    it had to be her.
At the Gold Tower of the West Wing,
                    he knocked on the Jade door:
Announcing himself to Little Jade
                    —and she told Shuang Cheng,
That the Emperor of the people of Han
                    had sent an envoy.
In the nine-flowered canopy
                    the faery's dreams were broken;
Holding her clothes, pushing the pillow,
                    she rose, walking unsteady.
Winding, opening the pearl door,
                    the inlaid silver screens.
Her cloud-like hair, floating on one side,
                    —just brought from sleep.
Her flower-cap unadjusted
                    she came down the hall,
Wind blew her elegant sleeves
                    floating, floating up—
Seemed like the "Rainbow Skirt",
                    the "Feathered Robe" dance.
Her jade-like figure small and alone,
                    she scattered her sad tears:
As though one branch of a blossoming pear
                    was holding the whole Spring's rain.

Restraining her feelings, cooling her look,
                    she told him to thank the Emperor;
"With that parting our two forms
                    were split by the World's vast shifting;
After Zhaoyang temple,
                    our love was cut off.
Here in Raspberry-tangle Palace
                    the days and months are long—
I look down, hoping to see
                    lands where humans dwell,
I never see Chang'an
                    but only dusty haze."
Then taking some ancient treasures
                    rich in deep feeling,
An inlaid box, a gold hairpin,
                    to be delivered back,
Keeping a leg of the hairpin,
                    keeping half the box,
Breaking the gold of the hairpin,
                    box cut in two—
"If only our hearts are strong as
                    this gold hairpin,
Above in heaven, or among men,
                    we will somehow meet.
Go back swiftly
                    tell him this message:
For it tells of one Vow
                    that two hearts know,
In the seventh month on the seventh day
                    in Long-Life Temple.
At midnight, no one about,
                    we swore together
If in heaven, to fly as
                    the 'paired-wing' birds;
If on earth, to grow as
                    one joined branch."
Heaven lasts, Earth endures,
                    —and both will end;
This sorrow stretches on
                    forever, without limit.

No Nature

How Poetry Comes to Me

It comes blundering over the
Boulders at night, it stays
Frightened outside the
Range of my campfire
I go to meet it at the
Edge of the light

On Climbing the Sierra Matterhorn Again After Thirty-one Years

Range after range of mountains
Year after year after year.
I am still in love.

4.X.40086, *On the summit*

557

The Sweat

For John and Jan Straley

Now I must sit naked.

Socks and glasses tucked into my moccasins,
Wearing only earrings and a faded tattoo—

On a cedar bench too hot to touch,
Buttocks take it—legs fold,
Back cases on to the burning wall
Sweating and the in-breath cooled
Through a wet-soaked towel
—old Aleut trick—
And look out the small window
On a snow-capped volcano
And inside toward the stove, the
Women who sweat here
And groan and laugh with the heat,

The women speak of birth at home.
Of their children, their breasts hang
Softer, the nipples darker,
Eyes clear and warm.
Naked. Legs up, we have all raised children,

I could love each one,
Their ease, their opened—sweet—
    older—still youthful—
    womanly being bodies—

And outside, naked, cooling on the deck
Midsummer's far northern soft dusk eve,
Bare skin to the wind;
Older is smarter and more tasty.
Minds tough and funny—many lovers—
At the end of days of talking
Science, writing, values, spirit, politics, poems—

Different shoes and shirts,
In little heaps—sit naked, silent, gaze

On chests and breasts and knees and knobby feet
    in the tide smell, on the bleached deck planks,
Like seals hauled out for sunning,

Crinkles by the eyes,
Limber legs crossed,
Single mothers—past parenting—
Back to college—running a business—
Checking salmon for the Fish & Game,
Writing a play, an article, a novel,
Waitressing and teaching,
In between men friends, teen-age son—
Doing a dissertation on the Humpbacked Whales,
Doing tough-assed poems—

Naked comfort, scant fear,
Strong soul, naught to hide,

This life:
We get old enough and finally really like it!
Meeting and sweating
At a breezy beach.

                    VI.87, Baranoff Island, Alaska

Building

We started our house midway through the Cultural Revolution,
The Vietnam war, Cambodia, in our ears,
    tear gas in Berkeley,
Boys in overalls with frightened eyes, long matted hair, ran
    from the police.
We peeled trees, drilled boulders, dug sumps, took sweat baths
    together.
That house finished we went on
Built a schoolhouse, with a hundred wheelbarrows,
    held seminars on California paleo-indians during lunch.
We brazed the Chou dynasty form of the character "Mu"
    on the blacksmithed brackets of the ceiling of the lodge,
Buried a five-prong vajra between the schoolbuildings
    while praying and offering tobacco.
Those buildings were destroyed by a fire, a pale copy rebuilt
    by insurance.

Ten years later we gathered at the edge of a meadow.
The cultural revolution is over, hair is short,
    the industry calls the shots in the Peoples Forests,
Single mothers go back to college to become lawyers.

Blowing the conch, shaking the staff-rings
    we opened work on a Hall.
Forty people, women carpenters, child labor, pounding nails,
Screw down the corten roofing and shape the beams
    with a planer,
The building is done in three weeks.
We fill it with flowers and friends and open it up.

Now in the year of the Persian Gulf,
Of Lies and Crimes in the Government held up as Virtues,
    this dance with Matter
Goes on: our buildings are solid, to live, to teach, to sit,
To sit, to know for sure the sound of a bell—
This is history. This is outside of history.
Buildings are built in the moment,
    they are constantly wet from the pool
        that renews all things
      naked and gleaming.

The moon moves
Through her twenty-eight nights.
Wet years and dry years pass;
Sharp tools, good design.

Off the Trail

for Carole

We are free to find our own way
Over rocks—through the trees—
Where there are no trails. The ridge and the forest
Present themselves to our eyes and feet
Which decide for themselves
In their old learned wisdom of doing
Where the wild will take us. We have
Been here before. It's more intimate somehow
Than walking the paths that lay out some route
That you stick to,
All paths are possible, many will work,
Being blocked is its own kind of pleasure,
Getting through is a joy, the side-trips
And detours show down logs and flowers,
The deer paths straight up, the squirrel tracks
Across, the outcroppings lead us on over.
Resting on treetrunks,
Stepping out on the bedrock, angling and eyeing
Both making choices—now parting our ways—
And later rejoin; I'm right, you're right,
We come out together. *Mattake,* "Pine Mushroom,"
Heaves at the base of a stump. The dense matted floor
Of Red Fir needles and twigs. This is wild!
We laugh, wild for sure,
Because no place is more than another,
All places total,
And our ankles, knees, shoulders &
Haunches know right where they are.
Recall how the *Dao De*
Jing puts it: the trail's not the way.
No path will get you there, we're off the trail,
You and I, and we chose it! Our trips out of doors
Through the years have been practice
For this ramble together,
Deep in the mountains
Side by side,
Over rocks, through the trees.

Word Basket Woman

Years after surviving
the Warsaw uprising,
she wrote the poems of ordinary people
building barricades while being shot at,
small poems were all
that could hold so much
close to death   life
without making it false.

Robinson Jeffers, his tall cold view
quite true in a way, but why did he say it
as though he alone
stood above our delusions, he also
feared death, insignificance,
and was not quite up to the inhuman beauty
of parsnips or diapers, the deathless
nobility   at the core of all ordinary things

I dwell
in a house on the long west slope
of Sierra Nevada, two hundred mile
swell of granite,
bones of the Ancient Buddha,
miles back from the seacoast
on a line of fiery chakras
in the deep nerve web of the land,

Europe forgotten now, almost a dream—
but our writing
is sidewise and roman, and the language
a compote of old wars and tribes from some
place overseas. Here
at the rim of the world
where the *panaka* calls in the *chá*—the heart
words are Pomo, Miwok, Nisenan,
and the small poem word baskets
stretch to the heft of their burden.

I came this far to tell
of the grave of my great-

grandmother Harriet Callicotte
by itself on a low ridge in Kansas.
The sandstone tumbled,
her name almost eaten away,
where I found it in rain drenched grass
on my knees, closed my eyes
and swooped under the earth
to that loam dark, holding her emptiness
and placed one cool kiss
on the arch of her white
pubic bone.

VI.89, Carneiro Kansas
XII.87, Kitkitdizze

Right in the Trail

Here it is, near the house,
A **big** pile, fat scats,
Studded with those deep red
Smooth-skinned manzanita berries,
Such a pile! Such droppings,
Awesome. And I saw how
The young girl in the story,
Had good cause to comment
On the bearscats she found while
Picking blueberries with her friends.
She laughed at them
Or maybe **with** them, jumped over them
(Bad luck!), and is reported
To have said "wide anus!"
To amuse or annoy the Big Brown Ones
Who are listening, of course.

They say the ladies
Have always gone berrying
And they all join together
To go out for the herring spawn,
Or to clean green salmon.
And that big set of lessons
On what bears really want,
Was brought back by the girl
Who made those comments:
She was taken on a year-long excursion
Deep in the mountains,
Through the tangled deadfalls,
Down into the den.
She had some pretty children by a
Young and handsome Bear.

Now I'm on the dirt
Looking at these scats
And I want to cry not knowing why
At the honor and the humor
Of coming on this sign
That is not found in books

Or transmitted in letters,
And is for women just as much as men,
A shining message for all species,
A glimpse at the Trace
Of the Great One's passing,
With a peek into her whole wild system—
And what was going on last week,
(Mostly still manzanita)—

    Dear Bear: do stay around. Be good.
And though I know
It won't help to say this,

Chew your food.

For Lew Welch in a Snowfall

Snowfall in March:
I sit in the white glow reading a thesis
About you. Your poems, your life.

The author's my student,
He even quotes me.

Forty years since we joked in a kitchen in Portland
Twenty since you disappeared.

All those years and their moments—
Crackling bacon, slamming car doors,
Poems tried out on friends,
Will be one more archive,
One more shaky text.

But life continues in the kitchen
Where we still laugh and cook,
Watching snow.

                    III 91, Kitkitdizze

Ripples on the Surface

"Ripples on the surface of the water—
were silver salmon passing under—different
from the ripples caused by breezes"

A scudding plume on the wave—
a humpback whale is
breaking out in air up
gulping herring
         —Nature not a book, but a *performance,* a
high old culture

Ever-fresh events
scraped out, rubbed out, and used, used, again—
the braided channels of the rivers
hidden under fields of grass—

The vast wild
        the house, alone.
The little house in the wild,
        the wild in the house.
Both forgotten.

              No nature

        Both together, one big empty house.

Mountains and Rivers Without End

Bubbs Creek Haircut

High ceilinged and the double mirrors, the
    calendar a splendid alpine scene—scab barber—
in stained white barber gown, alone, sat down, old man
a summer fog gray San Francisco day
I walked right in. On Howard Street
        haircut a dollar twenty-five.
Just clip it close as it will go.
    "Now why you want your hair cut back like that."
    —Well I'm going to the Sierras for a while
Bubbs Creek and on across to upper Kern.
    He wriggled clippers
"Well I been up there, I built the cabin
    up at Cedar Grove. In nineteen five."
    Old haircut smell.

Next door, Goodwill
    where I came out.
A search for sweater and a stroll
    in the board & concrete room of
    unfixed junk downstairs—
all emblems of the past—too close—
    heaped up in chilly dust and bare-bulb glare
of tables, wheelchairs, battered trunks & lamps
& pots that boiled up coffee nineteen ten, things
swimming on their own & finally freed
    from human need. Or?
    Waiting a final flicker of desire
to tote them out once more. Some freakish use.
The Master of the limbo drag-legged watches
    making prices
    to the people seldom buy.
The sag-asst rocker has to make it now. Alone.
    A few days later drove with Locke
down San Joaquin, us barefoot in the heat
stopping for beer and melon on the way
    the Giant Orange,
rubber shreds of cast truck retreads on the pebble
shoulder, highway 99.
    Sierras marked by cumulus in the east.

Car coughing in the groves,   six thousand feet
down to Kings River Canyon; camped at Cedar Grove.
          Hard granite canyon walls that
          leave no scree.

Once tried a haircut at the Barber College too—
sat half an hour before they told me
                    white men use the other side.
Goodwill, St. Vincent de Paul,
                    Salvation Army up the coast
for mackinaws and boots and heavy socks
          —Seattle has the best for logger gear
once found a pair of good tricouni boots
                    at the under-the-public market store,
                    Mark Tobey's scene,
                              torn down I hear—
and Filson jacket with a birdblood stain.

A.G. and me got winter clothes for almost nothing
          at Lake Union, telling the old gal
          we was on our way
to work the winter out up in B.C.
                              hitchhiking home the
green hat got a ride (of that more later).
Hiking up Bubbs Creek saw the trail crew tent
in a scraggly grove of creekside lodgepole pine
                    talked to the guy, he says

"If you see McCool on the other trail crew over there
tell him Moorehead says to go to hell."
Late snow that summer. Crossing the scarred bare
                    shed of Forester Pass
          the winding rock-braced switchbacks
dive in snowbanks, we climb on where
                    pack trains have to dig or wait.
A half-iced-over lake, twelve thousand feet
                    its sterile boulder bank
but filled with leaping trout:
                    reflections wobble in the
mingling circles always spreading out
          the crazy web of wavelets makes sense
          seen from high above.
A deva world of sorts—it's high

        —a view that few men see, a point
    bare sunlight
    on the spaces
empty sky
        molding to fit the shape of what ice left
of fire-thrust, or of tilted, twisted, faulted
           cast-out from this lava belly globe.

The boulder in my mind's eye is a chair.
          . . . why was the man drag-legged?
King of Hell
    or is it a paradise of sorts, thus freed
from acting out the function some
        creator/carpenter
thrust on a thing to think he made, himself,
    an object always "chair"?
      Sinister ritual histories.
    Is the Mountain God a gimp?
The halting metrics   and the ritual limp,
        Good   Will?

Daughter of mountains, stooped
    moon breast Parvati

    mountain thunder speaks
    hair tingling static as the lightning lashes
    is neither word of love nor wisdom;
    though this be danger: hence thee fear.
        Some flowing girl
    whose slippery dance
    en trances Shiva
        —the valley spirit/Anahita,
          Sarasvati,
dark and female gate of all the world
water that cuts back quartzflake sand
        soft is the dance that melts the
mat-haired mountain sitter
      to leap in fire
& make of sand a tree
    of tree a board, of board (ideas!)
    somebody's rocking chair.
A room of empty sun of peaks and ridges
a universe of junk, all left alone.

The hat I always take on mountains:
When we came back down through Oregon
                    (three years before)
at nightfall in the Siskiyou few cars pass.

A big truck stopped a hundred yards above
        "Siskiyou Stoneware" on the side
the driver said
he recognized my old green hat.
I'd had a ride
                with him two years before
a whole state north
                when hitching down to Portland
                        from Warm Springs.

Allen in the rear on straw
forgot salami and we went on south
all night—in many cars—to Berkeley in the dawn.

        Upper Kern River country now after nine days walk
        it finally rain.
                We ran on that other trail crew
        setting up new camp in the drizzly pine
        cussing & slapping bugs, four days from road,
        we saw McCool, & he said tell that Moorehead
                kiss my ass.

We squatted smoking by the fire.
        "I'll never get a green hat now"
the foreman says fifty mosquitoes sitting on the brim

                they must like green.
& two more days of thundershower and cold
        (on Whitney hair on end
        hail stinging bare legs in the blast of wind
        but yodel off the summit echoes clean)

        all this comes after:

purity of the mountains and goodwills.
The diamond drill of racing icemelt waters
        and bumming trucks & watching

buildings raze
the garbage acres burning at the Bay
the girl who was the skid-row
cripple's daughter—

out of the memory of smoking pine
the lotion and the spittoon glitter rises
chair turns and in the double mirror waver
the old man cranks me down and cracks a chuckle

"Your Bubbs Creek haircut, boy."

The Blue Sky

"Eastward from here,

beyond Buddha-worlds ten times as
numerous as the sands of the Ganges
there is a world called
　　PURE AS LAPIS LAZULI
its Buddha is called Master of Healing,
　　AZURE RADIANCE TATHAGATA"

It would take you twelve thousand summer vacations
driving a car due east all day every day
to reach the *edge* of the lapis lazuli realm of
Medicine Old Man Buddha;
East. Old Man Realm,
East across the sea, yellow sand land
Coyote Old Man land
Silver, and stone blue.

　　　　　　　　　　ℭ

Blue.　Belo, "bright colors of the flames"
　　　flamen / brahman,
　　　beltane, "blue fire"—
Sky.
　　　[The dappled cloud zone—
　　　Sanskrit *sku* "covered"
　　　skewed (pied)　skewbald (. . . "Stewball")
　　　skybald / piebald]—

　　　　　Horse with lightning feet!
　　　　　A mane like distant rain,
　　　　　the turquoise horse,
　　　　　a black star for an eye
　　　　　white shell teeth.

　　　　Pony that feeds on the pollen of flowers
　　　　may he
　　　　make thee whole.
　　　　　　Heal, hale. . . . whole.

The Spell of the Master of Healing.

Namo bhagavate bhaishajyaguru-vaidurya-
prabharajaya tathagata arhate samyak
sambuddhaya tadyatha om bhaishajye
bhaishajye bhaishajya samudgate
svāhā.

"I honor the Lord, the Master of Healing,
shining like lapis lazuli, the king, the
Tathagata, the Saint, the perfectly enlightened
one, saying OM TO THE HEALING
TO THE HEALING TO THE HEALER HAIL!
svāhā."

꣑

Shades of blue through the day.
T'u chüeh a border tribe near China
Türc
Turquoise: a hydrous phosphate of aluminum
a little copper
a little iron—

꣑

In the reign of the Emperor Nimmyo
when Ono-no-Komachi the strange girl poet
was seventeen, she set out looking for her father
who had become a Buddhist wanderer. She took ill
on her journey, and sick in bed one night saw

AZURE RADIANCE THUS-COME MEDICINE
MASTER

in a dream. He told her she would find a hotsprings
on the bank of the Azuma river in the Bandai mountains
that would cure her; and she'd meet her father there.

꣑

"Enchantment as strange as
the Blue up above" my rose of San Antone

Tibetans say that goddesses have lapis lazuli hair.

Azure   Old French *azur,*
            Persian *lazhward,* "lapis lazuli"
—blue bead charms against the evil eye—

(Tim and Kim and Don and I were talking about
what an awful authoritarian garb Doctors
and Nurses wear, really, how spooky it is.
"What should they wear?"

—"masks and feathers!")

Ramana Maharshi Dream

I was working as a woodcutter by a crossroads—Ko-san was working with
me—we were sawing and splitting the firewood. An old man came up the
lane alongside a mud wall—he shouted a little scolding at some Zen monks
who were piling slash by the edge of the woods. He came over and chat-
ted with us, a grizzled face—neither eastern nor western; or both. He had
a glass of buttermilk in his hand. I asked him "Where'd you get that buttermilk?" I'd been looking all over for buttermilk. He said, "At the O K
Dairy, right where you leave town."

Medicine, measure, "Maya"—

Celestial. Arched cover . . . *kam.*
Comrade: sharing the same tent or sky,
a bent curved bow.

Kama, God of Love, Son of Maya,
bow of flowers.

Shakyamuni would then be the lord of the present world of
    sorrow;

Bhaishajyaguru
Yao-Shih Fo
Yakushi Nyorai,
"Old Man Medicine Buddha"

The lord of the lost paradise.
    (Glory of morning, pearly gates,
    tlitliltzin, the "heavenly blue.")

ℊ

Thinking on Amitabha in the setting sun,

    his *western* paradise—
    impurities flow out away, to west,
    behind us, *rolling,*

    planet ball forward turns into the "east"
    light-years beyond,
    Great Medicine Master;
    land of blue.

    The blue sky

    the blue sky.

    The Blue Sky

    is the land of

    OLD MAN MEDICINE BUDDHA

    where the eagle that flies out of sight

    flies.

The Flowing

Headwaters

Head doused under the bronze
    dragon-mouth jet
    from a cliff
    spring—headwaters, Kamo
    River back of Kyoto,
    Cliff-wall statue of Fudo
Blue-faced growling Fudo,

Lord of the Headwaters, making
Rocks of water,
Water out of rocks

Riverbed

Down at the riverbed
    singing a little tune.
    tin cans, fork stick stuck up straight,
    half the stones of an old black campfire ring,

The gypsy actors, rags and tatters,
    wives all dancers,
    and the children clowns,
    come skipping down
    hop on boulders,
        clever—free—

Gravel scoop bed of the Kamo
    a digger rig set up on truck bed with
    revolving screen to winnow out the stones
    brushy willow—twists of sand

At Celilo all the Yakima
    Wasco, Wishram, Warmspring,
    catching salmon, talking,
        napping scattered through the rocks

Long sweep dip net held by a
foam-drenched braced and leaning man
on a rickety scaffold rigged to rocks

the whole Columbia River thunders
beneath his one wet plank

the lift and plume
of the water curling out and over,

Salmon arching in the standing spray.

Falls

Over stone lip
   the creek leaps out as one
   divides in spray and streamers,
   lets it all   go.

Above, back there, the snowfields
   rocked between granite ribs
   turn spongy in the summer sun
   water slips out under
   mucky shallow flows
   enmeshed with roots of flower and moss and heather
   seeps through swampy meadows
   gathers to shimmer sandy shiny flats
   then soars off ledges —

Crash and thunder on the boulders at the base
   painless, playing,
   droplets regather
   seek the lowest,
      and keep going down
   in gravelly beds.

There is no use, the water cycle tumbles round —

Sierra Nevada
   could lift the heart so high
   fault block uplift

thrust of westward slipping crust—one way
to raise and swing the clouds around—
thus pine trees leapfrog up on sunlight
trapped in cells of leaf—nutrient minerals called together
like a magic song
to lead a cedar log along, that hopes
   to get to sea at last and be
     a great canoe.

A soft breath, world-wide, of night and day,
  rising, falling,
The Great Mind passes by its own
  fine-honed thoughts,
  going each way.

Rainbow hanging steady
  only slightly wavering with the
swing of the whole spill,
   between the rising and the falling,
    stands still.

I stand drenched in crashing spray and mist,
and pray.

Rivermouth

Mouth
you thick
vomiting outward sighing prairie
    muddy waters
    gathering all and
    issue it
    end over end
      away from land.
The faintest grade.
Implacable, heavy, gentle,

—O pressing song
    liquid butts and nibbles
    between the fingers—in the thigh—
    against the eye

curl round my testicles
drawn crinkled skin
        and lazy swimming cock.

Once sky-clear and tickling through pineseeds
        humus, moss fern stone
        but NOW

the vast loosing
            of all that was found, sucked, held,
            born, drowned,

sunk sleepily in
to the sea.

                The root of me
                hardens and lifts to you,
                thick flowing river,

                my skin shivers. I quit

                making this poem.

Arctic Midnight Twilight Cool North Breeze with Low Clouds Green Mountain Slopes, White Mountain Sheep

Dibée

Song

Green mountain walls in blowing cloud
white dots on far slopes, constellations,
slowly changing   not stars   not rocks
"by the midnight breezes strewn"
cloud tatters, lavender arctic light
on sedate wild sheep grazing
tundra greens, held in the web of clan
and kin by bleats and smells to the slow
rotation of their Order living
half in the sky—damp wind up from the
whole north slope and a taste of the icepack—

the primus roaring now,
here, have some tea.

    A broad bench, slate surfacing
    six sheep break out of the gorge
    skyline brisk trot scamper

        Pellet piles in moss
        a spiral horn in the grass
        long tundra sweeps and the rise of slopes
        to a peak of Doonerak,
        white sheep dots on the far green
        One chases one, they run in circles
        three move away. One cuts a tangent.
        On the shade side canyon wall
        scree patch rock slides, serried stepped-up
        ledges, a host of sheep hang out.

Sunshine across the valley, they choose
the chilly shade. Perched on cliffs
napping, scratching,
insouciant white head droops
over gulfs of air;

Low sun swings through the twenty-four hours
never high, never gone, a soft slant light,
miles of shadows, ever-dappling clouds,

> a sheepskull forehead with its horn prongs
> sitting on a boulder—
> an offer of the flower of a
> million years of nibbling forbs

> to the emptiness of intelligence,

> sheep impermanence, sheep practice,
> sheep shapeshifting—vows of beings—
> Vajra Sheep teaching the Koyukuk waters
> suchness for each—

"The beat of her unseen feet"
which the wild sheep hear
at the roof of the planet, the warp
of the longitudes gathered,
rips in the wind-built tent
of sky-sea-earth cycles, eating the
green of the twenty-four hours,
breaking the cloud-flock flight
with floods of rising, falling,
warmer, cooler, air-mass swirls
like the curls
of Dall sheep horns. The "feet"
of the onward paces of skulls and pellets—
clouds sublimate to pure air
blowing south through passes
feeding the white dot Dall sheep—dew.

> A sheep track followed by a wolf track
> south of the lake.
> A ewe and lamb in the sunshine, the lamb

tries to nurse, it's too old,
she lies down.
In the scoured-out gullies
thirty-one sheep.

Climbing Midnight Mountain sliding rock
find a sheep trail goes just right:
on the harder scree at the bases of faces,
follow it out, over ledges, find their hidden
sheltered beds.

Sweet rank smell makes the heart beat,
dusty and big pebbles whisked out
so it's softer, shaped,
sheep dreaming place—

   Sheep time.
   All over the world.
   At rest in a sheep bed
   at the cliff-edge of life and death
   over endless mountains
   and streams like strips of the sky.

Up the knife ridge
the trail crosses over and heads down a glacier,
tracks fade in the snow.

Sheep gone, and only endless twilight mountains.
Rest awhile among the rocks
arise to descend to unbuild it again,

 and hear the Koyukon riddle:

"It really snowed hard
in opposite directions
on my head

   who am I?"

 —*dibée*

  a mountain sheep.

Walking the New York Bedrock
Alive in the Sea of Information

Maple, oak, poplar, gingko
New leaves, "new green" on a rock ledge
Of steep little uplift, tucked among trees
Hot sun dapple—
    wake up.

Roll over and slide down the rockface
Walk away in the woods toward
A squirrel, toward
Rare people! Seen from a safe distance.
A murmur of traffic approaching,
Siren howls echoing
Through the gridlock of structures,
Vibrating with helicopters,
    the bass tone
        of a high jet.

    Leap over the park stone wall
    Dressed fast and light,
    Slip into the migrating flow.

New York like a sea anemone
Wide and waving in the Sea of Economy,
Cadres of educated youth   in chic costume
Step out to the nightlife, good food, after work—
In the chambers of prana-subtle power-pumping
Heartbeat buildings   fired
Deep at the bottom, under the basement,
Fired by old merchant marine
Ex-fire-tenders gone now from sea
    to the ships stood on end on the land:
        ex-seamen stand watch at the stationary boilers,
    give way to computers,
That monitor heat and the power
    webs underground;   in the air;
In the Sea   of Information.

Brisk flesh, keen-eyed, streams of people
Curve round the sweep of street corners

---

cardboard chunks tossed up in truckbed.
Delicate jiggle, rouge on the nipple,
            kohl under the eye.

Time and Life buildings—sixty thousand people—
Wind ripples the banners
    stiff shudder shakes limbs on the
    planted trees growing new green,

Glass, aluminum, aggregate gravel,
Iron. Stainless steel.
Hollow honeycomb brain-buildings owned by

Columbia University, the landlord of
Anemone
        colony
Alive, in the Sea of Information

    "Claus the Wild man"
    Lived mostly with Indians,
    Was there as a witness when the old lady
    "Karacapacomont"
    Sold the last bit of Washington Heights, 1701
    Down deep grates hear the watercourse,
    Rivers that never give up
    Trill under the roadbed, over the bedrock.
    A bird angles way off a brownstone
    Couloir that looks like a route.

Echo the hollowing darkness.
Crisscrossing light threads
Gleam squeals up the side streets,
One growl shadow
    in an egg of bright lights,
Lick of black on the tongue.
Echoes of sirens come down the walled canyons
Foot lifts to the curb and the lights change—

And look up at the gods.
Equitable god, Celanese god, noble line,
Old Union Carbide god,
Each catching   shares of the squared blocked shadow
Each swinging in sundial arc of the day
            more than the sum of its parts.

The Guggenheims, the Rockefellers, and the Fricks,
Assembling the art of the world, the plate glass
Window lets light in on "the water lilies"
Like fish or planets, people,
Move, pause, move   through the rooms,
White birch leaves shiver in breezes
While guards watch the world,
Helicopters making their long humming trips
Trading pollen and nectar
In the air
        of the
Sea of   Economy,
    Drop under the streetworld
    Steel squeal of stopping and starting
    Wind blows through black tunnels
        spiderwebs, fungus, lichen.

Gingko trees of Gondwanaland. Pictographs,
Petroglyphs, cover the subways—
Empty eye sockets of buildings just built
Soulless, they still wait the ceremony
    that will make them too,
        new, Big
        city Gods,
Provided with conduit, cable and plumbing,
They will light up, breathe cool air,
Breathe the minds of the workers who work there—
The cloud of their knowing
As they soar in the sky, in the air,
Of the Sea
Of Information,

    Cut across alleys and duck beneath trucks.
    "Under Destruction"—trash chair at the curb—
    Stop to gaze on the large roman letters
    Of writing on papers that tell of Economy,

Skilsaw whine slips through the windows
Empty room—no walls—such clear air in the cellar
Dry brick, cooked clay, rusty house bodies
Carbide blade Skilsaw cuts bricks. Squalls
From the steps leading down to the subway.
Blue-chested runner, a female, on car streets,
Red lights block traffic but she like the

Beam of a streetlight in the whine of the Skilsaw,
    She runs right through.
    A cross street leads toward a river
    North goes to the woods
    South takes you fishing
    Peregrines nest at the thirty-fifth floor

Street people rolling their carts
    of whole households
Or asleep wrapped in light blue blanket
    spring evening, at dusk, in a doorway,
Eyeballing arêtes and buttresses rising above them,
    con domus, dominion,
        domus,
    condominate, condominium
Towers, up there the
Clean crisp white dress white skin
    women and men
Who occupy sunnier niches,
Higher up on the layered stratigraphy cliffs, get
More photosynthesis, flow by more ostracods,
    get more sushi,
Gather more flesh, have delightful
Cascading laughs,

    —Peregrine sails past the window
    Off the edge of the word-chain
    Harvesting concepts, theologies,
    Snapping up bites of the bits bred by
    Banking
        ideas and wild speculations
    On new information—
        and stoops in a blur on a pigeon,

As the street bottom-feeders with shopping carts
Slowly check out the air for the fall of excess,
Of too much, flecks of extra,
From the higher-up folks in the sky

        As the fine dusk gleam
        Lights a whole glass side of
        Forty some stories

Soft liquid silver,

Beautiful buildings we float in, we feed in,

Foam, steel, gray

Alive   in the Sea of Information.

New Moon Tongue

Faint new moon arc, curl,

again in the west. Blue eve,

deer-moving dusk.

Purple shade in a plant-realm—

a million years of sniffs,

licks, lip and

reaching tongue.

Macaques in the Sky

Walking the trail with Wang Ch'ing-hua, Red Pine, Lo Ch'ing, and Carole from Nanren Lake, we see a clear spot in the jungle canopy of leaves—
a high point arch of heavy limbs, a lookout on the forest slope—

    A mother monkey sits and nurses,

    A couple perching side by side,

    A face peeks from another leaf screen, pink cheeks,
    shining eyes,

    An old male, silver belly, furrowed face,
    laid back in a crotch

        harsh little cough-calls echo

    faces among the leaves,
        being ears and eyes of trees
    soft hands and haunches pressed on boughs and vines

Then—*wha!*—she leaps out in the air
the baby dangling from her belly,

they float there,

—she fetches up along another limb—
    and settles in.

Her
arching like the Milky Way,
mother of the heavens,
    crossing realm to realm
    full of stars

as we hang on beneath with all we have

enjoy her flight.
Drink her light.

Rhesus macaque.

Raven's Beak River at the End

Doab of the Tatshenshini River and the Alsek Lake, a long spit of gravel,
one clear day after days on the river in the rain, the glowing sandy slopes
of Castilleja blooms & little fox tracks in the moose-print swales, & giant
scoops of dirt took out by bears around the lupine roots, at early light a
rim of snowy mountains and the ice fields slanting back for miles, I find
my way

> To the boulders
>> on the gravel   in the flowers
> At the end of the glacier
>> two ravens
> Sitting on a boulder
>> carried by the glacier
> Left on the gravel
>> resting in the flowers
> At the end of the ice age
>> show me the way
> To a place to sit
>> in a hollow on a boulder
> Looking east, looking south
>> ear in the river
> Running just behind me
>> nose in the grasses
> Vetch roots scooped out
>> by the bears in the gravels
> Looking up the ice slopes
>> ice plains, rock-fall
> Brush-line, dirt-sweeps
>> on the ancient river
> Blue queen floating in
>> ice lake, ice throne, end of a glacier
> Looking north
>> up the dancing river
> Where it turns into a glacier
>> under stairsteps of ice falls
> Green streaks of alder
>> climb the mountain knuckles
> Interlaced with snowfields
>> foamy water falling

Salmon weaving river
    bear flower   blue sky singer
As the raven leaves her boulder
    flying over flowers
Raven-sitting high spot
    eyes on the snowpeaks,
Nose of morning
    raindrops in the sunshine
Skin of sunlight
    skin of chilly gravel
Mind in the mountains, mind of tumbling water,
    mind running rivers,
Mind of sifting
    flowers in the gravels
At the end of the ice age
    we are the bears, we are the ravens,
We are the salmon
    in the gravel
At the end of an ice age
Growing on the gravels
    at the end of a glacier
Flying off alone
    flying off alone
    flying off alone

Off alone

Cross-Legg'd

for Carole

Cross-legg'd under the low tent roof,
dim light, dinner done,

drinking tea. We live
in dry old west

lift shirts bare skin
lean   touch lips—

old touches.
Love made, poems, makyngs,

always new, same stuff
life after life,

as though Milarepa
four times built a tower of stone

like each time was the first.
Our love is mixed with

rocks and streams,
a heartbeat, a breath, a gaze

makes place in the dizzy eddy.
Living this old clear way

—a sizzle of ash and embers.
Scratchy breeze on the tent fly

one sip tea, hunch on bones,
we two be here   what comes.

We Wash Our Bowls in This Water

"The 1.5 billion cubic kilometers of water on the earth are split by photosynthesis and reconstituted by respiration once every two million years or so."

A day on the ragged North Pacific coast get soaked by whipping mist, rainsqualls tumbling, mountain mirror ponds, snowfield slush, rock-wash creeks, earfulls of falls, sworls of ridge-edge snowflakes, swift gravelly rivers, tidewater crumbly glaciers, high hanging glaciers, shore-side mud pools, icebergs, streams looping through the tideflats, spume of brine, distant soft rain drooping from a cloud,

sea lions lazing under the surface of the sea—

>   *We wash our bowls in this water*
>   *It has the flavor of ambrosial dew—*

                              ⚘

        Beaching the raft, stagger out and shake off wetness like a
              bear,
        stand on the sandbar, rest from the river   being

        upwellings, sideswirls, backswirls
        curl-overs, outripples, eddies, chops and swells
        wash-overs, shallows   confluence turbulence   wash-seam
        wavelets, riffles, saying

    "A hydraulic's a cross between a wave and a hole,
            —you get a weir effect.
    Pillow-rock's a total fold-back over a hole,
            it shows spit on the top of the wave
    a haystack's a series of waves at the bottom of a tight
            channel
            there's a tongue of the rapids—the slick tongue—the
            'v'—
    some holes are 'keepers,' they won't let you through;
    eddies, backflows, we say 'eddies are your friends.'
    Current differential, it can suck you down
    vertical boils are straight-up eddies spinning,
    herringbone waves curl under and come back.
    Well, let's get going, get back to the rafts."
            Swing the big oars,
                  head into a storm.

We offer it to all demons and spirits
May all be filled and satisfied.
Om makula sai svaha!

℘

Su Tung-p'o sat out one whole night by a creek   on the slopes of Mt. Lu.
Next morning he showed this poem to his teacher:

>   The stream with its sounds   is a long broad tongue
>   The looming mountain   is a wide-awake body
>   Throughout the night   song after song
>   How can I   speak at dawn.

Old Master Chang-tsung approved him. Two centuries later Dōgen said,
>   "Sounds of streams and shapes of mountains.
>   The sounds never stop and the shapes never cease.
>   Was it Su who woke
>   or was it the mountains and streams?
>   Billions of beings see the morning star
>   and all become Buddhas!
>   If *you,* who are valley streams and looming
>   mountains,
>   can't throw some light on the nature of ridges and rivers,
>
>   *who can?"*

Earth Verse

Wide enough to keep you looking

Open enough to keep you moving

Dry enough to keep you honest

Prickly enough to make you tough

Green enough to go on living

Old enough to give you dreams

Finding the Space in the Heart

I first saw it in the sixties,
driving a Volkswagen camper
with a fierce gay poet and a
lovely but dangerous girl with a husky voice,

we came down from Canada
on the dry east side of the ranges. Grand Coulee, Blue
Mountains, lava flow caves,
the Alvord desert—pronghorn ranges—
and the glittering obsidian-paved
dirt track toward Vya,
seldom-seen roads late September and
thick frost at dawn; then
follow a canyon and suddenly open to
  silvery flats that curved over the edge

  O, ah! The
  awareness of emptiness
  brings forth a heart of compassion!

We followed the rim of the playa
to a bar where the roads end
and over a pass into Pyramid Lake
from the Smoke Creek side,
by the ranches of wizards
who follow the tipi path.
The next day we reached San Francisco
in a time when it seemed
the world might head a new way.
And again, in the seventies, back from
Montana, I recklessly pulled off the highway
took a dirt track onto the flats,
got stuck—scared the kids—slept the night,
and the next day sucked free and went on.

Fifteen years passed. In the eighties
With my lover I went where the roads end.
Walked the hills for a day,
looked out where it all drops away,

discovered a path
of carved stone inscriptions tucked into the sagebrush

    "Stomp out greed"
    "The best things in life are not things"

words placed by an old desert sage.

Faint shorelines seen high on these slopes,
long gone Lake Lahontan,
cutthroat trout spirit in silt—
Columbian Mammoth bones
four hundred feet up on the wave-etched
     beach ledge; curly-horned
        desert sheep outlines pecked into the rock,

and turned the truck onto the playa
heading for know-not,
bone-gray dust boiling and billowing,
mile after mile, trackless and featureless,
let the car coast to a halt
on the crazed cracked
flat hard face where
winter snow spirals, and
summer sun bakes like a kiln.
Off nowhere, to be or not be,

    all equal, far reaches, no bounds.
    Sound swallowed away,
    no waters, no mountains, no
    bush no grass and
       because no grass
    no shade but your shadow.
    No flatness because no not-flatness.
    No loss, no gain. So—
    nothing in the way!
    —the ground is the sky
    the sky is the ground,
    no place between, just

    wind-whip breeze,
    tent-mouth leeward,

time being here.
We meet heart to heart,
leg hard-twined to leg,
        with a kiss that goes to the bone.
Dawn sun comes straight in the eye. The tooth
of a far peak called King Lear.

Now in the nineties desert night
        —my lover's my wife—
old friends, old trucks, drawn around;
great arcs of kids on bikes out there in darkness
        no lights—just planet Venus glinting
by the calyx crescent moon,
and tasting grasshoppers roasted in a pan.

        They all somehow swarm down here—
        sons and daughters in the circle
        eating grasshoppers grimacing,

singing sūtras for the insects in the wilderness,

—the wideness, the
foolish loving spaces

full of heart.

        Walking on walking,
                under foot   earth turns

Streams and mountains never stay the same.

        The space goes on.
        But the wet black brush
        tip drawn to a point,
                lifts away.

                Marin-an 1956–Kitkitdizze 1996

New Poems

Icy Mountains Constantly Walking

for Seamus Heaney

Work took me to Ireland
a twelve-hour flight.
The river Liffy
ale in a bar,
So many stories
of passions and wars—
A hilltop stone tomb
with the wind across the door.
Peat swamps go by:
people of the ice age.
Endless fields and farms
the last two thousand years.

I read my poems in Galway,
just the chirp of a bug
And flew home thinking
of literature and time.

The serried rows of books
in the Long Hall at Trinity
The ranks of stony ranges
above the ice of Greenland.

Summer of Ninety-seven

West of the square old house, on the rise that was made
when the pond was dug; where we once slept out;
where the trampoline sat,

> Earth spirit please don't mind
> If cement trucks grind
> And plant spirits wait a while
> Please come back and smile

> Ditches, lines and drains
> Forms and pours and hidden doors
> The house begins!

> Sun for power
> Cedar for siding
> Fresh skinned poles for framing
> Gravel for crunching and
> Bollingen for bucks!

> Daniel peeling
> Moth for singing
> Matt for pounding
> Bruce for pondering
> Chuck for plumbering
> David drywalling
> > staining, crawling;
> Stu for drain rock
> Kurt for hot wire
> Gary for cold beer
> Carole for brave laugh
> > til she leaves,
> > crew grieves,
> Gen for painting
> > each window frame
> > Gen-red again

> Garden cucumbers for lunch.
> Fresh tomatoes crunch.

Tor for indoor paints and grins
Ted for rooftiles
Tarpaper curls
Sawdust swirls
Trucks for hauling
Barrels for burning
Old bedrooms disappearing

Wild turkeys watching
Deer disdainful
Bullfrogs croaking,

David Parmenter for bringing
        flooring oak at night,
Though his mill burned down,
He's still coming round.

Cyndra tracing manzanita
On the tile wall shower,
Sliding doors
Smooth new floors —

Old house a big hall now
Big as a stable
To bang the mead-stein on the
        table.
Robin got a room to write a poem,
& no more nights out walking to
        the john.

Carole finally coming home
Peeking at her many rooms.
Oak and pine trees looking on
Old Kitkitdizze house now
Has another wing —

So we'll pour a glass and sing —
This has been fun as heaven,
Summer of ninety-seven.

*IX.*97

This present moment:

That lives on,

To become

Long ago

Chronology

1930   Gary Snyder born (8 May) in San Francisco, California, first of two children born to Harold and Lois Wilkie Snyder.

1932   Snyder's family moves to country land near Lake City, Washington and starts a small dairy. Sister, Anthea, born.

1942   Family moves to Portland, Oregon.

1943–5   Enters high school in Portland, works summers at camp on Spirit Lake, Washington. Summer of 1945 climbs Mt. St. Helens.

1946–7   Joins the Portland Mazamas, mountaineering club. Works summers for United Press and as copy boy for the Portland *Oregonian*. Graduates from Lincoln High School. Climbs a number of Pacific Northwest snowpeaks.

1947   Summer, backpacks in the southern Washington Cascades. Climbs Mt. Rainier. Begins undergraduate study at Reed College, Portland, Oregon.

1948   Summer, hitchhikes to New York City, gets seaman's papers and ships out in the Marine Cooks and Stewards Union. Visits Colombia and Venezuela.

1949   Summer, works on trail crew for the U.S. Forest Service, Columbia National Forest (now the Gifford Pinchot.)

1950   Publishes first poems in Reed College student publication *Janus*. Summer works for U.S. Park Service excavating the archaeological site of old Fort Vancouver.

1951   Spring, graduates from Reed with BA in anthropology and literature, senior thesis, *The Dimensions of a Haida Myth*. Summer works as timber scaler on Warm Spring Indian Reservation, backpacks in the Olympic Mountains.
Autumn, begins graduate program in anthropology at Indiana University, Bloomington, Indiana, but stays only one semester.

1952   Spring, returns to San Francisco, does odd jobs, lives with poet Philip Whalen. Summer works as lookout at Crater Mountain, Mt. Baker National Forest.

1953–5   Graduate student, East Asian Languages Department, University of California, Berkeley.

1953   Summer, works as a lookout in Mt. Baker National Forest on Sourdough Mountain, works on *Myths & Texts*. Autumn meets Kenneth Rexroth.

1954	Summer and fall, works as choker-setter for Warm Springs Lumber Company, Oregon.
1955	Summer, works on trail crew, Yosemite National Park. Long backpack trip in the Minarets and headwaters of the Kern.
	Autumn, continues East Asian language study at U.C. Berkeley and translates Han-Shan. Meets Allen Ginsberg and Jack Kerouac in San Francisco. Poetry reading at Six Gallery in San Francisco. Lives with Kerouac in cabin in Mill Valley.
1956	May, by freighter to Kyoto, Japan, lives in Zen Temple Shokoku-ji. Studies under Miura Isshu Roshi. Summer, with Japanese climber friends, backpacks and climbs in the Northern Japanese Alps.
1957	August, boards *S.S. Sappa Creek* in Yokohama, works as wiper in engine room, visits Persian Gulf five times, Italy, Sicily, Turkey, Okinawa, Wake, Guam, Ceylon, Samoa, Hawai'i.
1958	April, disembarks in San Pedro, returns to San Francisco. Shares Marin County cabin with Lew Welch, spends nine months in the literary scene.
1959	Returns to Kyoto, Japan and begins study under Oda Sesso Roshi at the Daitoku-ji monastery. *Riprap* published, printed in Kyoto, and sold through City Lights Books, San Francisco.
1960	*Myths & Texts* published by Leroi Jones's Totem Press.
1960	Marries Joanne Kyger in Kyoto.
1961–62	Kyger and Snyder go to India by boat, travel extensively in Sri Lanka, India and Nepal. Join Allen Ginsberg in New Delhi. Visit with the Dalai Lama in Dharamshala.
1963	Allen Ginsberg visits Kyoto. Snyder and Ginsberg first meet poet, Nanao Sakaki.
1964	May, Snyder returns to the West Coast. Summer, long backpack trip in the Sierra in Bubbs Creek country. Fall teaches English poetry workshops and classes at U.C. Berkeley.
1965	Summer, Berkeley Poetry Conference (Robert Duncan, Charles Olson, Jack Spicer, James Koller, Lew Welch, Allen Ginsberg, and others). Long trip north with Ginsberg to British Columbia where the two climb Glacier Peak in the North Cascades.
1965	October, return to Japan. *Six Sections from Mountains and Rivers Without End* published by Grey Fox Press. Kyger and Snyder divorce.
1966	Meets Masa Uehara. Visits U.S., participates in the "Gathering of the Tribes" in Golden Gate Park. *A Range of Poems* published in England. Oda Sesso Roshi dies.
1967	March, returns to Japan. Summer at Banyon Ashram on Suwa-no-se Island in the East China Sea. Marries Masa Uehara there. Studies with Nakamura Sojun Roshi at Daitokuji in winter.
1968	Son, Kai, born in Kyoto. Returns to U.S., receives Levinson Prize from *Poetry* (Chicago), and is awarded Guggenheim Fellowship. Publishes *The Back Country*.
	Harold Snyder dies.

1969	Son, Gen, is born. *Earth House Hold* published. Summer backpacking with Nanao Sakaki in high Sierra, visits environmental activists around the U.S., distributes "Smokey the Bear Sutra" at Sierra Club Wilderness Conference, San Francisco.
1970	Moves to San Juan Ridge, north of the South Yuba river, in the foothills of the Sierra Nevada. Builds his house, "Kitkitdizze," with friends and students. Reads paper, "The Wilderness," at The Center for the Study of Democratic Institutions, Santa Barbara. *Regarding Wave* published.
1972	June, attends United Nations Conference on the Environment, Stockholm, Sweden. July travels throughout Hokkaido, Japan researching wildlife, climbs in the Daisetsu Mountain range.
1973	*The Fudo Trilogy* published, includes "Smokey the Bear Sutra."
1974	*Turtle Island* published.
1974–79	Appointed member of the Board of the California Arts Council.
1975	Awarded Pulitzer Prize for Poetry for *Turtle Island.* First MLA panel on Snyder's poetry held in San Francisco.
1976	First critical book-length study of Snyder's work published, Bob Steuding, *Gary Snyder.*
1977	*The Old Ways* published.
1979	*He Who Hunted Birds in His Father's Village:The Dimensions of a Haida Myth* (based on Reed College Thesis) published.
1980	*The Real Work: Interviews and Talks 1964–1979,* published.
1981	Summer, trip with family to Japan. Fall poetry readings in Australia with Nanao Sakaki.
1982	Summer, "Ring of Bone" Zendo built. Fall readings in Sweden, Scotland and England.
1983	*Axe Handles* and *Passage Through India,* published. Second critical study, *Gary Snyder's Vision* by Charles Molesworth, appears.
1984	Fall, travels in the Peoples' Republic of China as guest of the Writers' Union together with Toni Morrison, Maxine Hong Kingston, Allen Ginsberg, and others.
1986	Begins teaching at U.C. Davis. *Left Out in the Rain* published.
1987	Inducted into the American Academy of Arts and Letters.Travels in the Brooks Range of Alaska.
1989	Masa Uehara and Snyder divorce
1990	Yuba Watershed Institute established. Readings in Taiwan. *Practice of the Wild* published.
1991	Marries Carole Koda. Fall Snyder, Koda and Sakaki travel in Japan.
1992	Travels in Ladakh and readings in Spain. *No Nature* published.
1994	Travels in Botswana and Zimbabwe with Kai and Gen Snyder.
1995	*A Place in Space* published. Readings in Ireland. Fall trip to Nepal with Carole Koda and daughter, trek to Base Camp on Sagarmatha (Everest).
1996	Travels to France for cave art study. *Mountains and Rivers Without End* published.

1997   Awarded the Bollingen Prize for poetry.
1998   Travels to Japan for Bukkyo Dendo Kyokai (Society for the Propagation of Buddhism) award. Readings in Greece and in the Czech Republic. Lannan Award. Lila Wallace Reader's Digest Grant to support literary and educational programs in the rural Sierra Nevada.

Index